MODERN ARAB KINGSHIP

Frontispiece. Fiscal stamp of the "Arab Government,"
2 piasters, dated "al-Sham, 1338" (Damascus, 1919–
1920), created for the support of the Hijaz Railway.
Source: Timur Kuran Collection of Ottoman Revenue
Documents, with permission.

Modern Arab Kingship

REMAKING THE OTTOMAN POLITICAL ORDER IN THE INTERWAR MIDDLE EAST

Adam Mestyan

PRINCETON UNIVERSITY PRESS

PRINCETON & OXFORD

Published by Princeton University Press
41 William Street, Princeton, New Jersey 08540
99 Banbury Road, Oxford OX2 6JX

press.princeton.edu

ISBN 978-0-691-19097-6
ISBN (e-book) 978-0-691-24935-3

British Library Cataloging-in-Publication Data is available

Editorial: Fred Appel and James Collier
Production Editorial: Jill Harris
Production: Lauren Reese
Publicity: Kate Hensley and Charlotte Coyne

Jacket image: Haworth, W. B. *The Postage Stamps of the Hejaz*. London, Published for the Junior Philatelic Society by H. F. Johnson, 1922. Courtesy of World Digital Library / Library of Congress.

This book has been composed in Miller

10 9 8 7 6 5 4 3 2 1

The crisis consists precisely in the fact that the old is dying and the new cannot be born: in this interregnum, morbid phenomena of the most varied kind come to pass.

—GRAMSCI, *PRISON NOTEBOOKS*, 2:32–33 (1930)

CONTENTS

List of Illustrations · ix
List of Tables · xi
Principal Players · xiii
Glossary · xvii
Chronology of Events · xix
A Note on Transliteration · xxi

CHAPTER 1   Recycling Empire   1

PART I   A THEORY OF SOVEREIGN LOCAL STATES

CHAPTER 2   The Imperial Origin of Successor Political Orders   21

CHAPTER 3   Governing without Sovereignty   39

PART II   COMPOSITE ROUTES OUT OF EMPIRE

CHAPTER 4   Ottoman Genealogical Politics   65

CHAPTER 5   Utopian Federalism: Post-Ottoman Empires   89

PART III   FROM IMPERIAL TO LOCAL MUSLIM AUTHORITY

CHAPTER 6   Occupying Authority: The King of OETA East   119

CHAPTER 7   Authority and the *Shari'a* Apparatus in Post-Ottoman Egypt   147

PART IV   PATHS OF EXTRICATION

CHAPTER 8   The Syrian Making of the Arab Saudi Kingdom   173

CHAPTER 9   The Throne of Damascus, 1926–1939   202

                Afterword: Subordinated Sovereignty in the
                Twentieth Century   226

                    Acknowledgments · 233
                        Notes · 237
                     Works Cited · 275
                        Index · 317

ILLUSTRATIONS

Frontispiece. Fiscal stamp of the "Arab Government," 2 piasters, dated "al-Sham, 1338" (Damascus, 1919–1920), created for the support of the Hijaz Railway.

2.1. The header of *al-Taqaddum* (Aleppo), 8 August 1913.   35

2.2. The header of *al-Taqaddum* (Aleppo), 6 January 1919.   37

4.1. Sayyid Talib as Ottoman imperial patrician, 1904.   75

5.1. Sharif al-Husayn as Ottoman Emir of Mecca with other
     imperial officials (1908?).   97

6.1. Map of OETA, 1919.   121

6.2. Sharif ʿAli Haydar as Ottoman Emir of Mecca praying over a
     new telegraph line in Medina, 1916.   126

6.3. Map of the Kingdom of Syria; montage, around 1920.   130

8.1. The *Istiqlali* group (in the middle Sheikh Kamil al-Qassab)
     in Amman, 1922.   180

8.2. T. E. Lawrence greets Sharif ʿAbd Allah, 17 April 1921, Amman.   181

8.3. ʿAbd al-ʿAziz greets Amin Rihani (just arrived by plane).
     Also present are Hafiz Wahba and Yusuf Yasin, c.1926.   192

9.1. Ahmad Nami and his government of the State of Syria, 1926.   209

TABLES

4.1. The Sharifian Emirs of Mecca in the Age of Steam.   80

5.1. Principles of Imperial Utopias in Arabic, 1870s–1921.   91

6.1. The Legal Roles in the Ottoman *Nizamiye* Courts.   132

Ex-Ottoman Patricians in the Age of the League

ABBAS HILMI II (1874–1944): Ottoman Khedive of Egypt (1892–1914) under British occupation, businessman, after 1914 frequent candidate for thrones in Egypt, the Hijaz, Syria, and Palestine.

'ABD ALLAH (1882–1951): a *sharif*, son of al-Husayn (the Ottoman Emir of Mecca), deputy of Mecca in the Ottoman imperial parliament (1909–1914), Emir of British Transjordan (1921–1946), King of Jordan (1946–1951).

'ABD AL-'AZIZ (c.1880–1953): "Ibn Saud," 'Abd al-'Aziz of the Al Su'ud (the Su'ud clan), Emir of Riyadh, Ottoman governor of al-Ahsa, Sultan and later King of Najd, King of the Hijaz (1926–1932), finally King of the Arab Saudi Kingdom (Saudi Arabia, 1932–1953).

AHMAD NAMI (1873–1962): a rich Ottoman Circassian landowner, the "Damad," son-in-law of Sultan Abdülhamid II, president of the State of Syria (1926–1928), candidate for the Syrian throne in the 1920s.

'ALI HAYDAR (1866–1935): a *sharif*, born in Istanbul, member of the Ottoman State Council, vice-president of the Ottoman imperial parliament, last Ottoman Emir of Mecca (1916–1921), candidate for the thrones of the Kingdom of the Hijaz and the State of Syria in the 1920s.

FAYSAL (c.1883–1933): a *sharif*, son of al-Husayn (the Ottoman Emir of Mecca), declared king in Damascus in 1920, King of Iraq (1921–1933).

FUAD I (1876–1936): uncle of Abbas Hilmi II, educated in Italy and Istanbul, Sultan of Egypt (1917–1922) under British protectorate, King of Egypt (1922–1936).

AL-HUSAYN B. 'ALI (c.1853–1931): a *sharif*, born in Istanbul, member of the Ottoman State Council, Ottoman Emir of Mecca (1908–1916), leader of the Arab revolt, declared King of the Arabs, the Allied Powers recognized him as King of the Hijaz (1916–1924), declared himself caliph publicly in 1924.

HABIB LUTF ALLAH (LOTFALLAH) (1882–1954): from a rich Greek Orthodox Lebanese family in Egypt, Ottoman diplomat in the late 1900s and 1910s, financier and member of Syrian committees, Hijazi diplomat in the early 1920s, candidate for a possible throne in Lebanon, businessman circulating in interwar Europe.

SAYYID TALIB (1871–1929): a *sharif*, from Basra, Ottoman governor of the Najd, member of the Ottoman State Council, deputy of Basra in the Ottoman imperial parliament (1911?-1914), candidate for the throne of Iraq.

SHAKIB ARSLAN (1869–1946): a Druze emir, appointed district governor of Ottoman Shuf (Lebanon) in 1902, deputy of Hawran in the Ottoman imperial parliament, after the war lived mostly in Geneva, became Saudi-Hijazi citizen, interwar pan-Islamist activist.

Arab Internationalists

SELECTED "HIJAZI" OFFICIALS AND PARIS DELEGATION MEMBERS

'ALI RIDA AL-RIKABI (d. 1943): from Damascus, trained as military officer in Istanbul, Ottoman army general, military governor of OETA East from 1918, prime minister of the Syrian Kingdom in 1920, prime minister of Transjordan in 1922 and 1926.

'AWNI 'ABD AL-HADI (1889–1970): from Nablus, trained in law in Istanbul and Paris, accidental member of the Hijazi delegation to the 1919 Paris Peace Conference, secretary to Faysal in Damascus and 'Abd Allah in Amman in 1920–1921, later lawyer in mandate Palestine.

FU'AD AL-KHATIB (1880–1957): Sunni from Shuf (Lebanon), educated in Beirut at the Syrian Protestant College, teacher in the British Sudan, from 1916 propagandist for and advisor of al-Husayn in Mecca, foreign minister of the Kingdom of the Hijaz (1920–1924), advisor to 'Abd Allah in Transjordan (1926-33), later Saudi ambassador to Afghanistan.

MUHAMMAD RUSTUM HAYDAR (d. 1940): born in Baalbek to a Shi'a family, studied administration in Istanbul, studied history in Paris, school director in Ottoman Damascus and Jerusalem during the 1910s, member of the Hijazi delegation to the 1919 Peace Conference, personal secretary to King Faysal in Baghdad.

NURI AL-SA'ID (1888–1958): from Baghdad, trained as military officer in Istanbul, senior officer in the Hijazi army, member of the Hijazi delegation to the 1919 Peace Conference, created the Iraqi police, minister of defense in Iraq, several times prime minister of Iraq, killed in the 1958 *coup d'état*.

SELECTED ACTIVISTS OF THE
ISTIQLAL NETWORK (1920S)

FU'AD HAMZA (d. 1951): from a Druze family in Lebanon, English teacher in Jerusalem, from 1926 translator and foreign affairs advisor to King 'Abd al-'Aziz, later Saudi ambassador to France and the US.

KHAYR AL-DIN AL-ZIRIKLI (d. 1976): from a rich landowning Syrian Sunni family, student of al-Qassab, journalist, activist, writer, member of the first Transjordan government in 1922, Saudi diplomat from the 1930s.

MUHAMMAD KAMIL AL-QASSAB (1873–1954): a Syrian Sunni sheikh from Damascus, friend of Rida, worked in the Hijaz, exiled to Haifa, in regular contact with King 'Abd al-'Aziz, pardoned and returned to Damascus in 1933, became head of the Damascus *'ulama'*.

MUHAMMAD RASHID RIDA (1865–1935): Syrian Sunni sheikh living in Egypt, editor of the journal *al-Manar*, religious entrepreneur, activist, and writer, member of Syrian committees in the 1920s, in regular contact with Kamil al-Qassab and Fu'ad Hamza.

SHUKRI AL-QUWWATLI (1891–1967): rich Damascene Muslim absentee landowner, studied administration in Ottoman Istanbul, exiled in Cairo and Europe, organized resistance against the French, in contact with Rida-Qassab-Hamza, pardoned in 1930, later twice president of the State of Syria.

YUSUF YASIN (d. 1962): student of Rashid Rida before the war, studied law in Damascus, joined Saudi government in 1924, the most important foreign policy advisor of King 'Abd al-'Aziz.

fatwa (**pl.** *fatawa*). the legal opinion of a mufti. This opinion is not
   binding.
Grand Mufti. the mufti on whom a government confers the highest
   authority to issue legal opinions. In the Ottoman Empire, the mufti
   of Istanbul was the highest mufti, called *şeyhülislam*. The office of the
   grand mufti in a local state first emerged in the Ottoman khedivate
   of Egypt. In the new Arab polities of the interwar period, the office of
   grand ("state") mufti imitated the Egyptian solution.
Hanafi. one of the main four interpretations of Islamic law, the most
   authoritative body of legal thought in the Ottoman Empire and the
   official one in Egypt from the 1850s.
imam. (in the legal-constitutional sense) the highest authority in the Muslim community, the caliph.
khedive. a ceremonial title of the highest Ottoman imperial grandees; the
   special rank of the governor of Egypt in the Ottoman Empire between
   1867 and 1914.
khedivate. a distinguished status granted to the Egyptian province of the
   Ottoman Empire between 1867 and 1914.
mufti. a Muslim jurist who can issue a legal opinion (*fatwa*) as an answer
   to a question about a problem. A meta-constitutional interpreter of
   Muslim law.
qadi. a Muslim judge, with notary functions. In the Ottoman Empire, each
   province had a chief judge, sent from Istanbul.
şeyhülislam. the mufti of Istanbul, the highest imperial Ottoman jurist.
Shari'a **Court of First Instance, Supreme** *Shari'a* **Court**. the institutionalized *qadi* courts, the second being subordinate to the first, between
   1880 and 1955 in Egypt; first unique to the khedivate of Egypt, later
   introduced elsewhere.
sultan. the ceremonial title of the emperor of the Ottoman Empire; not a
   legal term although Muslim jurists often used it to mean "imam." The
   title was also used by the ruler of Egypt under the British protectorate
   (1914–1922) and by the ruler of Najd (1921–27). Many other Muslim
   rulers from East Asia to Oman to Morocco and sub-Saharan Africa
   have used the title.

wali al-amr. the "person in charge," the designation of the administrative functions of the imam in the vocabulary of Islamic law.

waqf. a pious endowment of private property in Islamic law; any sane and legally free private person may create one, and in theory it is perpetual.

CHRONOLOGY OF EVENTS

1876–1878 Declaration and Suspension of the Ottoman Constitution

1881 French protectorate of the beylik of Tunis established

1882 British occupation of the khedivate of Egypt begins

1908 "Young Turk" coup d'état and restoration
of the Ottoman Constitution

1914–1923 State of war between the Ottoman Empire
and Britain, France, and Russia

1914 British protectorate of the Sultanate of Egypt established

1916 Sharif al-Husayn's declaration of the Arab Kingdom

1917–1920 OETA zones in the Syrian provinces established

1920 Damascus assembly's declaration of the Syrian Kingdom

1921 Establishment of the Emirate of Transjordan

1922 British declaration of Egypt's independence,
end of the protectorate

1922 Turkish Assembly's abolishment of the Ottoman Empire

1923 Lausanne peace treaty, class "A" mandates come
into effect at the League of Nations

1924 Turkish Assembly's abolishment of the office of caliph

1925 French creation of the State of Syria, Saudi
occupation of the Kingdom of the Hijaz

1928 constitutional process in the State of Syria begins

1930 Submission of the French mandate's organic
law to the League of Nations

1932 Iraq joins the League of Nations, declaration of
the Arab Saudi Kingdom (Saudi Arabia)

1936 Egypt joins the League of Nations

1948 War in Palestine, declaration of the State of Israel,
the Palestinian Nakba

A NOTE ON TRANSLITERATION

TRANSLITERATION BECOMES SOMETHING of a political question when the period under consideration is the transition from the Ottoman Empire to new local states in the 1920s. Should I transliterate in Latin characters Ottoman words that are of Arabic origin occurring in a document in October 1918 in an ex-Ottoman Arabic-speaking city, let's say Damascus, according to an Arabic transliteration system or according to the way we transliterate Ottoman using the modern Turkish alphabet and pronunciation? Is the Muslim judge of Damascus already a *qadi* or still a *kadı* in October 1918?

In this book, my choice was the following: I strove to transliterate enough Ottoman words denoting imperial offices in the modern Turkish alphabet and pronunciation to preserve a feeling of the difference between imperial and Arab local contexts, but I went with the Arabic when the actors were clearly thinking in the Arabic language and the context was not Ottoman. When the reference was to Ottoman government-affiliated Turkish-speaking individuals and offices I used the modern Turkish transliteration (for instance, Abbas Hilmi II, Abdülhamid) but I use Arabic transliteration in the case of individuals associated with the Ottoman government who wanted to be remembered as Arabs even if they also spoke Turkish at home (for instance, 'Ali Haydar). I use the term "Turkey" in this book since the 1920s government accepted this English term, but, of course, I did my research in contemporary Türkiye.

In general, my guiding principle was to make reading easy for the everyday reader. Arabic words are transliterated following the system of the *International Journal of Middle East Studies* (IJMES) without the initial hamza and without diacritics. There is one point though that I wish to emphasize: I did not use the names that commonly appear in popular publications in the English language (for instance, Hussein and Ibn Saud) but opted for forms they used in signing their letters (such as al-Husayn and 'Abd al-'Aziz). Arabic and Turkish words found in the Oxford Dictionary of English are used accordingly (Koran, not *Qur'ān*; sheikh, not *shaykh*). Muslim months and days are transliterated according to Arabic vocalization, following the IJMES standard (Rajab and not Turkish Receb or Raceb; *jum'a*, not *cuma*).

MODERN ARAB KINGSHIP

CHAPTER ONE

Recycling Empire

WHAT COMES AFTER EMPIRE? As the world in the early 2020s watches the American withdrawal from Iraq and Afghanistan, the rise of a new Afghan emirate, and the prolonged conflicts in ex-Soviet countries, this becomes a pressing question. But it is a question for which history supplies no single clear-cut answer. After the fall of the Roman Empire we encounter city-communities, tribal Christian monarchies, and remote monastic settlements, and we can observe the rise of Byzantium. The first Muslims conquered both Byzantine and Persian territories, but their universal empire soon disintegrated into an array of small caliphates, emirates, and sultanates. In nineteenth-century India, British companies and armies transformed the Mughal Empire and small monarchies into an assemblage of colonies, provinces, and princely states variously subordinated to British rule. And, following the First World War, nation-states emerged from the wreckage of empires.[1]

Or did they? Historians and sociologists have increasingly challenged the commonplace assumption that the world after 1919 was a world of nation-states. Indeed, at a quick glance, we encounter quite a variety of political regimes—kingdoms, emirates, federations, mercantile city-states, domains controlled by warlords, and old and new imperial projects.[2] The scorched continents of Asia, Africa, and Europe after the First World War was a world profoundly shaped by the imperial order that preceded it. And just as empire is rarely a secular affair, so what came after empire in the 1920s was still defined by religious, dynastic, and, of course, ethno-nationalist principles.[3]

The suggestion about the postwar relevance of empire shouldn't be surprising given that empires ruled the world until 1919 and imperial formations remain today.[4] Among historians, to speak of the 1920s as a period of "imperial internationalism" under the League of Nations is now a commonplace.[5] But new imperial history also threatens to reproduce the categories of empire. If we are to understand the twentieth century and our complex present, we should then pose the question, "What comes after empire?" in more precise terms. If history did not proceed conveniently from empires to nation-states, then what was new and what was old in the twentieth century? And exactly *how* was empire the origin of successor political orders after the victory of Allied Powers? What does empire as an analytical category mean for political theory? If the concept of nationhood has not been the exclusive guiding principle in the construction of new political orders, then what kind of orders are these?

Modern Arab Kingship seeks to address these questions with regard to the new Arab governments born after the fall of the Ottoman Empire. I should make clear that this book is not a narrative history of the surprisingly slow Ottoman dissolution.[6] Building on primary sources and previous scholarship, I instead tell stories of Arab projects in the 1920s which do not fit in the empire-to-nation-state framework.[7] My argument is of two parts.

First, I suggest that in the 1920s the territories of the defeated Central Powers underwent a process that might be termed a "recycling of empire." This operation, I argue, saw the enforced repurposing of political, legal, economic, and ecological resources into new configurations. In terms of politics, this meant the recycling of modern Ottoman imperial institutions into local ones, similar to the transformation of imperial institutions in post-Habsburg polities.[8] Instead of characterizing the political order in such polities as *colonial* or *national*, I prefer to characterize it as *local*, so as to convey the locally-inflected use of multiple sources of authority (dynastic, genealogical, religious, and ethnic-national) left over from the previous imperial order. Hence, I call the governments in the post-Ottoman Arab regions "local states," except in Palestine. In sum, I suggest that recycling empire produced local states and new imperial projects among defeated peoples in the 1920s.[9]

Using and interrogating the term "local" enables us to historicize the uses of identity-based claims such as religion and ethnicity in postwar statemaking. It helps to situate the monarchical institution and other old forms of politics in the 1920s as transformed continuities of previous imperial institutions and practices. By using the term "local" especially in the Arab regions we can explain how the renewed French and British imperial projects continued a layered, vertical relationship to occupied, mandated, and treaty governments among the defeated peoples. Finally, the term "local" usefully conveys the often associative, modular logic of state-making, such as ideas and practices regarding associations, federations, and monarchical personal-unions.

The second half of the argument concerns the nature of Allied control in the occupied Arab regions. This control amounted to a new form of empire. The novelty consisted of legal sovereignty being incorporated into the techniques of domination because of the new norms at the League of Nations. In the 1920s, successor local polities were to be sovereign but subordinated to distant metropoles through contracts and military occupations. Similarly to the US in its occupation of 1920s Haiti (a sovereign polity in the League), the victorious British and French governments modified previous legal tools in order to rule over local Arab governments, whose sovereignty followed both from the Covenant of the League of Nations and from imperial recognition.[10] This modification of imperial rule has long been overlooked, I suggest, because the normative connection between sovereignty and the nation-state has occluded our vision. In historical scholarship, there has been a rhetorical inflation of the term "sovereignty," borrowed from law and political science.

What we today mean by "sovereignty" is often "independence" and "freedom," especially freedom from intervention; political scientists call this norm "Westphalian sovereignty."[11] For interwar French and British imperial advisors, however, sovereignty had a more narrowly technical meaning. It referred to the legal quality of domestic authority. It meant a government's right to issue title deeds for land ownership and its right to the adjudication of its subjects. Contrary to their actions in pre-1914 colonial situations, the British and French empires now conceded that there were some sovereign entities in the occupied Ottoman territories—but they at the same time intended their domination over these entities to be permanent.[12] By recognizing this bureaucratic sovereignty, therefore, the European administrators and jurists were not granting the occupied Ottoman territories freedom, but rather were embarking on a new strategy of domination. Governing without sovereignty, through administrative means and outsourced faculties of economy, was at the root of this new strategy. This was not the informal imperialism through trade and debt familiar from the nineteenth century.[13] The post-1919 formal framework was filled instead with new, yet-to-be-crystallized legal norms and practices, which connected newly designated regions through political, military, and economic contracts to old metropoles.[14] It is this sort of situation that I mean when I apply the apparently self-contradictory term "subordinated sovereign government" to the successor polities. These were sovereign local states.[15]

The title of this book is *Modern Arab Kingship* and some readers may expect a historical anthropology of transcendental authority in the twentieth century. They will be disappointed. Islamic law does not prescribe any particular form of political regime, and there is nothing inherently sacred in the institution of the Sunni imamate. In the 1920s, Sheikh Muhammad Bakhit al-Muti'i, the most respected Muslim jurist of post-Ottoman Egypt, argued that it does not matter whether the name of this office *caliph, imam, sultan*, or *king*, because "the meaning is important and not the titles."[16] When it came to establishing post-Ottoman Muslim polities, monarchy was only one among the available options. My story is about how, in the Arab world, Islam and monarchy became gradually reattached after the fall of the Ottoman Empire. Religion as a constituting element in the political order is an imperial feature. Sultan Abdülhamid II. (r. 1876–1909) had integrated the descendants of the Prophet (sing. *sharif*, pl. *ashraf*) and provincial patricians into the modern Ottoman political order between the 1870s and 1908. It was this Ottoman enhancement of Muslim Arab genealogical authority that attracted the attention of British and, to some extent, French, imperial planners. After a spate of short-lived though influential republican theorizing—largely the work of Indian Muslim thinkers and groups of young Arab bureaucrats—most Muslim Arab scholars of religion had by the mid-1920s reached the conclusion that dynastic rule alone could preserve Islam in the face of a purging of religious institutions such as they saw happening in the new Republic of Turkey and the USSR. As a result of meetings between European imperial planners and local activists, the new Arab local polities became somewhat counterrevolutionary, "Hamidian" regimes, without an actual ideology of kingship. Although historians often suppose a British preference for monarchies as opposed to a French preference for republics, we shall see that even French administrators considered the making of a monarchy in the new State of Syria until 1939. This is the story of modern Arab kingship.

A Theory of Transformation

To suggest that the "political cultural legacy" of empire is the origin of successor political orders is to state the obvious.[17] It is less obvious what the imperial political order in the early twentieth century consisted of and by what kind of alchemy defeated peoples adapted their former ways of life to the new League norms in a still imperial world.

Modern Arab Kingship is not about "governance," a concept that historians use to describe practices of government and domination (management

of peripheries, negotiated tax-collection, military conscription, legal categories of subjecthood, infrastructures, alliances among notables, and so
on).[18] My focus is, rather, on the "political order," the conceptual realm
behind political institutions. This we can analyze through the study of constituent events (moments when groups impose the constitutional form of
a new political society) and historical practices in legal institutions. I take
it for granted that the "political order" and the "legal order" are connected
at the deep constitutional level. This book is consequently one historian's
contribution to the political theory of empire in the age of steam and oil.

Historians and political scientists agree that an empire is a large economic, legal, and political organization with expansionist aims ("or with
memories of an expansionist past"), which manages diversity and repro-
duces differentiation and inequality among people.[19] Imperial officials
have often used ideas about racial and cultural superiority for legitimiz-
ing expansion in the eyes of the metropolitan public. We must consider
empire as an analytical category instead of a rhetorical one. I begin with
this crucial aspect.

The First World War was a long, global clash between two groups of
empires, the Allied Powers (Britain, France, Russia, Italy, and later the US)
and the Central Powers (the Ottoman, Austro-Hungarian, German, and
Bulgarian governments) between 1914 and about 1923.[20]

The prewar imperial political order, as I explain in Chapter Two in
more detail, was comprised of religious, ethnic-national, and dynastic
(occasionally presidential) sources of authority. Religion is important.
Empire accommodated plural temporal regimes, including religion-based
calendars, despite its bureaucratic preference for scientific time as appropriate to the age of steam. The modern Ottoman government, for example,
operated through such an arrangement, embodied in its bifurcated legal
system that encompassed both *qadi* (*shari'a*) and administrative, often
called "civil" (*nizamiye*), courts which used the Muslim calendar and the
imperial fiscal calendar, respectively, at the turn of the century. Scholars
argue that religious coexistence, as a body of thought and as reflected in
the practice of government, was "the ecumenical frame" of the Ottoman
Empire. From a political-legal point of view, this frame was made possible
by a modern form of imperial Muslim authority.[21]

What were the maneuvers through which, after defeat, imperial
authority became local? The revolutionary, total eradication of the past
is an exception in history. Far more common are constrained, negotiated,
often externally enforced transformations. To analyze these transformations, we need to take a genealogical approach to temporal change. We

need to understand that the birth of the present happens through the recasting of the past.[22]

Art historians understand such operations of recasting well as a result of their familiarity with what they term *spolia*. This Latin word means "spoils" (sing. *spolium*) as in "spoils of war." The term denotes materials and artifacts reused in buildings and art works and thus given "a form of new life" after some sort of dissolution and without reference to the original context. Spoliation is a transformation which ultimately diminishes anything original and authentic; "*spolia* are the survivors of violence."[23] Art historian Richard Brilliant has introduced the useful distinction between *spolia in se* (reuse of material) and *spolia in re* (reuse of form). He has suggested by this distinction that in addition to the reuse of materials, spoliation can be also virtual, "in style," for instance when motives and aesthetic energies are revived in new environments.[24]

Historians of technology and infrastructure also appreciate "repurposing" as an important operation, for instance when old machine parts are put to new uses.[25] In political theory, Eric Hobsbawm came close to describing this type of aesthetic action in politics when he coined the concept "invented tradition."[26] Philosophers would perhaps identify these genealogical operations with the Hegelian notion of *Aufhebung*, which expresses the change of something into a new quality through the reuse and synthesis of previous elements. Even anthropologists recognize the value of "imperial debris" as an analytical category.[27]

Since the 1990s, sociologists have employed the terms "bricolage" and "reworking" to characterize the rearrangement and repurposing of formerly Soviet political and economic institutions. They trace "paths of extrication" from the previous political-economic order to explain the advent of new institutions in post-Socialist polities.[28] Recent work on post-Habsburg polities similarly focuses on the social history of "local level transitions," fragmentation, imperial to Socialist internationalism, city-states, and deglobalization.[29] These studies about the remaking of previous orders all rely on a historical-genealogical approach to temporal change instead of postulating radical revolutionary breaks and the wholesale replacement of life-worlds.

Thus, at the center of this study lies the notion of the "successor society" and its hybrid political order. Successor societies and foreign powers often create local states in which the new political order contains recycled elements of the previous order, often without reference to or in explicit denial of their source. By focusing on instances of recasting and repurposing, we can translate fundamental questions whose vocabulary usually derives from normative international law and political science into the analytical terminology of empire and successor societies. In the case of the post-Ottoman polities, for instance, instead of asking "Is religion compatible with the nation-state and democracy?" we can ask "How did previously imperial institutions and practices of religion function in non-imperial polities?" and "How did practices of unelected and elected representation in empire change when faced with elected institutional forms of representation in successor societies?" Instead of seeing Islam as an authentic expression of an unchanging essence, we can ask "How did Muslim utopianism acquire a Western vocabulary in the 1920s and 1930s?"[30] Instead of taking nationalism at face value, we can ask, "What are the differences and similarities between race-talk in empire and in local states?"—especially when the subject is the interwar period of unprecedented white male domination. Such questions help us to redefine the landscapes of power, to find similarities and differences in state-making practices, to delaminate European and local agency in the political architecture of post-Ottoman polities, and to understand the programs which aimed at preserving the imperial management of diversity and inequality (what Burbank and Cooper call "the politics of difference") in new ways in the age of the League of Nations.[31] These questions help us to historicize transformations and map the logic of counterrevolutionary change; ultimately they lead us towards an empire-based theory of modernity.

The Social Birth of Local States in Global Legal History

The history of the modern Middle East is usually told very differently in scholarship. Instead of a transition from imperial to local authority, the conventional narrative starts with a revolution, led by a *sharif*. In 1916, Sharif al-Husayn, the Ottoman Emir of Mecca, led the Arabs, or at least some Arabs, against the "Turkish yoke" and received promises from the British government of a giant Arab state. But this "Arab revolt"—often portrayed as a nationalist movement—did not achieve its goals. The attempt by al-Husyan's son Faysal to create an independent Arab kingdom in Damascus ended with the French army's invasion in 1920. Due to infamous wartime agreements (Sykes-Picot and other lesser-known diplomatic deals) the British government did not help Faysal against the French—thus the story at this point often becomes a tale of British (and, in general, Western) betrayal.[32] Thereafter, so the master narrative goes, the League of Nations ostensibly gave mandates to the British and

French governments to administer the partitioned Arab territories. Historians transpose the terms of earlier European colonialism in Africa—or the terms of even earlier European colonization in the Americas—to the Allied attitude towards these mandated regions. British and French "colonial policy," we are told, created the "colonial state," which mediated "between the colony and the international economy." British administrators appointed puppet Arab rulers and co-opted landowners and tribal sheikhs, while the French institutionalized sectarian politics, and both the British and the French even went so far as to fashion an Arab nationalism to serve their own interests. Such interwar "methods of political organization," made "perhaps inevitable" the Arab military governments of the Cold War period.[33] A somewhat defensive version of this story uses, instead of "colonialism," the term "imperialism" and characterizes the interwar period as the "liberal age."[34]

There is a widespread conviction that "the post-Ottoman political order was European, not Ottoman."[35] In this view, the First World War completely "destroyed" the Ottoman imperial order.[36] The institution and terminology of Arab kingship were, according to scholars who hold this view, "a calque of 'king' or *roi* in the modern European meaning."[37] Some political scientists have focused on the arrival of the norm of "Westphalian sovereignty" in the "Arab world," while others investigate the relevance of empire purely as a European enterprise rather than a problem of the Ottoman past.[38] Revisionist "mandate studies" meanwhile struggle with the colonial-decolonial research framework.[39]

The agency of the Allied Powers—most often the British Empire—is best known in the popular formulation of David Fromkin. According to his "1922 settlement" thesis, acts and agreements—the distribution of the League mandates, the abolishment of the Ottoman Empire, and the British decisions—created what is known as the modern Middle East around 1922. The date had to be approximate since the British imperial conference in Cairo during which Secretary of the Colonies Winston Churchill and others settled borders and distributed the sons of al-Husayn (Faysal to Iraq, 'Abd Allah to Transjordan) occurred in fact in 1921. Fromkin concludes that this arrangement failed to ensure that the political systems they established would endure because "British policy-makers imposed a settlement upon the Middle East in 1922 in which, for the most part, they themselves no longer believed."[40]

The story I tell in *Modern Arab Kingship* covers a different range of topics through the lenses of recycling and spoliation. How does the 1920s emergence of the Arab world look if approached from within the Ottoman

Empire? How does the social birth of new states look if approached through religion and the modular logic of state formation instead of nationalism?

First, instead of a sudden break with the Ottoman Empire, I focus on the difficult and lengthy remaking of once imperial political and legal institutions. While many scholars use the term "post-Ottoman," they do not engage with what "Ottoman" as a modern imperial political order and legal bureaucracy meant in substantial terms in the 1900s and 1910s. When talking about empire, many consider only the European and American empires. The new Arab governments indeed stressed the importance of *not* being Ottoman. But the Ottoman Empire was a silent, immense, and long-standing obstacle for both local and Allied actors attempting to design successor polities. When I write "empire" I am often reflecting on the dilemma posed by the vanquished Ottoman world. This Muslim empire was not fully obliterated like the African pre-colonial empires and the Mughals in nineteenth-century India, or self-decomposed like defeated Austria-Hungary in 1918. Neither did the Arab provinces break off from the mother empire as the South American colonies did from Spain in the early nineteenth century.[41] Instead of a revolution there was an Allied occupation of Istanbul in 1919, unlike anything that took place in Berlin, Vienna, or Budapest in that year. The Allied Powers forced this empire to dissolve—and getting rid of empire was not an easy matter. For instance, historians have demonstrated the existence of imperial, dualist Arab-Turkish visions of order well into the 1920s.[42] In this book, I explore the consequences of these persistent imperial imaginaries and practices for the construction of local states.

Second, I focus on the role of local agency—including the rise of Arab activists—in the recasting of imperial political institutions. Alongside the grand narrative of French and British decision-making, scholars have taken note of violence and resistance on the part of local actors.[43] I demonstrate that elite and ordinary Arabs created the post-Ottoman Muslim monarchy as the model for a new imperial formation (ideally a new caliphate over an association of emirs). They considered this a useful regime form for managing religious and ethnic diversity and a potential locus of elite resistance to the Allied occupations.[44] The Allied planners struggled to reduce this invention to the subordinated, small princely regimes they desired. The Arab national monarchy thus became a fragile, counterrevolutionary institution, a somewhat Orientalist and self-Orientalizing political shell without significant ideological content. But we must understand that historical actors did not think in our categories. The Arabs were not alone. From Yugoslavia to

Afghanistan, monarchy was the agreed-upon counterrevolutionary regime for the political shaping of successor societies in the 1920s.[45]

Finally, instead of taking the artificial League mandate as a territorial framework, I consider a much larger Eastern Mediterranean and Red Sea trans-regional space as the political playground of once-Ottoman actors. By expanding the conventional "mandate" area to fit a larger frame we can follow, for instance, the emergence of the Arab Saudi Kingdom (Saudi Arabia) as a hybrid, pan-Arab, even global enterprise, and we can observe how it served some Syrians as an act of revenge on the French mandate. In this global framework, we can also trace 1920s Indian ideas about a Muslim republic in the Hijaz region (alongside the occasional post-Ottoman constitutionalism of Hijazi merchants) and the interregional making of a Muslim republic in the new State of Syria, long before Pakistan and Iran.[46]

Recentering the modern Ottoman Empire as a key point of origin for twentieth-century Arab polities, and indeed our contemporary world, does not invalidate the master story of Allied partitions, British, French, and Italian terror, and the Zionist colonization of Palestine. It rather invites us to address a new pool of questions about the spoliation, bricolage, extrication, reworking, and repurposing of previous Ottoman and Allied imperial institutions. To understand the emergence of the Arab world, we need to understand how the Ottoman and Allied imperial projects became conjoined in the 1920s. The 1923 Treaty of Lausanne, in which the new Turkey also recognized the independence of new Arab polities, gave rise to an immense body of paperwork, but the making of political orders was a more complex, regional matter.[47] The distinction between material and virtual reuse, *spolia in se* and *spolia in re*, is useful in this regard for it explains the process whereby, despite the rhetoric about "the Turkish yoke," Allied rule in Arab regions continued the style of earlier Hamidian politics. For it was the very reuse of once imperial Muslim bodies—for instance, the politicized descendants of the Prophet and the *qadi* courts—that brought about the obliteration of their Ottoman uses; so that in the virtual sense, there was no need for an actual caliph or "Ottoman" sultan if monarchy and religion were to remain constituent fictions in new local orders. In order "to attend to the evasive history of empire that disappears so easily into other appellations and other, more available contemporary terms," we must study the survival and integration of imperial ruins into new political programs.[48]

To approach the post-Ottoman world as an instance of recycled empire also highlights how exceptional Palestine was. This League-mandated region became neither a sovereign government nor a colony like Italian

Libya. The British Empire did not arrange for an ex-Ottoman dynast to reign, nor did it create an organic law for a government of Arab notables. Despite Palestine not being a colony, the League required the British government to allow Zionists to settle in this region, and this region alone, among the occupied Ottoman territories.[49] Interwar Palestine was not entirely immune from the post-Ottoman Arab federative projects, however. There were candidates for the throne of Jerusalem, but nothing came of such plans. As for the Palestinians, some hoped for spiritual subjecthood and protection from the new Arab kings, but in vain. In the midst of the 1930s Arab revolt, the poet 'Awad, from Nablus, is said to have written a poem on his prison wall to announce his bitter disappointment: "I thought the kings would lead us."[50] And indeed Jerusalem and the mosque of al-Aqsa are to this day subject to sharifian (Jordanian) claims.

Political scientist Adom Getachew conceptualizes anticolonial nationalism in 1960s Africa and the Caribbean with reference to the term "worldmaking," by which she denotes, *inter alia*, the idea of the regional federation as an alternative to the nation state. I too was tempted to use her term, because the 1920s saw the discursive birth of several worlds—the "Arab world," the "Muslim world," federations, and the rise of Arab internationalists. Ultimately, however, I concluded that the idea of "worldmaking" is of limited value for an enquiry into the social history of 1920s postwar state-making. Setting the idea of "worldmaking" in opposition to empire avails us little in conveying the temporal dimension of transformation (the operations of recycling and recasting), and leads us to overlook the fact that the practices and logic of modular state-making belong also to the imperial world (thus federations are imperial projects, too); furthermore, it risks both obscuring the keen Arab interest in the League of Nations, and exaggerating the utopian dimension of political thought. In fact, the main concern of post-Ottoman historical actors, including activists who applied to global ethical solidarities, was about their own regions, laws, economies, and governments, and not the wider world, and they often did not even consider building egalitarian societies. To describe the state-centered interest of defeated and empire-less peoples after the Great War we thus must start instead from an analytical critique of imperial programs.[51]

My approach, which may be called global legal history, has emerged from the new legal and intellectual history of empires.[52] It is a perspective useful for the critical study of large transformative processes in the twentieth century—among them "nation-building," shifts in territorial status, regime transformation, military occupation, the mandates, and "imposed constitutionalism"—for it brings together the tools of several productive fields, such as international history, area studies, historical sociology, and microhistory.[53]

As it is often used, however, the term "global legal history" means the mere collection of geographically diverse authors in a comparative frame to "denationalize" legal history.[54] Among historians, "global" has also been an adjective describing the *object* of history-writing, such as a story about the world-wide circulation of an individual or an object, the process of a locality's integration into the world economy, or as in the "globalizing" of a commodity.[55]

I use the term "global" chiefly in a methodological sense, as an adjective describing the encompassing, universal *perspective* of the historian. It conveys attention to the connections between international, imperial, and regional-local scales.[56] In this book, this attention often takes the form of microhistories of those constituent acts and events that were crucial moments of transformation when actors, operating at various scales, converged in the creation of a new political regime. "Global" is the social historian's attention to this convergence of scales—imperial, international, regional, local—that co-produced an often unintended outcome in a relatively short period.

In a book about the social birth of new local states, this "global" method is by definition legal because international, imperial, regional, and local actors all claimed measures of constituent power. While empire retained its claim to create sovereignty in constituent acts next to the League of Nations' distributive acts of sovereignty external activists also strove to critique and shape decisions in local institutions of representative self-determination. I also consider the legal aspects of military occupation and the question of authority in the administration of justice. This book provides selected examples of constituent actions and imaginations about legal authority from below and from above in the post-Ottoman regions.

National Projects in Composite Frameworks

The key Arab political schemes and practices in the period under investigation belong to the repertoire of ideas about modular and associative government. Modular (often layered) rule means that communities and regions are linked to a center through indirect means, such as contracts, administrative regulations, and, in the Ottoman case, through constitutional arrangements and symbols such as the recognition of the Ottoman sultan as imam (caliph).[57] As the European Union prompts new questions about sharing sovereignty, composite polities have been at the forefront of historical thinking about early modern European history.[58] European empires sought to control colonies in the form of subordinated confederacies, and activists also often imagined a better future through autonomy. We should seriously consider similar ideas about composite formations during the emergence of successor Arab polities from the Ottoman debris.

In analytical terms, the Arab paths out of the Ottoman Empire present us with two main dimensions of political thought on the subject of composite polities.[59] The first dimension is *organizational*: both Arab and Allied planners envisioned post-Ottoman federative associations in the 1910s and 1920s. The nation-state, despite the Arabs' appeal to the principle of self-determination in 1919, was not primary, let alone the sole form of imagining and making sovereign societies.[60] In the past hundred years, the pan-Arab "unity projects," first the interwar "Hashemite" and then the "radical" projects of the 1950s and 60s, have fascinated historians and political scientists.[61] Finding the first composite political ideas proposed in the late Ottoman context and in post-Ottoman constituent events helps us to rethink the question of why the practices of national homogeneity did not displace the logic of imperial organization. The post-Ottoman composite projects typically presupposed that Islam, ethnicity, dynasty, and regional economy would be the bonds connecting autonomous polities.[62]

The second stream of thought addresses the domestic *constitutional* dimension, including the regime form and the sources of authority in Arab successor societies. The preference for monarchy can be ascribed to larger concerns about the management of diverse post-Ottoman societies, anti-Bolshevik interests, and the continued relevance of Islam. European administrators, ex-Ottoman grandees, and, ultimately, Muslim activist-nationalists conceived the monarchical regime as a means of retaining diversity and inequality, and a tool of integration into the League's world. Simply put, the practical question for all of these counterrevolutionary groups was what kind of political regime would best preserve the texture of a once Muslim imperial society in a new composite polity.

The organizational and the constitutional imaginations and practices force us to reconsider the role of nationalist rhetoric in state-making. Ernest Dawn argued that the 1916 Arab revolt in Mecca was neither an instance of Arab nationalism nor a struggle for the caliphate, but was rather an internal uprising against the Ottoman government, in which "one element of the ruling class" utilized the ideology of Arabism "as an instrument of conflict with its rivals within that class."[63] Building on Dawn's old argument, we can further explore the possibility that repudiating empire was a rhetorical alibi for creating new imperial-composite projects.

There is a debate between historians who emphasize the composite, often cosmopolitan, modes of modern state-making and those who maintain the importance of nationalism and the nation-state in the twentieth century. The latter often point out that the nation-state triumphed despite federalist and cosmopolitan "fantasies."[64] Historians of imperial programs in successor societies certainly have a methodological point, though. For instance, my suggestion of thinking in terms of the sovereign local state as opposed to the national or colonial state in successor societies retains the imperial ambience and hierarchical organization without allowing a moral or an identity-based category to hijack the descriptive force of the argument in excavating the post-imperial difficulty. In my examples this allows us to follow how religion functioned in 1920s local state-making from above and from below. We can also use the history of failed projects to unearth disagreements from which new counter-movements often originated, hidden branches of dissent that much later resurfaced in changed forms.

How can we reconcile this empire-based theory of successor state-making with the claim that nationalism was the ruling public ideology of the time? In this book I will use the term "national project" to denote the ideas and practices that nationalist ideological groups advocated in the interests of codifying norms and laws in new polities. (Hence, I also subscribe to the use of the term "nationalizing states.").[65] Former Ottoman Arab military officers and patricians used the rhetoric of nationalism in the 1910s, but in the 1920s and 30s a new generation wanted to bring these ideas to fruition. Like socialism, a national project is a utopian enterprise. Achieving authenticity was the major problem faced by national projects within the imperial frames of the interwar period.[66] The path that would make "Ottomans into Arabs" involved significant cultural engineering.[67] The interwar period saw secular-nationalist projects that purported to be "authentic," based on the "traditional" authority of native monarchs and their religious apparatus.[68] The tension was that while the monarchical form maintained the imperial politics of diversity and inequality new racial-national imaginaries tended to erase the diversity of peoples in the Arab provinces, rendering peoples of Turkic, Kurdish, Albanian, Sudanese, Armenian, and other origins invisible in new nationalizing Arab governments. In chronological terms, it was possible that a strong national project might attain an exclusive position for some time and then collapse, leaving the political order once more subject to plural sources of authority.

Importantly, when considering national projects I consider not just people's domestic activism in their own "homeland" polities, but also the transregional activities of the previously intra-imperial Ottoman activists, especially in the case of one Syrian grouping, the "Independence (*Istiqlal*) Party" in the Eastern Mediterranean. The Allied occupations in fact produced communities of exile *before* they took up the work of making new polities. These diasporas began their quest for polities during the war, first by lobbying at the Paris Peace Conference and later by upgrading transnational, trans-Mediterranean, trans-Atlantic cultural-economic networks to form political networks. Typically, Muslim Arab diasporas, unlike the better-connected Zionist and Maronite ones, could promote the construction of "external homelands" only indirectly, through press propaganda and petitions. The end of the Ottoman Empire resulted in both in successor polities and in what I shall call "successor diasporas" in this book.

The Post-Ottoman Age

Do we still live in a post-Ottoman age? Where does the historical scope of "the post-Ottoman world" begin and end? What exact period does "post-Ottoman studies" cover?[69] Erik-Jan Zürcher argued that, far from there being a complete rupture between the Ottoman and Republican periods, the "Young Turk era" continued all the way from 1908 to 1950. In this Turkey-centered periodization, the "Young Turk era" refers to the post-war continuity of individuals and their political ideas, associated with the Committee of Union and Progress (CUP), which dominated the Ottoman government from 1912.[70] Historians have problematized the smooth republican transition. They have uncovered cases of anti-Atatürk CUP-secret agents with changing loyalties; the Turkish recycling of Armenians as "secular dhimmis" (protected peoples in Islamic law) in the 1920s; Muslim discontent with the abolishment of the caliphal position; the Ottoman roots of republican ideological dissent; and even cite Muslims in the new Yugoslavia fighting "to define a place for an Ottoman legacy" until the 1940s.[71]

In terms of their political order, the post-Ottoman Arab polities lie in the long shadow cast by Sultan Abdülhamid II. Exactly how long this shadow extends is a complex question. Historians have coined the somewhat nostalgic concept of an "Ottoman twilight," by which they most often mean the period between 1918 and the 1940s.[72] Others focus on memories as "the ghosts of empire" in the post-Ottoman context.[73] Keith Watenpaugh's pioneering work on the (Christian) Alepine middle class follows the Turkey-centric timeline, running between 1908 and the 1940s.[74] Michael Provence has proposed a sensible chrono-social category he calls "the last Ottoman generation": those individuals from the provinces who were educated between the 1880s and 1910s in Istanbul as imperial civil bureaucrats and higher military officers. Provence argues that their "Ottoman experience" was just as important as the "European colonial legacy" and that both were regional "commonalities" until the 1940s.[75] Cyrus Schayegh argues that the Ottoman twilight ended, at least in Greater Syria, around 1930, when the solidification of Arab states set off a "prolonged process of decolonization."[76] Anthropologists, however, have suggested that Ottoman practices persisted in rural Turkey well into the 1970s; and Ottoman family law is still important today in both Lebanon and Israel.[77]

In this book, the post-Ottoman era comes to two endings. The first marks the end of Arab political thinking in terms of Muslim imperial authority and can be dated around 1926. The second covers the decade from the 1948 Arab war with the new Zionist state and the resultant Palestinian Nakba. It does so because the events of 1948 brought an end to what had previously been an important, though often overlooked characteristic of the interwar decades. The post-Ottoman regimes, codifications, national projects, infrastructures, interwar techno-capitalism, and all regulatory activity—including in Palestine—were about the future.[78] Imperial *spolia* were the matter, literally, of Arab futures. Several temporalities, life-worlds, and uncertainties were jammed together within a framework of military occupation and transformation. A feeling of suspension, preparation, promise, and waiting prevailed. The shattering experience of 1948 ended the future-oriented character of the post-Ottoman Arab regimes, which now suddenly found themselves in the present. Composite projects, however, continued to instruct Arab politics up to the 1970s.

The Structure of This Book

I am writing this study in politics as a preparation for my next research project on material histories. I accept in part that "the forms of legitimation of political authority [. . .] have always been linked to the way we use the world."[79] But in this book I can only gesture towards the effects of technological and ecological circumstance (railways, steam-shipping, airplanes, and storms, plagues, and drought) on human decisions. The only material phenomenon I treat at some length is the Ottoman Hijaz railway between Damascus and Medina, which was the infrastructural spine of sharifian imperial projects between 1916 and 1924. But even in that case, human decisions finally overwrote material conditions.

It would be hard to deny that the contemporary Middle East is the product of the largest constitutional experiment in world history. During and after the First World War, Arab patricians and military officers, British and French administrators, and ordinary people reconfigured the Ottoman imperial order, and they did this even before discussing exact borders (many demanded "natural" borders), resources for agriculture, and new markets. We know well the British and French maps, the Allied armies' need for oil, the Zionist settlement project, and Syria's evaluation by French merchants. We can also find economic considerations in Arab federative ideas. But the claims to authority preceded the practices. In Marxist terms, they started with the superstructure instead of the base.

This book tells a story about the rise and fall of the sharifian Arab Kingdom (by the 1920s a bloc of genealogical monarchies) and how a new idea about a Saudi-led Muslim association attempted to replace it. It was never really a rise and never a complete fall (the Kingdom of Jordan is still with us). The material avatar of the Arab Kingdom was the forgotten Kingdom of the Hijaz, a sovereign local state, and founding government of the League of Nations. By focusing on the amobatic, almost tentacular, expansion of the Arab Kingdom I also explore how the State of Syria came into being, for this region was the linchpin of the new Middle East in the 1920s. And Syrian political events were closely connected to politics in the French metropole, to British Egypt, and to the making of Transjordan and the Saudi polity in the late 1920s. I can only hope that the conceptual tools I propose will be useful to researchers studying other post-imperial regions as well.

———◆———

In four sections, *Modern Arab Kingship* presents chapters that address the same question: namely, how the shift from imperial to local political order took place. This is a question of political theory that I answer by means of an empirical analysis of historical documents, employing the tools of microhistory and historical anthropology. Bringing together social history and legal theory helps us to access the disjuncture between composite practices and the norms of League-sovereignty.

In the first section, "A Theory of Sovereign Local States," I suggest a theory of the imperial political order (Chapter Two) and then describe the legal history of the new form of domination that I call "governing without sovereignty" (Chapter Three). I begin the second section, "Composite Routes Out of the Ottoman Empire," in Chapter Four, with an overview of the modern Ottoman composite order and the imperial upgrade of some Arab *ashraf* into their new roles as Ottoman grandees in the age of steam.

In Chapter Five, I describe the phenomenon I call "utopian federalism," which in the 1900s envisioned means for changing the Ottoman Empire into a composite polity, possibly as a Muslim association of sharifian monarchies. The third section, "From Imperial to Local Muslim Authority," consists of two case studies on the difficulties encountered by attempts to transform Ottoman imperial authority under Allied occupations. Chapter Six is a micro-historical study, based on court records, of legal authority in the *qadi* and *nizamiye* courts in occupied Ottoman Damascus—the Kingdom of Syria—in the period between 1918 and 1920. Chapter Seven explores the transformation of imperial authority in Islamic legal theory in the socio-legal *shari'a* apparatus of post-Ottoman Egypt as a reaction to the new monarchical regime. The fourth section, "Paths of Extrication," provides a connected, transnational history of the late 1920s. In Chapter Eight I focus on the pan-Arab, especially Syrian, making of the Arab Saudi Kingdom (Saudi Arabia) at the intersection of inter-polity and intersovereign law. Chapter Nine describes the political construction (and the many monarchical visions) of the State of Syria, the latest sovereign Arab local polity and the first Muslim republic in the late 1920s. The Afterword formulates conclusions relevant to comparisons with other successor societies and to studies of the Cold War and contemporary history. There is a "Note on Sources" in the Works Cited section.

PART I

A Theory of Sovereign Local States

CHAPTER TWO

The Imperial Origin
of Successor Political Orders

IF EMPIRE IS THE CRADLE of capitalist modernity, then the imperial political order is the cradle of successor political orders. In this chapter I explain this simple argument and I explore some of its consequences for political theory.

The imperial political order as a category of modernity has not been the subject of much theoretical reflection. This is because political scientists, sociologists, historians, and activists connect the term "political order" with the norms of democracy and the nation-state.

Benedict Anderson has proposed the most convincing theory about the emergence of nationalism. He has argued that the loss of the dynastic realm, the shift from the imperial to local languages, and technology (most prominently printing) transformed the human imagination in Christian Europe, replacing the religious apprehension of time with a technology-based temporality. The cultural idea of nation, he writes, inhabits this new empty time apprehension in our imagination.[1] Several critics have modified the scope of this brilliant argument.[2]

For an empire-based theory of successor political orders, however, the issue is not nationalism. The flames of the First World War forged new mixtures of ethnic-national, religious, and dynastic sources of authority. National projects did not create homogenous orders even if activists and politicians claimed that this was what they were doing. Religion and genealogical authority (or, forms of aristocracy) have remained instructive for successor societies in so-called nation-states. Instead of the complete loss of the dynastic realm and religious apprehensions of time, we thus need to account for their changed continuity in the twentieth century. Instead of nationalism, we have to study the imperial political order as the origin of modernity.

Investigating new regimes in terms of the old ones requires a deep understanding of those pasts. For our present purposes, this means that we need to understand the world of industrializing empires as they existed in the 1900s, especially the Ottoman Empire. In this chapter, I explore the modern imperial political order as a category of analysis and then engage with its two important elements: the dynastic realm and plural temporalities, including religious ones.

The Political Order as a Sociological Category of Empire

Let me start with a critical reflection on the key term "political order," which I use to analyze ideas and practices of domination and management. It is a somewhat unclear and relatively new usage in the English language. In the nineteenth century, writers rarely used it, and if they did they mostly meant "principles of government," referencing moral ideas inherent in the regime form of a country. Today, grand historical sociology uses the term "political order" in an expansive sense, including territorial organization and even issues pertaining to borders.[3] My definition is more restricted. As a category of analysis, the political order is an assembly of sources of authority, norms, and practices which regulate domination and enable identification with one governmental bureaucracy.

The roots of "political order" as a category of analysis grew in a collapsing empire. About 1919, during the German defeat, Max Weber defined the term *Herrschaft*, which is translated into English usually as "authority" or "legitimate domination," in a functional way as "a certain minimum of assured power to issue commands." He made the famous distinction between three ideal types of authority: legal, traditional, and charismatic.[4] A republican liberal who wrote a dissertation on the Roman Empire, Weber loved the German Empire but disliked its emperor. By 1913 he had already sketched his theory of domination, but the First World War interrupted his work. He was disturbed by the peace as well: in May 1919, Weber was called to Versailles to back up the German delegation in their difficult negotiations over the peace treaty. For about ten days, he helped to compose the German critique of that fateful treaty, to which we will return in the next chapter. The point is that the final shape of the Weberian theory of domination is the product of the short period between the summer of 1919 and his early death in June 1920. Weber polished the section on domination in what became *Economy and Society* after returning from Versailles, bitterly disappointed over the ratification of the treaty.[5]

It is hard to prove that Weber had in mind the stability of the German Empire when he formulated his abstract categories of domination, but the Weberian theory's influence on the foundations of twentieth-century political science was certainly related to its focus on political stability. A quick search in "Google Books" shows that the term "political order" only became common in the English language after the Second World War.[6] Based on Weberian ideas, 1950s American political science understood *Herrschaft* as "political order." This classic, relational (state-society) approach defined it as a bundle of relationships between "social forces" or the "culture of society" and "political institutions." These relationships defined the degree to which a government might effectively govern. The key concern was to explain the sources of stability.[7] The term "political order" became so commonplace in American political science (often simply put as "order vs. disorder") that major scholars today do not even take care to define it.[8]

In contrast to this stability-oriented political science, Hannah Arendt after the Second World War critically redefined the English term "authority" as a form of transcendental government. In her eyes, it was a historical (Greek) form of "obedience in which men retain their freedom" through a relationship to the past. In her metaphor, the structure of such "authoritarian" government was a pyramid (while tyranny was an onion). Authority in this sense, for Arendt, has ceased to exist in the modern world.[9] Nevertheless, anthropologists of Islam today frequently use her definition to understand "religious authority" in contemporary Muslim societies; or, for instance, to establish a notion of "solidarity" as a transnational, non-state-centric form of authority.[10] Historians, too, often look back to old empires to study non-European (non-Christian) forms of authority.[11]

Foucauldian and neo-Marxist political theories are a third alternative approach to the issues of domination. Scholars of this persuasion reject the notion that ideas and law establish "legitimacy;" they conceive of the state instead as an assemblage, an "effect" of human and nonhuman actors. Power means not effective government but describes instead a distinct sphere of violence, technical innovations, and capitalism through which small groups dominate societies; and the locus of this power is not confined to government institutions.[12]

In contrast to the static nature of these approaches but combining their analytically useful elements, a genealogical approach that sees the political order as a dynamic, historically changing assemblage of authority sources in both imperial and nonimperial contexts enables us to describe the emergence of new political orders in terms of the past. By introducing the notions "temporality" and "empire" to the logic of political organization, we gain a powerful tool for investigating constituent events and acts in periods of grand political transformation. William Sewell, in a perhaps Eurocentric way, posited "rupture" as the main form of a historical event, taking as his prime example the French Revolution.[13] An "eventful interpretation" of state-making does not, however, require European revolutions to explain change. Unfortunately, history provides a range of ruptures: from imperial constituent acts to war and military occupation to uncertain, prolonged negotiations over the fate of a previous regime. These operations of recycling the previous order in the making of successor political orders can be evaluated only if we first understand the imperial political order.

Sources of Authority in Imperial Political Orders

In this section I sketch a theory about the sources of authority that together build the political order in imperial formations. We will need to enter a somewhat abstract discussion.

To theorize empire as a political order requires more of us than analyses of written constitutions and an interpretation of ideology (of how imperial actors themselves theorized their empire), even if said interpretation extends to "the study of social practices" and "world-view."[14] Our inquiry should instead begin with a meta-reflection, a type of constitutional anthropology, on the main sources of authority and political institutions in the imperial order.[15]

Historians discuss imperial constitutional systems through various lenses: administrative law, the written constitution, and constitutional law; they also call for the inclusion of everyday acts as being constitutional in legal history.[16] By taking an anthropological perspective, we often are able to identify as well multiple uncodified sources of authority that operate alongside the written constitution and which create a sense of legality and validity. Among them are monarchy, genealogy, God, ethnicity, and the nation. Capitalist imperial government depended on an ability to arrange these plural sources and deploy them in differing combinations in distinct political "zones."[17]

But what exactly does "political" mean in an imperial context? To understand the full dimensions of this term, we must enter the realm of culture. The "political" is in my view a recognition whereby individuals make sense of themselves as members in a particular community. This is how a nation is usually imagined. But empire as a community is also an imagined thing. And at this deep level, imperial projects also present us with cultural ideas, imaginings that generate and enforce recognition and loyalty, which are produced both from above and from below. These ideas provide matter for imperial social imaginaries, which is to say world-views.[18] The assemblage of these ideas and identifications builds up the platform of politics.

Let me explain the nature of the ideas which inhabit this realm from a sociological-legal theory point of view. They are what we might term "constituent fictions," by which I mean ideas which create a sense of belonging to a group which constitutes a polity. Constituent fictions are cultural products, but in political and legal theory we call them a source of authority. They can "constitute" a recognition of belonging because they have a narrative form—not only the nation but also gods and dynasties are embodied stories. Constituent fictions provide foundations for obedience often through enforced identification with a powerful bureaucracy. They serve as sources of law and secure the temporal continuity of laws. They are "political" ideas in this very basic sense and populate the mental space of human relations.[19]

As an illustration, we might look at one of the better-known classes of ideas in the political order, namely "constitutional conventions," a concept widely familiar to legal scholars. Constitutional conventions are unwritten *norms* that regulate institutional behavior and inhabit a sort of ideologi-cal, moral space, outside of the machinery of government. Such unwritten norms are most important in situations where there is no written, central document that defines the final carrier of authority, as in Great Britain; or where aspects of regularity are not defined with full precision, as in the case of the US presidency.[20]

My definition of constituent *fictions* goes one level deeper than the level of constitutional conventions, however. Constituent fictions are mas-ter concepts. They are not norms, conventions, and ideals, but rather ideas and narratives, whose matter is cultural, rather than legal. They stand out-side of the law because it is they themselves that provide the foundation of legal rationality. They articulate the values on which we premise legal doc-trines and social imaginaries. Even if legally unrecognizable, they establish an authority-claim that serves as the basis for the legal superstructures of obedience.

Legal theorists in the twentieth century—with some notable excep-tions, such as the controversial jurist Carl Schmitt—tend not to engage with the idea of the political order. Many have considered the "legal order" to be an autonomous social domain. Indeed, normative scholars must maintain the autonomy of the legal order. Opposed to this "law as autonomy" approach, the idea of "law as integrity" has, especially in the American context, called attention to practices.[21] Still, none of the major theorists of jurisprudence make a distinction between imperial and non-imperial legal orders. They tend to assume a single constitutional standard regardless of the norms of socio-political organization, though implicitly they are often describing the democratic nation-state. For instance, Hans Kelsen has defined the basic norm of a legal order as a binding document, the most ancient one, which "commands" one to behave as "the fathers of the constitution and individuals authorized by the constitution command." This document is presupposed to be valid, and it is "the basic norm of a national legal order."[22] Herbert Hart has proposed that situations in which a rule of recognition is accepted and used for identifying primary rules of obligation are the "foundations of the legal system."[23] Whether a basic norm or a rule of recognition, legal philosophers interpret the legal order as based on one single commanding act, regardless of the political order in society. They are not concerned with the identification by which the legal order as a whole becomes meaningful to the individual. Kelsen has explicitly critiqued the idea of the "source of law."[24] At most, interwar jurists tend to attribute functions of the previous imperial sovereign to the new international society.[25]

Historians and anthropologists, however, should be attentive to the historical difference between imperial and national norms and practices, and to the way in which legal acts explain their authority and meaning to their subjects. In descriptive terms, the legal order has no complete autonomy in empires and local states; and it rests on a pluralistic political order. The emergence of the nation as a new constituent fiction in Europe did not entail the complete disappearance of previous imperial sources of authority, but it did push them lower in the queue of claims to loyalty and obedience. National projects helped European imperial governments to camouflage metropolitan imperial centers as nationalizing polities distinct from their overseas domains, to hide the violence of empire from their home audiences, and to reframe difference in racial terms.[26] But at the level of constituent fictions, religion and descent continued to remain narrative sources of authority in centers and peripheries both in European and non-European empires, next to ethno-national imaginaries.

Monarchs as Constituent Fictions

The period between the 1860s and the 1920s did not witness the end of the dynastic realm. It was instead a *Sattelzeit* of monarchical reconfiguration, when empires answered ideological and economic challenges by minting new traditions and incorporating new sources of authority into their political repertoires. In this section I describe monarchy as a constituent fiction, and in the next I discuss the proliferation of modern monarchs.

The central source of authority in imperial constitutional orders was monarchy, often dynastic monarchy. The centrality of monarchy was due not only to the violence of the ruler but also to the fact that it was both a narrative source of authority (the story of a founder and of a dynastic lineage), a constitutional norm, and a political institution with established rituals, images, memories, and laws.

Nineteenth-century republican imperial projects, such as the United States of America and France, created strong presidential institutions, whose powers resembled monarchical powers in many aspects, though absent the dynastic element. In fact, in France the republican presidency alternated with monarchy until the 1870s and French monarchism has remained strong. Apart from such rare exceptions, the dynastic realm continued to define imperial authority in most polities until the First World War.[27] And indeed this state of affairs continued long thereafter: alongside the continuing British, Japanese, Danish, Dutch, and Ethiopian imperial dynasties, in the 1920s minor monarchies became the regime form in local states from Afghanistan to many post-Ottoman and post-Habsburg polities.[28]

In recent decades, the "othering of monarchy" has been a prevalent trend in history writing.[29] Its proponents evaluate modern monarchies as embodying merely the "modernity of the outmoded,"[30] with scholars of various ideological camps arguing that capitalism and monarchy are fundamentally antagonistic.[31] Samuel Huntington famously described "the king's dilemma" by which he meant that capitalist modernization leads to the erosion of "traditional" forms of government, such as monarchy, which can then only be maintained through increased violence.[32] From a Marxist point of view, Benedict Anderson has also argued that "serious" (by which he meant absolute) monarchy "lies transverse to all modern conceptions of political life."[33]

The European (re)construction of non-European polities in colonies and other domains led a distinct group of scholars, inspired largely by historical anthropologist Bernard S. Cohn, to argue that at a local level, entirely new local political orders were invented. The general assumption in these studies is that "hollow" dynasts represented the ethnographic expectations of European imperialists, while some scholars go as far as to suggest that these expectations *created* the local dynasts, who were entirely out of touch with the societies over which they reigned.[34] Perhaps for this reason, historical anthropologies of "serious" kingship have remained focused on pre-industrial societies.[35]

A monarchy is a material regime form in which human bodies and objects carry the constituent fiction of the ruler.[36] We need not concern ourselves here with ontologies and historical varieties of sacral rulership.[37] Monarchy is not only an elite construction. Ruling groups and popular movements alike have developed visions about monarchical justice and politics. Monarchs exist in human flesh—unlike God or a nation (which exist only in narrative forms of imagination: in sacred texts, histories, the law, novels, and rituals).[38] The temporal continuity of laws in a monarchy is guaranteed either through genealogical descent or through the institution of monarchy itself. This representative corporeality can associate itself with other narrative constituent fictions. Dynasts may, for example, claim to represent descent, God, and the nation—even the universal *umma*— simultaneously, uniting narrative fictions within one physical body. Emerging often from conquest, a monarchy offers a new form of life to the subjugated, one that promises to obliterate the memory of the violence at its origins.[39] Historians even argue that monarchy ("imperial sovereignty") guaranteed property rights in Western European history.[40] Monarchs who control the means of violence often claim to be a stronger source of authority than the nation or even God, and accordingly absolute monarchs often provide laws of their own.

The Imperial Production of the Local Dynastic Realm

Political scientists describe an "affinity between monarchy as a regime type and state-building."[41] But monarchy was not a national but an imperial method of organizing subjugated peoples and regions. When building new local polities through delegation and through decentralized and modular governance, empires produced subordinate monarchs well into the twentieth century. In fact, European imperial and colonial expansion instead of reducing the numbers of monarchs—as one might assume would have been the natural consequence of the industrialist, expanding empires absorbing smaller entities—increased the number of local kings, princes, and emirs in the age of steam.

Under a layered system of rule, empires either delegated imperial or inter-imperial authority to an individual to reign in a subordinated local polity; or they simply acknowledged a strong local ruler as an imperial representative. Until the 1940s, in British-ruled Indian princely states elite leaders regarded this management technology, whereby the local dynast served as the node of subordinated sovereignty, as a possible way of trans-forming an empire into a federal union.[42] As we shall see, some Ottoman Muslim Arab emirs and activists entertained a similar vision of Ottoman federalization as early as the 1890s. Chapter Four will offer a separate treatment of the Ottoman practices concerning subordinate Muslim and Christian monarchs.

Let us now survey practices of sovereignty-granting in nineteenth-century Europe, which will serve us as one pre-history of the 1920s recycling of previously imperial patricians into local rulers in defeated regions. Despite the rejection of the Holy Alliance treaty proposed by Russia, in post-Napoleonic, "new, self-consciously Christian Europe" sovereign local polities could only emerge as legal entities if there was inter-imperial acknowledgement of a Christian monarch.[43] Under such an agreement, coalitions of Christian empires would confer "sovereignty" upon new local polities, thereby recognizing a particular dynast's authority over a demar-cated territory. Imperial sovereignty and what statesmen called domestic "legitimacy" were thus jointly incarnated in the persons of individual rul-ers. Instead of the nation-state, thus we can follow the emergence of local states and new imperial projects in the nineteenth century.

Defeated French diplomats were the first to come up with this arrange-ment, in their invocation of "the principle of legitimacy"—*le principe de la légitimité*—embodied in the dynasty of a constitutional, hereditary French monarchy, guaranteed by the coalition of victors.[44] During the Congress of Vienna in 1814 this notion, which essentially proposed a fundamen-tal relationship between monarchy and legitimacy, acquired the force of a territorial ordering principle. Emperors assumed new titles as signs of possession, as for example in the Kingdom of Lombardy-Venetia (ruled by the Austrian emperor as king) and parts of Poland (ruled by the Russian czar as king).[45] Next, a series of inter-polity agreements between 1815 and 1821 articulated European peace as a new inter-imperial Christian principle. The Vienna Congress created the Netherlands as a sovereign local king-dom in a federal union with Belgium in 1815. After the successful revolt of the Belgians, however, Leopold, from a minor German princely house, was the only acceptable solution to the problem of stability.[46] In this *Frieden-skultur*, the Holy Allies asserted the right to intervene when revolutions threatened "the legitimate government" of any country.[47] Friedrich Gentz, the secretary of the Congress of Vienna, took the view that "states of the second, third, and fourth rank" should "submit tacitly" to the empires' decisions.[48]

"The Courts of Great Britain, France, and Russia, duly authorized for this purpose by the Greek nation, offer the hereditary Sovereignty of Greece to Prince Frederick Otho of Bavaria, second son of His Majesty the King of Bavaria."[49] With this declaration, a coalition of empires in 1832 acknowledged a version of the post-Ottoman Greek national project, "under the sovereignty" of the new king.[50] (The Habsburg Empire quietly agreed.) The import of the word "sovereignty" in this treaty is very clear: it is a status that can be offered by an association of empires to an individual, or through an individual to a people and region. Empires recognized in law that sovereignty derives from the nation but they delivered it in an act of distribution. Serbia, Romania, and Bulgaria soon followed as similar post-Ottoman local monarchies, acknowledged as sovereign through inter-polity pacts among empires. Albania was perhaps the last such post-Ottoman local princedom, recognized as "sovereign" through a prince in February 1914, just a few months before the outbreak of the First World War.

The nineteenth century also saw the maintenance and production of subordinate, non-sovereign dynasts within empires. The Ottoman Empire, as we shall see in Chapters Four and Five, attempted to continue to rule through such subordinate monarchs, both Christian and Muslim, until the 1870s and even later. Christian empires often adopted similar practices, with racializing discourses framing the subordinate "native ruler," a non-Christian representing a lesser stage of civilization than the European metropoles.[51] In British India, the East India Company had created what a contemporary observer called "a fictious history of India," in which the "native princes" were regarded as independent from the Mughal caliph. It proved a useful legal fiction when the British Empire later co-opted them.[52]

While the discussion of civilizational hierarchy justified imperial rule to liberal audiences at home, European administrators clearly understood these subjugated rulers (sultans, princes, emirs, kings, "chiefs") as partners in government to whom legal authority was delegated. They expected them to draw on both imperial and local chains of authority to manage the people and economic resources under their direction. This ethnographic policy of segmented rule through conquest and association did not only produce new regimes and infrastructures of knowledge, but also translated and integrated earlier local loyalties into new imperial frameworks.[53]

Although historians associate indirect rule through subordinated rulers most often with the British Empire, all industrializing empires, especially the French, used this technique. Chateaubriand, the French foreign minister in the 1820s, tried to convince Spain to send Bourbon princes as rulers to the American colonies. He called this plan the "monarchical emancipation of Spanish colonies"—an imperial dream that was eventually fulfilled but ended in disaster in 1860s Mexico.[54] Also, it was functionaries in Napoleon III's service who first proposed a subordinated Arab Muslim kingdom as a means of governing an autonomous Algeria (an idea that was never realized).[55]

We can observe here an important discrepancy between imperial practice and political theory. The proliferation of local kings, princes, emirs, sultans, and maharajas did not result in new theories on monarchy. Instead, in the nineteenth century, a new *monarchomachia* arose against the modern monarchical order: both nationalists and anarchists targeted emperors, empresses, kings, pashas, and sultans. The Italian rebel-nationalist Giuseppe Mazzini wrote in 1832 that "we will not attempt any alliances with kings" (and bitterly condemned the later royalist making of Italy).[56] A young Marx wrote in the 1840s: "The monarchical principle in general is the despised, the despicable, the dehumanised man." [57] By the 1910s, only imperial administrators clung to and in some cases even developed further a theory of subordinated rulers.

Let us consider the two best-known theories of subordinated monarchs in the early twentieth century. Both British administrator Frederick Lugard, once governor of Nigeria and a member of the 1920s Permanent Mandates Commission at the League of Nations in Geneva, and French General Hubert Lyautey, the Resident General in the French protectorate of Morocco between 1912 and 1926, advocated the theory and the practice of using local dynasts to manage subordinated regions. Lyautey translated the sultan as the office of the "crowned imam" in Morocco and, like Lugard, maintained his preference for empire as an organizational principle of inter-polity relations even after the war. He lobbied that the Moroccan monarchy be a subordinated but distinct monarchical polity as opposed to a directly governed region in the interwar French empire.[58]

In a work written in 1922 to justify empire as a better mode of inter-polity relations than the League, Lugard took the view that the subordinated ruler possessed "native authority" in constitutional terms. This power, he argued, derived from the British "Suzerain," and thus the "native chiefs" were "trusted delegates." (He even framed one category of "native chiefs," the Nigerian Muslim emirs, in Islamic legal terms, calling them "Wakils"—a term that means "representative" in Arabic). As delegates, "native chiefs" could appoint and dismiss their subordinates in the native administration. Yet the commands of these subordinate rulers, if disobeyed, could be only enforced by the armed forces supplied by empire. In Lugard's eyes, this system therefore comprised not two sets of rulers but only one ruling entity, in which the native chiefs would have "well-defined duties."[59] In order for this ideal state of affairs to function smoothly, subordinate rulers would have to recognize the "community of interest" between the empire and themselves.[60] The most significant mark of their authority would be their power of jurisdiction over land allocations and disputes, because the imperial administrators believed that "the prestige of native authority depend[ed]" on land-related issues. This was the case also in Lyautey's Morocco. For instance, the first circular of the Moroccan grand vizier after the French occupation in 1912 was about domestic authority. It stated that the Moroccan government—the sultan—had the authority to issue titles to landed property through the local *qadis*, and that land sales to foreigners should not be possible without the local government's permission.[61]

This brief overview of modern imperial uses of the dynastic realm has highlighted an important issue in the history of legal sovereignty. This is the difference between inter-imperial sovereignty in nineteenth-century (Christian) Europe on the one hand, and empire as a composite, layered inter-polity system on the other. [62] New Christian rulers in Europe received the legal quality of sovereignty as an inter-imperial grant, whereas in non-Europe (non-Christian) rulers received limited territorial authority as an imperial grant. The first was the consequence of a collaboration between empires, the second resulted from decisions undertaken within individual empires. As we shall see in the next chapter, these two disparate conceptions about the source of sovereignty persisted into the 1920s (and possibly up to the 1970s).

From Imperial to Local Time: The Example of Late Ottoman Syria

Beside the imperial production of the local dynastic realm, we must also pay attention to temporal practices and forms of imagination in industrializing empires. The non-revolutionary change from empire to local states did not involve a complete erasure of religious temporalities. In this section, instead of a European polity or a colony, I bring the example of late Ottoman Syria as an illustration of how temporal practices change in the moment of enforced imperial transformation.

Empires have sustained an empty form of time, the rhythm of taxation, within their repertoires of plural temporalities. For empires, fiscal temporality, dictated by the rhythm of nature (the time of harvest), had been always crucial to their economic well-being. In the nineteenth century, the increasing bureaucratization of economic management and industrializing agriculture subordinated nature and local religious apprehensions to the government's requirements.[63] Just as nineteenth-century European expansion led to the proliferation of local monarchs, so the globalization of scientific time subordinated local religious calendars to imperial regimes of fiscal time-keeping. By "local time," I mean the bundle of temporal cultures that exists under the imperial umbrella and what emerges in successor polities after the collapse of an imperial regime. "Local time" thus contrasts with "imperial time."[64]

In this section, I trace this shift with reference to the examples of Aleppo and Damascus, two Syrian cities in the late Ottoman Empire, between the 1900s and 1920. The Ottoman Empire may be an unlikely subject for studies of imperial modernity, but its uses of religious and bureaucratic temporalities tell us more about our contemporary world than narratives about secularizing the metropolitan cores in Western European empires. In both modern Aleppo and Damascus, important provincial Ottoman capitals, journals, and law courts used plural temporalities simultaneously with the imperial fiscal calendar until 1918. In that year, the moment of Allied occupation, there occurred a chaos in time, after which local time replaced the former imperial calendar.

A calendar is the codified framework of a temporal culture (a "temporal culture" is the way individuals experience time through practices and emotions).[65] The Ottoman fiscal calendar was an important manifestation of imperial time, but it was not neatly analogous to the calendar of what is today called the "fiscal year," the fixed period of fiscal accountancy in government and in the corporate world. Its main unit was the *sene-i maliye* (SM), "the fiscal year" in Ottoman Turkish. Solar months were used to calculate a twelve-month fiscal year, starting with the *hijra* (the move of the Prophet from Mecca to Medina) as year one (622). The fiscal year began on 1 March and the months had so-called Syro-Macedonian names (for instance, Kanun al-Thani, Shubat, Adhar, etc., names with origins in the Babylonian calendar, which is still used in West Asia). The Ottoman fiscal solar months were not precise solar months as calculated by

the sixteenth-century Gregorian reform, but rather the months of the
Julian calendar. A "leap year" was thus inserted every thirty-three years
to synchronize with the lunar *hijri* (Muslim, AH) calendar. Although this
fiscal calendar had been in use since the sixteenth century, it was officially
adopted by the Ottoman government only in 1789, and fully codified as the
formal calendar of the empire in 1840. It was used in trade, in the *nizamiye* courts, and in the central and provincial bureaucracies (see more on
this in Chapter Six). Government almanacs printed in Istanbul ultimately
replaced even *hijri* dates with SM dates on their title pages after 1908,
bringing the whole empire into uniform fiscal time. Only global capitalism could disrupt this state of affairs; for example, although the year SM
1288 (1872–3) should have been a leap year, and thus skipped over, Ottoman
debt coupons were printed for the year, thus requiring it to be calculated.
This codified fiscal time gave a secular character to the modern Ottoman
bureaucracy.[66]

The Muslim *hijri* calendar competed with the fiscal calendar in the
Ottoman Empire. Sultan Abdülhamid II (1876–1909) celebrated his birth-
day according to the *hijri* calendar but the anniversary of his accession
according to the fiscal calendar; by contrast, the next sultan, Mehmed V
(1909–1918), celebrated both occasions according to the fiscal calendar
until 1918.[67] In some indirectly ruled Ottoman regions, a local calendar
was used for fiscal purposes also, as was the Coptic calendar in the Ottoman khedivate of Egypt, where the local bureaucracy did not use the
imperial *maliye* calendar. In the directly ruled Syrian provinces, Arabic
journals and almanacs often referred to the fiscal calendar as the "eastern"
(*sharqi* or *rumi*; perhaps here the best translation is "imperial") calendar
as opposed to the "western" (*gharbi*) calendar, by which these Syrian publications meant Christian solar time (most often, the Gregorian calendar).[68] Adding to this cacophony of calendrical regimes, Muslim jurists
kept on using the *hijri* calendar in dating notarized certificates, verdicts,
and juridical opinions.

As an example of multi-calendrical imperial time, let us consider Figure 2.1. The image shows the header of *al-Taqaddum*, an Arabic-language
journal that was published twice weekly in Ottoman Aleppo. The header
is dated 8 Ab 1913 (8 August 1913, i.e., the Gregorian year with the solar,
Syro-Macedonian month); 6 Ramadan 1331 (the *hijri* date with the lunar
month); and 26 Tammuz 1329 (the fiscal date with the *hijri* year and the
solar, Syro-Macedonian month).[69]

The significance of the fiscal calendar as an imperial organizing
device is best attested by the consequences of its subsequent cessation.

FIGURE 2.1. The header of *al-Taqaddum* (Aleppo), 8 August 1913.
Source: author's photograph.

For instance, the *nizamiye* courts of 1900s Ottoman Damascus used the
fiscal calendar to register certificates and verdicts, and in their communications with the provincial offices and the imperial center (usually in
the Ottoman Turkish language). The *kadı* (*shari'a*) court of Damascus,
meanwhile, used *hijri* dates in Arabic certificates and verdicts; importantly, however, *kadı* court scribes used both fiscal and *hijri* dates for
bureaucratic correspondence.[70] As we shall see in Chapter Six, the *nizamiye* and *kadı* courts together administered all aspects of life in Damascus
and in the villages in its judicial district.[71] The fiscal calendar thus represented the official presence of the empire in everyday legal transactions.
The reign of the Ottoman fiscal calendar came to an end when the Allied
Powers occupied Damascus in October 1918. In mid-September 1918,
as hostilities were drawing to a close, the government courts of the city
were still registering cases according to the Ottoman civic calendar, that
is, registering their dates as Eylül (Aylul) 1334, which was *maliye* time
for September 1918. However, at the end of September, around the time
when Ottoman army units were retreating in the face of Allied advance
and chaos prevailed, scribes switched to the Muslim *hijri* calendar.

This switch from fiscal-imperial to religious-local time in the scriptural
temporality of 1918 Damascus deserves a closer look. The reversion to
the *hijri* calendar lasted only few days, just until the immediate shock of
occupation passed. In the registers of the Damascus Court of Appeals, for
example, the practice of registering correspondence in Ottoman Turkish
with *maliye* dates suddenly ended after a final entry dated 28 Eylül 1334
(28 September 1918), with only a casual line drawn in black ink to mark

the transition. On the next page, registration began anew in the Arabic language in *hijri* dates with an entry dated 27 Dhu al-Hijja AH 1336 (28 September 1918; i.e., the same day as the previous entry in Turkish), and with new registration numbers starting from scratch.[72] In the first week of the occupation, scribes in this government court used only *hijri* dates.[73] After a few days, however, the occupied city switched to a new local temporal regime. Instead of Ottoman fiscal time, which had eclipsed all other calendars, we now find the simultaneous use of *hijri* lunar and Christian solar dates. In the above-mentioned Court of Appeals registry, after only five entries with *hijri* dates, the scribe registered the first letter with both the *hijri* dating and a solar, Christian dating of 7 Muharram 1337 / 12 Tashrin al-Awwal (12 October) 1918.[74] This solar calendar used the Syro-Macedonian names of the months, counted in Christian years, and began the year on 1 January (1 Kanun al-Thani). To all intents and purposes, it was the Gregorian calendar. It soon came to dominate scribal-legal dating in the government courts, where some registers show particular care in recording the beginning of 1919.[75] Before long, all government courts switched to this calendar. Soon, solar dates appeared even in *qadi* court registers. In journals, this calendar was often called *miladi*, "according to the birth [of Jesus Christ]" most effectively signaling the advent of Gregorian dates.

Was this change also the advent of a new, non-Ottoman, mode of secularism? Did the use of the Georgian calendar indicate that the temporality of the Allied Powers had fully conquered the regions of the Ottomans? Not quite. The *hijri* calendar remained a competing temporal regime in occupied Syria, alongside the solar calendar. Scribes in the "civil" courts continued to use *hijri* dates from time to time, while the *qadi* courts of course continued using the Muslim calendar. The earliest journals printed after the establishment of the Allied occupation that I have seen, which were published in Hama and Damascus, used both the Muslim calendar and solar years with Syro-Macedonian names for the months.[76] *Al-ʿAsima*, the official journal of the Hijazi occupation government, also used both calendars beginning with its very first issue in February 1919; and all nongovernmental newspapers followed suit.[77] One such journal was the Aleppo newspaper *al-Taqaddum*, whose header from 1913 we saw above; by 1919, *al-Taqaddum*'s header looked very different, as we can observe in Figure 2.2.

The temporal architecture of local societies in occupied regions in 1919, such as Damascus, Aleppo, and their environs, exemplifies what came to be known as secular-religious tension in the later twentieth century, and this solar Christian-*hijri* duality persisted after the French takeover in

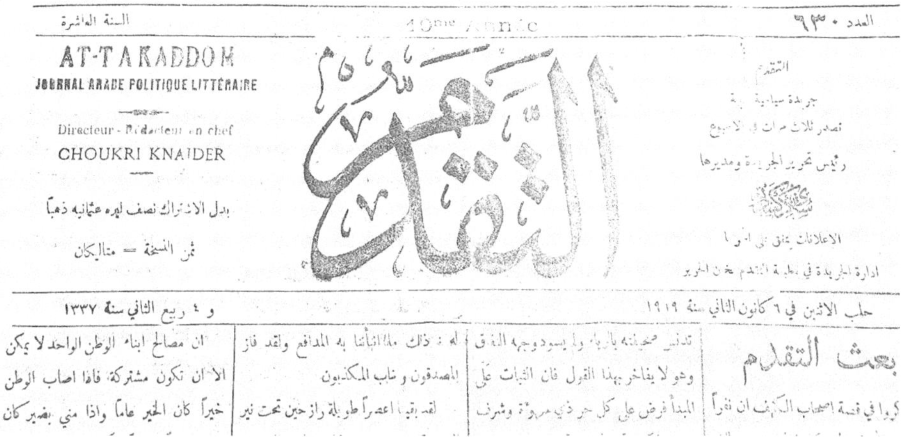

FIGURE 2.2. The header of *al-Taqaddum* (Aleppo), 6 January 1919. *Source*: author's photograph.

1920. In 1921, for example, an important Damascene daily journal, owned by a Greek Christian, printed on its title page the solar Christian (Gregorian) date, the *hijri* date, and the old Julian date (without identifying this latter as such).[78] Even in the new Turkish republic, the official gazette retained *hijri* and *maliye* dates until 1926. The law abolishing the caliph's position and banishing the Ottoman dynasty from Turkey in 1924 March was still dated in both systems.[79] In the Arab lands, where there was neither full integration into a new empire nor radical official secularism (such as existed in Soviet Russia and in the Turkish republic), a plurality of temporal cultures remained in play throughout the twentieth century and down to the present day.

Conclusion

Only an empire-based theory of political order accounts for the continuity of plural sources of authority in successor societies in the twentieth and twenty-first centuries. Instead of nation-states, successor societies come into being in local states and new imperial projects after large transformations. These new orders typically repurpose institutions and practices from the previous imperial order, including monarchy and plural temporalities. Instead of capitalism and technology leading to nationalist or egalitarian revolutionary eradication, these forces rather rearrange the imperial order in local configurations. In the nineteenth century, empires adapted to the challenges of nationalism and remained the fundamental way in which the masses made sense of the world. The dynastic realm, the co-existence of imperial and local languages, and religious apprehensions of time thus continued to characterize political orders well into the twentieth century.

The defeat of the Central Powers in 1918 meant that German, Austro-Hungarian, and Ottoman imperial traditions were no longer active organizing principles for the lives of peoples in the now occupied territories. The question thus presents itself: how did a world of imperial authority become a world of local political communities? How did landscapes of imperial administrators, subordinate rulers, monarchical hierarchies, and zones of subordination act in response to the norms of the League of Nations? How would the once imperial assemblage of religion, dynasty, and ethnic-national claims continue to define the political order in successor polities in the absence of any new imperial sovereign? To explore the new mode of Allied domination which made the spoliation of the Ottoman world possible, I turn in the next chapter to an alternative history of international law.

CHAPTER THREE

Governing without Sovereignty

HISTORIANS OVERWHELMINGLY AGREE that the League of Nations
was a site of "imperial internationalism." Over the course of its existence
between 1919 and 1947, it functioned not so much to eliminate Great
Power competition as to regulate it.[1] Some have further argued that the
League's international law was a prolongation of nineteenth-century economic colonialism.[2] Andrew Fitzmaurice adds that, in order to legitimize
European imperialism, nineteenth-century European jurists expanded
"the idea of occupation" to create a "theory of territorial sovereignty
appropriate to commercial expansion."[3]

The Allied jurists, however, inaugurated an age of administration
instead of conquest by modifying inter-imperial legal institutions after
the First World War. In this chapter, I argue that between the 1880s and
1940s British and French jurists and politicians experimented with an
alternative framework of legal control—one that did not involve the idea
of occupation. I characterize this alternative legal framework as "governing without sovereignty."[4] By this I mean the enduring *administrative* management of a region and its legally sovereign local government,
usually following military occupation and an agreement among other
imperial powers.[5]

After 1919, new norms scripted in the Covenant of the League of
Nations enabled the rise of subordinated sovereign polities. The design-
ers of the League originally specified the old imperial genre of "organic
law" as the administrative constitution for such arrangements in the class
A mandate territories. As it turned out, the repurposing of this imperial
legal instrument was ultimately implemented only in the French mandate
of Lebanon and Syria. This chapter will close with remarks on this unique

experiment and, as a concrete example, with the consequences of subordinated sovereignty in land administration practices.

Governing without sovereignty differed from governing a protectorate in that it did not entail a treaty between the local government and the
administrator polity, such as would have transferred selected rights from
the former to the latter.[6] Whereas in a protectorate there was inevitably
a measure of ambiguity about where exactly sovereignty lay, governing
without sovereignty involved an explicit prohibition on the administrator
polity's acquisition of sovereignty. Norms following from contracts *forbade*
the administrator from engaging in practices of sovereign authority such
as issuing title deeds to property, adjudicating crimes among local subjects, or delegating authority. However, French and British officers did not
in fact need sovereignty in order to regulate the post-Ottoman mandated
regions. By the terms of the League's class A mandates, administrative
authorities could issue regulatory laws because the League's Covenant
granted stronger administrative rights than those resulting from the local
government's sovereignty, which was also granted by the League. The
main norms of the class A mandate were thus similar to the Hague rules of
military occupation codified before the war, which also banned occupiers
from establishing sovereignty over an occupied region.[7] In this legal sense,
administrative authority was the opposite of political, sovereign authority.

Suspending the Right of Conquest: The Case of British Egypt

Governing without sovereignty has been the basic form of international
administration for the past hundred years. Scholars and practitioners of
international administration usually understand by the term "administration" any international organization: the League of Nations, the United
Nations, the World Health Organization, and so on.[8] My use of this
term is more restricted. By administration I mean the external military-
bureaucratic management of a region, its peoples, and its government,
and those norms, resulting from external agreements, that provide legality
for this state of affairs.

A French legal expert made a distinction around 1923 between "colonial occupation" and "military occupation which is temporary [. . .] and
which is a guarantee to execute the terms of the (peace) treaty." He pointed
to the British occupation of Egypt as the first such experiment.[9] Scholars
often trace the emergence of international administration to the idea of
the protectorate as it was articulated in the nineteenth-century laws of

peace.[10] By contrast, I suggest that it is more accurate to locate the origins of this legal arrangement in the suspension of the right of conquest as articulated in the laws of war. The British occupation of the Ottoman khedivate of Egypt that began in 1882 was indeed one of the first experiments in governing without sovereignty through the suspension of the right of conquest, and without a treaty.

During the occupation, the British government's relation to Egypt was unique in its legal structure. Between 1882 and 1914, the British Empire was a non-belligerent occupying power in this Ottoman province. No war had been declared between the Ottoman and British governments. The British Empire was not sovereign in Egypt; the occupiers in 1882 did not claim the right of conquest; and there was no treaty of protection between the khedive and the British government. Inter-imperial agreements and conventions (1885, 1887, and later) regulated the British presence, which was secured by a small occupying army. The famous Lord Cromer, Britain's representative, held no rank higher than consul-general during his long tenure between 1884 and 1907. Alongside delegating an Ottoman High Commissioner in Egypt, the Ottoman sultan also continued to delegate legal authority to the khedive of Egypt as his representative in matters of administrative and Islamic law. The *kadı* of Cairo remained a sultanic appointee and was sent from Istanbul; he was a permanent, though largely silent, member of the local legislative council (*Majlis Shura al-Qawanin*). The khedive was not a "native ruler," as for example an emir in British Nigeria, because he was not a British *wakil* (agent) but was rather, in Ottoman administrative law, a *vezir* (minister) and *vali* (governor), and in Islamic law the representative (*na'ib*) of the imam (the sultan). Khedivial Egypt under British occupation continued to pay tribute to the Ottoman government (or more precisely, to the Bank of England as repayment for earlier Ottoman loans). Sultanic power was in effect only at the constitutional level, and even there was distinctively weak, because both the khedive and multiple foreign powers claimed segments of legal authority.[11]

This complex situation changed dramatically in December of 1914, after the Ottoman declaration of war against the British Empire. Although British statesmen discussed annexation, they opted instead to establish a unique war protectorate in Egypt, based on a unilateral proclamation rather than a treaty, in view of the fact that Egypt was now "enemy territory." Britain's fellow Allied Powers—at that time France and Russia—had no objections. While, as we shall see below, the proclamation clearly violated the Hague rules of occupation, the British government could, if it wished, have argued that as the occupation predated the Hague agreements, it lay outside of their scope. The proclamation of December 1914 thus brought to a close both the first British occupation and four centuries of Ottoman rule in Egypt.[12]

In December of 1914 the British Empire did not become the sovereign ruling power *of* Egypt in a direct and permanent way. Rather, it became a sovereign *in* Egypt. In my interpretation, the British government assumed sovereignty only for the moment of proclamation in order to sever Egypt from the Ottoman Empire. The British administrators replaced the Ottoman-friendly Abbas Hilmi II (1892–1914) with Husayn Kamil (1914–1917), another ruler from the same family, and granted him the title "sultan of Egypt." Following the declaration, the British legal advisor's understanding was that the rights once belonging to the Ottoman government in Egypt were instead "accruing" to this new local dynast. This Egyptian sultan now held a status resembling that of a "native ruler" in a British domain because the empire had activated the right of conquest but had not concluded it. As in the British colonies in Nigeria, legal advisors viewed the British officials as "trustees for the inhabitants of Egypt."[13]

The protectorate was not a fully implemented legal system because there was no treaty between the governments. Instead, martial law gave the British army effective control over Egyptian affairs while the sultanic government in early 1915 affirmed that "the exceptional powers and the bodies which exercise these are authorized to [continue to] exercise all rights that follow from the Ottoman treaties and firmans until now."[14] The British administrators eased the land tax burden in November 1914 and decided to engage in the large-scale purchase of Egyptian cotton as a means of raising the regime's popularity (as a consequence, the cotton price steadily rose during the war, booming in 1919). Some British administrators hoped that the protectorate would be seen not as an act of annexation but rather as "progress towards self-government." One such figure was Henry McMahon, who was the High Commissioner and the foreign minister in the new Egyptian sultan's government, beginning in January of 1915.[15] In 1917, upon the death of Husayn Kamil, the first sultan, McMahon appointed Fuad, another member of the khedivial family, to the post. He called on Fuad "to assume that dignity for yourself and for your heirs according to such order of succession as shall be established by agreement between His Majesty's Government and Your Highness."[16] The imperial nature of succession was no secret: the public sultanic "prescript" on 10 October 1917 used the same words.[17] A tripartite system of government—empire, army rule through martial law, and a local monarch—remained in place until 1922.

Despite the British proclamation of December 1914, the question of Egypt's territorial status was not entirely settled, not even among the Allied Powers, and certainly not among Egyptians. In October 1917, when Fuad, yet another khedivial Ottoman aristocrat, was inducted as the new sultan, the diplomatic representatives of many Allied and neutral powers (from the United States to Denmark) attended the accession ceremony "without their staffs, not in uniform and in a separate room at the Abdine Palace" because they had not yet officially recognized the British proclamation or the new Egyptian regime.[18]

Ceremonies like this one give valuable insights into prickly political and legal situations from perspectives that official sources do not offer. Another instance is a reception in February 1918 at which foreign judges of the Mixed Courts (courts established in 1876 to adjudicate cases involving non-Egyptians) were expected to appear in Egyptian uniform. An invitation to this affair prompted a letter from Pierre Crabitès, the Louisiana-born American judge delegated to the Mixed Courts, to the US Department of State. He drew attention to the fact that the Ottoman Empire still claimed sovereignty over Egypt (!) and underlined that "from the point of view of the United States, Egypt at the moment technically" formed a "part of the Turkish Empire, a sovereign state against whom the United States of America have not declared war." He also noted that neither Italy nor the United States had yet recognized "the new Egyptian government as *de jure* government." Moreover, a British-French-Italian commission had started to redesign extraterritorial regulations and the British administrators now considered the Mixed Court judges as Egyptian employees. Crabitès urged the US government to continue to affirm *de jure* Ottoman sovereignty in Egypt—which would have helped Crabitès and other foreigner Mixed Courts judges to remain foreign representatives instead of Egyptian employees; which in turn would have enabled them to attend palace parties in their evening suits instead of uniform.[19]

The protectorate was indeed not the legal form through which British officers wished to govern Egypt and the other occupied Ottoman regions. The pre-1914 mode of governing without sovereignty was still much the preferred mode. Until the fall of 1918, for example, the British administrators of the Iraqi provinces believed that their occupation system in "Mesopotamia" would be similar to that which Lord Cromer had previously established in Egypt.[20] In fact, British officials frequently pointed to Cromer's administration of the khedivate as an example of the sort of governance envisaged by the League of Nations' new class A mandate. In November 1919, Lord Milner, British imperial administrator and a participant in the Paris peace conference, happily noted that the mandate was the "kind of system which we have in practice been trying to work out in Egypt" and, responding to a request from Lord Cecil, he wondered whether the British Empire could categorize "Egypt on the same footing as 'mandated' Syria." However, this did not happen. When Milner travelled to Egypt in late 1919 to investigate the situation after a huge Egyptian uprising in the spring, powerful members of the Ottoman-Egyptian elite, among them Sarwat ('Abd al-Haliq Tharwat) Pasha, expressed his preference that Egypt remain a British protectorate instead of being placed under League control. 'Abd al-'Aziz Fahmi, a nationalist lawyer, considered giving up the Suez Canal in return for the Sudan, thinking to re-establish an independent Egyptian mini-empire.[21] Lord Milner suggested finally that Egypt be instead granted a constitution—an organic law—"along mandatory lines" by the British Empire because he was not convinced that the League system would work properly.[22]

In February 1922, the status of Egypt was once again redefined. In response to passive resistance to the British protectorate by Egyptian bureaucrats and at the insistence of Lord Allenby, the new High Commissioner, the British government unilaterally declared Egyptian sovereignty. Egypt now became a sovereign local state under military occupation. The relation of the British Empire to Egypt reverted to governing without sovereignty. Fuad, formerly sultan, now became king, as Chapter Seven will explore in more detail. Thus began the second occupation of Egypt.

The declaration was rather hurried, and in the wake of the move some British officials expressed concerns that Egyptian sovereignty might endanger imperial communications with India. Thus, in March 1922, a month after the declaration, they proposed that in order to maintain secure communications they should create a distinct "state" in the Suez Canal region, as the United States had done in the Panama Zone, and this Suez-state might be under a League mandate. However, legal advisors were quick to point out that an 1888 Ottoman-British agreement conferred upon the khedive "rights and privileges in connection with the protection over the Suez Canal" and that following a peace treaty with new Turkey these rights would accrue directly to Britain. They argued that it would be better to leave the League out of Egyptian matters.[23] The British army went forward with the plan for a special administration of the Canal Zone, albeit without League involvement. It was not until the British-Egyptian treaty of 1936, the first one ever between the two governments, that British military occupation in Egypt formally came to an end (though the treaty specified that occupation would continue in the Suez Canal Zone).[24]

In sum, the legal situation of governing without sovereignty was in effect for two periods during the British military occupation in Egypt. In the first, between 1882 and 1914, the British army occupied a distinguished Ottoman province. The second period, between 1922 and 1936, saw the military occupation of a sovereign local state, with a special administration functioning in the strategic zone of the Suez Canal. During these periods, the British government refrained from claiming that occupation conferred sovereignty. In the years between, from 1914 to 1922, there was a war protectorate without a treaty, in which the British ruler appointed subordinated sultans. During the later years of the protectorate, the British Empire refused to cede Egypt in 1919, and then in 1922 the Suez Canal Zone, to the control of the League. Empire remained the source of Egyptian sovereignty until 1936 when Egypt became a member of the League.

Denying the Right of Conquest?

By establishing control over Egypt in December 1914, the British Empire was activating the "right of conquest." Legal experts argued that this right followed from the Ottoman declaration of war. It allowed the British Empire to declare the khedivate of Egypt enemy territory. Thus, the legal status changed from a state of "non-belligerent occupation" to "belligerent occupation." In order to appreciate the significance of this move, it may be useful here to clarify the difference between these two legal situations and to give insight into the curious career of the right of conquest in the period under consideration. The norms and principles by which this right was enshrined, often challenged but rarely completely disregarded, acquired salience during the First World War, when large regions came under long-standing occupations, and when governing without sovereignty became a global phenomenon.

Today, in public international law, belligerent occupation is defined as a situation where "the forces of one or more States exercise effective control over a territory of another State without the latter State's volition" and without the existence of a state of war.[25] However, until 1949, the existence of a state of war had been a precondition for legally identifying a situation as "belligerent." Jurists identified all parties in such a situation as "belligerents," and applied the laws of war to all the activities of all said parties on occupied enemy territory, including administration.[26] By contrast, until 1949, instances of military occupation without a state of war had been categorized as non-belligerent or "pacific" occupation. Non-belligerent occupation was a somewhat murky legal concept for, in the absence of a state of war, it must necessarily lie outside the scope of the agreed laws of war. Since the Second World War, jurists have generally regarded the category as outdated, but it still defined the period under review here.[27]

The most important change in the global history of norms concerning war occurred in 1899. At the Hague a group of states, including the Ottoman Empire, agreed to and ratified basic rules of warfare, which they reaffirmed, again at the Hague, in 1907.[28] Article 55 of Annex II (in the 1899 Convention) and of Annex IV (in the 1907 Convention) declared: "The occupying State shall be regarded *only* as administrator and usufructuary of public buildings, real estate, forests, and agricultural estates belonging to the hostile State, and situated in the occupied country."[29] (Italics added.) The novelty of this new principle was that the parties affirmed that belligerent occupation no longer granted title to land and people. Earlier, before the Hague Conventions, the right of conquest had been understood as "the right of the victor [...] to sovereignty over the conquered territory and its inhabitants."[30] The 1899 and 1907 agreements meant the suspension of two claims on territory: the original government's sovereignty (which became latent) and the occupant's right of conquest.

Like conquest, belligerent occupation was modelled on property law, in that it was premised on the idea of tenancy. The belligerent occupying power became a tenant of the occupied belligerent government. Article 55 in both Annexes to the Hague agreements continues with a second sentence: "[The occupying army] must safeguard the capital of these properties, and administer them in accordance with the rules of usufruct." Usufruct means the use of another person's property that should be returned after use to the original owner, in this case, to the original sovereign. While today's international legal experts consider this "sovereign-to-sovereign" approach outdated in the face of new situations of conflict and occupation, the idea of occupation as usufruct is key to understanding the legal logic of First World War occupations.[31]

Beyond the Hague laws, there was also a group of agreements among the Allied Powers that seemed to presage the suspension and denial of the right of conquest. These agreements, such as the 1915 Treaty of London (a British-Italian agreement); the secret Sykes-Picot agreement in 1916 (French-British-Russian); and the 1917 treaty in Saint-Jean-de-Maurienne (specifically about Ottoman Anatolia, concluded among Italy,

France and Britain), articulated territorial claims among the Allied Powers but included no provisions as to the recognition of conquests-yet-to-be-concluded.[32] The Principal Allied Powers in October 1918 affirmed that occupied territories could not be annexed by the individual occupying country.[33] By establishing this last point as a universal principle, the October 1918 agreement stamped a collective, joint character upon all Allied occupations, and did much to shape the events of the next few decades.

The Contractual Framework of Administration, 1919–1940s

Governing without sovereignty in post-1882 British Egypt was something of an anomaly in a world of protectorates and colonies. In the years after the First World War, however, the Allied Powers' occupations turned it into a widespread phenomenon. As a collective entity in law, the "Allied Powers" became the new owner of legal sovereignty in many occupied regions. The emergence of this purely virtual legal entity in contracts was central to the reconstitution of the world in 1919. In this section, I explain how it led to a formal framework of government without sovereignty. Since the Allied governments had agreed to exclude the right of conquest as a legitimate source of sovereignty-acquisition, they typically acquired sovereignty through contracts. Accordingly, for the Allied jurists at the peace conferences during 1919 and later, "sovereignty" meant a textual formula: "the rights and title" to manage and adjudicate over a region and its inhabitants. In this contractual mode of acquisition, sovereignty transfer functioned like property transfer in law. The analogy runs as follows. Property transfer presupposes two legal persons: an owner and a receiver. The owner transfers their title and rights to property in a contract to the receiver. As the result, the receiver becomes the new owner. The transfer of sovereignty likewise presupposes two legal persons: an original owner and a receiver. The original sovereign in a contract (a treaty or articles in a treaty) transfers their title and rights over a region and its peoples to the receiver. As a result, the receiver becomes the new sovereign (the new owner of "rights and title").[34]

We can identify four types of contractual sovereignty transfer in the agreements and peace treaties concluded in 1919 and later. In the first type, the Allied Powers recognized a successor government as sovereign, that is, as the new owner of rights and title to a region and its peoples, by entering into a treaty. The second was a simple legal operation whereby one defeated government transferred its rights and title to another, victorious government. In the third case, a defeated government would transfer its rights and title to a collective legal entity (usually the "Principal and Associated Allied Powers"). In the fourth scheme, a collective legal entity (the signatories of the Covenant) *decided among themselves* in a contract (the Covenant) about the sovereignty of new, virtual "nations" in originally non-sovereign regions. In the last two cases, the establishment of a new, purely virtual sovereign necessitated an additional, external administration (sometimes, this was the contract's explicit political goal), which entailed the appointment of administrators who governed without sovereignty. I will describe these types one by one.

1. RECOGNIZING SOVEREIGNTY THROUGH TREATY

Peace treaties indirectly recognized the defeated or successor government as sovereign in a contractual relationship. For instance, the June 1920 peace treaty between the "Principal Allied and Associated Powers" and the Kingdom of Hungary recognized this new local polity as sovereign following the dissolution of the Austro-Hungarian Empire. The preamble stated that "the former Austro-Hungarian Monarchy has now ceased to exist, and has been replaced in Hungary by a national Hungarian Government," and that "from that moment and subject to the provisions of this Treaty official relations will exist between the Allied and Associated Powers and Hungary." Article 73 added: "The independence of Hungary is inalienable otherwise than with the consent of the Council of the League of Nations." The League was the source of Hungarian sovereignty.

There was no need and in fact no possibility of a transfer of title and rights over the "Hungarian" regions from the old Austro-Hungarian imperial government to the new owner of sovereignty. The existence of the peace treaty, of which the Covenant of the League of Nations was the first part, along with the signatures of the parties, constituted the recognition of sovereignty of this successor government in accord with the terms of the treaty. The transfer of sovereignty entailed only an act of renunciation on the part of the new sovereign government in favor of the composite entity in Article 75: "Hungary renounces, so far as she is concerned, in favor of the Principal Allied and Associated Powers all rights and title over the territories which previously belonged to the former Austro-Hungarian Monarchy."

2. TRANSFER OF SOVEREIGNTY BETWEEN
INDIVIDUAL LEGAL ENTITIES

The transfer of sovereignty between individual governments was a simple legal operation. The 1919 Allied peace treaty with Germany will serve as an example. It clearly articulated the transfer of sovereignty over the German colony of Kiaochow (Jiaozhou Bay, China) to Japan: "Germany renounces, in favour of Japan, all her rights, title and privileges, particularly those concerning the territory of Kiaochow, railways, mines and submarine cables which she acquired in virtue of the Treaty concluded by her with China on March 6, 1898, and of all other arrangements relative to the Province of Shantung" (article 156); "Germany shall hand over to Japan within three months from the coming into force of the present Treaty the archives, registers, plans, title-deeds and documents of every kind, wherever they may be, relating to the administration, whether civil, military, financial, judicial or other, of the territory of Kiaochow" (article 158). Although for various reasons this region did not in the end come under Japanese rule, the legal operation was a simple transfer of sovereignty from the German government to the Japanese government as the result of a contract (the articles in the peace treaty).

3. TRANSFER OF SOVEREIGNTY FROM
INDIVIDUAL TO COLLECTIVE LEGAL ENTITIES

The transfer of sovereignty to a collective legal entity was also an uncomplicated operation, but it entailed further transfers of selected rights. Let me first recount the steps in an abstract, ideal description. The defeated government would transfer rights and titles to a receiver, here of course a legal collective entity, which was most often "the Principal Allied and Associated Powers" or "the Principal Allied Powers," or more rarely "the various States." (These terms differed according to whether the defeated government was at war with all Allied powers or only with selected ones). This transfer to a collective legal entity, existing only on paper, was the first step in the process. In the second step this composite entity would transfer (or, according to some interpretations, simply entrust) the received sovereignty to the League of Nations. The contract effecting this second transfer occurred—between, let us say, "the Principal Allied and Associated Powers" and the League—could be either the Covenant, some later agreement or agreements, or may have rested simply on an understanding that required no further back-up. In a third step the League of Nations, having no personnel for actual administration, would outsource the right of administration over the region in question to a government, which would then begin to exercise control without being sovereign. This third step involved a contract (the terms of the mandate) between the League and the administrator polity establishing the terms of administration.

Importantly, these transfers that I have described in the abstract often did not happen in neat temporal succession. While, as we have just seen, the Covenant theoretically should have constituted the second step in the transfer procedure, in practice the establishment of the Covenant preceded steps one and three: indeed, its establishment was the foundation of the post-war world, featuring as the first part of the 1919 Germany peace treaty. All subsequent sovereignty transfers were thus required to conform with the Covenant's terms.

Let us consider an example of how such a transfer took place. By the terms of the peace treaty with Germany in 1919, the Allied Powers received sovereignty over the district of Memel in German East Prussia (today part of Lithuania). Germany renounced "in favour of the Principal Allied and Associated Powers all rights and title over the territories" of Memel (article 99). In February 1920, the French army took over Memel's administration from the Reichscommissar "on behalf of the Allied Powers." An external party, the Lithuanian government, wanted to annex—acquire sovereignty over—Memel. The Lithuanian foreign minister used very precise language in a note: "The Allied and Associated Powers will be good enough to adopt a decision regarding the transfer to Lithuania of all rights and titles to the Memel Territories which they hold by virtue of Article 99 of the Versailles Treaty." He requested a simple transaction from the collective legal entity to his government, without even mentioning the League. However, "the Allied and Associated Powers" was a virtual entity, existed only on paper. Thus, on their behalf, the Conference of Ambassadors at the League of Nations sent an investigative commission. But whom did this commission represent? We must conclude that either the collective virtual owner of sovereignty over Memel entrusted a League organ to represent it, or that it transferred, in some unknown way, the sovereignty over this territory to the League. All the while, the French army administered the region without sovereignty until 1923.[35]

4. ARTICLE 22: SOVEREIGNTY AS THE
RESULT OF COLLECTIVE DECISION

Finally, unlike the other three types of contractual sovereignty transfer, the fourth did not have as its first step the transfer of sovereignty from a defeated government. Instead, a collective entity (the Allied Powers, or the original signatories of the Covenant) acquired sovereignty by means of activating the right of conquest and, in a contractual agreement among themselves (the Covenant), through *recognition*, they then accorded sovereignty to new, to-be-created governments in the occupied territories. The Allied Powers in 1919 thus distributed sovereignty, similarly to the "monarchical emancipation" by groups of European empires in the nineteenth century.

This fourth type of sovereignty transfer applied to those occupied Ottoman regions that Britain and France in the Sykes-Picot agreement agreed to take under their spheres of influence. Article 22 of the Covenant outlined three provisions for these regions. The first provision stated that "as a consequence of the late war [certain German and Ottoman territories] have ceased to be under the sovereignty of the States." We cannot interpret this statement in any other way than as the declaration of the right of conquest on behalf of the signatories and in disregard of the Hague laws. The second provision was the formal recognition by signatories to the Covenant of the existence of "independent nations" in the "former" Ottoman territories—a recognition which, as we shall see, later jurists interpreted as conferring sovereignty upon governments in these regions. The third was a directive for mandatory powers to "assist" these nations. In this way, Article 22 codified in a few sentences the governing of sovereign polities without sovereignty.

The nature of this contractual transfer becomes clearer if we compare the status of post-Ottoman Arab regions with the situation in post-Habsburg Hungary, where there was a contractual acknowledgment of sovereignty. While in both cases parties recognized independent nations, they did this by means of two different types of contracts. The locus for the recognition of sovereignty in the post-Ottoman Arab regions was the Covenant of the League of Nations, a contract to which neither the Ottoman government nor any post-Ottoman successor government (other than the Kingdom of the Hijaz, see Chapters Six and Eight) was party at the time. This contract meant that the League-system included and guaranteed as-yet unspecified post-Ottoman legal sovereigns. By contrast, the

1920 Trianon peace treaty was concluded between a composite entity and Hungary, a discrete post-Habsburg government. In this second case, the government recognized as sovereign was a contractual party to the contract wherein recognition was conferred.

The aforementioned three provisions in Article 22 of the Covenant help explain why both the 1920 Sèvres treaty with the Ottomans (which featured the Covenant as the first part of its text) and the follow-up 1923 Lausanne treaty made no mention of transferring "rights and title" or "sovereignty" from the defeated government, but instead required the Ottoman/new Turkish government to recognize as entities Mesopotamia, Hijaz, Palestine, Syria and other polities *that, according to the treaties, already existed in law.* For instance, in the case of the Kingdom of the Hijaz, "Turkey, in accordance with the action already taken by the Allied Powers, hereby recognises the Hedjaz as a free and independent State, and renounces in favour of the Hedjaz all rights and titles over the territories of the former Turkish Empire" (Article 98). In these cases, there was no contract stipulating the transfer of sovereignty because the Covenant had already taken sovereignty from the Ottomans and, by the recognition of "independent nations," now transferred said sovereignty to the new governments.

The profound consequences of Article 22 did not become immediately clear. In the early 1920s many European politicians and lawyers remained confused about the status of the occupied Ottoman territories.[36] For instance, in 1921, the British Foreign Secretary Lord Balfour took the view that the "Allied Powers" were sovereign in "certain portions of the Turkish Empire."[37] Mark Frank Lindley, a leading British jurist in the 1920s, compared the mandate to a protectorate (in which the protector has some measure of sovereignty) because he was not entirely sure about its constitutional structure.[38] The source of confusion was, and to some extent still is, that Lindley and other jurists wanted to define the mandate as a single normative category even though the Covenant specified "independent nations" in the class A mandates only and not in class B and C regions (the former German colonies in Africa and the Pacific). Eventually, the legal experts at the League clarified that neither the League of Nations, nor the Allied Powers, nor the mandatory powers, were sovereign in the class A mandates.[39]

The Ottomans did not ratify the Sèvres treaty, and as a result the state of war continued in the occupied regions until 1923, when the government of new Turkey agreed to peace in the Lausanne treaty.[40] The duration of the state of war also prolonged the confusion among statesmen. In

July 1920 Eric Drummond, the new League of Nations' secretary general, described Syria in a private letter as belonging to France "by right of military occupation."[41] In August 1920, the Council of the League accepted a report that stated: "Syria is still part of an enemy country."[42] In December 1920, the French Foreign Ministry told the Sénat representatives that "the present legal regime in Syria is [. . .] still military occupation."[43] In 1921 January, the British and French governments agreed that the League must acknowledge that the administration of the occupied regions would continue according to the terms of the draft mandate until the question of sovereignty was settled in a treaty ratified by the Ottomans.[44] The continued state of war meant also that the 1921 British Middle East Conference in Cairo decided that the "Mesopotamia" and "Palestine" High Commissioners were in fact titular commanders-in-chief and that the new Arab army in Iraq should take over "the British line."[45]

In closing this complex discussion of contracts, it would be well to summarize the legal norms as they applied in the occupied Ottoman regions. Until the signature of the League's Covenant in June 1919, the principles enshrined in the Hague laws of war protected Ottoman sovereignty in its occupied territories. In June 1919, the situation changed: the Allied Powers and other Covenant signatories, *together* exercising the right of conquest in Article 22, alienated the occupied territories from Ottoman sovereignty and codified this separation in the Covenant. At the same time, Article 22 established a new legal norm, whereby the Ottoman regions that subsequently became class A mandates were identified as "independent nations." Some French and British occupation administrators immediately understood that this new norm challenged their previous methods of imperial rule.[46] From that moment on, the League, as enshrined in the Covenant, would be a competing source of sovereignty with empire. Empire no longer had the legal capacity to delegate authority in the class A regions; sovereign governments, as norms, were *already* there. France and Britain, without sovereignty, were to govern sovereign polities.

The Administrative Constitution: The Organic Law

Governing without sovereignty was not a formally codified legal regime. Jurists did not regard League administration, premised on the laws of peace, as remotely resembling military occupation, premised on the laws of war. Only the League class A mandate texts contained what I call an "administrative constitution" and what the jurists of the time called the "organic law" (*loi organique*). Although governments and historians have often obscured the importance of this legal instrument, it is vital to understand the contradictions inherent in governing without sovereignty. In this section, I consider how the nineteenth-century imperial genre of organic law became the administrative constitution for the French class A mandate regions.

First, a definition. Organic law is an administrative code that manages and regulates provinces and autonomous regions in empires. Among the best-known early examples are the sultanic administrative laws (*kanunname*) that governed Ottoman provinces in the fifteenth and sixteenth centuries. In nineteenth-century dynastic and republican empires, administrative laws (decrees, organic laws, agreements) created and regulated subordinate regions and polities.[47] In the early nineteenth century, Napoleon issued an organic law (*statut organique*) to codify the French Italian republic.[48] Russia used a similar instrument in Poland in 1832, after abolishing the Polish national constitution.[49] The latter half of the nineteenth century saw many organic laws regulating administrative autonomy in intra- and inter-imperial relations in the Mediterranean region. For instance, in 1861 the Great Powers agreed to issue an organic law (known as a *règlement organique*) to regulate the administrative councils in the province of Mount Lebanon in the Ottoman Empire. This law constituted the inter-imperial legal architecture of what the Ottomans called a "distinguished province" in Mount Lebanon.[50] Similarly, by the terms of the Berlin treaty of 1878 the Great Powers developed what they called a *statut organique* for Ottoman Rumelia.[51] The Ottoman ambassador also used the term in an 1881 letter to the French foreign minister to characterize what is today called the first Tunisian "constitution." At that time, on the eve of the French invasion, the ambassador emphasized that the Tunisian law in question was only an administrative law *within* the Ottoman Empire, thereby asserting Tunis' subordination to Ottoman rule in the hope of discouraging French aggression.[52] In khedivial Egypt, the occupying British authorities used the term "the Organic Law" both for the 1883 administrative law and the follow-up administrative law of 1913.[53] The Ottoman government also issued an organic law for its provinces, providing for representative councils, in 1913. Organic law was thus a tool both for denying sovereignty and for creating limited, distinct territorial authority.

Organic laws have also featured in the composite system of the United States of America. Today, the term is often confusingly applied to the Declaration of Independence, the Constitution, and other fundamental texts, in the general sense of "basic law." However, in the nineteenth century there was a clear distinction in the United States between an organic law and the Constitution. The organic law was the administrative code of a single member state—for instance, there was "the organic law of the Territories of Wisconsin and Iowa"[54]—while the Constitution was the foundational, sovereign law of the federation. There have been many American legal compendiums that contain "the organic law" of a state and the "Constitution" as two distinct texts.[55]

In 1919, the makers of the new world order borrowed the genre "organic law" for the legal articulation of autonomous territories under the administrative supervision of other states. It was the regulatory guarantee of an entity's separate territorial existence. The League of Nations' Convention, for example, specified that a commission would create a *statut organique* for the former German territory of Memel under the trusteeship of Lithuania.[56] William Ormsby-Gore, the main British architect of the League's "indirect international supervision," remarked in a 1920 publication that the supervising power would not be able "to amend the organic law without the approval of the League of Nations."[57] The League thus acquired the previous position of an empire with regard to the organic law.

The design of the class A mandate contained organic laws at its core. The so-called "American draft" of the mandate text (the first draft of 1919) required that "the Mandatory Power [. . .] undertakes to frame an organic law within (one) year from the date of this Mandate [. . .] in consultation with the native authorities." In this draft, the organic law was supposed to "contain provisions designed to facilitate the progressive developments of [the mandated territory] as a Self-Governing State and the ultimate cessation of this Mandate."[58] In December 1920, both the French draft text for Syria and Lebanon and the British draft text for the mandate of Iraq ("Mesopotamia") contained references to the establishment of an organic law. Only the British draft text for Palestine did not contain such a condition.[59] The requirement for the establishment of an organic law was one of three fundamental directives for the class A mandates—the other two being bans on military conscription and on the direct exploitation of natural resources—that the League's Assembly recommended to the Council on 18 December 1920.[60]

In the end, however, only the first article of the mandate text for Syria and Lebanon required a *statut organique*, an organic law, "in agreement with the native authorities" to be presented to the League of Nations within three years, by 1926.[61] Historians, and even legal scholars, often confuse the organic law with the Syrian and Lebanese national constitutions.[62] Others state that "no one had a clear idea about what the *statut organique* was in 1923."[63] However, the French *parti colonial* knew exactly what it was: an administrative law that out-ranked the local political order. By tracing the way in which the Allied Powers re-used the organic law in the League's legal architecture I wish to highlight how central imperial constitutional law was for League internationalism.

In 1923, the French mandate for Syria and Lebanon was the only such mandate to come into being with the requirement that it be granted an organic law. Henceforth, the *statut organique* would be no longer an imperial but rather an international instrument. The text embodying authority above the organic law was the Covenant of the League, rather than the mandatory power's own basic law. Once submitted to the League, the mandatory power could not change this law. Recognizing this bind, the British government decided to substitute its 1920 text requiring the establishment of an organic law for the mandate in Iraq with a less onerous treaty drawn up in 1922, which was then submitted to the League as the text for the mandate. Although this treaty stated that the Iraqi king agreed "to frame an organic law for presentation to the Constituent Assembly," it specified that said law "shall contain nothing contrary to the provisions of the present treaty" (Article III).[64] In Palestine, the closest document to an organic law was the series of Orders-in-Council issued by the Crown in 1922 and 1923, which British legal advisors considered to compose a "constitution."[65] Hence, the organic law retained its original function only in the French mandate text.

The organic law in the French mandate was to be the codification of the new Federation of the States of the Levant, a composite polity that the French High Commission created—partly as an answer to local visions of a post-Ottoman federation (see more on prewar Ottoman federalism in Chapter Five). Like many French legal acts in the mandate, the initial French conception of an organic law was based on an Ottoman imperial law, in this case the 1913 Law of Provinces (see more on this law in Chapter Five). As in all cases dating to the military occupation period, in legal terms the High Commission stepped into the shoes of the previous Ottoman government. This is why, in 1923, when the mandate came into effect at the League of Nations, Prime Minister Poincaré expected that the High Commission as an imperial organ would issue the *statut organique* of this sub-federation.[66] Poincaré interpreted the "agreement" of "native authorities" as merely a *consultation* about the already compiled code.[67]

After 1925, however, the French parliamentary left reinterpreted the meaning of "in agreement with the native authorities" as authorizing elected assemblies that would make their own basic laws in the mandate. This reinterpretation prompted both local groups and the French High Commission to engage with institutions of elected representation. Even the Druze rebels in August 1925 demanded an "organic law" created by a free Syrian assembly.[68] While the Lebanese assembly, under the control of a French official, produced their basic law with little difficulty in 1926, the Syrian constitution of 1928 became the subject of an immense struggle between ex-Ottoman patricians, Syrian groups, the French High Commission, and the League, as we shall see in Chapter Nine. The French High Commission created the constitutions of the smaller mandate polities (the Alawite state and the Djebel Druze). After changing the anti-mandate articles of the 1928 Syrian constitution, the French government then in 1930 submitted all of these texts together to the League as the organic law of the mandate. Thus, the organic law became the administrative constitution of governing without sovereignty only in the class A mandate for Syria and Lebanon, an example of how imperial constituent acts survived in the age of the League of Nations.[69]

Bureaucratic Sovereignty: The Example of Syrian Land Administration

Let me emphasize once again the utility of understanding administrative sovereignty as a category of practice. In this last section of the present chapter, I tell briefly the story of the land survey service that came into being in the French mandate in the early 1920s. This will serve as an example of how imperial methods changed because administrators now had to deal with the legal quality of sovereignty as part of domination.

When it comes to property practices in post-Ottoman Lebanon and Syria, scholars have argued that modern Ottoman and colonial French reforms designed to separate religion from the economy replaced an earlier Muslim notion of legitimate territorial Ottoman sovereignty; and, further, that 1920s land surveys served French financial interest and they were a French attempt at laying "covert" claim to sovereignty in the mandated regions.[70] Building on these arguments, but leaving out the term "sovereignty," I would suggest that the French making of a land survey office in the mandate demonstrates instead the emergence of governing without sovereignty as a new form of domination. The possibility of a local sovereign government forced French administrators to give up direct, colonial means of administration and bypass Syrian bureaucratic sovereignty through private contracts.

During the occupation period (1918–1923), High Commissioner General Gouraud and his staff, especially the chief of administration Robert de Caix, acted as a military government substituting for the Ottoman imperial government. They spent these early years preparing for eventual French sovereignty by establishing departments of various affairs directly controlled by the High Commission. The High Commission was all but in name a mini-imperial government presiding over a bloc of small, newly created, subordinated local polities. The Syrians were not oblivious to these French practices. For instance, in April 1920 the government in Damascus declared that the High Commission had no right to authorize a bank in Beirut to issue bank notes to be used in all Syrian occupied zones because: "this right belongs to the prerogatives of absolute sovereignty."[71]

Another such prerogative was the issuing of property titles. After the invasion of Damascus and the internal territories (which I shall explain more fully in Chapter Six), the French High Commission, in July 1921, established a land administration office (*Services Fonciers*). Directed by Philippe Gennardi, a legal expert, it included a department devoted to land surveys, directed by Camille Duraffourd, a topographic engineer. The office was a veritable spoliation of the previous bureaucratic practice. The two Frenchmen had been studying Ottoman and local land codes and practices, the bureaucratic procedures of the Defterhane (the Ottoman imperial land registry), and the Ottoman agrarian credit system. Duraffourd had actually spent time in Istanbul in 1919 to study the Ottoman central land administration. They pored over old Ottoman materials and even translated a page of an Ottoman land register page into French as a sample. Meanwhile the High Commission created a separate department, under Muslim jurists, for the management of pious endowments, with Gennardi serving as a "delegate." Duraffaurd quickly trained land surveyors in Beirut. In 1922, he carried out an experimental land survey and cadaster in one Syrian sub-district to estimate the technical challenges, required personnel, and the expenses of such undertakings.[72]

The new legal norms, however, soon challenged this grand preparation. At the end of 1921, the new Turkish Grand Assembly signed a separate peace treaty in Ankara with the French government. In October 1922, the bureaus of the League of Nations sent out their first questionnaire to the French government about its administration of the mandate. In August 1923, the Turkish government ratified the treaty of Lausanne, in which they recognized sovereignty transfers to new local governments. In light of these developments, the High Commission's legal office repeatedly warned the French generals and bureaucrats of their obligations following from the treaties and League texts, and especially about the requirement for an organic law. For instance, Charles Puech, the main legal advisor, emphasized, sometime in 1923 in a lecture addressed to French agents, that "you have no authority to intervene in a [local] juridical issue." As to the administration, a note from the legal office even as late as 1926 suggested that "we have to be seen more 'mandatory.'"[73]

After Puech's warnings and an explicit order from Paris, the High Commission abolished its Land Administration office in December 1922. First, they experimented with a federalized land survey system with local offices, following the Swiss model. Then, in July 1923, Duraffaurd resigned from the service of the High Commission. The abolishment, federalization, and his resignation were steps aimed at managing land and fiscal territoriality without sovereignty.

Instead of imitating a French colony, for instance Algeria, the financial advisor to the High Commission suggested the contractual method of land surveys in the "liberated territories" of France as a model. Duraffaurd then created a private company of land survey, a "management" (régie), with 250,000 francs capital. This company contracted with the post-Ottoman governments in June-July 1923. Local "governors" signed the contracts but the French financial inspectors, Gennardi, and the High Commission also approved them; the marketization of land surveying thus remained an internal French affair. The main arguments for this arrangement included the provision of identical services in all local states, the supposed shortage of local technical expertise, the advantage that work would continue unobstructed regardless of the changing territorial-political conditions of the new states, and economies of scale. In his official reports, Duraffaurd neglected to mention that this management was a private, capitalist enterprise which charged ten percent profit on all expenses. Legal and technical hurdles meant that the work of the land survey did not begin until 1925 (which meant that prewar Ottoman agrarian fiscal practices continued at the everyday level for many years). Soon, the storing of title deeds and technical information raised complications, as local judges had to be involved in the cadastral process when legal title was added to any demarcated piece of land. For my argument here, the important issue is that the new legal norms forced French administrators to outsource sovereign practices to semi-private agents.[74]

Conclusion: The Rise of League-Sovereignty

Legal historians of Europe and practicing jurists should be familiar with governing without sovereignty as the basic form of Western dominance in the post-1919 world system. Jean Bodin's sixteenth-century theory articulates clearly that a contract can bind the sovereign. He famously did not find contradiction between the indivisibility of sovereignty and the fact that the ruler can be bound by contracts, both by his subjects and by other sovereigns. The logic in this non-imperial articulation of sovereignty is that a contract entails mutual recognition.[75] The fact that sovereigns can become parties to a contract without their knowledge, and even without their existence, was not yet a problem for Bodin. Yet this was precisely the situation in what I have termed "League-sovereignty" in the post-Ottoman Arab lands after the First World War.

In this chapter I have argued that the period between the 1880s and 1940s witnessed an increasing number of legal instances of administrative control over a region. In such situations, jurists and politicians did not invoke the idea of occupation to justify their acquisition of rights and title to regions. Instead, they disavowed the right of conquest and increasingly premised their domination on contracts. Transfers of title and rights to collective virtual entities (the Allied Powers) and to unspecified, individual legal entities ("nations") resulted in enduring military occupations and mandate class A administrations. Specifically in the French mandate, the organic law changed from an imperial to a League-instrument, an administrative constitution. Thus, there emerged a legal framework for subordinated sovereign states, connected to a metropolitan center, similar to Bolshevik practices in the same decade.[76]

We must remember that the League's "mandate system" was not a single, undifferentiated phenomenon; in fact, despite the League's terminology and bureaucracy, it was not a "system." The Covenant created both local sovereignty and the right to administer only in post-Ottoman territories comprising the mandate class A, and not in the former German colonies comprising the mandate class B and C regions. In Palestine, the mandate's text contradicted the Covenant. The League's PMC supported the Zionist settlement even against occasional episodes when the British put a halt to colonization.[77]

As we move now into a more detailed discussion of the making of local political orders under the conditions that we have sketched in the post-Ottoman world, it is imperative to bear in mind that the Covenant of the League of Nations became a new source of legal sovereignty, competing with empire outside Europe. The main dynamic of the interwar period was competition between League-sovereignty and imperial sovereignty. This competition had massive practical dimensions: for instance, the British Empire decided in 1932 that it would be easier and cheaper to rule Iraq without the mandate category.[78] The new Arab governments were in fact legal sites where this competition occurred in the 1920s and 1930s. As we shall see in the remainder of this book, the British and French empires were faced with the challenge of finding ways to respect League-sovereignty even as they aspired to permanent domination. To this end, administrative domination contrived a constrained form of local agency in the making of successor political orders. This rest of the book tells this story.

PART II

Composite Routes
Out of Empire

CHAPTER FOUR

Ottoman Genealogical Politics

SOMETIME IN 2016, I met a descendant of the Prophet Muhammad in Cairo. Salah was a taxi driver. After a tiring day in the archive, I got him to drive me home because the next day I was scheduled to make an early start for Amman, Jordan. When I mentioned my trip to Salah he joked: "Give my greetings to my cousins!" He cheerfully explained that he was a *sharif* (pl. *ashraf*), a "noble person," that is, a descendant of the Prophet Muhammad, and that his distant "cousins" were the Jordanian royal family who were also *ashraf.* I was somewhat reluctant to credit this claim by a taxi-driver in Cairo. Salah leaned over to the glove-compartment and produced a stamped "certificate of descent" (*bitaqat nasab*), a sharifian ID, issued in 2008 by the Cairo office of the "verifier of the Prophet's descendants" (*naqib al-ashraf*).[1]

This marked the start of my fascination with the descendants of the Prophet Muhammad, whether taxi drivers or kings. Since then, I have learned that Saddam Hussein, the executed dictator of Iraq, also claimed to be a *sharif,* and that experts estimate that tens of millions of Muslims around the world claim this distinguished lineage.[2] The king of Morocco is one of them, of course. The Saudi monarch is not. Still, in Saudi Arabia, some *ashraf* in Mecca maintain a genealogical website, in which a blog post in 2021 recommended the Arab science of genealogy to modern kings because, the author argued, it "strengthens the grip of sultans" and because European Orientalists drew on this science to advance "European colonization."[3]

As a historian I was curious about the larger story behind Salah the taxi driver's sharifian ID. Was this a new form of managing Muslim descent? And why would a Meccan *sharif* take the view that genealogy helps the "grip of the sultans" and assisted European colonization in the past? The tale I uncovered begins in fin-de-siècle Cairo, about a hundred years before my meeting with Sharif Salah.

Genealogy and Empire

In February 1914, 'Abd Allah, later emir and king of Jordan, decided that he wished to postpone a trip from Cairo to Istanbul. This young son of the Ottoman Emir of Mecca was enjoying the hospitality of the Ottoman khedive of Egypt, but he was due to board a Romanian steamship in Alexandria, leaving soon for the imperial capital.[4] He asked his "benefactor," Khedive Abbas Hilmi II, the rich dynast, to allow him to stay a little longer in his palace in British-occupied Cairo. "Sharif 'Abd Allah Bey," as the Arabic and Turkish press called this Ottoman Arab patrician, liked such breaks in khedivial Cairo; later in the summer of 1914 he would stop again, while *en route* for the session of the Ottoman imperial parliament, where he was the deputy for Mecca.[5]

Here were the young *sharif* and the khedive, members of the steam-based Ottoman imperial nobility of the early 1910s. The phrase "Sharif 'Abd Allah Bey" expresses a double role: he was a *sharif*, a descendant of the Prophet, and a *bey*, holder of an Ottoman imperial rank. He stood at the intersection of empires, between the Red Sea and the Eastern Mediterranean. He commuted between Mecca, Cairo, and Istanbul, spoke both Arabic and Turkish, and knew well what empire was. We will take up his story again before long.

In this chapter, I argue that prophetic descent became a source of imperial authority, and was more important than ever in the Ottoman project of the 1900s.[6] 'Abd Allah was the product of what I call "genealogical politics." I mean by this phrase the modern Ottoman (and later British) political use of Muslim Arab claims to descent from the Prophet Muhammad. If we are to understand the 1920s' recycling of descent and dynasty in post-Ottoman Arab polities, we first must understand the earlier Ottoman attempt to institutionalize descent as a source of imperial authority. The steam-based *ashraf* were not an invention of tradition in the sense of being a "use of ancient materials to construct invented traditions of a novel type for quite novel purposes," but they were nevertheless a significant instance of repurposing, an institutionalized upgrade over the previous imperial management of this special group of Muslims.[7]

Genealogical politics was the political dimension of what Ussama Makdisi termed "Ottoman Orientalism" in the late nineteenth and early twentieth centuries. It defined the way the government represented and, consequently, treated Arabs and nomadic populations, often justified by racial and civilizational imaginaries.[8] But it was far more than a "discourse" or an "official iconography," and it had more than "symbolic legitimacy."[9] Genealogical politics was in fact a constitutional strategy. Ottoman ethnographic policy included an unelected but representative Muslim composite and cosmopolitan order, a genealogical-religious alternative to nationalizing empire.[10] This was the sultanic government's reaction to the growing links between the Egyptian khedives and the Meccan *ashraf*, and to the fact that European empires had also discovered the potential of the Meccan *ashraf* as possible caliphs for their own Muslim populations in their colonies and overseas possessions.[11] Over the pages that follow I relate a story about the struggle for control over the genealogical capital of the descendants of the Prophet, waged between the Ottoman government and the expanding European empires.

While a "systematic and analytically informed history of the Sharifs of Mecca and Medina in the Ottoman period" is still missing, we can nevertheless reconstruct in some detail how the sultanic government established a pantheon of *ashraf* within the political and administrative order of the empire in the nineteenth century.[12] Some of these *ashraf* were able to turn their genealogical capital into imperial positions and economic capital. These descendants of the Prophet enjoyed heritable salaries, financial support for palaces along the Bosporus, and lucrative positions in government institutions. In the late imperial political order, printing and the coal-based technical infrastructures that supported Ottoman sea and land routes disseminated sharifian authority.[13] In competition with European Orientalists, the Ottoman and khedivial governments encouraged the editing and printing of medieval Arabic manuscripts and commissioned new works on prophetic lineage.[14] In 1908, the coup d'état by army officers affiliated with the Committee of Union and Progress (CUP, the "Young Turks") and the restoration of the Ottoman constitution disturbed this world of the *ashraf* (from now on they would have to be elected if they were to participate in the imperial government) but their claims remained useful; the CUP governments continued to employ *ashraf*. Hence, we find printed sharifian genealogies, whole books devoted to the science of genealogy, and we see sharif-beys and sharif-pashas on steamships in the Red Sea, riding in first-class wagons on the new Hijaz railway, and in summer palaces in Istanbul. We come across them on imperial councils and as governors of distant regions, as emirs of Mecca, and as ministers until the end of the Ottoman Empire.

MANAGING PROPHETIC DESCENT

Let me explain first what a *sharif* was in preindustrial Muslim imperial societies, especially in the early Ottoman Empire. I follow Kazuo Morimoto who has established "sayyido-sharifology" as a distinct branch of scholarship devoted to researching the global history of claims to prophetic descent. He has suggested that we should understand such claims as bids for symbolic capital, and that we should interpret being a *sharif* as a social category conveying tokens of both "strangerness" (by this Morimoto means, for instance, the situation of newly arrived Muslim immigrants) and association. Importantly, he has highlighted the historical "affinity" between such kinship claims and the leadership of mystical Sufi brotherhoods.[15]

"When there is a blast on the trumpet, on that day there will be no kinship between them, nor will they question each other," says the Koran (23:101). The Prophet Muhammed sought to refute the importance of kinship, the pre-Islamic instrument of group identity, by emphasizing that Islam was a cosmopolitan and universal religion. He needed to do so because in late antique Arabia both Arabs and Jews had grouped together based on their descent; and thus his first followers were mostly clanless Arabs, Ethiopians, and other enslaved foreigners. The Prophet, however, failed. Kinship remained a recognized and much-debated source of identification in later Muslim societies. One might say that kinship became a source of kingship when prophetic descent or at least affiliation with the Prophet's clan became part of the self-legitimation of early Muslim dynasties. There exists a host of sayings posthumously attributed to the Prophet which endorse genealogy, the Arab science of descent (*'ilm al-ansab*).[16]

One reason for the continued importance of prophetic kinship in Muslim societies was migration between Muslim polities (for instance from Central Asia to India) and the consequent use of lineages as markers of membership in ruling groups and for purposes of claiming protection. As early as the eighteenth century, Indian Muslim scholars reflected on the social uses of such claims. They criticized forged genealogies and underscored the fact that respectability based on kinship could arise from both socio-economic status (*hasbi*) and descent (*nasbi*). Margrit Pernau summarizes their critiques in Mughal Delhi: "Status may follow from genealogy, but historically usually the opposite path was taken."[17] To this day, kinship remains a way to imagine and claim association and protection in both urban and desert societies and a means of creating a community of memories among oceanic and intercontinental Arab diasporas.[18]

Despite its emphasis on equality among Muslims, the Koran does contain references to the household of the Prophet (*ahl al-bayt*), and there are many sayings attributed to the Prophet about his family.[19] A special category of kinship is the claim to direct descent from the Prophet Muhammad himself. Such a claim combines assertions of ethnicity (of being an Arab), clan affiliation (as a member of the Prophet's clan, the Quraysh in Mecca), religion (as being of the Muslim faith), and of the moral distinction that follows from prophetic descent. There are two Arabic words to denote a person who claims such descent: *sharif* ("noble," "patrician," pl. *ashraf*) and *sayyid* ("lord," "master," pl. *sada*). In Mughal India, the term *sharif* denoted the general category of a noble Muslim, and within that category a *sayyid* was a descendant of the Prophet. Today in Egypt these are interchangeable categories; in other countries there is a difference based on which grandchild of the Prophet one claims as an ancestor. In order for the claim to be valid, a family tree must reach back to either Hasan or Husayn, the two grandchildren of the Prophet through his daughter Fatima and her husband 'Ali (who was also a cousin of the Prophet). (In some interpretations, the *sayyid* title can be also carried by descendants of other relatives of the Prophet, such as uncles, cousins, and so on.)[20]

The status of *sharif* and *sayyid* can be claimed through either paternal or maternal lineage. The early Muslims who advocated for the political leadership of these individuals were the first Shi'i. But Sunnis also held the Prophet's family in esteem. The eighteenth century, in particular, was a golden age for *ashraf* from Mughal Delhi to Ottoman Aleppo. In this city, by some estimates, more than eighty percent of Muslim elite families held approved *ashraf* status. It should be noted that being a descendant of the Prophet did not automatically entail elite status, but elites had the ability to use their attribution of descent to claim special salaries and favored treatment in courts.[21]

Over time, the Ottoman rulers perfected the management of such claims and individuals. They granted exceptional legal status, tax-exemption, and in certain cases monthly stipends to verified *ashraf* and *sada*. In the early sixteenth century the Ottoman government revived the Abbasid and Mamluk administrative position of the "verifier of the Prophet's descendants" (*naqib al-ashraf*) and appointed deputy "verifiers" in many provincial towns. These were legally trained individuals, usually with past experience as *qadi* or mufti, who were themselves descendants of the Prophet. Their task was to evaluate the claimed status and thus the claimed legal-economic privileges, through the examination of witnesses, documents, and genealogical trees, and to issue sharifian certificates (*hüccet* in Ottoman Turkish, *hujja* in Arabic). Importantly, the *nakibüleşraf* in the imperial capital was the first official to pledge loyalty during the investiture ceremony of a new sultan and to say prayers for him. In the early centuries the provincial "representatives" (s. *kaimakam* in Ottoman administrative language, but locally also called *naqib al-ashraf*) of the imperial *nakibüleşraf* may have been sent from the center. By the eighteenth century the postholders were usually members of local families, in keeping with the general "verticalization" of empire in that century, and it was only the confirmation of their appointment that they received from the Ottoman metropole.[22]

Claims to genealogical prophetic distinction was not a source of political authority in the preindustrial empire. (The special case of Mecca and its *ashraf* will be touched on below.) This was partly because the Ottoman ruling dynasty was itself unable to claim sharifian status: as a Turkic clan whose members did not marry Arabs, it was excluded from the line of prophetic descent. As a consequence, in the early centuries of Ottoman rule imperial propaganda downplayed the significance of genealogy, and instead emphasized continuity with Byzantium, propagated the Muslim warrior (*ghazi*) image, and encouraged mystical ideas about the caliphate.[23]

MAKING DESCENT A SOURCE OF AUTHORITY: THE *NAKIBÜLEŞRAF* IN THE AGE OF ABDÜLHAMID II

In the nineteenth century, however, the *ashraf* did become a source of political authority. A number of causes led to this upgrade in status: the weakness of the Ottoman government, the establishment of Christian European rule over significant Muslim populations, the time-space compression brought by steam technology, and the *ashraf*'s own ambitions. Ulrike Freitag has explored how South Arabian *sayyid* communities outside of the Ottoman sphere looked at the Ottoman center for protection against the British, for instance by sending their children to Istanbul to study.[24] Wilson Chacko Jacob suggests the rhetorical term "*sayyid* sovereignty" to describe the political visions of these individuals.[25] Michael Laffan explores in an analytically more useful way the relationship between

Ottoman imperial consuls and the *sayyid*-communities in the world of the Indian Ocean. A feature of Ottoman imperial globalization was the protection extended to Arabian merchants—who practically all claimed descent from the Prophet—in Dutch Indonesia from the 1880s.[26] Building on an imperial version of Engseng Ho's argument about genealogy and mobility, I would describe the *ashraf* of this period, and especially the holders of the *nakibüleşraf* position in the imperial capital, as the architects of a new Ottoman order in which lineage and empire became connected.[27] The imperial use of prophetic descent as a new source of authority was a genuine Muslim-Ottoman alternative to the uses of the national idea in nineteenth-century empires.

An indication, or perhaps a cause, of the new imperial interest in the postholders of *nakibüleşraf* was the publication of the book *The Genealogy of the Verifiers (Devhat ün-Nükaba)* by an Ottoman accountant called Ahmed Rıfaat in 1866 in Istanbul. This short, popular, lithographed work identifies and gives brief biographies of the holders of the imperial *naqib* position from the early days of the empire to the 1860s.[28] By the late nineteenth century, many provincial holders of the position—from Baghdad to Damascus to Cairo—were also heads of Sufi orders and counted among the elite representatives of the local community. Their social prestige was high and their reach in society surprisingly deep, because they controlled male networks and family communities in the Sufi brotherhoods. As the *Devhat* indicates, many also benefitted from mid-century land reforms and became large landowners. By the late nineteenth century, imperial administrators—Ottoman, but also British, French, Russian, and Italian—had taken note of the *naqib* families in provincial cities and recognized their political potential. But it was Sultan Abdülhamid II who, beginning in the late 1870s, realized this potential as part of his new imperial order.

There were three important *nuqaba' al-ashraf*, one of them is an imperial *nakibüleşraf* in the Hamidian genealogical experiment. The best-known was Abu al-Huda al-Sayyadi (his birth name was Muhammad b. Hasan Wadi), an opportunistic Sufi from the Syrian countryside. He was appointed to the position of *naqib al-ashraf* first in a small town close to Aleppo, and then in the city of Aleppo itself in 1873. Both times he travelled to Istanbul and there received his appointments from the government, despite having no previous connection to these locales. Researchers assume that he enjoyed the support of circles close to the sultan already at this early time. He certainly enjoyed the favor of Abdülhamid II, the new sultan, from 1877, when the sheikh moved to the capital, and was appointed as the head of all Sufi orders in that city; later he also attained the highest grade in the

Ottoman *'ulama'* hierarchy, that of the *kazasker* of Rumeli (the chief military judge of Rumeli). The most important service that Abu al-Huda did for the sultan was to help spread the Rifa'iyya Sufi order in the provinces and to undertake what we can call a genealogical restructuring: he channeled a number of smaller Sufi orders into the ranks of the Rifa'iyya or at least associated their lineages with the legendary Ahmad al-Rifa'i, an Iraqi Sufi, who was a descendant of the Prophet Muhammad. This insured that all individuals claiming a Sufi family lineage, including himself, would become *ashraf* in novel genealogical networks of patronage, especially in the Iraqi and Syrian provinces. He was one of "the black cabinet of four sheikhs" in the sultanic court, to borrow Thomas Eich's appellation; the other three being Ahmad As'ad (in charge of Arabia), Muhammad Zafir al-Madani (in charge of Tripoli), and Sayyid Fadl al-Malabi (in charge of the Indian ocean). Abu al-Huda had a reputation for exchanging influence for money, and critics considered him the *bête noir* of the sultan. After the 1908 coup d'état, perhaps unsurprisingly, the CUP government imprisoned the sheikh. He died in prison in 1909.[29]

Hamidian genealogical politics channeled prophetic descent as an alternative means of legitimating the sultanic caliphate. With the goal of scripting an uncodified constitutional system loyal to the sultan, Abu al-Huda and his circle issued hundreds of publications between 1880 and 1908 in Arabic. These texts defended both the Ottoman caliphate and absolute rule as an Islamic principle, and incidentally also proved his own sharifian lineage. The sheikh himself acted as a genealogist.[30]

On the politics of this situation, I would cite an early pamphlet (c. 1880) with a title that I will roughly translate as *The Call of Reason for Union and Obedience* (note the slight echo here of the later the CUP, the Young Turk "Committee of Union and Progress"). Butrus Abu-Manneh has analyzed this text already, but will be useful to examine it within the context of a constituent history. Abu al-Huda (or his team) argues that an imam is a necessity for Muslims (*fard wajib*), that the Ottoman sultans are the best defenders of the faith, and that obedience to such perfect imams is compulsory. Throughout the text he uses the word "king" (*malik*) to denote the sultan, stating for instance that "the just king is like abundance in all times, or, like the soul in the body."[31] References to prophetic sayings and Sufi maxims and poems about obedience serve to enforce the argument. This monarchical propaganda also contributed to the new valorization of Muslim unity, because Abu al-Huda emphasized that "Muslims and their hearts unite in the service of the ruler."[32] This call for monarchical loyalty, one must remember, was written around 1880, after the suspension of the Ottoman constitution and in the midst of an Ottoman-Russian war.

Abu al-Huda's power was institutional. Between 1877 and 1905, as the imperial *nakibüleşraf*, he appointed or confirmed 289 deputies, provincial holders of the post *naqib al-ashraf*, who received salaries from the Ministry of Pious Endowments and the Imperial Treasury. He sent the names he had chosen to the sultan whose offices issued an order of appointment, which was then sent to the provincial postholder. Every year he investigated and renewed the appointments as long as the postholders were giving satisfaction.[33]

The second important individual, whom we shall meet again later in this book, is Talib of Basra, usually referred to as Talib al-Naqib, Sayyid Talib, or Talib Pasha al-Naqib (1871–1929).[34] Talib, whose grandfather and father occupied the post of *naqib al-ashraf* in this important South Iraqi merchant city, traced his lineage back to the Prophet through the Sufi mystic Ahmad al-Rifaʿi (which made him a distant, imagined cousin to Abu al-Huda). They were in charge with maintaining the tomb of Ahmad al-Rifaʿi in a Southern Iraqi village. The family's wealth came from acquiring lands around Basra after the 1858 Ottoman land law was issued and through their control of pious foundations; they mediated often between the sheikhs of Kuwait, Najd, and the Ottoman imperial authorities. Talib studied Turkish, Persian, English, and "Hindustani." Through the recommendation of the Ministry of Sultanic Pious Foundations, he received, "from among the honorable *sada* of Basra" (*Basra'da sadat-i kiramdan*), the imperial rank of "bey" (of second degree) in 1896.[35] In 1899 he travelled to the imperial metropole, where he was granted the *mirmiran* imperial rank and warmly welcomed by Abu al-Huda and the sultan.[36] At Talib's request, the sultan replaced the governor, his family's enemy, in the Basra province. Sayyid Talib then turned an Ottoman imperial grandee in charge of Arabian matters, becoming the district governor (*mutasarrif*) of the Najd district in the period 1902–1904. The sultan elevated Sayyid Talib to the high imperial rank of Rumeli Beğlerbeği and bestowed Ottoman decorations upon him, his father Rajab (who was the *naqib* in Basra), and his mother (!). As governor of Najd, Sayyid Talib imprisoned a local notable and searched his house in Qatif, where he found British correspondence and weapons and also made off with some of the household's money—which led to huge scandal.[37] In 1904, he settled in Istanbul and the sultan appointed him to the State Council (*Meclis-i Şura-yi Devlet*), a body which hosted many other *ashraf* as well (more on this below).[38]

Figure 4.1 shows Sayyid Talib, "Naqibzade" (the son of the *naqib*) as Ottoman sources called him, in his imperial grandeur, just as he himself wanted the public to see him in 1904. The image is from a volume of laudatory poetry (*mada'ih*) published in khedivial Egypt. Two such books were printed in Egypt in that year. Sayyid Talib arranged for these publications and for the free distribution of hundreds of copies in Basra, in response to the government's request that the sultan receive praise. He used this occasion to advertise himself as well, paying for a full page with his own photograph and laudatory poems in the Cairo journal *al-'Umran*.[39] In the caption next to his photo, Sayyid Talib is described as "most loyal in his servitude to the exalted throne" who lodged in Istanbul with his "uncle" Abu al-Huda.[40] The book was a celebration of the "Islamic caliphate" and the world of *ashraf* and contained Arabic poetry by Sayyid 'Alawi al-Saqaf, the Meccan *naqib al-ashraf*, and others—among them the mufti of Basra. It provides a good view of fin-de-siècle Arabian politics through poetry. The texts praise the sultan, numerous *ashraf* (including the father of Abu al-Huda and the father of Sayyid Talib), and local dynasts in the Gulf. And of course, they praise Sayyid Talib who was at the peak of his imperial career in 1904, having helped to quell a rebellion in Southern Iraq which earned him the *bala* rank (the third highest imperial rank after *muşir* and *vezir*) from the sultan.

A third important, although usually forgotten, Hamidian *naqib al-ashraf* was Muhammad al-Bakri of Cairo (1870–1932). Al-Bakri hailed from an Egyptian sharifian family, leaders of Sufi orders, who had been allied with the Ottoman governors of Cairo since the sixteenth century. They had also often filled the *naqib al-ashraf* position since the late eighteenth century. Under the governor Mehmed Ali pasha (r. 1805–1848) and his descendants, the Ottoman Egyptian *naqib al-ashraf* lost juridical power, though he remained in control of *ashraf* endowments. (In other Ottoman Arab regions, for instance in Jerusalem, the *naqib* maintained informal jurisdiction over the descendants of the Prophet until the twentieth century.)[41] Al-Bakri was educated together with the male children of the khedivial family in Cairo, but instead of following them to the Theresianum in Vienna, he remained in Cairo to complete his education there. He became both the leader of all Sufi orders and *naqib al-ashraf* in Egypt in 1892 but had to resign from this last position after a clash with the khedive in 1895. At this point, Sultan Abdülhamid II invited him to the imperial metropole, where the sultan decorated this Egyptian *sharif* with high honors and then appointed him to the old imperial position of *kazasker* (chief military judge) of Anatolia. The young man returned to the position

FIGURE 4.1. Sayyid Talib as Ottoman imperial
patrician, 1904. *Source*: Yusufzade, *Asna Matalib
al-Arib*, title page verso.

of *naqib al-ashraf* in 1903 in Cairo, likely under sultanic patronage, and
remained in that post until 1911 when his mental state deteriorated. His
most important book, *The Dynasty of al-Siddiq* (*Bayt al-Siddiq*), a genealogical apotheosis, enumerated the various lineages that connected him to
the Prophet and the Prophet's clan, mixing lineage lists with stories of Sufi
sheikhs and descriptions of Sufi rituals. Although he was not intimate with
the innermost circles of the sultan like Abu al-Huda and Sayyid Talib, he
remained loyal to the Ottoman caliphate.[42]

Thus did prophetic descent became a source of political authority in the Ottoman Empire. The promotion of *ashraf* to government
positions was part of Ottoman "Arab" and "official faith" policy, which
included the employment of ethnically Arab, or at least Arabic-speaking,

provincial notables in high government positions and support for loyal
Sunni sheikhs. It is more than possible that these Hamidian men also
looked to the British Raj and the princely states of India as models of
empire and gave thought to imperial reforms and decentralization along
the princely lines.[43]

Sultanic policy and the ambitions of local Arab lords both contributed
to the growth of Arab enclaves in the imperial metropole. And it was not
only *ashraf*, merchants, and bureaucrats who arrived in the age of steam.
For our purposes it is important to note yet another forgotten Arabian
notable, 'Abd Allah Al Thunayan, a candidate for rulership in the emirate of Riyadh in the Najd, who settled in Istanbul in the late nineteenth
century. As we shall see, his Turkish- and French-speaking son Ahmad
would become important for Emir 'Abd al-'Aziz (the later king "Ibn Saud")
during the First World War.[44] It was into this social milieu in Istanbul that
the holders of provincial *naqib al-ashraf* positions and their family members integrated.[45] And at the center of the Ottoman genealogical empire
were the *ashraf* of Mecca.

THE RE-INVENTION OF THE SHARIFIAN EMIRATE:
AN OTTOMAN NATIVE RULER?

Ahmad Zayni Dahlan, a jurist in late nineteenth-century Mecca, wrote a
history of the *ashraf* emirs of the Holy City. His colleague, the imam of the
central mosque in Mecca, contracted a printing house in khedivial Egypt
to publish Dahlan's history in 1888. In the printed book's margins there
is yet another book, a history about the city of Mecca, which serves as a
guarantee that readers will recognize the bond between this special place
and sharifian genealogy. In Dahlan's narrative, a "dynastic state of *ashraf*"
(*dawlat al-ashraf*) in Mecca between the tenth and the twelfth centuries
was just the beginning of what would become a glorious lineage.[46] Dahlan
also describes in glowing words the Ottoman takeover of Egypt and the
control it exercised over the Hijaz until the arrival of a sultanic telegraph
message in 1882, which appointed a certain Sharif 'Awn al-Rafiq to be
the "emir of the Hijaz."[47] We know that the Meccan mufti maintained a
deep interest in the histories of the descendants of the Prophet and had
extensive *sayyid* networks in South Arabia.[48] Dahlan, himself a *sharif*,
and his colleague the imam, thought it important to advertise the relationship between territory and genealogy and their new sharif-emir in a
printed record.

Dahlan's narrative aimed at restoring the image of the Meccan emir as a local rulership—the "Grand Sherif of Mecca," as both Ottoman administrators and European travelers and spies liked to call this position. The book touted the historical relationship between Sharif 'Awn al-Rafiq, the Ottoman emir who hailed from a local sharifian clan, and the city of Mecca. This was a method that worked from "from below," serving to combine Islam, descent, ethnicity, and territory within an imperial framework.

It is not easy to unearth the story of the re-invention of the Meccan emirate in the second half of the nineteenth century because twentieth-century regime changes in Arabia have rendered the historiography of the city a contested domain. Apart from Dahlan and the writings of Egyptian and Ottoman pashas, there are two significant reflections on Mecca's twentieth century history. The first is a manuscript work by 'Abd Allah al-Ghazi (d. 1946), a Meccan scholar, and the second a book by Ahmad al-Siba'i, a fascinating journalist and the first theatre-owner in Mecca (d. 1984). Al-Siba'i, who published his *History of Mecca* first in the 1950s, relied on al-Ghazi's manuscript (itself partly based on Dahlan's work) which remained unpublished for a long time.[49] In 2001, Darat al-Malik 'Abd al-'Aziz (DMAA), the private archive of the Saudi princes, commissioned Ibn Duhaysh, a scholar in Mecca, to edit al-Ghazi's manuscript for publication. However, DMAA did not publish the edited manuscript, so finally Ibn Duhaysh published it himself in 2009, with the permission of DMAA.[50] In the absence of access to primary sources, especially to the most important *shari'a* court records, due to Saudi archival politics, one must read between the lines of these published works.[51]

The Meccan descendants of the Prophet's grandson Hasan have always claimed that theirs is the most distinguished status among all *ashraf*— not least against any claims of the Medina-based descendants of Husayn, the other grandson. In the tenth century, the originally Zaydi and Shi'i *ashraf* of Mecca and Medina aligned with the Fatimid Shi'i caliph in Egypt because they relied on Egypt for food. From the late fourteenth century, the *ashraf* of both Mecca and Medina joined the new Sunni formation of the Mamluk sultans, who created a "vice-sultan" position in Mecca and directly controlled Jidda, the important port of the region. Hence, when the Ottomans conquered Egypt in 1517, they found the son of a Meccan sharifian vice-sultan sitting hostage in Mamluk Cairo. Instead of proceeding to occupy the Hijaz, the sultan decided to send the son back home carrying with him an invitation for submission. From then on, the *ashraf* of Mecca acknowledged the Ottoman sultans as imams of the Muslim community, and the sultans, in return, sent appointment letters to the new emirs as employees of the empire. The Ottomans restricted Portuguese expansion in the Red Sea; and Mecca and Medina remained places of exile for Muslim political dissidents and retired eunuchs. (However, no single Ottoman sultan ever made the pilgrimage to Mecca.) The empire institutionalized the previous tradition of supporting the Hijaz by rendering large revenues from the ports and from the provinces (almost ten percent of the Egyptian budget in 1596–7) to the *ashraf* in the Hijaz. Over the next centuries, two Hasanid sharifian clans, the Dhawi 'Awn and the Dhawi Zayd, fought each other for position and wealth.[52]

A letter by Sharif Ghalib (of the Zayd clan), the Ottoman emir of Mecca at the close of the eighteenth century, written to Napoleon in French-occupied Egypt in 1799 provides a good window into the economic and food reliance of the Hijaz on Egypt just before the age of steam. After asking protection for the Hijazi coffee trade to Egypt, Sharif Ghalib requested millions (possibly in *diwani* piasters) as due to the *ashraf* and the Holy Cities from the Egyptian provincial administration, to be sent with the scribe and accountant of the pilgrimage caravan.[53]

In practical terms, the emirate of Mecca ceased to exist in the first global age of revolutions in the late eighteenth and early nineteenth century. The series of strikes to the Meccan *ashraf* started with occupation by the clans led by Saudi emirs in the early 1800s. These fighters from the Najd region in Eastern Arabia followed a puritan brand of Islamic teaching. After the establishment of Najdi power in 1805, the sharifian emir had to govern the city and its environment in the name of the Najdi ruler, who sent his own judge (a Hanbali *qadi*) to administer justice in the city between 1805 and 1812. The Ottoman imperial government, suffering from internal and external turmoil, could only request that Mehmed Ali, the governor of the post-French Egyptian province, reconquer the Holy Cities. The violent and clever pasha obliged them and in 1812–13 reconquered the Hijaz. Next, the pasha sent his son Ibrahim to the Najd to destroy the Saudi base in Eastern Arabia—a task that he and his eclectic army duly accomplished. In 1818, Mehmed Ali sent the Saudi emir, in chains, to Istanbul for execution. Despite this display of loyalty, the pasha of Egypt also toyed with the idea of keeping the Holy Cities for himself. The Hijaz remained under Egyptian military and administrative rule until 1840.[54]

It was Mehmed Ali's occupation which finally destroyed the old world of the *ashraf* in Mecca and initiated the age of Istanbulite Meccan *ashraf*. In 1827, Mehmed Ali asked for a blank appointment letter from the sultan and appointed *sharif* Muhammad b. 'Abd al-Mu'in b. 'Awn (d. 1857), who lived in Egypt and was loyal to the pasha, as emir of Mecca. This appointment of a member of the 'Awn clan came as a grave injury to the young 'Abd al-Muttalib (d. 1887), son of Ghalib, of the Zayd clan, who in Mecca meanwhile had been appointed emir by the local Ottoman governor. After a rebellion and many adventures, in 1832 'Abd al-Muttalib did briefly serve as an Ottoman anti-emir in opposition to the Egyptian-supported Muhammad b. 'Awn; but as he was unable to enter the Hijaz, he and his brothers finally settled in Istanbul, close to the imperial government. But there was worse to come: for several years, beginning in 1836, the emirate ceased to exist, while Mehmed Ali ruled the Hijaz directly from Cairo from 1836. (Muhammad b. 'Abd al-Mu'in failed to subjugate the region of 'Asir and was requested to again stay in Egypt with his son). Only the 1840 inter-imperial agreement in London, by which the Europeans undertook to protect the unity of the Ottoman Empire, forced Mehmed Ali to give up his sub-empire and restore the Meccan emirate to the care of the sultanic government.[55]

The sultans now exploited the rivalry between the two *ashraf*, Muhammad and 'Abd al-Muttalib. In 1851, Muhammad and his sons were invited to Istanbul where 'Abd al-Muttalib was already established.[56] The transfer of the old fight between the 'Awn and the Zayd clans from Mecca to the imperial capital, the product of Mehmed Ali's ambitions, meant the integration of a local rivalry into the highest level of imperial governance. This state of affairs persisted, with the rivals for the post of the Meccan emir alternately occupying the position until the end of the First World War. We can observe the back-and-forth of the officeholders in Table 4.1.

Beginning in the 1850s, the Meccan *ashraf* strove to rebuild the public image of the emirate under the Ottoman umbrella while at the same time challenging the empire in their capacity as imperial patricians. They could challenge the sultan because the pilgrimage and province of Hijaz province had become a target of competition among the new British, French, and Russian "Muslim powers" and the Ottomans.[57] Sharif 'Abd al-Muttalib of the Zayd clan twice managed to secure appointment to the position of Emir of Mecca (in 1851–56 and 1880–82), but showing himself on both occasions to be unreliable he had to return to Istanbul. Importantly, the Hijaz was also a center of other *sayyid* groups, such as the Hadramawti merchants, whose rise to prominence—and their Ottoman privileges—in Jidda from the 1850s onwards Philippe Pétriat narrates in his fascinating *Négoce des lieux saints*.[58] The 1860s emir of Mecca, Sharif 'Abd Allah, the son of Muhammad from the 'Awn

Table 4.1. The Sharifian Emirs of Mecca in the Age of Steam

Hijri dates of office-holding	Approx. Gregorian date of office-holding	Name of *sharif*	Name of clan
1202–1228	–1813	Ghalib	Zayd
1228–1242	1813–1826/27	Yahya	Zayd
1242–1248	1826/27–1833	Muhammad	ʿAwn
1248	1833	ʿAbd al-Muttalib	Zayd
1248–1267	1833–1851	Muhammad	ʿAwn
1267–1272	1851–1856	ʿAbd al-Muttalib	Zayd
1272–1274	1856–1858	Muhammad	ʿAwn
1274–1294	1858–1877	ʿAbd Allah b. ʿAwn b. Muhammad	ʿAwn
1294–1297	1877–1880	Husayn b. Muhammad	ʿAwn
1297–1299	1880–1882	ʿAbd al-Muttalib	Zayd
1299–1323	1882–1906	ʿAwn al-Rafiq b. Muhammad	ʿAwn
1323–1327	1906–1907	ʿAli b. ʿAbd Allah b. Muhammad	ʿAwn
1327	1908	ʿAbd al-Ilah b. Muhammad	ʿAwn
1327–1334	1908—1916	Al-Husayn b. ʿAli b. Muhammad	ʿAwn
1334–1337	1916—1919	ʿAli Haydar b. Jabir b. ʿAbd al-Muttalib	Zayd

Source: Uzunçarşili, *Mekke-i Mükerreme Emirleri*, Tables 1 and 2; *Salname-i Hicaz* (1304), 143–144; *Salname-i Hicaz* (1309), 121–122; Al-Batatuni, *al-Rihla al-Hijaziyya*, 86; BOA.

clan, followed a loyal course. In the late 1870s, anticipating the imminent fall of the Ottoman Empire, Emir Sharif Husayn, also of the ʿAwn clan, reached out to the British consul with plans for an alliance and an offer of assistance in Afghanistan (I discuss the context of this overture in the next chapter). After this daring *sharif*'s assassination in 1880, old ʿAbd al-Muttalib's second two-year tenure as emir ended with accusations of British collaboration in 1882, at the moment of the British occupation of Egypt.[59]

Hamidian genealogical politics was thus also an imperial reaction to the activity of the Meccan *ashraf*. The value of a loyal sharifian emir of Mecca rose considerably once European empires became overlords of millions of Muslims. The sultan thus left the long-reigning emir Sharif ʿAwn al-Rafiq (r. 1882–1905), the fourth son of Muhammad b. ʿAwn, some freedom of action to create a subordinated princely government. By the 1890s, centralizing Ottoman imperial bureaucrats regarded the Meccan emirate, "the most privileged province," as an obstacle in the way of their ambitions, but Sultan Abdülhamid II decided to maintain Meccan autonomy as being a less costly solution than direct rule. In order to oversee and constrain the Emir's activities, an Ottoman governor—usually an army general—was appointed to the province. Michael Christopher Low explores how the Ottoman government experimented with a "frontier techno-state" in the Hijaz by expanding technology and by disciplining Arabian subjects, educating tribal children, installing a telegraph line, new hygiene infrastructure, new water infrastructure, the Hijaz railway between Damascus and Medina, and a water distillation steam-machine in Jidda. The Emir 'Awn al-Rafiq attempted to create something of a monopolized business from the now steam-based *hajj*. As Low and Mostafa Minawi both demonstrate, the Ottoman governor and Emir 'Awn al-Rafiq colluded in several acts of corruption. The empire attempted to control the emirate by making Mecca rather than Jidda the capital of the Hijaz *eyalet*, a move that contributed to the assimilation of the emirate into the province—or, on the contrary, to the increase of the Meccan emir's power over this imperial province.[60]

In sum, the Meccan *ashraf* provided the genealogical component for Hamidian imperial authority in the 1880s. They joined the holders of *naqib al-ashraf* positions as a special ethics-based group of imperial patricians, a status founded on the principle that prophetic descent conveys moral distinction. Although the sultan always suspected their loyalty, he decided not to deny their claims to distinction, but rather to make use of them and even to grant the *ashraf* greater esteem. In the late nineteenth century, as religion became an argument for European intervention—when, for instance, the Russians and French intervened in the affairs of the empire by alleging that their aim was to protect Orthodox and Catholic Christians in Greater Syria—the Hasanid *ashraf*'s association with Islam's most holy place became a precious source of authority in the Ottoman constitutional order.

INSTITUTIONALIZATION: 'ALI HAYDAR
AND AL-HUSAYN B. 'ALI

To what extent did genealogical politics contribute to the rise of sharifian local polities after the First World War? To answer this question we have to look backward to explore the political imaginary of the Meccan *ashraf* under the Ottoman empire. As an illustration, I turn to the life of 'Ali

Haydar (1866–1935), a grandson of 'Abd al-Muttalib, and the last Ottoman emir of Mecca (who in fact never entered the city in this capacity), and with whom we shall meet again in the following chapters. His nemesis in imperial Muslim politics was al-Husayn b. 'Ali, from the 'Awn clan, the leader of the 1916 "Arab revolt" against the Ottomans, later King of the Arabs, and father of the young Sharif 'Abd Allah Bey who we saw enjoying khedivial Cairo in 1914. We will encounter these individuals in the next chapters.

Examining 'Ali Haydar's forgotten life is crucial for contextualizing al-Husayn and his family, the "Hashemites" who are well known in modern history-writing, but whose Ottoman-era origins have often been obscured by later ideological agendas. Their life in fin-de-siècle Istanbul provides us with a window into the late Ottoman world of genealogy, Islam, and steamships. The institutionalization of these Meccan *ashraf* ensued from their appointment to a variety of administrative positions, the granting of a "sharifian stipend" (*şerafet-i maaş, şerafet maaşı*), and the conferral of membership in the Council of State (*Meclis-i Şura-i Devlet*) of the empire. By disclosing the imperial institutions that so profoundly influenced the lives of the Meccan *ashraf*, we can also gain a glimpse into their imperial imaginary.

The Ottomanization of young Sharif 'Ali Haydar was the outcome of a conscious strategy. At the mid-century, 'Abd al-Muttalib's first three sons, Hashim, 'Ali, and Jabir, received the high rank of *beğlerbeğ* and learned the ways of the Ottoman imperial patricians, including the use of the Turkish language. Their competition with the 'Awn clan and the vacillating fortunes of their father saw them travelling the steamship route between Mecca and Istanbul with ever-greater frequency. It is into this world that 'Ali Haydar was born, as the first son of Jabir b. 'Abd al-Muttalib in 1866. He travelled with his father to Mecca around 1876, where he spent two years studying Arabic and socializing with Meccan society, then returned to Istanbul. His grandfather 'Abd al-Muttalib appears to have selected this grandson to be his successor, preferring him even over his sons. After the child's return from Mecca to Istanbul, one day in 1879 old 'Abd al-Muttalib brought his grandson for an audience with Sultan Abdülhamid II in the Yıldız Palace. The sultan and his sons kissed the hand of the old *sharif*, whom they appear to have much respected. Abdülhamid and the old *sharif* agreed that 'Ali Haydar should be educated together with the Ottoman princes. In the palace school, he developed lasting connections with the sons of the previous sultan, Abdülaziz, and with the sons of Abdülhamid II. Having thus spent most of his youth in the imperial metropole, he continued to use Turkish as his main language until the end of his life.[61] When his grandfather was appointed for the last time in 1880 to the emirate of Mecca, 'Ali Haydar was left behind in Istanbul, both as a hostage and in order to complete his education. His father Jabir worked as the representative (*wakil*) of 'Abd al-Muttalib in Mecca in 1880 but died soon thereafter. Once orphaned 'Ali Haydar completed school with the sultanic princes, but he was not permitted to leave Istanbul.[62]

What was private life like for a young *sharif* living as an imperial grandee? On the whole, we can safely suppose that 'Ali Haydar was quite happily situated. Home was an agreeable palace set within a small estate among the hills of Çamlıca on the Asian side of the imperial capital. There he had two wives: first he married Sabiha, an Ottoman woman, with whom he had a girl Hatice and three sons (Abdülmecid, Muhiddin—later an important musician in republican Turkey—and Mehmed Emin). His second bride was a British woman, Isobel Dunn, who converted to Islam and took the name ("Princess") Fatma, and with whom he had daughters Sefine (Sfyneh) and Musbah, and a son Mehmed Faysal. The children studied music and painting. Fin-de-siècle life in Istanbul for this Arab-Turk-British Ottoman elite family, descendants of the Prophet Muham-mad, would seem to have been quite free of cares, even as the sultan kept Haydar under close surveillance.[63]

The financial means for this *sharif*'s comfortable existence lay in the imperial coffers. When 'Abd al-Muttalib died in exile in 1886, the sultan raised his grandson's treasury-funded salary from 5000 to 7000 *guruş*.[64] In 1889, 'Ali Haydar was appointed to the Council of State with an addi-tional membership salary (*'azalık maaşı*) of 2000 *guruş*.[65] Before long, he received the imperial rank of *bala*.[66] Ten years later, the sultan ordered his privy council (ministers and other administrative leaders) to find a way of further raising 'Ali Haydar's and his brother Ja'far's income. The privy council decided that they should receive an extra stipend in recognition of his being a sharif (*şerafet vech-ile*).[67] Accordingly, in August of 1900, Ali Haydar's sharifian stipend became 10,000 *guruş*.[68]

The "sharifian stipend" was an institutionalized payment to distin-guished *ashraf*. Many early Muslim polities paid stipends to *ashraf* and *sada* and the sixteenth-century Ottomans followed suit, especially in the case of Mecca-based descendants of the Prophet. From the second half of the nineteenth century on, the Pious Endowments Ministry paid some of these sums.[69] When the Meccan *ashraf* moved to Istanbul, they requested that their salaries follow them. For instance, Sharif Yahya Bey, another grandson of 'Abd al-Muttalib who also lived in the capital, requested in 1893 that his sharifian stipend of monthly 1500 *guruş* from the treasury of the Mecca directorate (*Mekke-i mukarrama-i mudiriyet hazinesinden*), which had been part of the *sürre* (the amounts paid to tribes to maintain the security of the pilgrimage caravan), should be transferred and paid in Istanbul.[70] The sultanic government thus restructured an earlier payment to the provincial Meccan *ashraf* into an imperial salary within the metropole.

By the 1900s, the imperial budget included a special financial category, the *şerafet-i tertib*, "the sharifian allocation." (It also included the *muhtaciyet-i tertib*, "the allocation for those in need," from which certain *ashraf* received additional sums). The stipend from *şerafet-i tertib* was a heritable and transferrable amount. We know, for instance, that upon the death in 1912 of Jabir Efendi, a lesser Hijazi *sharif* in Ta'if, the local *kadı* court divided his stipend of 53 *guruş* and 10 *para* among his two wives, his daughter, and his son, and requested the Meccan emirate to notify the Finance Ministry in Istanbul of the adjustment.[71] Both 'Ali Haydar's competitor al-Husayn b. 'Ali and 'Ali Haydar himself likewise decided to distribute their own sharifian stipends, as well as the stipends they had inherited among their children. Al-Husayn b. 'Ali transferred the sharifian stipend he inherited from his father 'Ali to his first three sons 'Ali, 'Abd Allah, and Faysal, in 1900.[72] 'Ali Haydar transferred parts of his own sharifian and *muhtaciyet* stipends to his sons and daughters when he was appointed as the emir of Mecca in 1916.[73]

The Council of State (*Meclis-i Şura-i Devlet*), which paid 'Ali Haydar and others also a salary as members, was the institutional expression of Hamidian genealogical politics.[74] Established in 1867, it was an instance of Ottoman Muslim unelected representation (a brainchild of the reformer Midhat Pasha), as its members were nominated by provincial governors and appointed by the sultan. Being a member of this institution was a high social distinction in the imperial order. Although the Council of State had no control over the imperial budget and sultanic decisions, it remained the highest and most important body in imperial governance because it had the right to investigate the execution of laws. Its offices adjudicated administrative justice at the highest level. For genealogical politics, its importance lay in the fact that the sultanic government appointed many *ashraf* to this institution in various capacities, even though most of them took no part in the daily work of the bureaus at all. The earliest *sharif* I have been able to identify as a member, admitted in the 1870s, was Husayn Pasha, the son of Muhammad b. 'Awn, who as Meccan emir was assassinated in 1880. But there were many other *ashraf* and *sada* members, among them 'Abd Allah Pasha, 'Awn al-Rafiq, 'Ali Haydar (appointed 1889), al-Husayn b. 'Ali (appointed 1892), Mas'ud (appointed 1899), and Sayyid Talib (appointed 1904).[75]

The rival of ʿAli Haydar, al-Husayn b. ʿAli of the ʿAwn clan—known in Ottoman imperial correspondence at the time as *merhum Şerif Ali Paşazade utufatlu Şerif Hüseyin Bey* ("his Excellency Şerif Hüseyin Bey, the son of the deceased Şerif Ali pasha")—also received a handsome sharifian stipend of 9,000 *guruş* while he lived in Mecca in the 1880s (after being born in Istanbul and frequently commuting between the two cities in the 1860s and 70s); this stipend was paid from the *sürre* through the treasury of the Mecca emirate. When the sultan appointed al-Husayn to the Council of State in 1892, he received an extra 5,000 *guruş* for his membership.[76] He received other benefits as well. For instance, the sultan ordered a housing support (20,000 *guruş* yearly) for the rent of a small palace on the shores of the Bosporus (a *konak, sahilhane*) in Mirgün, after his family's return to the imperial capital in 1892.[77] The Ottoman "consort" (*halile*) of al-Husayn, Hatice Adile, applied for and received further support in the form of a partial tax-exemption for her properties in various districts of the imperial metropole.[78]

Genealogical authority thus secured substantial financial support and social capital for these individuals and families, a state of affairs that projected the propaganda of the Muslim caliphate with full force. It was also through the Palace that they could compete for the emirate of their distant region. Prominent *ashraf* participated in imperial ceremonies and personally knew the highest administrators of the empire. We know, for example, that Haydar entertained good relations with the members of sultanic family members and was closely integrated into the newly invented Ottoman "aristocracy." After his appointment to the emirate of Mecca in 1908, he and his sons became better acquainted with Abbas Hilmi II, the powerful khedive of Egypt, a node of exceptional wealth and force within the steam-based Muslim Ottoman aristocratic order. Perhaps they had known earlier, as their house was near the Emirgan palace of Ismail Pasha, the old ex-khedive of Egypt—whose grandson Abbas Hilmi II visited Istanbul regularly in the summers of the 1890s. And later in the 1910s, we saw already and shall see in the next chapter, the Egypt-Mecca relation acquired a special importance.

The Consequences of the 1908 Coup
on the Hamidian Ashraf

Historians agree that the 1908 coup d'état did not result in a complete revolutionary purge, but instead initiated a power-struggle in the imperial government.[79] The new regime had an adverse effect on the

Hamidian *ashraf* and other imperial Arabs though it did not eliminate
them entirely from the imperial government. Only the widely hated imperial *nakibüleşraf* Abu al-Huda was imprisoned, dying in captivity in 1909.
Others, though disgruntled, continued to play the imperial game now as
elected, instead of appointed, representatives. For instance, Sayyid Talib
retreated to Basra, joined the opposition "Liberal Party" (which collected
other Arabs and *ashraf* as well) and became a representative in the new
parliament. The Liberal Party was important in defending the private property of landowners against government appropriation, which increased
Talib's influence and status with wealthy families in Basra. In 1912, he visited Egypt and met Khedive Abbas Hilmi II, then travelled to India for
secret discussions with the British government. As we shall see in greater
detail in the next chapter, he probably converted to the idea of a federation
of Arab emirs under British protection around Arabia. It was a federation
that would include himself as the ruler of a Basra city-state. Talib engaged
in a private war against the CUP in Basra that resulted in his men killing a
number of CUP-loyalist Ottoman officers in 1913. In the summer of 1914,
the Ottoman government offered him the post of the Basra governorship,
combining genealogical politics with the logic of composite rule.[80]

The Meccan *ashraf* continued to compete for the emirate in Istanbul after
the restoration of the constitution. The CUP, whose chief goal was incremental,
technocratic improvement of the empire, valued genealogical politics as a
tool. As is well documented in histories of Arab nationalism, al-Husayn b.
'Ali received the appointment for the Meccan emirate in 1908, right after the
coup d'état. But 'Ali Haydar's imperial career was far from over. Although
the CUP terminated his membership in the Council of State, he retained his
sharifian stipend and remained a member of the Hijazi railway commission,
the mostly symbolic infrastructural project linking Damascus with Medina
and the last Hamidian investment in Muslim politics.[81]

In fact, Haydar became a CUP-*sharif*. In April 1909, after a pro-
sultanic uprising in the capital (often referred to as a "counterrevolution")
the suppression of which involved the dethronement of Abdülhamid II,
the government made sure that Haydar was the first person to publicly
pledge his loyalty to Mehmed V, the new sultan, whom he already knew
quite well. A *sharif* pledging loyalty was important because the counter-
revolt had a strong Islamic coloring. In Ottoman ceremonial tradition,
the first person to pledge loyalty to the new caliph should have been the
imperial *nakibüleşraf*, but with Abu al-Huda in prison, the government
deemed Sharif 'Ali Haydar a good substitute. In 1910 Haydar was even
appointed Minister of Pious Endowments; and in 1911 he was sent on a

propaganda tour through Beirut to Damascus and then on to Medina on the Hijazi railway. He was received everywhere he arrived by the salutations of the Ottoman army in his capacity as a high imperial dignitary. In his later memoirs, he provides extensive details about his plans to develop the techno-material infrastructure of the Hijaz—perhaps a case of retroactive self-justification. It appears that certain CUP-related military leaders, such as Mahmud Şevket Pasha (who became Grand Vizier in January 1913), respected Haydar and regularly sought his advice. In 1912, 'Ali Haydar was appointed vice-president of the Senate (*Meclis-i 'Ayan*), the non-elected upper house of the elected parliament, where other Hamidian dignitaries also continued to serve.[82] He intrigued for the Meccan emirate in the following years. Finally, as we shall see in the next chapters, in June 1916, when al-Husayn b. 'Ali started an open revolt in the name of Arabs, the CUP-government appointed 'Ali Haydar as the Ottoman emir of Mecca. He would be the last one in world history.

Conclusion: A Genealogical Empire?

There is a small dark room in the paintings section of the Dolmabahçe Palace Museum in Istanbul. It is a painter's studio, in which the wax figure of the artist is showcased painting a Bedouin figure on a large canvas. The artist is Abdülmecid Efendi, the last Ottoman caliph who held the post between 1922 and 1924. Driven by today's nostalgia for the imperial past, the museum thus commemorates the sad figure of the last caliph, who loved painting.

In another room of the museum, we can see the original photograph that served as the inspiration for the curators who created Abdülmecid's studio. And in that photo we can see who it was that acted as the caliph-painter's model. It was *sharif* 'Abd al-Majid in Bedouin clothes. This *sharif* was the eldest son of 'Ali Haydar and the husband of Rukiye, an Ottoman princess; himself thus representing the final act of Ottoman genealogical politics, the sexual merger of *ashraf* with the sultanic family.

The painting—and the staged studio—sum up the very modern imperial relationship between an Ottoman prince and a descendent of the Prophet as a representation of the imperial political order—and not without a touch of Ottoman racial Orientalism. The curators must have been aware of the obvious artistic play involved in Abdülmecid representing 'Abd al-Majid. (Or shall we use "Abdülmecid" according to Turkish orthography?)

The two Abdülmecids should remind us to the attempt to bind the shadow world of *ashraf* to the Ottoman dynasty and to the Istanbul-based modern imperial order. The non-territorial ways of migrant *sayyid*-existence and loyalty in the Indian Ocean worlds provided the empire additional tools to exercise control using genealogy outside of its borders. For a political theory of empire, the story of metropolitan genealogical politics—both as a policy from above and the ambition of selected individuals from below—limns the contours of a Hamidian Muslim princely constituent system between the 1890s and 1900s. As an arrangement of imperial governance based on Islam and inequality, it resembles the style of governance by which the British Raj ruled India.

The Ottoman imperial matrix changed after 1908. The CUP government imagined a new, bureaucracy-based imperial organization. Critics of Hamidian politics also proposed new, modular visions of using religion in transforming empire. Comparisons with federal Christian polities suggested instead a focus on ethnicity as a basis of territorial autonomy. The contradiction inherent in the old Hamidian policy had been that the *ashraf* became fitting leaders of separatist, Arab ethnicity-based visions of new Muslim imperial orders. This potential was not lost on their Muslim supporters and critics or British and French observers, and as we shall see in the next chapter, it did not escape the awareness of the *ashraf* themselves.

CHAPTER FIVE

Utopian Federalism

POST-OTTOMAN EMPIRES

IN THE MIDST of the First World War, the Allied Powers became extremely annoyed when Sharif al-Husayn, the Ottoman Emir of Mecca, proclaimed an Arab kingdom on 29 October 1916. This *sharif* was supposed to lead an uprising against the Ottoman center, nothing more. The Meccan Arabic propaganda journal *Al-Qibla* was reporting, however, that local notables were now swearing loyalty to al-Husayn as "king over the Arabs" (*malikan 'ala al-'Arab*) and, moreover, as "their religious authority (*marj'an diniyyan la-hum*)," on account of his descent from the Quraysh clan and, specifically, from the Prophet.[1] The French government blamed this debacle on their political officer at the emir's court having failed to "guide" al-Husayn. The British officials were particularly angered by what they perceived as al-Husayn's arrogance; as far as they were concerned, al-Husayn was only one, albeit presently the most valuable, out of a host of local leaders in Arabia. They were so surprised by the kingship declaration that a later British memorandum called it a "*coup d'état*."[2]

Historians of the modern Middle East generally recount the story of political utopias, such as the sharifian Arab kingdom, from the perspective of nationalist claims.[3] Many claim that al-Husayn's kingship was a British invention—but wartime British spies and administrators were also astonished by this development. Building on recent scholarship, I instead seek to situate the emergence of Arab monarchical ambitions against the backdrop of organizational visions that sought to transform the Ottoman Empire into a federative polity between the 1870s and 1921. Historians have pointed to a number of such "federalist moments" in modern history, both in empires and post-imperial colonies up to the 1960s.[4] Ideas about decentralization and federalization were also heavily debated in the 1900s Ottoman Empire. And these visions of order are instances where imperial institutions were repurposed in one way or another. Most often, the (imperial) dynasty remained the key political institution of such imagined decentralized polities.

I use the term "utopian federalism" to characterize visions of post-Ottoman composite polities.[5] These visions of order belong to a wider political phenomenon seen in such late nineteenth- and early twentieth-century imperial reformist programs as plans for Irish "home rule" in the British Empire, a Slavic "Duna-federation," a *Grossösterreich*, and a United States of Austria.[6] In the same period, Ottoman Arab visions of decentralized and composite polities compose an archive of political futures, alternatives to the unitary norm of the nation-state. Ottoman genealogical politics was only one imperial use of descent that enabled these visions. We have to understand a much larger catalogue of religious-dynastic-ethnic modular projects, next to the *ashraf.*

There are two binary distinctions that, to my mind, have categorized Arab composite utopias: first, whether it was Islam or ethnic-regional self-administration that constituted their key federative principle; and second, whether these visions aimed at preserving or substituting the empire (which is to say, whether they were pro- or counter-Ottoman) (Table 5.1). I here understand a "pro-Ottoman" vision to be one that aspires to establish a reformed polity that retains the Ottoman dynasty at its head as Sunni caliphs, regardless of other organizational aspects of reform; and by a "counter-Ottoman" vision I mean one that instead aspires to establish a new polity, or association of polities, under an Arab caliph as a spiritual leader.

These ideas need not be mutually exclusive. Indeed, as we shall see, during this period the Ottoman polity was itself a combination of direct administration, Muslim dynastic, and composite semi-autonomous techniques of rule. Imperial patricians and provincial intellectuals constantly rearranged federative ideas in new configurations. The Arab thinking in empire as a mode of envisioning the future was an integral part of the larger discursive field of reform in Armenian, Greek, Jewish, Slavic, and other ethno-political groups in the late Ottoman-Habsburg-Russian intertwined spaces.[7] The Ottoman government and many of its most loyal ideologists were convinced that Islam should still underpin domestic relations in a reformed empire.[8] Still, by distributing the ideas along the binaries of pro- and counter-Ottoman visions, and by separating Islamic and ethnic federative principles within those visions, we can get an analytical grasp on the often confusing matrix of political utopias in this period.

Table 5.1. Principles of Imperial Utopias in Arabic, 1870s–1921

Vision of Order	Counter-Ottoman	Pro-Ottoman	Ethnic/Regional Administration as Federal Principle	Islam as Federal Principle
Arab Caliphate	x			x
Egyptian-Sharifian Dualism	x			x
Egyptian-Ottoman Dualism		x		x
Administrative Decentralization		x	x	
Arab Kingdom, 1916	x			x
Arab Republican Caliphate (Rida, 1916)	x		x	x
Turco-Arab Dualisms		x	x?	x

The word "utopia" is most often applied to universal visions of revolutionary human equality. It has been observed, furthermore, that such visions often reflect ideals that were developed and "lived" by exile and immigrant communities.[9] While fin-de-siècle Arab imperial visions of order lack such a broad commitment towards transforming humanity as a whole, it is nevertheless reasonable to class them as "utopias" because they articulate normative, universal ideals about Islam and ethnic-linguistic communities. Also, some of their makers did live in diaspora communities, such as the influential community of Syrians in khedivial Egypt. Cultural and political associations founded by members of the Syrian diaspora in Cairo and Egypt were major producers of reform visions, which they advanced through petitions both to the Ottoman and to the French and British governments.[10]

Imperial utopias figure prominently also in what I call the politics of "Muslim princely regions," which is to say communities ruled by Muslim Ottoman patricians whose authority derived from descent, violence, and sultanic appointment. As some of the visions aimed at a loose association among Muslim monarchs, they are often said to be the seeds of the ideologies that interwar European administrators, Orientalists, and today's researchers have termed "pan-Islamism" and "pan-Arabism." In addition to an analysis of these ideas, this chapter traces the emergence of middling individuals whom we can call activists of utopian federalism. Many of them remained involved deeply in the post-war politics, partnering or quarreling with Muslim emirs to create new monarchies, small sub-empires, under the Allied umbrella.

Tracing the emergence of imperial utopias in the late Ottoman Empire alters our understanding of at least four aspects of political history. First, we can see sophisticated ideas about inter-polity relations among emirates and city-states as diverse "routes out of empire," alternatives to the nation-state.[11] Second, these utopias tell us of hitherto overlooked Euro-Muslim imaginaries in which the caliph was not the political head of a Muslim federative polity. These clandestine visions complicate the supposed political importance of the caliphate even as they simultaneously highlight its theological-epistemological importance.[12] Third, following Ernest Dawn's suggestion about the use of Arab nationalism as a discursive tool in imperial competition, and instead of explanations revolving around "tribal claims," they reveal how the disgruntled *ashraf* of the Hamidian era in fact recycled an imperial vision of political order. And thus they open the door to an interpretation of the 1916 "Arab kingdom" of Sharif al-Husayn as the expression of a sharifian imperial utopia.[13] Finally, we can begin to see to what extent modular government was a shared fin-de-siècle political imaginary among European and Ottoman imperial patricians.

The Modular Ottoman Empire:
Muslim Princely Regions

In order to understand the thinking behind the reconfiguration of regions in the Ottoman Empire, we first need to consider Ottoman practices of layered government as they existed in the age of steam. Many prefer to start the story of the twentieth-century Arab polities with the designs of the British Foreign Office or its Indian Government as to the partitioning of the Ottoman Empire. But we can also start a narrative from within this Muslim imperial formation, with an account of the Hamidian *ashraf*'s discussions and visions about switching regions from Ottoman to British imperial frames.

Just two years before the announcement of an Arab kingdom, in the spring of 1914, when young Sharif 'Abd Allah Bey had those few days' holiday as the guest of Khedive Abbas Hilmi II in Cairo, these two Ottoman dignitaries did a bit more than attending receptions and enjoying excursions. With the support of the khedive, 'Abd Allah met the British consul

in Cairo to transmit a secret message from his father, al-Husayn, the Ottoman Emir of Mecca. The consular secretary reported to his superiors that
'Abd Allah had asked whether his father would be able to obtain an agreement with the British Empire "similar to that existing between the Emir
of Afghanistan and the Government of India."[14]

This Egyptian-Hijazi scheming in the 1910s was an instance of the
politics of Muslim princely regions. Between 1912 and 1914, Sayyid Talib of
Basra, another product of Hamidian genealogical politics, asked the Ottomans for decentralized government and then asked the British for a special
status for his region—his example was the distinguished province of Mount
Lebanon.[15] At the same time, as we shall see later, Ibn Saud, the imam and
emir of Riyadh, also performed a balancing act between Ottoman and British autonomous subordination. The modular, layered logic of territoriality,
as in the British Raj, defined the political imagination of imperial *ashraf*.

Like all empires, the Ottoman Empire from its emergence in the fifteenth century was no exception in making use of subordinated rulers.[16]
This practice evolved over time: commercialization in the eighteenth
century led to an Ottoman "networking society" and to "horizontal" imperial governance, a type of partnership with local leaders.[17]

With the advent of European military superiority in the nineteenth
century, the Ottoman government adopted two policies: one in which
the center exercised direct rule, and another where it reigned indirectly.[18]
Many emphasize the Tanzimat reforms of centralization but modular tools
of subordination also figured among the Ottoman tools up to 1922. Riding
the waves of the inter-imperial Mediterranean, the fortunes of self-made
Muslim men had been on the rise in the nineteenth century. They acquired
new technologies (steamships, land surveys, industrial agriculture) but
retained a subordinated relationship to the Ottoman center. The best-
known example is the Ottoman governor (later khedive) of Egypt who created a novel military machine in his rich province in the 1820s and 1830s.
The bey of Tunis similarly adopted a modernization program, sandwiched
as he was between French imperialism and Ottoman demands. The Grand
Sanusi's Sufi network-based oasis-polity in the Sahara is another telling
illustration. The Emirate of Mecca increased its importance as European
empires ruled more and more Muslims. In Arabia, the Ottoman government competed for the loyalty of the emir of Kuwait, the imam of Yemen,
the al-Idrisi in Asir, and the emirs of the Su'ud clan in the Najd in the face
of British and Italian offers of protection. All in all, the nineteenth-century
Ottoman Empire also had a layered structure, "a modular condition of
empire," alongside the directly ruled provinces.[19]

European intrusion in Ottoman administration also propelled the sultanic government toward indirect rule. A good example here is the interimperial contract through which the Christian-majority region of Mount Lebanon became a special, distinguished governorate (*mutasarrafiya*) after the 1860 disturbances. The agreement included the appointment of a nonlocal, Ottoman Christian as governor. Writing in the 1910s, Iskandar 'Ammun, a clever Lebanese lawyer in British Egypt (whom we will meet briefly again in the post-war sharifian empire) took the view, expressed in a pamphlet, that this arrangement offered the possibility of establishing a subordinated republic that would have its own elected representative local government and an elected president. He wrote that "the form of government in the mountain should be republican, without the slightest infraction of Ottoman sovereignty or international law."[20] In this case, the 1860s European intervention to create some autonomy based on religious affiliation—an origin of later institutionalized "sectarianism" very much advocated by the Maronite church—led to 1910s local imaginations about constitutional upgrade, a subordinated mountain mini-republic within a composite Ottoman Empire.[21]

Let us theorize further what territoriality means in a composite mode of imperial government where religion and monarchy are justifications for territorial autonomy. Scholars interested in an alternative conception of sovereignty to the nation-state point at the late Ottoman princely regions.[22] But it is important to underline that such practices of imperial government meant non-sovereignty for these regions. Thus, we have to start first with the way the Ottomans fused subordinated local dynasties with administrative units. The Ottoman ceremonial-administrative vocabulary indicated the status of the princely regions by means of the office and honorific title of the local leader. These ceremonial terms were distinct from the administrative vocabulary but conveyed specific meanings to those who understood the Ottoman imperial hierarchy. Mecca was both an *emirlik* and *şeriflik* (the Hijaz administratively an *eyalet*), Kuwait an *emirlik* (administratively a *kaza*), Tunis an *emirlik* and *beylik*, and post-1867 Egypt was a *hidiviyet* (administratively a *vilayet*), which in English came to be known as "khedivate." The autonomy of Christian princely regions could also be deduced from the status of the local prince, as in the case of the *baş-knezlik* of Belgrade after 1838 (it had earlier been a *voyvodalık*).[23] The Sanusi brotherhood was a network-based spiritual power in North Africa and Arabia. Its classification as a political-territorial unit caused problems even for the generally innovative Ottomans.[24] These titles and offices reflected informal practices in the imperial order that preserved the dignity of the sultan as the highest lord but operated with a certain flexibility to distinguish degrees of regional autonomy.[25]

There is a difference between what I term a Muslim princely region as a category of analysis and what the Ottoman government called a "privileged province" (*eyalet-i mümtaze*) as a category of administrative practice. Historians have described how "privileged province" as a term functioned in European and Ottoman legal-administrative texts in the late nineteenth century.[26] Fujinami Nobuyoshi has shown that in inter-imperial agreements during the first half of the nineteenth century the Ottoman government termed the privileges (pl. *imtiyazat*) given to local Christian princes (Wallachia and Moldova, Serbia) in French as *suzerainty*, whereas it termed those accorded to Muslim emirs (Samos, Algeria, Egypt) in French as *sovereignty*. He argues that the word *imtiyaz* gradually acquired the new meaning of "autonomy" in the Ottoman imperial administrative-legal vocabulary after the 1860s administrative reform. It is important for my own argument that the privileges enjoyed by a "privileged province" were initially granted to subordinated minor rulers: to the prince of Serbia, the khedive of Egypt, the governor of Tunis, the prince of the United Principalities (Romania), the bey of Samos, and the prince of Bulgaria. Through these local lords did the sultan convey administrative privileges to the communities in their regions. Crete, Bosnia-Hercegovina, and Cyprus were assimilated into the "privileged province" category quite late.[27] In the mid-1890s, Ibrahim Hakkı, an important Ottoman legal expert, listed the privileged provinces as being the "Bulgarian emirate," "Egyptian khedivate," "Tunis eyalet," "Samos emirate," Bosnia-Hercegovina ("temporarily under Austro-Hungarian administration"), and Cyprus.[28] The privileged provinces thus were not fully coextensive with what I call "princely regions." There are some territories that I call Muslim princely regions—such as the Hijaz—which were never categorized as a privileged province (in this last case, possibly because the Ottoman government always understood it as an exceptional region given the sacred cities). Until the 1870s, the representatives of the princely regions at the imperial center were mostly minor rulers and their agents.[29] Later, Ottoman legal experts borrowed the language of Western-Christian international law to characterize some of these Ottoman sub-polities, especially Egypt, as "quasi-sovereign" (*şibh-i saltanat*).[30]

The *regionality* of the princely region was equally important. Cyrus Schayegh uses the idea of "regionalization" to replace the nation-state paradigm with a trans-spatial, *croisé* theory of city-state-region development in Greater Syria (*bilad al-Sham*) between the 1830s and 1950s. For

Schayegh, the concept of a region, or meso-region, is a "heuristic device" defined by a combination of shared "structural traits," among them social, historical, and infrastructural features that result in connectedness.[31] Alongside the imperial administrative categories, Ottoman officials used the word "region" (*hıtta*, from Ar. *khitta*, pl. *khitat*, originally "land marked out for building upon"), "section" (*kıt'a*, from Ar. *qit'a* pl. *qita'*) and "domain" (*memleke*, from Ar. *mamlaka*, pl. *mamalik*) to refer to large territories and provinces under their direct or indirect control. Ottoman geographers also used terms such as *Kurdistan, Arabistan*, and so on, to denote the "lands" of ethno-linguistic communities. The Arabic geo-spatial vocabulary has always used the plurals of "lands" and "cities" to describe regions (*bilad, aqtar*), such as *bilad al-Sham* and *bilad al-Sudan*—all variant terms for the concept of region.[32]

My use of "princely region" as a category of analysis thus arises from non-European imperial ceremonial-hierarchical and spatial vocabularies. This category should not, however, be seen as an Orientalizing term. To use the term "princely region" instead of the vocabulary of the nation-state does not mean that territorial government and territorial legal authority were absent. For instance, in khedival Egypt an elaborate bureaucracy developed that called itself "the local government" (*al-hukuma al-mahalliyya*), a term that the Ottoman central administration also used when they described many of the provincial administrations. Local government underwent a process in the nineteenth century of increasing physiocratic and economic centralization, characterized not by strictly demarcated borders but by precise spheres of tax-collecting authority and a high regulatory consciousness. Even in the waters of the Persian Gulf, rulers observed nautical frontiers that they had agreed upon among themselves before the establishment of British-demarcated borders.[33] From the 1900s on, border-making among Ottoman princely regions under European occupation was an extremely difficult exercise with multiple overlapping imperial and local concerns.[34]

The ceremonies in 1900s Mecca provide a good illustration of the contradictory practices of an Ottoman princely region: dynastic ambitions combined with economic reliance on imperial sources. (Figure 5.1) For instance, on 5 November 1913, the Egyptian caravan carrying the cover of the Kaaba (*mahmal*) and the subvention from the Egyptian foundations for the Hijaz reached Mecca. Emir al-Husayn arrived on the scene with his tribal soldiers and greeted the delegation with a ceremonial fusillade of cannon shots; only after him did the Ottoman governor arrive with the commander of the imperial units. The same day, the Egyptian delegation's

FIGURE 5.1. Sharif al-Husayn as Ottoman Emir of Mecca (with white beard and a sword, standing to the right of the figure standing on the pedestal) presumably with the Ottoman governor and with Ottoman officials in 1908. *Source*: 1/1, Bowman Album, GB165–0034, MECA, with permission.

leader counted the money (which arrived with the *mahmal*) in the presence of the army commander. On the next day, there was a military parade before the emir; and the Egyptian and Syrian *mahmal* delegations mixed. Soon, the Egyptian delegation paid the sum due to the emir himself, then a further amount to cover administrative expenses, and finally the emir distributed the money for salaries to the Meccan institutions. At the end of the visit, the governor and the sons of the emir accompanied the *mahmal* delegation on their way out of the city.[35] Despite the pomp accorded to the emir, it remained obvious to contemporaries that the Meccan emirate was dependent on those who ruled Egypt, the Red Sea, and the Syrian lands.[36]

Princely regions thus reflect a practice of non-sovereign territoriality that began well before the age of the League of Nations.[37] We can characterize the nineteenth-century Ottoman princely regions as examples of religious and dynastic territoriality. These were non-European polities in which the governing dynastic power was subordinate to the imperial metropole. In some cases, as in mid-nineteenth-century Egypt, the local government attempted to mask its provincial status. In the 1860s, the pashas of Tunis and Cairo wanted to appear as independent rulers to their subjects and to foreigners (pride was at issue of course, and importantly also access to contract loans from Europe) despite the fact that they were subordinate to the imperial center.[38]

The Ottoman government for its part attempted to conceal the modular nature of its constitutional system. The written Ottoman constitution of 1876 makes only indirect reference to the khedivate, the emirates, or any other indirectly controlled regions. Its very first article declares that the Ottoman Empire is composed of "domains" (*memalik*), "regions" (*kıta'at* [!]; the contemporary French and English translation of this word was "possessions"), and "distinguished provinces" (*eyalet-i mümtaze*). In Art. 7, the "sacred rights" of the sultan include the right to "appointments in the distinguished provinces according to the privileges given," which was translated into French as *il donne l'investiture aux chefs des provinces privilégiées, dans les formes déterminées par les privilèges qui leur ont été concédés*. Once existing in a codified and public form, however, the question of what was meant by "privileged provinces" became a contested topic. When the government of the United Principalities (Romania) posed a question about their own status, they received the answer that the Principalities remained under Ottoman suzerainty, since the constitution's force extended to the Romanian regions as well as the khedivate of Egypt. This claim pushed the Romanians towards the announcement of full independence in 1877.[39]

It is tempting to see the existence of princely regions and notions about an Ottoman-Christian mountain republic as an alluring possibility of creating an Ottoman commonwealth, or in other words, a decentralized empire. This possibility was not lost to local intellectuals and European imperial planners.

A Counter-Ottoman Empire? The Arab Caliphate

For Ottoman Arab intellectuals, the problem was not with the imperial constitution but instead arose when it was suspended in 1878. They did not argue for a Romanian-style political break from the Ottoman Empire. Instead, the Ottoman government was faced with an upsurge of utopian thinking in Arabic that envisioned Islam as the constitutional principle behind a new composite project that, some thought, should entail the establishment of a non-Ottoman Arab caliph. Advocates of the Arab caliphate believed in a universal Muslim *umma*, where membership would be open to anyone who accepted the truth of divine revelation, but where at the same time there was an ethnic distinction between Arabs who were potentially eligible for the caliphal office and non-Arabs who were not.[40]

ETHNICITY AND THE CALIPHATE

In theory, there can only be one leader of the Muslim community (the *imam*). In practice, there were always many political imams. In Ottoman times, from the fifteenth century onwards the caliphal title "Commandant of the Faithful," was held not only by the Ottoman ruler, but by multiple other personages from Morocco to Oman. For instance, the Najdi scholars in Arabia called the rebellious Al Su'ud emirs *imam* and *khalifa* even after they were repeatedly defeated in the nineteenth century.[41]

Historians found evidence of clandestine talks about a future Arab caliph as early as the second half of the nineteenth century. In 1858, the British consul in Damascus noted that a group of Syrian notables, offended by *Tanzimat* religious equality, were discussing the possibility of a better and more virtuous Arab caliph in Mecca. In 1860, British officials considered that the emir of Mecca might not be a bad idea. He could perhaps act as a useful foil, a counter-caliph against the French influence in khedivial Egypt.[42] British agents and Muslim millenarians (as the *hijri* year 1300—Gregorian 1882–83—approached) thus went forward with this vision. In 1877, after the Queen of the United Kingdom became the Empress of India, officials advocated in the British press for the emir of Mecca's appointment as their own Sunni caliph to safeguard their interests among Muslims in India. In 1879, the British consul in Jidda advanced the idea of the *hajj* as a yearly meeting of Muslim "representatives" and called attention to the potential of the Hijaz as a locale for global exchange. When in 1879–1880, the sharifian Emir of Mecca offered his services to the British government to act as intermediary in the Anglo-Afghan wars, he also asserted the illegitimacy of the Ottoman ruler's claim to caliphal authority.[43]

Europeans contributed significantly to the popularization of the idea of an ethnicized Arab caliphate. The British nobleman-traveler Wilfrid Blunt (d. 1922) and a French journalist, Gabriel Charmes (d. 1886), wrote at length on the issue in both English and French. Blunt, who had spent time in the Hijaz and Egypt, wrote a memorandum about a potential new Arab caliphate to the Foreign Office in 1880. A year later he put out a series of articles in which he advocated that the emir of Mecca should be the Arab caliph under British protection. These articles were collected in an influential book, *The Future of Islam*, in 1882. Blunt's understanding was that the caliphate was analogous to a Muslim papacy. Trailing Blunt, Charmes published French articles in which he similarly advanced the Arab claims and collected the articles in another influential volume *L'avenir de la Turquie—Le panislamisme*, in 1883.[44]

The question of the relationship between a hypothetical Arab caliphate and the Egyptian khedivate became an issue in the politics of the Ottoman princely regions from the 1880s. Orientalists report that some Damascene notables took the view that the sharifian emir of Mecca should be the spiritual Arab head of Islam, while the khedive of Egypt should be "the temporary head" of a new polity.[45] Habib Antony Salmoné (d. 1904?), a British-affiliated Christian from Beirut, advocated for an Arab caliphate in a number of articles in Arabic publications.[46] In 1896, a Young Turk newspaper in Cairo published a plan to create an independent Arab caliphate, though in the view of historians "this was just a ploy to frighten the sultan."[47] British agents were almost always involved in these discussions, and in reaction the Ottoman ambassador in Paris regularly warned his government in the 1890s of the British schemes in the Hijaz, which aimed at separating the caliphate from the sultanate.[48]

A KHEDIVIAL CALIPH? THE EGYPTIAN CONNECTION

In these schemes and visions, the khedivate of Egypt often appears as an involved party. Khedive Abbas Hilmi II was, for a time, an active supporter of the anti-Hamidian caliphal discourse. An example: in the mid-1890s, Sultan Abdülhamid II and his imperial *nakibüleşraf* Sheikh Abu al-Huda decided to strip the khedive of income from the Kavala *waqf*, a wealthy endowment on the Aegean island of Thasos. This was bad news for the business-minded young khedive, who had been planning to rent out its properties to a Greek businessman. Abu al-Huda wanted to hand over this lucrative endowment to another, perhaps more loyal khedivial family branch. The sheikh allied with the notable Mehmed Yeğen and the journalist Hasan Husni Tuwayrani (d. 1897) to spread anti-Abbas and pro-sultanic propaganda in Egypt. Abbas Hilmi II, who knew about this alliance, tacitly opposed the seizure of the Kavala endowment, or at least allowed members of his household to oppose it on his behalf. Sympathizers who were associated with the CUP within the khedive's private administration attacked and threatened Mehmed Yeğen with death in 1896.[49]

The angry khedive used the caliphate-claim as a knife in the sultan's back. He amplified the talk of a caliphate. In an 1895 meeting in Istanbul, he discussed with Jamal al-Din al-Afghani (d. 1897), the old anti-imperialist

Muslim philosopher, the establishment of an "Arab caliphate."[50] 'Abd Allah Nadim, the khedivial agent in Istanbul between 1895 and 1896, reported to his master that Sheikh Abu al-Huda had told the sultan that al-Afghani and Nadim had sworn loyalty to the khedive as a caliph. In Nadim's words, the sultan then accused al-Afghani of attempting to create an "Abbasid" caliphate.[51] Whether or not there was a plan to establish such a caliphate, the khedive was certainly interested: he acquired treatises on Quranic verses and prophetic sayings concerning the caliphate and *shari'a* rules of good governance.[52] Some of his men called him "the Commander of the Faithful" in their letters. In 1911, Yemeni notables were ready to support his claim for the "the throne of the Islamic caliphate" (*'arsh al-khilafa al-islamiyya*).[53] The caliphate was an inter-Ottoman issue for Abbas Hilmi II—even though as a descendant of the Ottoman, possibly Turkish, Mehmed Ali Pasha he could hardly claim Arab ethnicity for himself.

THE CALIPHATE AS A MUSLIM FEDERATION

Abbas Hilmi II also cultivated a pious image in Greater Syria through symbolic acts; for instance, in 1896 he gave orders for the building of a mosque near to Damascus at his own expense,[54] and he encouraged Syrians to see Cairo as an attractive place in in which to do business. Ottoman subjects did not need a passport, and the British occupation provided some freedom for anti-Ottoman expression.

Under the reign of Abbas Hilmi II, Sheikh Muhammad Rashid Rida (1865–1935) and Sheikh 'Abd al-Rahman al-Kawakibi (1854–1902) two sheikhs in the Syrian community of British Egypt campaigned for political utopias framed as associations of Muslim polities. Both modular visions conceived of Egypt as part, if not the center, of post-Ottoman Muslim federations, considered Mecca as the spiritual center of these federations, and counted Muslim emirates, even potential ones such the demanded autonomy of Sayyid Talib in Basra, as the units of an association of governments. Unlike some of the clandestine schemes that we find attested only in archival evidence, these ideas appeared in print and were widely circulated.

These figures, and some of their followers, are often presented as grandfathers of "Salafism," a contemporary movement that promotes a very puritanical brand of Islam. Al-Kawakibi is also credited in historical scholarship as the father of pan-Arabism.[55] However, recent scholarship rejects applying the category of Salafism as a self-conscious ideological movement before the 1930s.[56] As to pan-Arabism, I suggest that we should see Muslim federalist ideas with an Arab caliph as part of the matrix of imperial utopias that aimed to reform the Ottoman polity or to imagine post-Ottoman empires.[57]

Sheikh Muhammad Rashid Rida, a clever religious entrepreneur and *sayyid* was born in al-Qalamun, a small town in Ottoman Syria, where he studied Muslim law and sciences. He migrated to Cairo in the late 1890s and found protection under the khedive, with whom he corresponded. In 1898 Rida established *al-Manar*, the "Lighthouse," a Muslim activist journal that would quickly achieve global outreach. In 1912, together with another young journalist called Muhibb al-Din al-Khatib (d. 1969), he founded a Muslim school (*Dar al-Da'wa wa-l-Irshad*), from which a number of important Syrians graduated (among them Amin al-Husayni, the later mufti of Jerusalem; and Yusuf Yasin, the later Saudi foreign secretary). We will meet with these men as they formed a network in the post-war years. Although Rida's role in the process of Islamic modernization is often exaggerated, he was nevertheless a gifted conspirator, a prolific writer, and an ambitious practitioner of *Realpolitik*. The role that his school played in bringing together Muslim activist teachers and students was more important for the interwar political landscape than his ideology. In his public writing, he remained a cautious Ottoman loyalist until 1914.[58]

The older Sheikh 'Abd al-Rahman al-Kawakibi (1854–1902) of Aleppo also moved to Cairo in the late 1890s. He was a learned man and a journalist. Over the course of a long career in provincial Ottoman Arabic journalism and business, al-Kawakibi had already written, in Aleppo, the draft of a book entitled *Umm al-Qura* ("The Mother of All Villages," meaning Mecca), which was published in 1900 in Cairo to huge acclaim. The book contains an explicit mention of an Arab caliph. Al-Kawakibi's sudden death in Cairo in 1902 gave rise to speculations about poisoning, but it might also have been a heart attack. *Umm al-Qura* was posthumously serialized in Rida's journal *al-Manar* in 1902, under pseudonyms and then printed separately.[59]

Within the opposition to Sultan Abdülhamid II, al-Kawakibi and Rida entertained an alternative theological-juristic action plan to the Young Turks' scientific materialism. They envisaged a society—an association of scholars—as a generator of Muslim progress, though not necessarily within the Ottoman Empire. Jamal al-Din al-Afghani, Blunt's *The Future of Islam*, and other writers inspired both of them.[60]

Rida, the younger man, was cautious. He understood well the renewed importance of Islam for the Ottoman Empire. He noted that the previous sultans' power had been based on group solidarity (*'asabiyya*) and executive authority (*mulk*).[61] In his new journal *al-Manar* in 1898, after a series of articles accusing Muslim leaders and scholars of corruption, there appeared an article stating that Abdülhamid II had "renewed" the caliphal office. The author noted that this renewal constituted a religious (*dini*) reform, as opposed to a political (*siyasi*) one. The article proposed the establishment of a worldwide society of scholars (and an accompanying journal), which would address a range of important tasks: the supervision of religious doctrine, legal unification, linguistic (Arabic) unification, reformed and centrally distributed Friday preaching, and proselytization. The author was careful to observe that the Ottoman caliph ought to support these activities. This worldwide society, embodying "religious leadership" (*ri'asa diniyya*), would be headquartered in the Hijaz; and for this reason, the Ottoman state must enhance the status of this territory by establishing a railway from Damascus and initiate agricultural development in the Hijaz. This reform would allow, according to the writer, the establishment of political unity among Muslim governments, even between the Iranian (i.e., Shi'i) and the Ottoman (i.e., Sunni) empires, and the creation of a federation, like the United States of America, in order to resist European imperialism.[62] In outlining this idea, the author of the article tacitly challenges the Ottoman sultan's claims to caliphal authority by proposing instead the establishment in Mecca of a corporate Islamic leadership.

In his book *Umm al-Qura*, the older al-Kawakibi proposed a political union of Muslims, essentially a federation of Muslim monarchs, as a remedy for social injustice. In describing an imagined meeting of Muslim scholars in Mecca in 1899, he proposed the establishment of a formal society of this type which would revive the principles of the Rightly Guided caliphs, the first four imams of Islam. The author emphasized that this reform should happen through the "purest" people, the Arabs. He accused the Ottoman Turks of negligence regarding piety and Muslim unity and praised the Arabs, specifically those of the Arabian Peninsula, as being "the only means to realize the religion's potential."[63]

Most notably, in an appendix to the book, al-Kawakibi made his case for an Arab caliph in Mecca, who would have no political authority. His argument took the form of an imagined conversation between an Indian scholar and an (Arab?) emir. The emir argues that the sultan cannot take the lead when it comes to the strengthening of religion (*i'zaz al-din*) because "religion is one thing and temporal power (*mulk*) is another." Historically, the emir claims, only the rightly guided caliphs and the Umayyad caliph 'Umar b. 'Abd al-'Aziz were qualified to exercise governance over both religion and administration (*mulk*). The Ottoman sultans had not strengthened Islam by conquering Byzantium, he maintained, but had instead betrayed Islam by exchanging Andalusia for Byzantium; and now in contemporary times the Ottoman army was reconquering the Yemen at the expense of Muslim lives. All of a sudden the fictional emir produced a document from out of his pocket and presented his solution: an Arab caliph should be established from among the Quraysh tribe—that of the Prophet himself—whose administrative authority should be restricted to the Hijaz and who should have no command over an army, though he would have the help of an elected consulting council. The caliph and the council should only decide religious issues. His name should be the first in the Friday prayer globally, after which would come the name of the actual Muslim ruler in each particular location. The caliph's name should not appear on coins, and his only political function should be to certify succession when a Muslim ruler dies. The main benefit of such an Arab caliphate, said the imaginary emir, would be to enable "the Muslims' union," to create something of a federal polity "similar to what the Germans and Americans had."[64]

Remaking empire from the inside met with external clandestine propaganda as well. In Adana, pamphlets appeared in 1905 that contained a declaration in French by "The League of the Arab Homeland," in which the authors demanded the establishment of an "Arab Empire" extending from the Tigris and Euphrates to the Suez Canal and on to Oman in the south. This was to have been a global sultanate with an Arab Muslim sultan. A second, independent "empire," the pamphlet continued, should be created in the Hijaz: a polity headed by an Arab caliph with universal spiritual authority. "Everything," the authors suggested, "is ready for liberation."[65]

Loyalist Ottoman Arab intellectuals were not fans of the idea. Rafiq al-'Azm (d. 1925), a rich Damascene intellectual, who was in fact a friend of Rashid Rida, took the view in 1911 that the example of the Prophet actually demonstrated the primacy of the Ottoman sultan's claim to the caliphate and that an Arab caliph would be nonsense.[66]

Dualism and Decentralization: An Administrative Ottoman Federation?

The vision of an Arab caliph reigning over a constellation of Muslim princely regions was not popular among the Arabs in the Ottoman provinces. There is no evidence that when censorship was lifted temporarily in late 1908, Arab caliphate plans were discussed anywhere in the region. On the contrary, as Rafiq al-'Azm's critique of the Arab caliphate idea indicates, Arabic-speaking intellectuals displayed instead a renewed hope in the empire. Instead of Islam, historians have identified dualist plans and administrative decentralization (*la-markaziyya, adem-i merkeziyet*) as the two predominant schemes for constitutional reform in the complex period between 1908 and 1914. They gave rise in 1913 to a "temporary" organic law of the provinces, which made possible representative councils through local (male-only) elections. Let me summarize these reforms briefly and highlight how the measures they proposed stood in contrast to the underground world of Muslim imperial utopias.

THE EMERGENCE OF THE DUALIST UTOPIA

In the fall after the 1908 CUP coup d'état and the restoration of the constitution, teachers and students prepared a school celebration in Damascus. The new (Turkish) superintendent of education in the province of Suriye took part in this event. After speeches in Turkish and Arabic, he came down and mingled among the students. He asked one of them, "To whom does the administration (*idara*) of Egypt belong?" The student answered that it belonged to the British. The atmosphere suddenly became frosty. A teacher hastily changed the subject, asking another student about the "relations" of Egypt to the Ottoman state. The student answered that Egypt was under Ottoman sovereignty (*tahta al-siyada al-'Uthmaniyya*), to which the superintendent remarked: "May God help that [Egypt] returns to our administration in the future!"[67]

Explicit dualist demands for Ottoman constitutional transformation were prompted not by a change in "imperial knowledge," as Laura Stoler claims, but by the reaction of the provinces to change in the metropole.[68] This change was, specifically, the 1908 restoration of the imperial constitution, which prompted hopes that Egypt might return to the empire in a new dualist configuration. Despite Abbas Hilmi's scheming, the khedivate's status as an Ottoman possession was of increased legal and political value for the Egyptian elite during the British occupation.[69] The transformation of the Ottoman Empire into a dualist union between the khedivate of Egypt and the central government, *à la* Austria-Hungary, had been a scarcely mentioned comparison in the Arabic press. Ottoman Arab journalists had a somewhat spotty understanding of the 1867 *Ausgleich*, which transformed the Austrian Empire into a dualist polity comprising the empire and the Hungarian kingdom and sharing common institutions and a common ruler.[70] A similar Ottoman-Egyptian union with a common ruler was obviously problematic as it would have involved eliminating the khedive while keeping the khedivate so as to allow the sultan to become a sultan-khedive, but some Egyptians nevertheless hoped for a dualist solution of some sort.

In September 1908, Muhammad Tawfiq al-Bakri, the Hamidian *naqib al-ashraf* in the Egyptian khedivate, proposed a transformation of the Ottoman Empire along the lines of the Austro-Hungarian empire in an interview to the leading nationalist journal *al-Liwa'*. The topic of the interview was the restoration of the Ottoman constitution in July 1908. Al-Bakri capitalized on the momentum to demand that Egypt be granted its own constitution. He emphasized "complete independence": "from now on we must make our program the full independence (*istiqlalan tamman*) of Egypt and the persistent unity with the Ottoman state like the unity of Hungary with Austria."[71] A month later al-Bakri published an article in *al-Liwa'* in response to criticism of his interview. He affirmed that his goal was a powerful Ottoman state of the kind that Japan was in Asia. In order to create such a polity Egypt must be "fully independent in a full unity (*ittihad tamm*) with the Exalted State." Al-Bakri argued that there were only three possible futures for Egypt: to remain fully part of the empire, to achieve administrative (*idari*) independence, or to achieve full independence in full unity with the empire. His logic here rested on constitutional considerations: in the first case, the khedive would only be able to provide rights as delegated by the sultan, in the second case the Egyptian constitution would be practically that of an independent country ("like Australia is independent of England"), and in the third case it would follow the Austro-Hungarian model or the German imperial one (he referred to the works of Bismarck among his sources). He added that the imperial tribute from Egypt might not be needed once the Ottomans had managed to stabilize their economy and that he did not see any problem with mentioning the names of the caliph and the khedive together in the Friday prayer (this was the symbolic Muslim recognition of sovereignty). His ultimate conclusion was that the dualist solution was the best because Egypt should never stand alone, outside the Ottoman Empire.[72]

Al-Bakri's idea of complete independence is different from what we mean today when we talk about independence as the "Westphalian sovereignty" of a nation-state. He calls "administrative" (*idari*) independence what we today would conceive as the status of a sovereign state in an imperial commonwealth, such as Australia or Canada. In al-Bakri's construction, this administrative independence did not apply to the Austro-Hungarian case. He took the view that administrative independence did not provide the same degree of absolute independence as did the third type of relationship, the dualist solution. It appears that for him "independence" had two meanings: independence as state sovereignty and independence as an autonomous (Muslim) existence, protected from Western dominance. For al-Bakri, the second was more important than—and preferable to—the first. It is no wonder, then, that *al-Liwa'* (whose editor 'Abd al-'Aziz Jawish became a fierce advocate for the Ottoman cause during the First World War) published an impressive leading article in the next issue in which the author declared Egypt among the most important components of the Ottoman Empire.[73]

DECENTRALIZATION: OTTOMAN DUALISM AS AN ETHNICITY-BASED IDEA, 1908–1914

After 1908, some Egyptians celebrated the Turk-Arab unity that they saw embodied in the restored constitution.[74] At the same time, others encouraged Arab autonomy, thus championing what was called *decentralization*.[75] By "decentralization" in the 1900s they meant a government in which the imperial constitution would formally codify provincial autonomies with local representative institutions and local language use. This move was yet again a shared momentum in the Ottoman-Habsburg discursive imperial: the official incorporation of formerly Ottoman Bosnia-Herzegovina into Austria-Hungary was achieved by means of the emperor providing a constitution in 1910 *without* a formal declaration of annexation. Austro-Hungarian legal experts debated at this time whether the Austrian constitution of Bosnia was a move towards decentralization in the empire.[76]

Within the Ottoman metropole, the idea of decentralization originated with Prince Sabaheddin (d. 1948), a disgruntled member of the sultanic family.[77] The French proto-sociologist Edmond Demolins's (d. 1907) theory about individualism as the basis of (British) success had a great impression on this Ottoman prince. Perhaps not unrelated to the Austro-Hungarian debates, Sabaheddin identified individualism with *administrative* decentralization. He supported the Young Turk movement and their Paris conference in 1902, and in his subsequent pamphlets introduced the idea of decentralization. His followers even established a "Society for Decentralization and Private Initiative." And yet, after the 1908 revolution, to the great sorrow of the prince, the CUP in government moved precisely in the opposite direction: towards even stronger centralization. Ottoman Turkish became the compulsory language in government schools and legal forums. The constitution was modified in 1909 and repeatedly thereafter.[78] In contrast, the Sabaheddin's program explicitly advocated administrative decentralization. In the tense imperial parliament Sabaheddin thus supported the "Freedom and Accord Party" (*Hürriyet ve I'tilaf Firkası*, in French known as *Entente Libérale*).[79]

The majority of the Arab provincial deputies, including the *ashraf*, in the Ottoman parliament gradually gravitated towards the "Freedom and Accord Party" in 1911. The idea of decentralization provided also an opportunity for restoring Arabic in educational and legal institutions. In this year Emrullah Efendi, a former minister, publicly wondered whether Sabaheddin wanted to transform the Ottoman Empire "by imitating" Austria-Hungary. Provincial elites in exile in Egypt and Paris made decentralization their main political slogan in this period. For many Syrians, decentralization meant the transformation of the empire in order to accommodate administrative autonomy for the "Arabs." A German Orientalist in Damascus observed that "belonging to the *al-Ahrar*" (the "Liberals") meant belonging to the "national party" in the city; and a reform committee demanded, among other things, the official use of Arabic in Beirut in the spring of 1913.[80]

At the same time, in January 1913, an "Ottoman Administrative Decentralization Party" (*Hizb al-La-markaziyya al-Idari al-'Uthmani*) emerged in Cairo. Its members—among them Iskandar 'Ammun, Rashid Rida, Rafiq al-'Azm, Muhibb al-Din al-Khatib, and others—often referred to the federal models of Switzerland or the imperial German federation. Finally, an Arab Congress in Paris in June 1913 formalized demands for decentralization in a united communication.

Among Ottoman Arab patricians in the early 1910s, decentralization and centralization were the two main poles of imperial reformist expectations. Although the grand narratives of Arab nationalism present the 1913 gathering as part of an Arab nationalist-separatist movement, it is quite clear that most participants wanted to retain a reformed empire; and it is also clear that centralist Ottoman Arabs held to the view that political decentralization would cause more harm than gain. The later pan-Islamist Shakib Arslan (d. 1946), a Lebanese notable and friend of CUP-leader Enver Pasha, for instance, argued that the decentralists made "mistakes of comparison" (*aghlat fi al-kiyas*) when they compared the situation of Arabs in the Ottoman Empire to German federalism and to Australia. Arslan was invested in portraying (experts even write "demonizing") the Decentralization Party as a secessionist movement.[81] In sum, decentralization and centralization were much more widely discussed among

Arabic-speaking intellectuals between 1908 and 1914 than the clandestine idea of an Arab caliphate.[82]

Historians have noted with interest that the German general Colmar Freiherr von der Goltz (d. 1916), who worked for the Ottoman army in the late 1880s, produced in 1897 an ethnicized account of Turks and Arabs as two Muslim imperial peoples, a short work that also appeared in Turkish in 1906 in Cairo (!). Von der Goltz tutored the sultanic princes in Istanbul and he encountered *sharif* 'Ali Haydar among them. He also regularly advised his former Ottoman military students to learn about the Arabs. In a long essay in May 1913, he emphasized the military importance of Arabs for the "Turkish half" of the empire. Yet he did not explicitly mention the Austro-Hungarian model in his essay, published as the lead article of the Viennese journal *Neue Freie Presse*. Many of his writings were translated into Turkish in the early 1910s, and they became an important foreign source of ideas for the CUP leadership. Von Goltz himself died in Baghdad in 1916, as a Central Powers German general defending the Ottoman Empire.[83]

Other external observers include the Zionist, later militant, Ze'ev Jabotinsky (d. 1940), who remarked in a Russian article in January 1909 that if a full-fledged Arab nationalist movement were to begin, this would mark the beginning of the "Austro-Hungarian" phase of the Ottoman Empire, after which, he thought, a multinational federation would emerge as the future and final stage (he hoped the same for Austria-Hungary itself).[84]

We might call the spring of 1913 "the spring of Ottoman dualism," as the idea gained attraction in government circles. The loss of Libya, the First Balkan War, the activity of the Decentralization Party in Cairo, the heated discussions in the Greater Syrian provincial cities, the attention given to Von Goltz's essay in May 1913, the June 1913 Arab Congress in Paris and many press articles, all these forces converged and placed immense public pressure on the Ottoman government to countenance, however reluctantly, imperial reform on a dualist ethnic basis. The British Ambassador to Istanbul remarked to his superiors in London that the CUP government now held that the empire should be transformed into a "Turco-Arabia" like Austria-Hungary, with the Sultan-Caliph as the link between the two elements.[85]

THE 1913 LAW OF PROVINCES: REPRESENTATION WITHOUT ETHNIC AUTONOMY

An organizational reform of empire does not abolish sources of authority, but it often rearranges them. In the "dualist" spring of 1913, the Grand Vizier Mahmud Şevket, an Ottoman military leader born in Baghdad, seriously considered the Austria-Hungarian model until his assassination in June that year. This general not only had sympathies for Arabs, but he had also worked with von Goltz in the 1880s and visited Germany several times.[86] His diary records how in March 1913 he worried about losing the Arab provinces.[87] Şevket's government instructed their Vienna ambassador, Hilmi Pasha, to analyze the Austro-Hungarian electoral law (tangentially, Şevket considered Hungarians to be friends of Turks).[88] Historian Hasan Kayalı writes that "in the Ottoman press other suggestions were put forward. Ahmed Ferid . . . criticized the notion of a biracial Turco-Arab empire on the Austria-Hungary model. According to Ahmed Ferid, Austria-Galicia-Bohemia-Carinthia provided a more appropriate analogy than Austria-Hungary."[89] Leading CUP intellectuals, such as the sociologist and Turkification advocate Ziya Gökalp, also preferred a scenario whereby two imperial nations (*millet*) coexisted in the Ottoman lands (at the expense of multinational equality).[90] Had Mahmud Şevket survived and remained Grand Vizier, he could have taken advantage of this momentum to remake the empire on a dualist basis in 1913.

What Mahmud Şevket did achieve before his death was to help frame a new organic law for the provinces in which elected local representation was incorporated. This was perhaps a way to appease the many ethno-religious demands—and not those of the Arabs only—by embracing the principle of representation without ethno-territorial autonomy. Had not the world war started in the next year, the Ottoman 1913 could have been a belated Austro-Hungarian 1867, a kind of composite consolidation for the empire. This organic law did not aim at the abolishment of either the dynasty or Muslim laws, but it did introduce locally elected, ethnicity-based representation as new sources "from below" of the imperial political order.

The Provisional Law of Provinces, as it was called, redefined the Ottoman provincial bureaucracy. It accommodated the principle of representation in the make-up of several local administrative bodies. Locally elected representatives would now serve on administrative councils (*mecalis-i idare*; article 62) at the provincial (*vilayet*), district (*liwa*), and sub-district (*kaza*) levels. The Council of State (*Şura-yi Devlet*), the empire's highest administrative body, would supervise the decisions of these councils (article 67). In addition, every *vilayet* was to have an elected general assembly (*meclis-i umumi*), chaired by the governor. Every 12,500 male electors could send one representative to sit for five years, and voting would take place in every *kaza*. Special care was taken to ensure that non-Muslim groups were not underrepresented. The elections were to be organized by the governor of the province in a time decided by him. Soldiers, members of the imperial assembly, and state bureaucrats were not eligible to run for the office. The general assembly's rulings would follow from the decision of an absolute majority (articles 103–120).[91]

Despite this step towards provincial self-government, Arab secret and not so secret societies continued to aspire to a dualist model. In the imperial capital in October 1913, the Ottoman Arab officers' "Covenant" society (al-'Ahd) enshrined in its founding document their intention "to work for the internal independence for the Arab regions, so that they will remain united with the Istanbul government, as Hungary is united with Austria."[92] The leader of this society, the Ottoman Egyptian-Circassian officer 'Aziz al-Misri (d. 1965), once surprised his military superior Cemal (d. 1922, a Young Turk general and the infamous governor of the Syrian provinces during the First World War) with a very angry outburst and a demand for Arab dignity. Later, Cemal remembered that, in his eyes, the Austria-Hungary comparison represented the most radical option among the various decentralist ideas circulating at the time.[93] "Independence" within a federative system, along the lines of what al-Bakri had proposed in 1908, was the preference of these Arab soldiers in 1913.[94] The CUP government arrested 'Aziz al-Misri and sent him with two younger Arab officials—one of them being Nuri al-Sa'id (later the prime minister of Iraq)—back to Egypt.

Activists Assemble: A Sharifian Commonwealth as Arab Kingdom?

By the time 'Aziz al-Misri arrived back in Cairo in 1913, composite visions of order were brewing. The idea of an association of Muslim princely regions, similar to the British Raj, became popular among disgruntled ashraf and decentralist activists as a critique of the CUP. As early as 1911, Sayyid Talib of Basra—who certainly knew the system of the British Raj—sent a letter to Emir al-Husayn from Istanbul in which he and a number of Arab representatives in the Ottoman parliament acknowledged that "only he [al-Husayn] [had] religious authority (al-sulta al-diniyya) over the Arab regions."[95] The ashraf and sada-alliances with merchants stuck to their political ambitions in many locations from Basra to Yemen well into the 1920s.[96]

The available evidence shows that Rashid Rida from Cairo was actively corresponding with Muslim emirs and ashraf over plans to create a political association around Arabia. He played two games: he was a member of the Ottoman Administrative Decentralization Party in Cairo, but he was clearly also invested in a Muslim regional federation, a new imperial project. Perhaps he was not the only one in the "party" running two simultaneous campaigns—a public one for decentralization and a secret one for a new empire. In 1912, on the way back from an Indian lecture tour, he stopped in Kuwait and Oman to promote the idea of an alliance among Muslim emirs. In his letters, Rida used the code-name "Namus" (best translated here as "revenge"); perhaps he had in mind a Damascus saying: "may your *namus* curse the police's *namus*" (*yi'lan namusak namus dabtiyya*).[97]

The outbreak of the First World War coincided with quite concrete actions for a post-Ottoman Muslim federation in relation to British war planning. In the summer and fall of 1914, Rida and Rafiq al-'Azm made contact with 'Aziz al-Misri and his younger colleague, Nuri al-Sa'id, both exiled in Cairo. They sent al-Sa'id and the journalist Muhibb al-Din al-Khatib as representatives of a certain "Society of Arab Commonwealth" (*Jam'iyyat al-Jami' al-'Arabiyya*) to stir up support from Sayyid Talib in Basra, the emir of Kuwait, 'Abd al-'Aziz the emir in Riyadh, the sultan of Oman, al-Husayn in Mecca, and other minor Muslim leaders. Sayyid Talib was certainly interested in continuing Hamidian genealogical politics in a new imperial formation. The mission was at first supported by the British authorities. Rida was ready to declare the formation of this Muslim political association and to suggest that al-Husayn, the sharifian Emir of Mecca, should be its head. The British authorities, however, cautious as always, feared the effects such a declaration would have on their Muslim subjects in Asia and Africa. An "intimation" was conveyed to Rida as to the inappropriate timing of such a move. Just as his envoys arrived in the Gulf in November 1914, at the uncomfortable moment of the British-Indian invasion of Ottoman Basra, the occupation army arrested and sent the activists either to India or back to Cairo.[98]

Although in this instance the British wartime authorities had opted not to support "The Society of Arab Commonwealth," Sheikh Rashid Rida held out hopes that Britain would back a decentralized Muslim-Arab sharifian association. In 1915, another Syrian sheikh, Muhammad Kamil al-Qassab, also joined the scheming Rida in wartime Cairo. Al-Qassab was educated in Damascus and Cairo at al-Azhar in the late 1890s, and in 1905 he had established a school in Damascus for Muslim children (the "Ottoman School," later called the *Kamiliyya*) that focused on the Arabic language. The school later educated some prominent Syrians, such as the politician 'Abd al-Rahman Shahbandar and the poet-writer-diplomat

Khayr al-Din al-Zirikli. After 1908, Sheikh al-Qassab was an openly anti-CUP Muslim activist. In 1915 he visited Cairo, possibly on behalf of Damascene activists, to exchange views with the Syrian diaspora in that city. While the exact nature of the connection between Rida and al-Qassab at this moment cannot be ascertained, they certainly were aware of great changes to come.[99]

The master narrative of Arab nationalism begins in 1915 with the negotiations between Sir Henry McMahon, the British High Commissioner in Egypt, and Sharif al-Husayn, the Ottoman emir of Mecca, over the Ottoman provinces."[100] At the same time, Rida submitted a counterproposal to the British Agency in Cairo: The "General Organic Law of the Arab Empire" would establish a republican caliphate-empire, which would inherit the Ottoman Arab provinces in a modular system: "each province is to be governed by a *vali* [governor]." In this draft law, the emirs in the Arabian Peninsula would be "subject to the Empire [only] in common affairs," because the empire would be "decentralized." A caliph was to be chosen from among the sharifs of Mecca who also "should recognize the organic law of the Empire." This caliph was to stay in Mecca and the distinct political government with a president (!) would be headquartered in Damascus.[101] In 1916, Rida affirmed publicly, too, that a post-Ottoman polity should be based on religious authority (*al-sulta al-diniyya*) as distinct from political authority.[102] However, in the midst of war, the idea of a republican caliphate submitted by a journalist-sheikh had no appeal to the British war machine, especially weighed against the richer potential of the sharifian emir of Mecca.

THE ARAB KINGDOM

Compared to the idea of a modular republican caliphate or a federation of *ashraf*, Sharif al-Husayn's announcement in Mecca in October 1916 about the establishment of a centralized Arab kingdom was a less sophisticated political vision. The British authorities, for their part, suspended their anger at al-Husayn's declaration until the end of war. They began to connect the decentralist activists to the sharifian government in Mecca. The journalist al-Khatib, the officer al-Sa'id, Sheikh al-Qassab, and others, together with a number of British Arab imperialists (usually working for the Sudan government) held offices from 1917 under the Hijazi government. From Damascus, Sheikh al-Qassab fled to Mecca, under the pretext of pilgrimage, to escape persecution directed at him by the Ottoman military governor after his return from wartime Cairo in 1916. The *ashraf* entrusted al-Qassab with public education in the Hijaz and he joined their "Arab government." Rida himself visited Mecca but clashed with al-Husayn, whom he saw as a new autocrat, and thus returned and waited in Cairo in dignified silence.

The regime form in the imagined polity of the Arab kingdom was the recycled Ottoman emirate, not too different from a subordinated Muslim princely state. Unsurprisingly, keeping with his son 'Abd Allah's 1914 offer that the Hijaz may switch empires, the new king implicitly acknowledged the sovereignty of the British Empire. Possibly he had the caliphate as a non-political office in mind. Sharif al-Husayn's famous first letter to McMahon had requested that Britain "agree" to the proclamation of an "Arab caliphate" in return for al-Husayn's authorizing a revolt against the Ottoman Empire.[103] The "oath" that the notables swore to al-Husayn in October 1916 could more accurately be described as a petition ('arida) requesting him to accept the position of king. The text is a curious one; it begins with a preface that so strongly highlights the special role of Arabs in the history of Islam that it appears at first reading to be a request for al-Husayn to accept the caliphate, but by the end the 'arida turns out to pertain to kingship instead.[104] As his discussions with British officials made clear, al-Husayn evidently considered himself as representing the British system of delegated sovereignty. For instance, in these years he regarded the treaties that the British Empire had signed with the other Arab leaders in Arabia "as if they were made by him" and he concluded that "Great Britain gave him authority over them."[105]

We can get a glimpse into al-Husayn's and his activist circle's understanding of the kingship in their answers to questions posed by the surprised British officers. On 30 October 1916, 'Abd Allah from Mecca called the British agent in Jidda. He argued over the telephone that "the people here declared him [al-Husayn, his father] to be the king of Arabs in order to show that they are not under any other power." As to the other Arabian leaders in Ottoman and British dependency, he argued that "it [was] not important whether those people would agree or not." He added that the kingship "is to prove to the Islamic World that the Hedjaz Government is actually independent and that its ruler is a Great Muslim King." Soon the new king al-Husayn himself called the agent, confirmed his son's statements, and added that there was nothing to worry about because as an independent monarch he would still allow the British government to choose his Minister of War(!). He stated that he publicly disavowed any claim to the caliphate. Al-Husayn even offered to publish a "Wahhabi" book, which, he claimed, would prove that there was no caliphate.[106]

Fu'ad al-Khatib, a British Arab delegate deputed to al-Husayn, also issued a statement appealing to military logic. He argued that the declaration of kingship was a necessary step to counteract the Central Powers' propaganda, which claimed that the Arabs wanted the Holy Cities to come under foreign control. Moreover, the oath at the Ka'ba by reluctant Hijazis had been, reasoned al-Khatib, effective in securing local loyalty. And finally, he underlined that the title "King of the Arab lands" made reconciliation with the Ottomans impossible, and that it signified that the "movement" (i.e., the revolt) was permanent.[107]

During the war, al-Husayn's Arab Kingdom idea represented a rejection of Rida's decentralized Muslim federal utopia. Both contained mixtures of religion, monarchy, and ethnicity but they took markedly different directions. Instead of a vertical empire based on an association of Muslim emirs or a republican caliphate with governors codified in a constitution, al-Husayn's Hamidian imagination projected an uncodified Muslim political order. And importantly, none of these ideas were nation-states.

Conclusion: Pre-War Utopias in Post-War Contexts

Let me conclude with the portrait of one last, unexpected activist of Muslim federalist utopia. Amin al-Rihani (Ameen Rihani), the Christian American-Lebanese writer, describes how he supported the Arab Revolt during the First World War—with his pen, from the distance. In 1916, he happened to be visiting the Alhambra in Spain, and he ventured into a room where another American, Washington Irving had set his famous *Tales of the Alhambra*, Rihani's favorite childhood book. And here, in this hyper-Orientalist literary space, Rihani heard voices talking about Arab nationalism (*qawmiyya*) and the Arab homeland. It appears that the voices mentioned King al-Husayn, the leader of the revolt in the Hijaz. In fact, Rihani may have actually heard al-Husayn's voice because the old *sharif* commissioned the writer to compose a book about "the Arabs" in 1922. The American published instead a sensationalist and witty book about his meetings with Muslim rulers, which became a bestseller in both Arabic (titled "The Kings of the Arabs," *Muluk al-'Arab*) and English.[108] Rihani was perhaps the first Arab American activist who made political (and even monetary) capital out of post-Ottoman utopianism.

Arjun Appadurai and others have proposed that we should imagine sovereignty without territoriality in contemporary history.[109] My analysis has shown that the opposite was true in the age of empire and steam: visions of territoriality without sovereignty were the rule in modular imperial projects. No one conceived of either ethnicity or religion as the *exclusive* source of the right to sovereignty; instead they conceived of all of them as operating in combination, as fitting with the imperial political order. No one wanted sovereignty without an imperial project.

By staging individuals, such as Rida, al-Qassab, and al-Khatib, usually regarded as "religious scholars" and others, usually regarded as "secular nationalists" such as 'Aziz al-Misri and Nuri al-Sa'id, as actors in one single story, all being involved in the fever of composite projects, I have not only confirmed arguments that contemporary Muslim puritan utopias such as Salafism or even jihadism only emerged in the second half of the twentieth century. Importantly, we have concrete examples about constitutional projects aiming at non-national polities in a period which is usually regarded as the formative period of Arab nationalism. These examples confirm that the imagined Arab routes out of the Ottoman Empire aimed at distinct forms of composite, even cosmopolitan, polities which retained religion as a source of authority.

Politicians, intellectuals, merchants, and military leaders continued to envisage emirates and city states, such as Basra, and federal unions until the mid-1920s. Even in the occupied imperial capital in 1919, politicians and intellectuals devised reforms to remake the Ottoman Empire.[110] And Austria-Hungary remained a model for imagining a post-war Muslim imperial formation. For instance, in the summer of 1917, two Syrian-run periodicals in Egypt printed a letter from Paris according to which the Ottoman government was proposing to change the constitution into a dualist ('*ala al-asas al-thana'i*) Turco-Arab regime, modelled after Austria-Hungary.[111] Another example is an abortive Hijazi peace proposal to the Ottomans in June 1918 that contained an offer to transform the Ottoman Empire along the lines of Austria-Hungary—now, given al-Husayn's title, there were grounds for an Arab kingship to be associated with an Ottoman emperor.[112] Even after the armistice, in November 1918 a Hijazi-British delegation sent a secret proposal for an Arab-Turkish federation to the Ottoman Grand Vizier. In 1920 February General Mustafa Kemal considered "unit[ing] in the form of a confederation, once each nation [had] established independence." In the spring, some political leaders in occupied Damascus also proposed Arab-Turkish unity.[113] In his unpublished memoirs, the journalist and activist al-Khatib—later a true Salafi—cried out: "Why couldn't we be with the Turks like Hungary was with the Austrians?"[114]

PART III

From Imperial to Local Muslim Authority

CHAPTER SIX

Occupying Authority

ON 21 OCTOBER 1918, the scribe of the *qadi* court in Damascus, the capital of the Suriye Province, started a new register with the following case:

> Al-Hajj Ahmad b. 'Umar b. Muhammad al-Halabi came [before the court]. He was a legally free, sane, adult Muslim Arab from among the inhabitants of al-'Ammara quarter in Damascus. The wife of Darwish, his deceased brother, also came with him. She was the lady Khadija b. Darwish b. 'Abd Allah Sa'd, a legally free, sane, adult Muslim Arab woman from among the inhabitants of the same quarter. They were properly identified according to the law by Shahad b. Hamid b. al-Shaykh Shahad al-Najjar from the Shaghur quarter in Damascus and by 'Abd Allah b. al-Shaykh 'Abd Allah b. al-Sayyid Salih Talu from among the inhabitants of the mentioned al-'Ammara quarter. Both of them are subjects of the Hasanid Arab State (*taba'at al-dawla al-'arabiyya al-hasaniyya*).
>
> The aforementioned al-Hajj Ahmad declared the following. These are his own true words: "Previously, on 12 Dhu al-Qa'da 1336 [19 August 1918], I came to this court. I took the obligation upon myself, by a legal certificate dated on the same day, to pay daily 35 standard piasters alimony to the daughters of my aforementioned deceased brother for their necessary expenses from that day. They are the legally adult Samiya and the minors Ifaqat and Salwa, who are in the guardianship of their mother who came with me. I did this because their sibling, the legally adult senior Muhyi al-Din, had been imprisoned in the Citadel of Damascus. But as their sibling Muhyi al-Din is around

now and is able to take care of their alimony I lift the alimony that I took upon myself and I ask to annul that action."

Upon first glance there is nothing unusual in this case. *Qadi* courts routinely handled issues of alimony (*nafaqa*), the obligation to provide maintenance to wives and minor children. In fact, the lady Khadija also made a statement. She stated that Muhyi al-Din was crippled so he had no ability to maintain her and her daughters even after his release from prison. She asked the judge to uphold the obligation of alimony on al-Hajj Ahmad. The judge decided otherwise.[1] There are millions of such cases in *qadi* court records in Muslim societies.[2]

The case of al-Hajj Ahmad and the lady Khadija, however, is unusual in that it offers a window into a world historical event. On the day of this hearing, the Ottoman city of Damascus was already under the occupation of the Allied Powers. It is hard to tell who the occupiers were exactly. The Australian cavalry of the Egyptian Expeditionary Force (EEF), under the orders of General Edmund Allenby, had chased the retreating Ottoman troops through this ancient city in late September-early October. Next the Hijazi Northern Army entered, under the orders of *sharif* Faysal Bey. He was the second son of al-Husayn, the former Ottoman Emir of Mecca and now-declared "King of the Arabs." General Allenby had created the Occupied Enemy Zone (OETA) East out of the occupied Suriye (Damascus) and Halep (Aleppo) provinces and had given its control over to the Hijazi Northern Army. The eclectic Hijazi army (ex-Ottoman officers, utopian activists, and tribal fighters), however, called themselves the "Arab government." Meanwhile, French troops occupied Beirut and the coast, now OETA North and West; while the British army retained direct control of Palestine, the OETA South. (See the map in Figure 6.1). All of these armies trumpeted their presence in the Ottoman regions as "liberation."[3]

In recounting the case of al-Hajj Ahmad and the lady Khadija, the *qadi* court register noted two important details about this chaotic state of affairs. The first was the identification of the litigants being "Arab." During the war, Ottoman courts, including the *kadı* courts, registered the citizenship status and the census-identification numbers of litigants. Now, in the place of "Ottoman" there appeared the term "Arab" although Islamic law does not require the identification of citizenship or ethnicity. Second, the characterization of the witnesses as subjects of the "Hasanid Arab State" is also striking. Indeed, the phrase itself was unusual. The Arabic word *dawla* (a temporal continuity of power) could mean "state" or "dynasty" in this context; Arabs had used this word to refer to the Ottoman Empire.

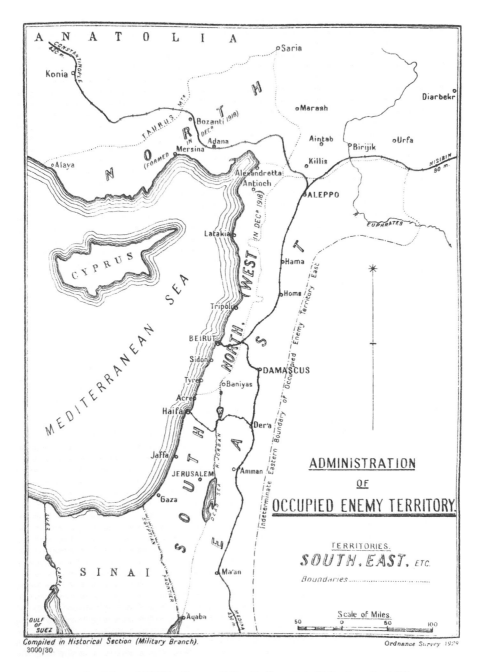

ANATOLIA

Konia

Saria

Bozanti (1918)
Adana
Mersina
Alaya

Maraah

Aintab
Killis
Birijik
Urfa
Diarbekr

NISIBIN
80 m.

ALEPPO

Alexandretta
Antioch

Latakia

EUPHRATES

Hama

Homs

CYPRUS

MEDITERRANEAN SEA

Tripoli

BEIRUT
Sidon
Tyre
Acre
Haifa

DAMASCUS
Baniyas

Der'a

Jaffa

JERUSALEM

Amman

Gaza

Ma'an

SINAI

GULF OF SUEZ

Aqaba

ADMINISTRATION
OF
OCCUPIED ENEMY TERRITORY.

TERRITORIES.
SOUTH. EAST. ETC.
Boundaries...............

Scale of Miles.
50   0   50   100

Compiled in Historical Section (Military Branch).
3000/30

Ordnance Survey 1929

FIGURE 6.1. Map of OETA. *Source*: Falls, Cyril, and A. F. Becke, eds. *Military Operations—Egypt & Palestine* (London: His Majesty's Stationery Office, 1930), 2:2:607 (Sketch 42).

The term "Hasanid," meanwhile, conveys the sense of being descended from Hasan, one of the two grandchildren of the Prophet Muhammad—a descent shared, for instance, by Meccan *ashraf*. For the ordinary Damascenes in the court, their new polity was a "Hasanid," that is to say, a genealogical empire. Or at least this was the case for a few days.[4]

The story of the Arab government in Damascus is often told as a "great man" narrative: the story of how Faysal Bey first changed into the image of an Orientalized Bedouin emir and "Prince" during the Paris Peace Conference, next into "King Faysal" of the Syrian Kingdom (in March 1920), and finally, after the French invasion of inland Syria, into the king of British Iraq (August 1921).[5] An alternative "great man" storyline focuses on the British agent T. E. Lawrence ("Lawrence of Arabia"), who played a major role in staging Faysal both in Damascus and Paris. More recently, historical scholarship has apotheosized the role of a third hero, namely our journalist-sheikh Rashid Rida. This Muslim activist for federal utopianism was the belated president of the Damascus assembly in the summer of 1920. Elizabeth Thompson observes that both Rida and Faysal "embraced the ideals of the 1908 [Ottoman] constitutional revolution" and suggests that we should see in their efforts an example of Muslim liberalism. In her telling, the tragic fate of the Syrian Kingdom is a story about "democracy denied" by the "West."[6] All these narratives frame the war as liberation from the "Turkish yoke."

Others, beyond the critique of Western policy, have studied the Allied occupation *as* occupation. They tell of the complexities involved in building a new polity from out of an Ottoman provincial administration and about the plethora of conflicting ideologies and popular movements.[7] The striking conclusion of Keith David Watenpaugh in his study on occupied Aleppo was that "Faysal could just as easily have been perceived as an alien opportunist allied with a Christian power against the legitimate leader of the Muslim community, the Ottoman sultan."[8]

This view is not far from how Muhammad Adib Al Taqi al-Din al-Hisni, a Damascene scholar and keen observer of the events, indeed described Faysal's arrival as the "head of an alien army." Al-Hisni mentions that Faysal himself, in a speech in May 1919, criticized those who thought that the Hijazi revolt was an act of "treason towards the people, the homeland, and the Ottoman community." Instead of a military occupation, Faysal emphatically explained, Syrians should regard their new situation as the result of a "revolution." This effort to equate occupation with revolution found adherents in later scholarship, but a number of Syrians left clues that they viewed Faysal as an occupier who stood in the way their own self-rule (which they in October of 1918 had imagined would be under the leadership of the al-Jaza'iri family).[9]

The spoliation of the Ottoman order meant the survival of the modular logic of territoriality but now as a vertical empire of the *ashraf*. In this chapter, I seek to explore at depth how a new type of Muslim authority took the place of Ottoman authority under the conditions of occupation. To what extent did the Meccan *ashraf*'s genealogical claims conform with the previous composite visions of order? I argue that, instead of bringing about democracy and revolutionary change, the Hijazi occupation enabled the revival of Hamidian genealogical politics. Through an analysis of court registers, I demonstrate that sharifian claims occupied the place of Ottoman imperial authority. In a virtual operation of *spolia in se*, the Kingdom of Syria was to become a Hamidian emirate under the reign of a sultan-caliph in Mecca.

There was, though, one change brought about by the events of autumn 1918 that one may reasonably regard as revolutionary. The language of administration switched entirely from Turkish to Arabic (with some English and French in supporting roles). In the Damascus and countryside courts, the Ottoman Turkish official seals were soon replaced by Arabic ones; and Ottoman Arab soldiers translated Turkish military expressions into Arabic for use by a new army.[10] This change occurred within a few weeks of the occupation, sometimes even within the course of a single court register.[11] Old Damascenes regarded the language change as natural, but they opposed the expulsion of bureaucrats identified as of Turkish origin.[12] The Damascus legislative council abolished the Ottoman ranks, but the people continued to use the titles "pasha" and "bey" in everyday life well into the 1950s.[13] While I focus primarily on the story of recycling authority in the courts, this chapter also looks at the change in the language of administration.

Gilded Tracks: the Hijazi Railway as a Sharifian Infrastructure

Let us begin with an instance of *spolia in re*, the material repurposing of an imperial infrastructure. The Syrian Kingdom emerged from an interaction between British imperial calculation, Muslim genealogical claims, utopian federalism, and a railway. The Hijazi troops arrived in Damascus following the tracks of the Hijaz railway, which connected Ottoman Medina in the Hijaz to Damascus, the heart of Syria. As is often the case with railway journeys, however, this one too was marked by delays: in mid-September 1918, Northern Arab Army units were still mounting attacks on the railway around Dara'a, and so they did not arrive in Damascus until after Australian units had already secured the city.[14]

Historians, anthropologists, and political scientists have argued that material infrastructure is a socially constructed technological formation which enables new forms of exclusion and political power.[15] As opposed to social infrastructures that connect people through "phatic labor," the making of material ones often creates great demands on imperial resources.[16] The Damascus-Medina railway had been a military project, with "railway battalions" building the tracks in the desert in the 1900s.[17] In January of 1914, the Ottoman government had transferred the legal title of the railway to the Ministry of Endowments as a measure against French pressure, thus granting tracks, land, and equipment the status of a pious endowment.[18] (This status, which Muslim activists claimed made the railroad unsellable, would cause much trouble in the 1920s and 1930s to the new governments and to the British and French authorities.) After the outbreak of the war, the Ottoman Ministry of War took over this pious railway as a strategic asset during the Allied Powers' sea-blockade in the Eastern Mediterranean.

Ottoman genealogical politics obscured the military aspects of the tracks during the war. The *ashraf* of the sultan and men of Enver Pasha, the Minister of War, used the railway to pursue their political business throughout Ottoman Western Asia. In 1911, 'Ali Haydar had taken a train from Damascus to Medina as part of the CUP campaign to propagandize among the Arabs. From the opposite direction, catching the train in Medina, Faysal Bey was twice able to visit Damascus, in 1915 and early 1916, ostensibly to offer help to the Ottoman army, though in actuality to scheme with Arab officers. In the late spring of 1916, General Fahri (Fahreddin) Pasha and a section of the Fourth Ottoman Army were transported quickly from Damascus to Medina and army units fortified the railway stations along Palestine and Transjordan.[19]

The 1916 revolt within the city of Mecca was possible only because, before the war, al-Husayn had prevented the extension of the railway to the holy city, which meant that the Ottoman authorities were unable to get troops into the rebel territory. When in June 1916 the Ottoman government appointed 'Ali Haydar instead of al-Husayn as the new Emir, General Fahri sent his trustworthy man, Tahsin Qadri, an Arab officer, up the railway to Damascus so that he could receive Haydar and his sons in that city first. Qadri brought the new emir and his sons back to Medina in a private wagon.[20]

Treasure and genealogical authority emblazoned the tracks. In Jordan, it is still rumored today that the Ottoman army buried gold during their retreat in 1918.[21] Islamic legal rules of treasure (*rikaz*) had framed the

Ottoman government's donation of coal-mines to the Hijaz Railway Company,[22] but the legend of gilded tracks is more likely a residue of the fact that the Ottoman government several times sent gold up the railway to Arabia. A CUP-secret agent and prominent man of Enver was, for example, once entrusted to deliver more than a third of a million gold liras to Yemen using the Hijaz railway, and despite his capture by the rebellious Meccan *ashraf*, the sum did arrive thanks to clever planning.[23] It is also possible that the Jordanian treasure-hunting legend derives from memories of Ali Haydar's trip in 1916, or Qadri's recounting of this journey. As Qadri tells the story, the train journey from Damascus to Medina took four days. On the way, the train suddenly stopped somewhere in Transjordan. 'Ali Haydar and his sons got off the train with a bag that Qadri assumed contained gold. They feared that the train had been stopped by Bedouin bandits, and so decided to hide the gold. As it turned out, the only thing obstructing the tracks was a cow. After the reluctant animal was chased away, 'Ali Haydar, the new Emir of Mecca, arrived in Medina for the Ottoman army's celebration on 1 August 1916.[24] The railway indeed promised treasures, especially political ones.

During 1918, the eclectic Northern Hijazi army advanced from Arabia following the railway tracks towards Damascus. Faysal Bey and British and French agents collected more tribal fighters, ex-Ottoman Arab soldiers en route and, by the end of summer 1918, even some residents of Transjordanian and Damascene activists (who switched sides over the summer). Their main task was to continue the obstruction of the Ottoman garrisons along the railway and to occupy villages and fortified stations. By September 1918, Allenby decided to call on this army to finish the campaign along the tracks and to occupy the final station, Damascus.[25]

While the *ashraf* and armies commuted back and forth following the tracks, British imperial strategists pored over their own plans in London. The Eastern Committee of the government disregarded the Sykes-Picot agreement in the summer of 1918. They were plotting an independent, Damascus-centered polity under British protection. In the early days of the war, British and French officials had agreed that "there [was] no person in Syria of a position fitting him to be a ruling prince."[26] Now, in 1918, the Eastern Committee was determined that the Hijaz government be excluded from Syria when it came to "secular matters" and that Faysal be regarded a "constitutional ruler" in occupied Syria, with the title "hakkam." As to old al-Husayn in Mecca, he should remain only King of the Hijaz. His polity was to remain a small, sovereign kingdom because it would in any case be impossible to establish a British protectorate over the

FIGURE 6.2. Sharif 'Ali Haydar as Ottoman Emir of Mecca praying over a new telegraph line in Medina, 1916. Atatürk Kitaplığı, Bel-Mtf.024750, with permission.

sacred cities of Mecca and Medina. These plans for what would resemble the British Raj's system of subordinated princes were not far removed from some of the visions of Arab utopian federalism before and during the war.[27]

Infrastructure, genealogical authority, and the idea of a composite polity continued to be linked during the existence of OETA in the Syrian provinces. The Hijazi delegation to the Paris peace conference themselves made this connection, fulfilling British logic and foreshadowing much later academic theories of pan-Arab nationalism. In Paris, in January 1919 Sharif Faysal and his men, including T. E. Lawrence, explained the situation to British politicians: "The unity of Arabs in Asia has been made more easy of late years, since the development of railways, telegraphs, and air-roads. In old days, the area was too huge, and in parts necessarily too thinly peopled, to communicate common ideas readily." But they also acknowledged that the Arabic-speaking Ottoman regions were quite diverse and declared it "impossible to force them into one frame of government." There should, for example, be a discrete Syrian polity comprising an "agricultural and industrial area" that could "manage its own internal affairs." Historian Arnold Toynbee, a member of the British delegation to the peace conference, approved this "statesmanlike" proposal—conceived half a year before by the Eastern Committee itself. [28]

The sharifian task now was to reconcile the idea of Syria as part of a genealogical polity with the various competing Arab-Ottoman composite visions. Already in the nineteenth century Damascene notables had romantic notions of creating their own kingdom in *bilad al-Sham*.[29] But in May 1919, back in Damascus, Faysal announced that Syria must be "independent" in an economic federation with Iraq and the other Arab regions. It was at this point that he called the Syrians to embrace "revolution" instead of occupation and proposed himself as head of the new Syrian polity.[30]

The aim of recycling empire in Damascus was to create a new composite formation. In the government journal, the Damascene journalist and lawyer Shakir al-Hanbali noted that Faysal's plan called for "United Arab Governments," and explained that what was meant by this was that the governments would share a "united foreign policy and a united domestic economy." Al-Hanbali also outlined four possible kinds of "composite" (*murakkiba*) governments. The fourth kind he called "federation," giving the example of the United States of America and Switzerland, where the federal government possesses "general federative sovereignty" (*al-hakimiyya al-ittihadiyya al-'amma*). The internal arrangement of such a polity would be based on "decentralization" (*la-markaziyya*).[31] In July 1919, this vision, in a slightly Americanized version and on a territorially smaller scale, became the constitutional model for the "United States of Syria" with Faysal as king, and it was proposed to the visiting American King-Crane Commission.[32] The Commission, originally conceived as an investigative Allied Powers delegation to find out which power the local peoples would prefer as their mandatories in the summer of 1919, was finally only composed of American members—Charles Crane, a millionaire and Henry King, the president of Oberlin College, and thus powerless. The Commission received 1863 petitions from local individuals and associations, of which 1,107 asked for what the Americans translated as "democratic monarchy," with 1,102 of these proposing Faysal as their king.[33] Even in Tripoli, which was under OETA West (French) rule, the carpenters' guild advanced similar points a similar plan (with a pointed remark about Palestine being "Southern Syria") and rejected the idea of an independent Lebanon. The guild's request for a "monarchical government under Emir Faysal" was something of an afterthought, appearing some way down their list of demands.[34] (The American millionaire Crane was to remain deeply involved in post-Ottoman affairs in the 1920s.)[35]

The enshrinement of genealogy, in the shape of a sharifian king from Arabia, as the main source of political authority in their new state was troubling for many Damascenes, Muslim and non-Muslim alike. To spur them on, in early 1920 Faysal warned a new Damascene assembly that the "Turkish" peace treaty was just around the corner.[36] The question of whether to adopt a monarchy was not a straightforward one. On 3 March 1920 Faysal's secretary, 'Awni 'Abd al-Hadi, read aloud Faysal's opening speech to the assembly, which defined as the assembly's first task deciding "about the regime form" and a constitution.[37] Demonstrators, led by the activist Sheikh Kamil al-Qassab, a friend of Rida, who had just returned to the city and whom we have already met and will encounter again, sent a note to the conference, stating: "If you want to proclaim Emir Faysal a king, let him thus be proclaimed as a constitutional, democratic, and just king."[38] During the following months, the constitutional committee considered the alternative of declaring a republic. In the end, however, they opted for a monarchy.[39]

As befits the composite logic of post-imperial organizational thinking, in addition to the Syrian assembly, Damascus also saw the establishment of a small consultative body composed of soldiers and a number of civilians of Iraqi background. The latter made up the "Baghdadi party," ex-Ottoman Iraqi officers under the leadership of ex-Ottoman soldiers Ja'far al-'Askari and Nuri al-Sa'id within the OETA East government.[40] They decided to announce the "independence" of the Iraqi region (*al-bilad al-'iraqiyya*), stating further that this new entity would enter into a "political and economic union" (*ittihad*) with the Kingdom of Syria, itself a composite polity. They proclaimed Sharif 'Abd Allah, the third son of King al-Husayn, "constitutional king" in Baghdad and his brother Zayd as his deputy (*na'ib*) and announced that the occupation was thereby terminated.[41]

Historians often explore the relationship between large technological systems and state-formation. For instance, some argue that the State of Israel was born first as an "infrastructural" entity in mandate Palestine. But imperial infrastructure can also prefigure local state-making. The March 1920 announcement of sharifian kingdoms was thus a melding of the *ashraf* ambitions, British calculation, pre-war Ottoman infrastructure, Arab utopian federalism, and genealogical politics. The Syrian Kingdom was to recycle both material and immaterial Ottoman institutions. Let us consider a piece of material propaganda: a genealogical-technological map of the State of Syria (Figure 6.3). The new polity was depicted with the Hijaz railway as its infrastructural spine and with Faysal as its head.[42]

The Bifurcated Legal Infrastructure of Ottoman Authority, 1910s

Max Weber famously distinguished between three ideal types of domination: legal, traditional, and charismatic, and argued that in the case of a legal bureaucracy "obedience is owed to an impersonal order."[43] Despite its imperial context, as explained in Chapter Two, the Weberian model does not readily lend itself to the study of political practice in empire. Instead of exploring ideal types, it is more fruitful to look at how imperial authority operates in a real-life legal bureaucracy. That is, how the political order intersects with the legal order at their foundations. Through such historical analysis, we will be able to consider our central topic: the remaking of imperial authority into local institutions under the conditions of occupation. But first, we must understand the modern Ottoman legal bureaucracy.

By the 1900s, there was an elaborate administration of justice in the Ottoman Empire, in which different legal actors adjudicated cases in the name of different authority sources, all of which were bound to the imperial government. As we saw in Chapter Two, there were two main types of legal forums, the *kadı* (*shari'a*) and the *nizamiye* courts.[44] The difference between them was not "religious" and "secular" according to the popular use of these terms today. In the first, the Muslim judge registered and adjudicated cases in the local language using the traditional Muslim sources

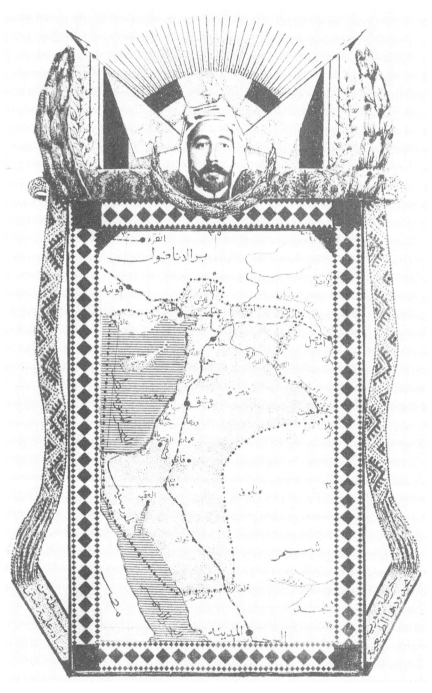

FIGURE 6.3. Map of the Kingdom of Syria, montage; late 1919–early 1920.
Source: 399 PAAP/135, Archives du Ministère de l'Europe et des Affaires étrangères—La Courneuve, with permission.

of *shari'a* and Muslim witnesses. In the second, magistrates (in theory, regardless of religion) adjudicated mostly in Ottoman Turkish applying the new government codes (which were codified *shari'a* norms), without the evidentiary requirements of the *qadi*.

Let me describe the modern Ottoman court system in some detail as it existed at the moment of the occupation of the Syrian provinces in 1918. By the 1910s, the Ottoman *qadi* courts were centralized in the provinces. In Damascus, there emerged a single central *qadi* court in place of the several small courts that had previously operated in the city's various quarters. The sultanic government appointed and sent the usually nonlocal judge (after the 1850s named variously as *kadı*, *naib*, or *hakim*). The imperial mufti's office (*şeyhülislam*) was in charge of this administration. The judges issued verdicts without mentioning under whose authority they were acting. It was understood that the verdict relied on revealed law and the sultan's power. After the 1880s, verdicts of the *kadı* were executed by the executive offices at the *nizamiye* courts. The *kadı* acted most often as a notary as we saw in the case of al-Hajj Ahmad. By the 1910s real estate transactions, except those pertaining to important pious endowments, and criminal cases were in theory outside of his jurisdiction. The commission for orphans (which handled significant wealth) also reported to this court. The *kadı* was fully under Ottoman government control and relied on imperial executive power, even though he represented a non-state-centered authority. In a final step, in 1917 the Ministry of Justice took over the control over the *kadı* courts from the *şeyhülislam*.[45]

The *nizamiye* courts, on the other hand, constituted a fully state-centered, imperial legal hierarchy. Ottoman government officials established judicial councils gradually from the 1850s on and institutionalized them as government courts in the 1880s. Beginning in 1879, a series of administrative laws gave final shape to the hierarchy. There was a Court of Cassation (*mahkeme-i temyiz*), the highest court of appeals, in the imperial center; a Court of Appeals (*mahkeme-i istinaf*) in each provincial capital; and a Court of First Instance (*mahkeme-i bidayet*) in each district. There were separate criminal (*ceza*) and civil (*hukuk*) sections of the appeal courts in large provincial centers. This reform created the new offices of government judge (*hakim*), public prosecutor, investigative magistrate with powers to detain suspects, court usher (who had to know how to read and write Ottoman Turkish), arbitration judge (from 1913 on), bailiff (to execute the judges' orders), and public notary, as well as the independent role of the lawyer (see Table 6.1 for the Ottoman-Arabic terms used for these new roles).

Table 6.1. The Legal Roles in the Ottoman *Nizamiye* Courts

Role	Ottoman use	Arabic use
judge	*hakim*	*hakim*
presiding judge (usually at appeal courts)	*reis*	*ra'is*
arbitration judge (*juge de paix*, for small disputes)	*sulh hakimi*	*hakim al-sulh*
public prosecutor	*müdde-i 'umumi*	*mudda'i 'amm*
chief investigative magistrate	*ser-müstantık*	*ser-mustantiq*
investigative magistrate	*müstantık*	*mustantiq*
court usher / scribe	*muhzir*	*muhdir*
bailiff	*mübaşır*	*mubashir*

Importantly, the *nizamiye* courts issued verdicts in the name of the sultan. The Ministry of Justice and the Council of State oversaw their activities. These courts applied the new government legal codes, such as the *Mecelle* (the Civil Code) and the Criminal Code, all of which contained rearranged and systematized *shari'a* principles mixed with (French) procedural regulations. These jurists could not cite *shari'a* texts; their law was not the jurist's law but the government's law, set down in Ottoman Turkish. However, given the *shari'a*-basis of the new codes, often *kadıs* doubled as *nizamiye* judges in the provinces. The new judicial organization may well have remained incomplete in many smaller provincial settings. In any case, the public prosecutor was the most "stable," purely government-related office in the legal administration.[46]

The Muslim jurisconsult (*mufti*) remained somewhat outside of both types of courts. The mufti is a jurist-theorist who provides nonbinding legal opinions (*fatwa*, pl. *fatawa*), and often publishes manuals, essays, and commentaries on particular legal problems. Their legal opinions become precedents to which later muftis can refer. (Islamic law differs in this regard from Anglo-Saxon law: it is not the judges' rulings that constitute legal precedent, but rather the muftis' legal opinions.)[47] Importantly, as opposed to the *kadı*, the Ottoman provincial mufti, though appointed by the sultan, was usually local (and wrote in the local language); after 1913, he was in theory elected locally and confirmed by the sultan. There were muftis in each province, often in subdistricts as well, who were members of administrative councils, heads of the *'ulama'*, and directors of religious schools.[48] In late Ottoman Damascus, the mufti even presided over the municipality in case of a mayor's illness and controlled the pious endowments. Ordinary people, bureaucrats, and judges requested legal opinions from the mufti, but they were not bound by the terms of the opinion they received. The Ottoman mufti, like the *kadı*, issued his opinions without reference to the sultan.[49] (See more on muftis in the Egyptian context in the next chapter.)

In light of the above, we can now turn to the legal administration of wartime Damascus, the capital of the Suriye province. In the period 1914–1917, General Cemal Pasha as military governor created an exceptional court martial, with nonlocal members, which sentenced activist and pro-French Syrian notables and their families to exile and execution.[50] After Cemal's iron fist, a Turkish individual called Tahsin Bey became governor of Damascus for a short time; he was an able administrator, and was frequently praised by local scholars.[51] During the war, the jurist Süleyman Rüşdi was the *kadı* of the Damascus court, whose registers were all written in Arabic, though its administrative correspondence was partly in Turkish. The mufti of the province was Abu al-Khayr ʿAbidin, from a distinguished local Damascene jurist family. The Suriye *nizamiye* system consisted of a province-wide Court of Appeals with civil and criminal sections, a public prosecutor and his assistant, and eight members. There was also a Court of First Instance, again with a public prosecutor and his assistant, and two members. In addition, there were a chief investigative magistrate and two arbitration judges (*sulh hakimi*). In most of the government courts Ottoman Turkish was the language of administration. Within this central bureaucracy of the province there were twenty-four rural sub-districts. Each of these had at least one *kadı* and one Court of First Instance with legal staff. In addition to its judicial functions, the provincial bureaucracy had many other law-related responsibilities and bureaus that dealt with them, such as offices of land registration and the cadaster (*defter-i haqani* and *tapu*), and directorates of pious endowments and state property.[52] In 1918, the Allied forces found these institutional spoils of war when they established the Occupied Enemy Territories Administration (OETA).

Occupation and Law

Given that OETA was a military occupation, the question arises as to how far the occupiers went in changing the Ottoman administration of justice that they found on the ground. In accordance with the Hague conventions, the 1914 edition of the British army's *Manual of Military Law*, which was likely the edition General Allenby possessed, states that "during the occupation by the enemy the sovereignty of the legitimate owner of the territory is only temporarily latent but it still exists and in no way passes to the occupant."[53] Allenby accordingly and regularly assured the British War Office that he was governing in harmony with these requirements: "Subject to the necessary modifications, the Turkish system of government and administrative machinery have been maintained in all areas."[54] He even announced in an OETA meeting that no one could abolish the "Turkish" laws, especially not the ones concerning taxation.[55]

The heads of OETA zones, however, embarked upon on a project to transform the legal administration of the occupied territories. During the occupation, the OETA zones became judicially independent of the Ottoman Empire. Allenby himself abolished the right to appeal to the Court of Cassation in Istanbul for the inhabitants of the OETA East and South zones in early 1919. Charles Puech, at the time the French Senior Judicial Advisor in OETA West and North, opined that Allenby's authorizing OETA South and East administrations to change existing institutions was "against international law." Nonetheless, Puech also argued that the Anglo-French declaration (in November 1918) meant that Syria was "liberated from the Ottoman yoke" and thus an "independent state." France could not change the local legal infrastructure but only study the legal situation until such time as a peace treaty would "sanctify the liberation" (*consacrera la libération*) and a new government would decide about the laws. Still, Puech suggested that a court of cassation (to be called a "superior" or "supreme" court), with French judges only, should be established "in order to express Syrian national sovereignty." Puech's idea of liberation also imagined French as the language of the new legal system and the appointments of French-speaking judges from the metropole and Algeria during a "transitory period" (between the would-be peace treaty and such time as Syrians became self-supporting).[56] In January 1920, Puech noted that whereas the creation of a supreme court is normally an act premised on the establishment of sovereignty, OETA was not a sovereign government. General Gouraud, the Commander-in-Chief of the French army in the Levant, contemplated sending appeals cases to Istanbul, although he saw this solution as damaging the loyalty of the Lebanese.[57] The best way to resolve this conundrum, Puech suggested, was to interpret a new supreme court in Beirut as "the council of the General Commander-in-Chief" (*conseil du Général Commandant en Chef*), with authority derived from the commander's duty to maintain order during occupation.[58] (Later, in a public talk, Puech referred to article 43 of the Hague laws which, in his interpretation, allowed military occupiers to establish juridical institutions).[59] Having thus established a new local supreme court, the French administration also moved the right of appeal of the inhabitants of OETA North (today part of Turkey) to the new supreme court in Beirut in early 1920.[60]

OETA South (Palestine) posed a different set of challenges. In the view of Colonel Norman Bentwich, Senior Judicial Officer and, incidentally, an important Zionist, OETA South became judicially independent from the Ottoman Empire, because the Ottoman judges had retreated with the Ottoman troops and "communication with Constantinople was cut off." In a 1920 essay, Bentwich stated that he, as Judicial Officer of the occupation, had "taken the place of the Ottoman Ministry of Justice." Unlike Puech, Bentwich noted the theoretically common judicial nature of all OETA zones from the perspective of occupation. In OETA South, there was no new supreme court but one Court of Appeals with final powers in civil cases, and the chief administrator functioned as a supreme court in criminal cases. Bentwich took the view that the Commander-in-Chief was the "fountain-head of justice," with final judicial powers over particularly important cases, such as those involving the death penalty, similar to a president or ruler in a polity.[61]

In OETA East (comprising largely the Suriye and Aleppo provinces), a more complicated administrative situation emerged due to the simultaneous presence of two occupation armies, the British and the Hijazi. Allenby appointed 'Ali Rida al-Rikabi, an ex-Ottoman general from Damascus, to take charge as the general military governor (al-hakim al-'askari al-'amm) of OETA East. Syrian and foreign historians consider al-Rikabi a controversial figure: he was a good administrator but an opportunist, a practical nationalist who thought there was no sense in resisting the French, and who therefore only reluctantly cooperated with the Meccan ashraf in Damascus and in Transjordan two years later.[62]

Before we proceed to address in detail the question of legal authority in OETA East, it will be useful to familiarize ourselves with how the Suriye provincial legal system changed—in the scriptural-visual dimension of law, according to the court records. Three signs indicated the end of direct Ottoman control in the Damascus nizamiye records: a black line after the last notice in Ottoman Turkish on the pages, the change of language to Arabic, and the restarting of the numeration of notices from one. On 3 October 1918, al-Rikabi abolished the arbitration courts and transferred all criminal cases from the court of appeals to a separate diwan.[63] He soon affirmed, however, that all financial contracts and agreements which had been formulated "among the people or with the government" "before the announcement of Arab independence" must be adjudicated based on existing Ottoman laws and regulations.[64] All buildings and government offices which were in the possession of the people before "independence" had to continue to pay the previous Ottoman taxes.[65]

The Ottoman infrastructure of justice also continued in place, despite the fact that many officials had fled. The people wanted their issues adjudicated. Al-Rikabi was surprised that municipality officials asked him about legal appointments in October 1918, and so he ordered the establishment of a legislative council, called *majlis al-shura* in Arabic. Respected Muslim jurist and scholar Sheikh 'Abd al-Muhsin al-Ustuwani served as its vice-president, along with a number of non-Damascene Muslim and non-Muslim jurists. Although this body's Arabic name conveys the sense of a "parliament," its members imagined it as the local equivalent of the legislative-regulatory office of the Ottoman parliament. Rikabi ordered the application of laws issued by this newly-formed body. For instance, the *majlis* declared that all Ottoman government buildings considered to be "spoils of war" now belonged to the new government—a move of material spoliation that was clearly in breach of the Hague laws of occupation.[66]

The legislative council created a "temporary" law of the courts which was "approved by the emir [Faysal]," but it did not provide enough guidance for judges and legal personnel in its first draft. So, in January of 1919 the council, following consultation with more legal experts and after studying the Ottoman experimental law in the Edirne province, changed the law. In its remarkable new version, the council specified the continued existence of the Ottoman *nizamiye* (or, now, in its Arabic transliteration, *nizamiyya*) and *shar'iyya* legal domains, and acknowledged military courts and religious councils as the only additional juridical bodies (article 1). The law maintained the *shari'a* (*qadi*) courts' jurisdiction in personal issues and in the administration of the pious endowments, but it called attention to the fact that anything else was under the purview of the "justice" (*'adliyya*) government courts. In retrospect, we can see how this last choice of words foreshadows the imminent disappearance of the Ottoman word *nizamiye*, replaced by the Arabic *'adliyya* to denote the old-new government court. The law required changes in personnel and procedures but preserved in force all previous Ottoman laws and regulations "which do not contradict this present law" (article 21).[67]

Conventional narratives frequently report that the new Arab "state" then suddenly became an accepted fact, attracting "all Arabs who had previously been in the Ottoman administration," plus others who flocked from abroad.[68] However, some of the newly-arrived did not come out of patriotism. Take for instance the story of Saʻd Shuqayr Pasha, a Lebanese official serving in the British Sudanese system. The status of OETA East as an administration outsourced to the Hijazi army posed a problem of imperial management. It was a threat to the British Treasury because al-Rikabi spent the British subsidy without supervision, a state of affairs that was liable to cause difficulty because the Lords of the Treasury expected the next budget to attract parliamentary scrutiny.[69] In March 1919, the "Hijazi" soldiers revolted in Amman and Karak because they had not received their pay.[70] For this reason, the British authorities in Cairo made a number of new appointments to OETA East. Saʻd Shuqayr was assigned the role of financial advisor. Iskandar ʻAmmun, the old Lebanese legal expert in British Egypt (whom we encountered previously in Chapter Five, articulating his vision for the establishment of a mountain republic), came to serve as minister of justice.[71] These British appointees did not last long in OETA East, and most of them soon returned to Cairo, Shuqayr explicitly preferring to serve the British authorities rather than the Arab government in the spring of 1920.[72]

Authority in Government Courts

It is in this context that we can now turn to investigate the challenge of authority as a practical question in the administration of justice. The local-Ottoman legal order, especially the *nizamiye* courts, required a new political regime. We will take a close look at two instances.

DIVIDING OCCUPATION AUTHORITY

In 1919, a basic conflict over authority arose between the legal administrations in the occupation zones. It involved the British army in OETA South, the Arab government in OETA East, and the French army in OETA North and West. The disagreements centered on two issues in the domain of law.

The first concerned the collective occupation. General Allenby, as the Commander-in-Chief of the British-Egyptian Expeditionary Force, was the highest authority and source of regulations in all OETA (as he wrote to his wife once: "I am supreme in Egypt, Palestine, and Syria"). As we have just seen, Allenby's regulative authority was challenged by rival army leaders, the French General Gouraud, Emir Faysal, and by the legislative council in Damascus. But, even if Allenby had delegated his authority to the OETA zone administrators, they were not fully in charge: postal and railway matters remained under the British army.[73]

The second point of contention among and even within OETA zones concerned the exact jurisdictional scope of the courts. Ottoman legal administrators had all shared a common status in the provincial hierarchy, but now they were not only separated but also appeared to be subordinated to British officers in Jerusalem. For instance, accused persons arrested in "Syria" were to be given over to "Palestine" if the appropriate British officer in Damascus so requested.[74] The Damascus legal office, however, firmly informed the court in Jerusalem that it had "no right to bring about a verdict concerning the rights of those who are in the territory of the Arab government unless the [military] governor orders it otherwise."[75] The Arab government, however, also understood OETA East as one legal zone, despite the fact that it included both the Suriye and Halep provinces. This meant that the administrative reach of Damascus extended over Aleppo and other cities in the North. For instance, British monetary aid flew through Damascus and al-Rikabi then distributed the financial allocations and verifications to the courts in the Aleppo province. In the new Ministry of Justice in Damascus, the committee for appointing legal personnel appointed judges in the Aleppo court of second instance and its subordinate courts, too, together with those in Damascus, Ba'albak, Hama, Hims, 'Ajlun, Hawran, al-Karak, al-Salt, Amman, and elsewhere.[76]

WHOSE ADMINISTRATION?

In OETA East, the most fundamental struggle over authority was a rift between 'Ali Rida al-Rikabi, whose authority flowed from General Allenby, and Faysal Bey and his brother Zayd, two *ashraf*, who claimed authority based on their father's being the King of Arabs. From October 1918 on, General al-Rikabi gave orders directly to the legal center of the provincial administration. The legislative council reported to al-Rikabi and not to the emir's office. The former's fiery temper did not ease the situation. For instance, he did not accept the resignation of Misbah Efendi, a member of the legal appointments committee, and sent a short note: "I want to see Misbah Efendi's signature also, Rikabi."[77] No wonder that when the popular Faysal returned from Paris in May 1919, al-Rikabi felt forced to publicly announce that he was still the "general director" of OETA East and that his orders were based on the military power of General Allenby.[78]

The conflict between these parties can be construed as a conflict between authority in an administrative sense and authority in a political sense. In this way, claims to military-administrative and political-civil authority clashed over issues of jurisdiction. That Faysal Bey was regarded as a civil individual rather than an Allied army leader was a deliberate outcome of British calculation.[79] The key component in the plan was to associate Faysal with the local civilian population. At first, Allenby had regarded Faysal as a subordinated officer, but by late 1918 he acknowledged him instead as a representative of "locals."[80] This acknowledgment took place through a simple declaration: Allenby declared Faysal the "supreme authority in Syria in all Arab matters," thus failing to assign him any role in the OETA chain of command.[81] It appears, however, that Faysal did see himself as military leader. When he wrote from Paris in January-February 1919, his letterhead was emblazoned in Arabic "Leadership of the Northern Arab Army"—"The Emir's Office" (*qiyadat al-juyush al-'arabiyya al-shimaliyya—diwan al-amir*).[82] He did not shy away from asserting his status as an Allied army leader when it suited him to do so: during his negotiations in Paris, he on one occasion proposed that, if the British and the French armies retreated, he would also withdraw his Hijazi soldiers from Syria.[83]

The appointments of judges, and the administration of justice in general, went to the question: By whose authority were appointments made? And by whose authority were verdicts issued over local individuals? As it happens, the appointment formulas were clear spoils from the previous Ottoman government. In Damascus, the emir's office acted as a political organ while Faysal was in Paris. At first, military governor 'Ali al-Rikabi appointed new judges and prosecutors, but soon the emir's office assumed the right to appoint judges and prosecutors. The way these "appointments" worked was that the letters sent to appointees included the phrase "the committee for selecting the legal employees appointed you as XXX in XXX and His Highness the Emir agreed. Go to your place of appointment immediately!" or "His Highness the Emir issued a decree agreeing to the appointment of XXX as XXX in XXX."[84] This last phrase "His Highness the Emir issued a decree" (*sadarat iradat Sumuww al-Amir*), appearing at a time when Faysal himself was physically in Paris, indicates that sharifian political authority echoed Ottoman sultanic authority in its use of the languages of decrees (*irade*). It still fell to al-Rikabi, as military governor, to appoint legal personnel, but after February 1919 his appointments were restricted to office staff, and, as we shall see, the judges henceforth operated under sharifian authority.[85]

The establishment in Damascus of a supreme court, whose function was to determine whether verdicts issued in the courts were in conformity with the constitutional system, was premised on the existence of a sovereign political order. As General Allenby blocked the way to appeal to the Ottoman Court of Cassation in Istanbul, al-Rikabi gave orders to execute the decisions of the legislative council and to create a Court of Cassation (*mahkamat al-tamyiz*) as the highest court in the administrative hierarchy. In March 1919, the government rented a new office-building in the Suq Saruja neighborhood to house both this new supreme court and the courts of first and second instance, to which all Ottoman registers and papers were to be transferred. The supreme Court of Cassation would henceforth adjudicate all criminal, civil, and even *shari'a* cases, although it is unclear on which constitution they based the debated verdicts. The appointment of former Ottoman *shari'a* jurists as members of this highest court indicates that Rikabi and the Damascene committee considered revealed law to be part of the post-Ottoman local order.[86]

The government courts in Damascus clearly acknowledged the authority of the King of the Arabs in 1919. Even though Emir Faysal, or rarely al-Rikabi, appointed the judges and prosecutors, the surviving registers of the newly termed "civil" (*huquq*) courts of first and second instances show that legal appointees derived their legal authority from King al-Husayn and not from the Ottoman sultan. As an example of this legal spoliation of monarchy, in one court of first instance a case begins with the following sentence: "In the ongoing trial in the court of first instance which is permitted to issue a verdict in the name of His Majesty, the King of the Arabs, may God support him, XXX accuses XXX [. . .]." The verdicts in this register refer to the articles of the Ottoman Civil Code (*Mecelle*) and, "if necessary," to the new regulations issued by the *majlis al-shura*.[87] In a later register (relating cases tried between 28 January and 5 May 1920), the reporting begins, "A complaint, dated XXX, was submitted to the court of first instance in Damascus which is permitted to execute a trial and issue a verdict in the name of His Majesty the King of the Arabs, may God support him." The verdicts in this register, like those in the earlier one, apply both the *Mecelle* and some new regulations.[88] Another register documenting the activity of the court of second instance (between 6 August 1919 and 25 May 1920) records decisions as follows: "[This is] a legal notice from the session held at the court of second instance which is permitted to adjudicate and issue verdicts in the name of his Majesty Sultan [!] Husayn I." In the early entries in this register, the scribe alternates uncertainly between the titles "Sultan" or "King of the Arabs," but by the end he routinely uses the latter formulation.[89] These seemingly subtle changes in the language of the court allow us to witness, at the level of minute detail, the remaking of Ottoman sultanic authority into its Arab imperial successor.

The change of authority at the court reflected the new assembly's announcement of the establishment of a Syrian Kingdom with Faysal as its king on 6 March 1920. The *huquq* courts immediately switched to this new political fiction. After this date, the notices in the register of the aforementioned court of second instance register began: "[This is] a legal notice from the session held [. . .] at the court of second instance which is permitted to adjudicate and to bring about judgments in the name of his Majesty the King of Syria, Faysal the First, may God the Almighty support him." [90] In another court of second instance register (cases between February and December 1920), we can trace three regimes of authority in succession. The court at first issued judgments in the name of "His Majesty, the King of the Arabs, Husayn the First, may God support him," but from 15 March 1920 they began to adjudicate "in the name of his Majesty, King of Syria, Faysal the First, may God support him." The third change happened after 19 Tammuz (July) 1920, when the French army invaded OETA East. The first case recorded after the establishment of the French occupation, on 29 Tammuz (July) 1920, does not indicate the source of authority. Although the case in question had actually begun on 26 February 1920, when verdicts still referred to the name of al-Husayn, in the late July copy we find only the simple sentence: "this is a register of minutes of the session on Thursday, 26 Shubat (February) 1920 by the judge of the court of second instance in Damascus."[91] The register continues without reference to political authority until its end.

Authority in the Qadi *Court, 1918–1920*

During the two years of the Hijazi OETA East, the construction of the political order relied on sharifian genealogy as a source of authority. This attempt to revive Hamidian politics met with subtle opposition not only from Muslim activists such as Kamil al-Qassab and Rashid Rida, but also from local Muslim jurists.[92] Let us turn now to the question of Muslim authority and the *qadi* court.

In the fall of 1918, the Meccan *ashraf* embarked upon the project of recasting a new imperial imamate with al-Husayn as its head. During the Northern Arab Army's advance, Faysal sent letters to local notables referring to the decree of his father as a *firman* (a very Ottoman word denoting the sultan's decree).[93] At the moment of his entry into Damascus, Faysal in a printed public letter took the bold step of calling his father "the Commander of the Faithful."[94] In a turn of speech quite typical to instances of spoliation, he also thanked the people of Damascus people for acknowledging his father as "sultan" and "Commander of the Faithful."[95] Faysal's men occupied the cities in the Suriye province in the name of al-Husayn. In Aleppo, the notables swear loyalty for al-Husayn through his representative Faysal in the new Arab Club, previously the CUP Club. In Beirut, journalists started to call al-Husayn their "sultan." When the French army prohibited the mention of his name in the mosques of Beirut, some Muslim scholars protested, writing that "the Syrian Muslims accept al-Husayn as their religious authority" (*al-sulta al-diniyya*).[96]

The recycled style of empire is again plainly visible in the appearance of references to the "Hasanid Arab State" in the Damascus *qadi* court records in October 1918. The Turkish judge of Damascus had fled the city in late September, leaving the local *shari'a* scholars to negotiate with the occupiers. They pledged their loyalty to Faysal, and he appointed a new, local *qadi* Muhammad Khayri al-Mahasini, from a distinguished Damascene jurist family. It is unclear how al-Mahasini secured the appointment, but he had been previously the chief scribe of the *kadı* court, so it is possible that he simply continued his work. His court was functioning within two weeks after the entry of the Allied forces into Damascus. The Ottoman-appointed mufti of the Suriye province, Muhammad Abu al-Khayr 'Abidin, remained in his office for some months, but Faysal soon deposed this elderly scholar and instead appointed Muhammad Ata Allah al-Kasm as the new mufti of Damascus. Judge al-Mahasini and mufti al-Kasm were to remain the chief *shari'a* jurists in the following years, well into era of the French regime.[97]

The designation "Arab" appeared in the place of "Ottoman" in the *qadi* court's records during the first few weeks of the new regime. The earliest cases marking the shift that I have found are dated 9 Muharram 1337 (15 October 1918). In a register dedicated to recording alimony cases, the first that the new judge al-Mahasini adjudicated regarded the allocation of a sum for the benefit of two children from their deceased father's inheritance to their mother, Amina bint Muhammad b. 'Ali al-Aza'i. The text identifies the lady Amina as "a legally free, sane, adult, Muslim, and Arab woman." Three weeks earlier that last adjective would have been "Ottoman." The text also indicates that Amina and the witnesses, her brother Darwish and 'Isa b. Mustafa b. Muhammad al-Hamawi, were "Muslim Arabs" (*al-muslimin al-'arabiyyin*[!]).[98] In another register, the same case is copied, but with a slightly different language: the scribe of this latter text indicated that the widow and her two witnesses were "subjects of the Arab dynastic state" (*taba'at al-dawla al-'arabiyya*).[99] In yet another transcript of the case, composed six days later in yet another register, the text contains the adjective "Hasanid" next to "Arab State." In that register, this identification is used for only nine more days. The designation "Arab" disappears after the end of October.[100] There was much confusion. In a case recorded in another register, a certain sheikh Muhammad Tawfiq Efendi had come to court to demand legal control over a sum whose guarantee was a share in an endowed house; in the transcript he, too, was characterized as an Arab.[101] In an entry on 11 Muharram 1337 (17 October 1918), in the probate case of the deceased Saliha bint 'Abd al-Qadir, one of the heirs was her son, Khalid b. Yasin, still serving in the "ranks of the imperial army" (al-'asakir al-shahaniyya). But the witnesses were all "subjects of the Northern Arab State" (tab' al-dawla al-'arabiyya al-shimaliyya).[102]

Not all cases registered in this period, however, troubled to characterize people as being Arab. One such case, adjudicated by the judge al-Mahasini, involved a claim by a certain Munira bint 'Abd Allah, who was from Edirne (but for some reason stayed in Damascus during the war) against her former husband, who was unwilling to return her bridal dower after their divorce. The two parties were not identified as Arabs, nor were their local witnesses identified as subjects of the Hasanid Arab State.[103] As James Gelvin has demonstrated, there was in Damascus at the time considerable disagreement over nationalist ideology. Some disregarded the ashraf and saw the Damascenes themselves as the only legitimate authority. For instance, in the private journal al-'Uqab the only mention about ashraf at the time was in the context of a motion by the "administrative council of Suriya" and the Damascus municipality to send a letter authorizing Faysal to represent them in the Paris Peace Conference in February 1919.[104]

Perhaps this is the reason why an even larger campaign for sharifian claims soon began in the occupied provinces. In February 1919, al-'Asima, the new journal of "the official government," appeared with al-Husayn's picture on its title page. Its inaugural issues serialized a history of "The Exalted Sharifs of Mecca" authored by Iskandar Ma'luf.[105] In the same month, 'Ali, the first son of al-Husayn, after a long siege finally took the city of Medina from the Ottoman army, and once again he accorded his father the title "Commander of the Faithful."[106]

Recycling empire without revolution meant the preservation of the Ottomans' bifurcated imperial legal framework. Although there were proposals to abolish the qadi courts—even an article about "Socialism and Equality" by Fa'iz al-Khuri appeared in the official journal during Ramadan.[107] But for the ashraf and most local notables there was no question of abolishing revealed law or replacing the Mecelle in the regions under their power. In February 1919, the legal office called attention to the fact that in alimony cases "if the *qadi* issues a verdict by legal notice (*hukm bi-mawjib i'lam shar'i*)" then the execution of the verdict was compulsory (*wajib*) and could not be canceled under any circumstances because the alimony was not a "debt" but a legal obligation, prescribed by God.[108]

Faysal Bey also assumed Muslim authority in place of the Ottoman caliph and his own father. He appointed, or agreed to appoint, new administrators of pious endowments in Damascus and the occupied regions; and it was in his name that both *nizamiye* judges and *shari'a* personnel, including the countryside muftis, were appointed.[109]

The *qadi* al-Mahasini and other *'ulama'* actively intervened in the legislative process. In 1919, for instance, al-Mahasini sent a letter to the *majlis al-shura* telling them that their decision that the *shari'a* courts should execute their own decisions would cause huge difficulties and delays because of a shortage of trained personnel and space. He pointed out that after two offices of arbitration had been abolished and the work of their justices transferred to the executive offices of the civil courts in Damascus and Aleppo, the operation of these bureaus had slowed. He now demanded that the execution of *shari'a* decisions should be given back to these offices, as in Ottoman times, because it would take time for new legal personnel to learn the procedures. He suggested a new text for article 17 of the Law of Judicial Reforms: "the procedures of execution should remain as these were before the latest uprising." The use of the word "uprising" (*inqilab*) instead of revolution (*thawra*), incidentally, suggests that al-Mahasini was not entirely pro-sharifian.[110]

In terms of the constitutional dimension of the *shari'a*, the continuation of the Ottoman caliphate without its actual imperial control did remain an obstacle to finalizing a new order in the occupied regions. The British government, fearing a violent reaction from its Indian Muslim subjects, had not allowed Sharif al-Husayn to use titles associated with the caliphate. The Friday prayers—the public mark of Muslim authority—had continued to include the name of the sultan in many occupied regions. Thus, for instance, when in June 1916 Hijazi mosques started mentioning al-Husayn in the Friday prayers, they continued at the same time to mention the sultan also. As we saw in Chapter Five, Ottoman Muslim activists had no objections to pairing the names of the caliph and the local ruler in the Friday prayer. In January 1918, however, al-Husayn prohibited mention of the sultan's name in the Hijaz. Instead, Friday prayers would now cite his name only as "king of the Arab countries and *sharif* and emir of Mecca." This shift gave rise to confusion as some overzealous imams began to label him "Commander of the Faithful," that is, the caliph; but they were quickly notified of their error—they were too early.[111] After the occupation and his sons' announcements, in December 1918 al-Husayn had to make clear once again that "this title [the Commander of the Faithful] pertained only for the caliphate." He announced that all should address him "with the title the country had bestowed on him," namely *malik*.[112]

The sharifian spoliation of Ottoman authority was somewhat unsuccessful in these early years. In terms of *shari'a*, authority remained an unsettled issue in the occupied regions. In Baghdad in June 1918, some sheikhs named al-Husayn as caliph, others the Ottoman sultan, and yet others simply omitted the name of any authority in Friday prayers.[113] In October 1918, at the moment of occupying Damascus, the Ottoman-appointed local mufti Abu al-Khayr 'Abidin acknowledged the *ashraf* as the ruling authority; but he did so in a somewhat lukewarm manner, which prompted Faysal's entourage to accuse the mufti of being an Ottoman loyalist.[114] The Druze leaders declared that while they recognized Faysal as emir over Syria (possibly they meant the Suriye province), his authority did not extend over their territory, and neither the Hijazi nor the Syrian government had any political or administrative agency over their tribes.[115] Elsewhere, especially in Aleppo, sharifian claims were also frowned upon. Following the French invasion in 1920, the Friday prayers in Aleppo straightaway restored the name of the Ottoman sultan.[116]

Conclusion

The March 1920 proclamation of the Syrian Kingdom, a Hamidian polity ruling over the Syrian provinces as part of a larger composite polity of emirs, represented a compromise between advocates of federal utopianism and the sharifian occupiers. Its end in July by the invading French army brought about chaos in Damascus and, like his entry, so too the exit of Faysal was accompanied by the loss of life. His bodyguards killed an Arab soldier by mistake.[117]

Historians often characterize the decision by British imperial administrators in 1921 to appoint Faysal king of Iraq as an act of arbitrary colonialism. Indeed, until that point Sayyid Talib of Basra, another descendant of the Prophet, was the most likely candidate for a new throne or presidency in those occupied provinces. However, in the light of Faysal's own effort to translate Hamidian genealogical politics into a sharifian monarchy in Damascus, and the local and British imperial plans for a federation of emirs, his appointment appears a logical counterrevolutionary extension of the previous Hamidian policy. Even his person was not as arbitrary as it seems. The ex-Ottoman Arab army officers who sustained the sharifian kingdom in Damascus did imagine a *sharif* monarch in Baghdad and they—chiefly Nuri al-Saʿid—had a major role in staging Faysal as a new monarch-imam in the new local state of Iraq.

This chapter has shown an often-unarticulated discrepancy between religion and genealogy in a political order, on the one hand, and older institutionalized and codified legal forums tending towards a Muslim secular system, on the other. The Faysali regime in 1919–1920 inherited this situation from the Hamidian era because in the short period between 1908 and 1918 the CUP did not fully abolish the Hamidian imperial project. This discrepancy between the political (plural sources of authority) and legal (tending towards homogeneity) orders should be the subject of further thinking and research.

The use of genealogical authority and the reuse of Ottoman attributes in the making of new legal and political institutions pose larger questions about government and the political order after the empire. Unlike Mustafa Kemal, the leader of the new Turkish army, who, after 1922, decided to abolish revealed law as a source of authority in the new constitutional order, former Ottoman patricians and the French and British occupiers continued to uphold revealed law in the 1920s Arabs regions. In the next chapter, I study this problem in constitutional terms with particular focus on the example of Egypt.

CHAPTER SEVEN

Authority and the *Shariʿa* Apparatus in Post-Ottoman Egypt

AT 10 O'CLOCK on the morning of 21 December 1914, the ministers of the Egyptian government gathered in the ʿAbdin Palace in Cairo for an important meeting. The British High Commission had just declared martial law and the establishment of a new state, the Sultanate of Egypt, under a British protectorate. Until that moment, Egypt had been a province of the Ottoman Empire under British occupation. Sultan Husayn Kamil, Egypt's newly appointed ruling dynast (r. 1914–1917), chaired the session, at which the government made several key decisions. First, they abolished the position of "*Qadi* of Cairo" and declared that the subordination of Islamic law in Egypt to the authority of the "Turkish sultan" was terminated, effectively ending Ottoman sovereignty over Egypt. Following this declaration, the government decided that the Code of the *Shariʿa* Courts had to be amended. They appointed "a president and a representative of Egyptians" at both the Supreme *Shariʿa* Court and at the Cairo *Shariʿa* Court of First Instance. A committee was also set up in the Justice Ministry in order to consider further legal amendments. Finally, the ministers and the new sultan sent the aging Grand Mufti into retirement and appointed the energetic Muhammad Bakhit al-Mutiʿi as the new Grand Mufti in the Sultanate of Egypt.[1]

There has been extensive debate among political scientists and scholars of law about the relationship between *shariʿa*, state, and democracy. Wael Hallaq has denied the compatibility of *shariʿa* with the Western concept of the state, arguing that premodern *shariʿa* was "a non-state order," which was "contaminated" by the modern state.[2] Others, including Gudrun Krämer and Noah Feldman, have argued the opposite, namely that democracy, state, and Islam can comfortably coexist.[3] More recently, Andrew March has argued that Muslim intellectuals in the interwar period invented the notion of Islamic popular sovereignty as a direct challenge to the Western concept of nation-state sovereignty.[4] Specifically with regard to interwar Egypt, Abdeslam Maghraoui has contended that "formal political institutions are misleading indicators of democratization when they are decoupled from the substantive issues of citizenship and political community."[5] Rachel Scott has explored how *shari'a* became state law in modern Egyptian constitutions, premising her argument on a distinction between "religion" and "politics."[6]

The perspective of imperial transformation helps to historicize these normative arguments.[7] Instead of seeing religion and politics as two static categories, we might rather focus on the transition from the Ottoman to a local political order as the key to understanding how and why Muslim doctrines of government changed in Egypt. It is an important issue since, I propose, imperial forms of Islam differ from the forms of Islam in local states. Specifically, the post-Ottoman period is a laboratory where doctrines and concepts were revised. Aziz al-Azmeh has argued in a memorable passage that "ideas of Western origin have implanted themselves in Arab countries and become our own; they are the foundations of modern political life, or rather they constitute the foundations of the current modern political discourse."[8] The Western epistemological implantation and imbrication of Muslim Arabic thought had its beginnings in late Ottoman times, but Westernized forms of Islamic concepts started to claim authenticity and hegemony only in successor societies such as post-Ottoman Egypt.

What prompted a transformation in the doctrine of Muslim authority in 1920s Egypt was not, I suggest in the pages that follow, the norm of the nation-state, nor was the loss of the Ottoman caliphate entirely responsible. The more critical component behind the change was the immediate prospect of the establishment of a local, Egyptian absolute monarchy. Despite the fact that by 1926 the "Ottoman religious-political order was dead," Muslim thinkers still had to deal with Ottoman *spolia in se*, such as the threat of a khedive-turned-sultan-turned-king without the Ottoman imperial oversight.[9] Before 1914, there had been moments of imagining Egypt without its khedivial lords. Some Muslim jurists had concluded that it was the khedives who were the cause of the country's sorry state rather than the British occupation.[10] Yet in post-war Egypt imperial norms continued to define the political order in the shape of dynastic state. Finally, even some Muslim scholars viewed the monarchy as the only solution to the question of how a previously subordinated Muslim polity could integrate simultaneously into the British Empire and the League-world while preserving Islam.

I shall begin by exploring the making of the post-Ottoman Egyptian monarchy; then move on to explore the history of what I call the "*shari'a* apparatus," including the courts and the office of the Grand Mufti. Finally, I identify the main features of the Ottoman Hanafi doctrine of imperial authority, which was the ideology behind the *shari'a* apparatus. In the 1920s, jurists changed this ideology by reviving an old doctrine that saw nonimperial Muslim authority as a form of contractual representation. This reworked ideology came to be called "Islamic popular sovereignty" in the second half of the twentieth century, and it became the public ideology of the Society of Muslim Brothers, known today as the Muslim Brotherhood.

By "*shari'a* apparatus," I mean an institutional-discursive domain which includes the Grand Mufti, the *qadi* (*shari'a*) courts, their judges and lawyers, their schools and publications, and the laws and regulations that prescribe their sphere of jurisdiction. Occasionally, even non-*shari'a* jurists became part of this conglomerate by publishing opinions, questions, or essays in the specialized *shari'a* law journals. This ensemble of professionals, institutions, and ideas emerged in nineteenth-century Egypt as a local *shari'a* realm, and it came to define Egypt's post-Ottoman period up to 1955 and even later. In other post-Ottoman local states we can observe similar hierarchical institutionalizations, so often in fact that scholars label the *'ulama'* in the twentieth century as "clergy."[11] When local rulers in the 1920s acquired an official body of local Muslim jurists, the structural conditions required for feudalizing Arabs in the twentieth century were complete.

In terms of ideology, the jurists who reactivated the old idea of representation included *shari'a* practitioners such as the Grand Mufti Bakhit, activists such as Sheikh Rashid Rida, and non-*shari'a* lawyers such as the famous 'Abd al-Razzaq al-Sanhuri (1895–1971). In historical writing, these individuals stand at the center of their own distinct narratives: Bakhit, for instance, figures in the study of Islamic doctrines, while al-Sanhuri is celebrated as the writer of the 1940s and 50s civil codes in Egypt, Iraq, and Syria.[12] In this chapter, I will, however, de-center their stories, situating the young al-Sanhuri alongside old Bakhit and many other jurists in the 1920s *shari'a* apparatus.

Dynastication, 1919–1923

The story begins with the making of a new Egyptian sultanship and kingship under the British Empire. After the death of Husayn Kamil, a new dynastic regime was hastily put together between 1919 and 1923 for new Sultan-turned-King Fuad. This process of "dynastication" involved imperial declarations, sexual politics, and local legal measures. The goal was to obstruct the establishment of a republic in Egypt and the return of the Ottoman khedivate—a pressing need for the British Empire in this period of post-war uprisings.

What was indeed at stake in Egyptian domestic politics under the British iron umbrella in the 1920s was whether the country would become a Muslim republic instead of a monarchy.[13] A group of nationalist landowners, led by the legendary Sa'd Zaghlul, were openly against the new monarchy; Muslim scholars were divided; and there were constant demonstrations, pro- and contra-Palace. It took some time for the *shari'a* apparatus to decide. In November 1924, at the height of tensions between Fuad and Sa'd Zaghlul, Azhari students incited demonstrations and shouted "[There should be] no president, only the king!"[14]

How then is a king made? In Egypt the situation was quite unlike that of 1920 Damascus, where ambitions to establish a post-Ottoman monarchy were immediately assailed by multiple challenges. The combination of a long-established khedival family in Cairo and firm British overlordship ensured the smooth emergence of a new dynastic regime. The British High Commission made a pact with Sultan Fuad who had nervously watched the negotiations over Egypt's status in the wake of the 1919 revolt. He had much to lose: as things stood, he received an annual sum of 150,000 EGP from the government budget for his personal expenses.[15] When al-Azhar University issued declarations demanding a British withdrawal in late 1919, visiting Lord Milner immediately asked High Commissioner Allenby to persuade Fuad "to exercise that authority to defend our own. It was for him and not for us to deal with [. . .] the leaders of the Muslim religious community." Fuad, somewhat reluctantly, talked to Grand Mufti Bakhit and the rector of al-Azhar the same afternoon.[16] In return, Milner assured the sultan that any British-Egyptian agreement would "put him and his Ministers in the forefront of any settlement."[17]

Alongside British imperial support, sexual politics also played a role in strengthening Fuad's position. He was hitherto unmarried and feared that due to his lack of a son and heir, he might one day be forced to abdicate. To redress this danger, in 1919 he married Nazlı, from a Franco-Ottoman Egyptian family, who in January 1920 bore him a son called Faruq.[18] High Commissioner Allenby, in the name of the British king, immediately stated that regnal succession would henceforth be by male primogeniture. Zaghlul's Wafd party rejected the validity of Allenby's proclamation, possibly acting in unison with resentful princes.[19] In their protest, submitted to all foreign diplomatic representatives in Egypt, the Wafd recognized monarchical rule as legitimate, but they denied the right of the British Empire to legislate matters of succession. "Only [the Egyptian nation] alone has the right to establish this order."[20] Another party, the "National Party," protested that the British had acted in disregard of international law and pointed out that their revision of the order of succession was an act of imperialism.[21]

Fuad's action in creating a constitutional system before there was a written constitution was based on the principle of imperial recognition, a familiar usage in other contexts of transformation where local kings were considered legally indispensable to maintaining an imperial relationship.[22] Upon the proclamation of independence, on 15 March 1922, Sultan Fuad assumed the title "King of Egypt." One Foreign Office official cynically commented, "The Sultan can call himself Majesty or Grand Panjandrum or anything else he likes."[23] Nevertheless, the Foreign Office suggested that the British ruler should use the occasion to bolster relations and send his congratulations, even if he did not like this "debasement of the coinage of current language."[24] In doing so, one Foreign Office official wrote, the British king would be responding in the same way as to the enthronements of Sharif al-Husayn in Mecca, Prince Nicholas in Montenegro, and Prince Ferdinand in Bulgaria, all of whom had assumed the royal title at some point.[25] In fact, the title that Fuad had initially wanted to assume, and which the Ottoman-Egyptian patricians supported, was "King of Egypt and the Sudan," the latter being a bid towards securing recognition of the Sudan as an Egyptian and not a British territory. The first drafts of the 1923 constitution contained this title, but the High Commission forced the committee to delete it. The question whether the Egyptian ruler was also the ruler of the Sudan (and even the Hijaz in the late 1920s)—a truly mini-imperial idea that foresaw Egypt as a Red Sea power—was to create much tension until the 1960s.[26]

Over the course of 1922, Fuad issued a royal decree (*amr karim*) establishing succession by primogeniture (n. 25/1922), and a series of other orders that hastily built up a legal structure for the dynasty before the proclamation of a constitution. (In June 1922, a drafting committee started to discuss its articles). These decrees significantly reconfigured the previous social hierarchy of the Ottoman khedivial elite, promoting some to new positions and removing others from long-held positions of privilege; at the same time, they also created a legal and financial basis whereby Fuad could control the various branches of his immediate family. Fuad additionally created a special royal court to decide matters of personal status in the dynasty, comprised of Muslim members only. This measure enabled him to restrict the political activities of family members.[27] The court, an anonymous explanation argued, was based on *shari'a* and the "laws of the kingdom," and bound the princes and princesses to the king.[28] The regulation of this royal court-council was eventually spelled out in a complicated 65-point royal decree in July 1922.[29]

In the light of continued British military presence and Fuad's own manipulations, the text of the 1923 constitution made the already codified monarchical regime a meta-constitutional system. The constitution announced that "the form of government of Egypt is hereditary monarchy," "and its [regime] form is representative" (*wa-shakluha niyabi*) (article 1).[30] The drafting committee, especially members 'Abd al-'Aziz Fahmi and Husayn Rushdi, were veterans of British-affiliated legal institutions and knew the ruler's expectations.[31] Fuad himself had studied the Belgian constitution while others looked at the Romanian one, seeking to determine how best to create a constitutional order for an independent monarchy.[32] The king, at the end, viewed the constitution as a "dishonest farce."[33]

During the sessions of the constitutional committee in 1922, which considered only drafts already framed by a drafting committee, the regime form was indirectly debated. Members, such as ex-Grand Mufti Muhammad Bakhit, could not openly oppose the regime form prescribed by the old khedivial elite and the British authorities. One lengthy discussion was devoted to decision n. 51 of the drafting committee (in the first draft constitution it became article 36 and in the final text article 38) which concerned the right of the king to dissolve the elected lower house of the parliament (*haqq hall majlis al-nuwwab*). Bakhit, and others, opposed giving this right to the king in the constitution. The ex-Grand Mufti burst out "there is no such right in any constitution! And if there is, show me the text which gives right to the king to dissolve parliament in case of disagreement between him and the parliament!" As a response, the royalist 'Abd al-Latif al-Makbati noted that opposition to this right might lead to the accusation that the committee wanted to create a republic, as "recent events in Europe led to the acceptance of the republican regime and the general rejection of the monarchical regime and led to the spread of Communist ideas (*al-afkar al-shuyuʿiyya*)." The members had already voted to enshrine the principle of the *umma* as the source of sovereignty. To avoid the spread of republican-Communist ideas, al-Makbati was quick to insist that "here we must protect our monarchical order because it is the only one which fits our nature and customs." Thus, he suggested keeping the king's right to dissolve parliament as a means to avoid giving too much power to the elected representatives; because "we have to have the most modern principles while we also protect the monarchical regime form" because constitution-makers should "protect the *umma* from itself."[34]

There was no further question about the regime form registered in the printed proceedings of the committee. The constitution as a text appeared as part of a royal order (*amr malaki*) (n. 42/1923), which constitutes its preamble.[35] For this reason, legal experts and historians later debated whether the constitution was a "grant from the king" (*minha min al-malik*), that is, whether the king stood outside or within the constitution. In either case, the 1923 Egyptian constitution was an act of explicitly counterrevolutionary constitutionalism.[36]

A POST-OTTOMAN HEADACHE

The last threat to the new local monarchy was the Ottoman past, embodied in the person of ex-khedive Abbas Hilmi II. In the early months of the war, a saying circulated among Egyptian peasants: *Allah hayy . . . ʿAbbas gayy* ("God lives . . . Abbas returns"). To this day one finds it inscribed on jewelry and talismans.[37] Ex-khedive Abbas had engaged in propaganda activities for the Ottoman government during the war, and subsequently advocated for Egypt remaining "attached to Turkey."[38] Throughout the 1920s, he remained a post-Ottoman headache for both the Allied Powers and Fuad. In June 1922, an Arabic pamphlet appeared in Egypt in which he disputed Fuad's very right to rule.[39] Fuad's answer was yet another special decree issued in July 1922, whereby he liquidated all the ex-khedive's property and restricted his rights, going so far as to ban him from entering Egyptian territory. While this decree had the effect of marginalizing the ex-khedive, it also had the unintended consequence of making him once again extremely wealthy again, as the liquidation netted him an immense sum of money.[40]

The resolution of the khedive's claims is a somewhat complicated story of post-Ottoman internationalism. The new republican Turkish government had returned Abbas Hilmi's properties in new Turkey and granted him Turkish citizenship.[41] Fuad hoped to tar Abbas Hilmi's reputation within Egypt by spreading rumors that he was behind an assassination attempt against Sa'd Zaghlul. In 1924, the king temporarily managed to achieve the restriction of Abbas Hilmi's movements in Europe. Soon after, however, Turkish president Mustafa Kemal intervened on Abbas Hilmi's behalf, securing permission from the French government for Abbas to remain in Paris. Perhaps in return, Abbas Hilmi acknowledged and supported the Turkish suspension of the caliphate in 1924.[42] The French government saw an opportunity to eliminate the source of tension: they allowed the ex-khedive to reside in France as a Turkish subject if he declared that he had renounced his Egyptian citizenship and ceased his maneuvers. The ex-khedive, somewhat embarrassed, signed the declaration in February 1925 in a small office of the French Foreign Ministry. King Fuad was satisfied.[43]

The Shari'a Apparatus and the Rise of the Grand Mufti

Historians have shown how missionary activity tested the concept of religious freedom in Egypt during the transition to the world of the League of Nations.[44] In this section, I seek to explore how the Egyptian shari'a apparatus made sense of the monarchy and the new territorial status in terms of Islamic law. In their own ways, these religious thinkers also wanted to protect the umma from itself.

Let us first consider the rise of the shari'a apparatus and its relations to the other court-systems in Egypt.[45] Like all other Ottoman provinces, Egypt by 1914 already possessed a bifurcated legal domain: there were qadi (shari'a) courts and there were administrative or "civil" courts. But unlike the administrative courts (called nizamiye in Ottoman Turkish) in other provinces, the khedivial administrative courts were called "local" (ahli in Arabic; the British occupiers called them "native" courts). In both shari'a and ahli courts, Arabic was generally the language of administration. From 1876, there existed a third legal platform: mixed courts with European judges that adjudicated disputes between Europeans and the khedivial government, and between Europeans and local subjects. These mixed courts usually operated in French and Italian, and used a special code of law. As a result of the Capitulations, consular courts also maintained their own jurisdictions for their subjects.[46]

In Egypt, the scope and sway of Ottoman imperial legal authority was severely reduced in the course of the long nineteenth century. The core of the *shari'a* apparatus was its court-system, which was still "Ottoman" in a constitutional sense until 1914. The sultan's legal power flowed through the *kadı* of Cairo.[47] In 1856, the governor Said Pasha took over the sultanic right of appointing judges in the Egyptian province, except in the juridical district of Cairo (Cairo and Suez), which remained under direct sultanic authority until 1876.[48] The *kadı* of Cairo remained a contested position between the sultan and the khedive. In 1880, the courts became codified administratively as a *shari'a* court "system." In 1914, it consisted of two summary courts—one in Alexandria and the other in Cairo—for smaller cases; numerous courts of premier instance; and a supreme court in Cairo. The *shari'a* courts' jurisdiction was confined to personal law and the administration of the important pious foundations. As elsewhere in the Ottoman Empire, both before and after the war, *shari'a* judges brought their verdicts without reference to political authority. This three-tier hierarchy remained essentially in place until 1955.[49]

To some extent, the *shari'a* apparatus also included the "government"—local, administrative—legal system until the 1880s, just as the *nizamiye* courts did in the directly governed Ottoman regions. The administrative court was an autochthonous development of legal reform in late Ottoman Egypt. Beginning in 1852, the khedives set up judicial councils (sing. *majlis*) in the cities and countryside, whose members included local notables and *shari'a* jurists, to adjudicate offenses based on the Ottoman Penal Code. The khedivial legislative council extended the *majlis*-system in the 1860s and institutionalized it in 1871; the councils were now able to adjudicate issues such as inheritance that had hitherto come under the jurisdiction of *qadi* courts. Through a sequence of reforms in 1881 and, after the establishment of the British occupation, in 1883 these legal forums came to be reorganized as "local" (*ahli*) "courts." Now they were sharply distinguished from the *qadi* courts and thus placed outside of the *shari'a* apparatus. Similar to the central *nizamiye* reforms in the 1880s, in khedivial Egypt new legal roles emerged, such as that of the public persecutor. These shifts took time, however, and a shortage of personnel meant that it was not until the end of the 1880s that the *ahli* courts took over the functions of the judicial councils in the countryside.

In civil cases, the *ahli* judge issued his verdict in the name of the khedive and not in the Ottoman sultan. The earliest such verdict that I found in print is from the Mansura primary court in 1885, issued "in the name of His Majesty the Khedive" (*bi-ism al-khadra al-khidiwiyya*).[50] As late as December 1914, verdicts were still issued "in the name of the Khedive of Egypt Abbas Hilmi Pasha, the most exalted khedive" (*bi-ism al-Janab al-Khidiwi al-Afham 'Abbas Hilmi Basha Khidiw Misr*).[51] Soon after the beginning of the war and the British declaration about ceasing Egypt's Ottoman status, however, the *ahli* judges gave their verdicts "in the name of His Grandness Husayn Kamil, Sultan of Egypt" (*bi-Ism Sahib al-'Uzma Husayn Kamil Sultan Misr*), and after 1922, they did so in the name of King Fuad. Importantly, in criminal cases the *ahli* judges issued their verdicts without any reference to authority. (From 1883 on, the courts ceased applying the Ottoman Penal Code, adopting in its place a new British-Egyptian Penal Code.) In civil cases, the judges applied the Egyptian Civil Code, which was a mixture of *shari'a* principles and French law; and they often looked at the Ottoman *Mecelle* as comparison.[52]

Importantly, the *shari'a* judges were only one part of the apparatus. There was also the legal jurisconsult (*mufti*) to consider, who in khedivial Egypt attained a much more important role than in other Ottoman provinces. Emad Helal has demonstrated that the khedivial government appointed an army of muftis to various government offices to harmonize administrative decisions between the 1850s and the 1910s. Often, legal historians postulate a sharp contrast between the *ahli* courts and the *shari'a* apparatus, but in fact the relationship between the two systems was more complicated. For instance, muftis provided opinions about murder cases for the *ahli* courts until 1920.[53]

In the post-Ottoman period, the Grand Mufti sat at the top of Egypt's *shari'a* apparatus. The 1914 abolishment of the somewhat depleted office of the Ottoman *kadı* of Cairo left the local Grand Mufti as the highest institutional authority on revealed law. This office as part of official bureaucracy had begun to be formed under Mehmed Ali and was formalized when Said Pasha issued an order in 1855 that only the Hanafi mufti of Cairo was authorized to issue legal opinions (*ifta'*). Europeans began to call the holder of this office "the Grand Mufti of Egypt," but officially the title remained "the mufti of the Hanafi lords in the Egyptian lands" (*mufti al-sada al-hanafiyya al-diyar al-Misriyya*), and often the honorific title *shaykh al-islam* was attached to it. Only in 1886 did the office become "the mufti of the Egyptian lands" (*mufti al-diyar al-Misriyya*). Thus was born, in Egypt, the government office of "Grand Mufti."[54]

Wael Hallaq has regarded legal bodies presided over by a ruler in the early period of Islamic law as "extrajudicial," representing the state's (the ruler's) "interference" with *shari'a*.[55] While there is little empirical support for his theory in the Ottoman period, it certainly seems to apply to the post-Ottoman age.[56] After 1914, the most important goal of the *shari'a* apparatus was to ensure that revelation remained an integral part of Egyptians' legal life, and it worked hard to maintain a sharp distinction between *shari'a* and non-*shari'a*. The normative tools of this enterprise were the legal opinions of muftis and Grand Muftis. Approximately 21,000 Grand Mufti legal opinions were issued between 1914 and 1945.[57] Today, despite the 1955 abolition of the *shari'a* courts, the Grand Mufti in Egypt is still in charge of explaining and interpreting legal principles in those domains where the Egyptian government acknowledges *shari'a*, such as marriage and inheritance laws.[58]

Despite some scholars belittling their importance, the *shari'a* courts played a key role in the social life of the interwar occupied Kingdom of Egypt.[59] Their jurisdiction continued to be confined to personal law (marriage, divorce, and inheritance) and to matters involving pious endowments (if the endowed assets, or at least the most valuable ones, lay within their juridical districts or if the trustees lived there).[60] But even this limited jurisdiction gave them enormous influence over the everyday lives of millions of Muslim Egyptians, including the Muslim elite of the country. The administration of the courts fell to the Ministry of Justice, under a distinct office called the Administration of *Shari'a* Courts. The judges had to be properly educated scholars of Muslim law. Between 1907 and 1930, a special school for *shari'a* law (*Madrasat al-Qada' al-Shara'i*) trained specialized personnel: judges, muftis, lawyers. (There was constant rivalry between al-Azhar mosque-university and this school.) The lawyers also needed specialist training, and thus until the 1950s there existed a distinct group of *shari'a* lawyers. The Grand Mufti, the courts, their personnel, the professors in the schools, and the lawyers together formed the main components of the interwar *shari'a* apparatus.[61]

Allied armies and the new Arab governments in the 1920s considered the Egyptian *shari'a* apparatus a good model for repurposing the Ottoman *qadi* courts into the new local systems. In all occupied Ottoman territories, the *shari'a* courts were accordingly refashioned on the Egyptian model. In Palestine, OETA South established a Central *Waqf* Committee in Jerusalem to replace the Ottoman Ministry of Pious Endowments in 1920. After lengthy negotiations, in 1921 the new High Commissioner Herbert Samuel established the Supreme Muslim Council, which controlled endowments, and appointed both the judges in *shari'a* courts and the muftis in Palestine (two independent functions in the late modern Ottoman system). As is common in instances of *spolia in re*, Council members regarded their institution as continuous with the Ottoman *şeyhülislam* office.[62] In 1921, in the French-occupied territories, the French High Commission created a *Côntrole générale des waqfs musulmans* that encompassed all territories under their mandate, and which reported directly to the High Commissioner.[63] From 1926, the Lebanese Shiʻi community possessed their own courts, and Shiʻi scholars adjudicated endowment cases in these new Jaʻfari courts, although they still reported to the *Côntrole générale*.[64] In British Iraq, the 1921 "temporary" law regarding *shariʻa* court procedures confirmed the courts' jurisdiction over *awqaf*.[65] In 1923, King Faysal of Iraq designated territories where two judges (a Sunni and a Shiʻi—Jaʻfari) could be appointed. The Jaʻfari courts could hear cases involving endowments where the endower was shiʻi.[66]

These changes in the local legal administrations completed the remaking of the Ottoman imperial legal system. New Arab governments copied the Egyptian example and appointed Grand Muftis while they simultaneously abolished all provincial *qadi* offices as unwanted reminders of Ottoman power (a typical example is Lebanon in 1932). The institution of the Grand Mufti thus emerged as the epitome of a new *shariʻa* in the divided, post-Ottoman world.

Who Is the Imam? The Ottoman Hanafi Doctrine of Muslim Executive Authority

The ideology of the *shariʻa* apparatus played a profound epistemic role in creating a new logic in Muslim constituent thought.[67] Its sources lay in the Ottoman Hanafi doctrines of Muslim government to which the parties comprising this apparatus subscribed, and which had a central place in the empire until its end. Thanks to some outstanding work in the last thirty years, it is possible now to reconstruct a picture of these doctrines.[68] We should consider these features of the Ottoman imperial ideology for the light they shed on the *spolia* of Islamic law in the postwar Arab world.

In the Ottoman Empire, Muslim jurists used the Arabic words *imam*, *wali al-amr*, *sultan*, and *amir* to denote the highest governing office in the community. (Although rarely they also used the term *khalifa*, professional jurists preferred *imam* and *wali al-amr* when referring to the executive-legal function of the ruler.) These expressions denote a Muslim leader who holds effective administrative power, without making any explicit ascription of the caliphal office. All of these words *can* pertain to a caliph, of course, and did so in the Ottoman context. Yet, they also made it possible to apply universal principles to local circumstances, when the actual Muslim ruler was not a caliph, or was only the caliph's representative, as in the case of the khedive, the governor of the Egyptian province.[69]

In imperial Hanafi doctrine, the imam did not have a representative relationship to the Muslim community. The Ottoman imam was not an artificial person. To borrow Kantorowicz's formula, there were no "two bodies" of the imam. Although a contractual theory of the imamate (caliphate) had existed in pre-Ottoman Muslim polities, Ebu-Su'ud, the influential sixteenth-century imperial Hanafi mufti of Istanbul (şeyhülislam in Turkish), ignored it and instead advanced the idea of a hereditary imamate, which directly represented God.[70] This doctrine remained in use until the end of the empire. The 1876 and 1908 Ottoman constitutions maintained the principle that the caliphal office devolved hereditarily within the Ottoman dynasty.

The sultan as imam was a source of law. The post-sixteenth-century Hanafi jurists held Ottoman imperial ordinances (qanun) to be indispensably authoritative, but not absolute. The mufti of Istanbul, the şeyhülislam, installed the Ottoman sultan and could legally depose him.[71] The sultan's imperial decree could not change a qadi's decision.[72] The imam was only one source of jurisdiction, although his existence was indispensable for the functioning of other sources of law: shari'a and local custom. The Muslim jurists and the imam shared jurisdictional abilities.

The imam—the sultan—in the legal Ottoman empire had the power to issue ordinances in harmony with revealed law. According to Ebu-Su'ud, the imam was a legislator and legal interpreter. He was the distributor of the Muslims' common property (thus his decision could impact property rights). The imam also guarded God's rights to punish people guilty of fornication, drunkenness, robbery, and theft on Earth. He was required to punish these sins. Importantly, in theory he had no right to punish homicide because that right belonged to individuals, not to God. The Hanafi school also prescribed the imam's authority to perform the main Muslim duties in worship. For instance, the Friday congregational prayer was only valid if the imam or his delegate led it. This requirement clearly benefitted a centralized, imperial hierarchy of Muslim preaching.[73]

Ottoman Hanafi jurists used the expression wali al-amr ("the person in charge") to denote the imam's function in deciding practical, economic issues. One of their late successors, Jad al-Haqq (d. 1996), a famous Hanafi Grand Mufti of Egypt and Rector of al-Azhar in the 1980s, helps to explain this concept's legal genealogy. In a case that related to finance, al-Haqq once opined that the idea of wali al-amr did indeed have an economic origin, being based on a saying attributed to the Caliph 'Umar: "I took the same position concerning God's wealth as the legal guardian of an orphan (wali al-yatim). I took it when I was in need and when my circumstances improved I returned it. If I had plenty of wealth I stayed away from it." In Jad al-Haqq's eyes, this saying authorized Egypt's republican military government in the 1980s to function as the final authority over the Muslims' economic interest. He highlighted that al-Shafi'i (d. 820), the godfather of the Shafi'i legal school, had codified this principle of the imam's guardianship. Jad al-Haqq stated that "the imam's position in relation to the subjects is the same position as the legal guardian of an orphan." He sought also to attach (Ottoman) Hanafi authors to this principle, thus rooting it soundly in Hanafi genealogy as well.[74]

In the Ottoman province of Egypt, *wali al-amr* meant the sultan and his governor—the khedive in the late nineteenth century—as his representative (*na'ib*). As we have seen, the sources of law were plural: Islamic jurists; selected Ottoman imperial laws; the khedive's "exalted order" (*al-amr al-'ali*; issued in his capacity as the representative of the sultan); for brief periods legislative assemblies, and for foreign subjects consular jurisdiction (as a result of the Capitulations). After the establishment of British occupation in 1882, the laws were still issued in the name of the khedive by exalted orders, because the sultan (through his representative the khedive) remained the imam of Egypt until 1914. Certain Ottoman imperial laws continued to be applied in Egypt. For instance, lawyers and courts recognized that the Ottoman Law of Mines (1869) and the law on the ownership of land by foreigners (1867) continued to regulate properties in 1900s Egypt.[75]

In sum, the imperial Ottoman Hanafi doctrine of government accommodated 1) the hereditary imamate; 2) the legislative power of the imam; 3) his delegation of jurisdictional and ritual functions; and 4) his distributive role in property matters. At the same time, however, the doctrine 5) did not accept the absolute indivisibility of the basis of legislation; and 6) it upheld that neither God nor individuals delegated *all* their natural rights to the imam. The imperial caliph was not a sole, indivisible, law-making artificial person, an "authority" in the Hobbesian sense but was instead an "authority" (*wali al-amr*) in the imperial sense of Ebu-Su'ud Efendi. The imperial ideology of Muslim government was shared by the Egyptian *shari'a* apparatus because the khedivate remained a subordinated Ottoman princely region until 1914.

Wali al-Amr *as a Transformer:*
Monarchy and Popular Sovereignty, 1914–1928

How did the *shari'a* apparatus react to the making of a constitutional monarchy after the war? How did the Ottoman imperial ideology change into a local Muslim one? The Grand Muftis' legal opinions, court decisions, and the many essays in the journals of the *shariʿa* lawyers attest to three basic challenges.

First, the apparatus had to explain the very existence of a Muslim polity, Egypt, outside of the still-existing Ottoman caliphate, and under the British protectorate during the war. Second, they had to accommodate the simultaneous establishment of a dynasty and a national constitution during the years 1922 and 1923. Finally, they had to make sense of the crisis resulting from the collapse of the Ottoman caliphate in 1924. It was this last issue that posed the biggest intellectual challenge, since the loss of the caliphate was a stark affront to the Ottoman Hanafi doctrine, which conceptualized the imperial imamate as the fundamental glue in Muslim law in Egypt. In fact, even as these difficulties remained unresolved, the *shariʿa* courts continued going about their business; and, in any case, muftis tacitly acknowledged the new government and King Fuad as *wali al-amr* in the 1920s. What was needed was a new *shariʿa*-based ideology that could respond simultaneously to the challenges posed by an autocrat Muslim ruler and to the advocates of Western secular constitutionalism.

To this end, the Egyptian *apparatus* adapted the core elements of the imperial Hanafi doctrine to the new political status quo by creating a binding ideal, an "authority" in the Hobbesian sense, of the imam in legal doctrine. This entailed replacing Ottoman-era norms with norms dating back to the pre-Ottoman period, namely: 1) no longer recognizing the imam as a law-maker and legal interpreter in theory, and 2) reframing the Muslim community as the source of the imam's authority (*wilaya*) in a *contractual* form. The project's aim was to harmonize Muslim doctrine with the 1923 constitution, as a contractual understanding of the imam's authority better lent itself to modern constitutional thinking about the will of the populace. The *shariʿa*-men also began to apply various canons of Islamic law interchangeably, although the Hanafi doctrines remained the central norms.[76] Let us address their challenges one by one.

1. ENDING THE OTTOMAN CALIPHATE IN EGYPT

During the First World War, the *shariʿa* apparatus resolved the first of the three afore-mentioned challenges by opting not to reflect on the problem. Sultan Husayn Kamil himself announced that he was now the highest Muslim executive authority in one of his first decrees (n. 16, 20 June 1915): he declared to have "general legal authority" (*al-wilaya al-ʿamma al-sharʿiyya*) in matters involving pious endowments. As *wali al-amr*, he appointed the Minister of Pious Endowments temporary trustee of those pious endowments whose administration was changing (i.e., the endowments whose administrators remained Ottoman—enemy—subjects, such as the ex-khedive) until the courts designated new administrators as stipulated by the founders.[77]

Muhammad Bakhit, the Grand Mufti appointed in December 1914, took a cautious approach to the question of the imperial imamate between 1914 and 1920 when he was deposed. This becomes apparent when we consider the case of the Friday prayer, which was, as noted in the previous chapters, one of the symbolic markers of Muslim authority.[78] The December 1914 government declaration that severed Egypt from the Ottoman sultanate did not include an explicit declaration about the status of the caliphate in Egypt. Soon however, Bakhit (and Salim al-Bishri, the rector of al-Azhar at the time) declared that the Friday prayer should include the name of Husayn Kamil, and not that of the Ottoman caliph.[79] In one legal opinion issued during the war, Bakhit affirmed the previous Hanafi imperial interpretation: only the imam of the community (the caliph) or his representative could lead the Friday prayer. He did not specify, however, who that imam was. But he did mention that the Shafi'i and Maliki schools did not stipulate that the imam should assign the leader of the Friday prayer, and by this gesture, he offered a solution to this sensitive question.[80] We have seen that neither the Syrian sheikh Rashid Rida nor other Muslim utopian activists objected to declaring Sharif al-Husayn a purely spiritual caliph in Mecca in the 1910s. Some, such as Mustafa al-Maraghi, the *Qadi* of the Sudan, privately suggested to the British High Commission in 1915 that the British authorities should allow the sultan of Egypt to become a caliph, arguing that Qurayshi descent (that is, Arab ethnicity) was not a precondition for the Muslims' obedience. Sultan Husayn Kamil indeed preferred himself to Sharif al-Husayn as the candidate for a new caliphate in 1916–17.[81]

When, after the 1919 uprising, the visiting Lord Milner interviewed the Grand Mufti in December of that year, Bakhit declared that "Turkey has no political rights in Egypt, only religious rights."[82] Lord Milner was surprised and took the view that this was incorrect given that the Ottoman sultan clearly had political rights in pre-1914 Egypt. The only explanation for Bakhit's argument is that Bakhit also accepted the idea of a purely religious, pope-like caliph at the time. The nationalist Grand Mufti may also have calculated on retaining some type of relationship between Egypt and the Ottoman caliph after the war concluded, but at the same time would have wanted to uphold Egypt's independence in the eyes of the British politicians. Egyptian elites had generated a myth about the existence of a pre-1914 independent Egypt in order to bolster their demands to send a delegation to the Peace Conference in 1919, at the height of the Wilsonian moment. Bakhit appears to have emphasized this claim to Lord Milner in the same year. Perhaps unsurprisingly, within a year Bakhit was removed from office.[83]

2. DYNASTY AND CONSTITUTION

The second challenge, namely explaining in Islamic terms the establishment of a dynasty and a national constitution, came to the fore in the fateful spring of 1922 when Fuad simultaneously declared independence and his own accession to kingship. This was a clear instance of imperial constitutionalism in which regime form and legal sovereignty were bound together. I have been unable to find any public comments from the Egyptian *shari'a* apparatus on the monarchical form of government, apart from Bakhit's outburst in the 1922 committee meeting. In public, ordinary Egyptians received the announcements with cold indifference. In Port Said on the Suez Canal, Egyptian workers and efendis were unenthusiastic and skeptical because they still saw British soldiers on the streets.[84] Privately, even elite Egyptians expressed hatred of the dynasty.[85] A student's essay in the *Shari'a* Law School's journal of August 1922 took the view that if the people were free to choose an imam, the position would be more like that the president of a republic than a king. But Egyptians "preferred," he added sarcastically, "a king like the British."[86] Law professors, such as Ahmad Ibrahim (1874–1945), a student of reformer Muhammad 'Abduh and a prominent teacher in the *Shari'a* Law School, argued that in the age of elected parliaments, an imam could be also elected like the president of a republic, or affirmed through dynastic succession (*wilayat al-'ahd*) if a law were to codify this option.[87]

In order to reconcile a monarch and a codified popular constitution, the *shari'a* apparatus needed to find a way of restricting the king's authority in a manner that simultaneously affirmed their own importance. Rather than debating the respective merits of republican and monarchical orders, the jurists simply accepted the monarchy—though with a number of conditions. For instance, when the Egyptian government first considered abolishing the office of the Grand Mufti, the now ex-Grand Mufti Bakhit issued a pamphlet to defend the office by claiming that if there were no such position, the executive authority (*wali al-amr*) would risk becoming a sinner (*athim*). Bakhit referred not only to the example of the Prophet, who appointed his own representatives— among them officials whom Bakhit interpreted as "muftis"—but also to Ibn Khaldun, who prescribed legal interpretation as part of the duty not only of the caliphate, but also of "executive kingship" (*al-mulukiyya al-sultaniyya*).[88] Such arguments cemented an ideological relationship between the local monarch and the local shari'a apparatus in the 1920s in the language of constitutionalism.

3. IDENTIFYING REPRESENTATION WITH THE CALIPHATE: RIDA, BAKHIT, SANHURI

The third problem (how to respond to the Turkish Assembly's restriction of caliphate authority to matters of religion in late 1922, and its eventual abolishment of the office in 1924) posed a mighty epistemological challenge. Soon, in 1928, the Egyptian *shari'a* apparatus also had to cope with the fact that King Fuad proclaimed a new constitution with almost unlimited monarchical power. Confronted with these challenges, the apparatus reconfigured the Ottoman doctrine of the unelected imperial imam into the concept of an imam who contractually represented the Muslim community.

After 1922, figures such as Rashid Rida set aside their earlier ideas of a non-political Arab caliphate (discussed in previous chapters), and now instead identified the caliphate and imamate as the political leadership of Islamic government (*ri'asat al-hukuma al-islamiyya*).[89] This may have been a consequence of the ideas from the Indian Khilafat movement and, specifically, due to the engagement of Abul Kalam Azad, the movement's leader, with the caliphate. In an Urdu book whose Arabic translation was serialized in Rida's *al-Manar* between January and December 1922, Azad argued that the office of the caliph was a political position: "He is a ruler and sultan in reality."[90] By 1923, changing colors, Rashid Rida, too, depicted the caliphate as an Islamic political government, in which the caliph was elected by the representatives of the Muslim community. In the Egyptian context, the invocation of the Muslim community's power (*sultat al-umma*) was not only a message to secularists, but also a Muslim argument for a constitution and against the monarchical autocracy of Fuad. Rida identified the jurists (*ahl al-hall wa-l-'aqd*) as the carriers of the undivided caliphate in the age of global division.[91]

Rida's opinion was arguably only a well-advertised thought-experiment, but there was another, professional legal debate ongoing among the practicing Muslim jurists in Egypt. Ahmad Ibrahim, the aforementioned professor in the *Shari'a* Law School, wrote in October 1922 that the caliph was the *qa'immaqam* (the "representative," an Ottomanism in Arabic) of the Prophet in both the religious and administrative spheres.

The caliph, he wrote, is "like water: you cannot take one element out of it without terminating its being." Striking here was Ibrahim's use of the Arabic word *mulk*: "If the authority of the caliph ceases to exist in matters of administration (*mulk*), he is no more a caliph and there is no more a polity (*mulk*)."[92] He rejected the notion of a purely religious, pope-like caliph which had been widely held among Muslim activist thinkers just a few years before.

'Afifi 'Umar, a judge in the Matariyya *Shari'a* Court, took up the debate directly with the Turkish assembly. He argued in an article that there had been no distinction between religion and empire (*mulk*) until the Turkish Assembly's act of separation. His main question was whether the new, diminished caliph would have any executive power, even if only indirectly or partially. If not, the caliph would become a sort of head of a Sufi order and would be of no use to the community. 'Umar suggested one potential solution, which was perhaps the last instance of the caliph-as-pope-concept. The caliph would remain sultan in name only, and a political administration (*mulk*) would be established alongside him, with a parliament that would fashion laws according to *shari'a* principles.[93] What he suggested was to reform, and not to abolish, the imperial political order.

When in 1924 the office of the Ottoman caliph was finally abolished, there ensued a debate in the Egyptian *shari'a* apparatus. A hastily assembled committee announced that no one was now caliph, and that a caliph could be created only by Muslims swearing an oath (*bay'*) or by succession (*istikhlaf*).[94] The debate continued in 1925 with *Islam and the Foundations of Government*, a well-known publication in which the author, 'Ali 'Abd al-Raziq, a rich Azhari sheikh, argued that the caliphate was a religious office only—just as al-Kawakibi, Rida, and others had proposed before 1922. But in 1926 'Abd al-Raziq was put on trial and deprived of his position at al-Azhar; Rashid Rida now loudly argued for the political importance of the caliphate. We can perhaps interpret the decision to prosecute 'Ali 'Abd al-Raziq as an act of self-discipline by the *shari'a* apparatus and public repudiation of its previous flirtation with the idea of a pope-like caliph.[95]

In this debate, ex-Grand Mufti Bakhit adopted a modified version of Rida's new argument that the caliphate was an all-encompassing entity. On the surface, Bakhit's *The True Essence of Islam* would appear to reject 'Ali 'Abd al-Raziq's argument for the purely religious nature of the caliphate by the assertion that the caliph was in fact both a religious and political leader. But Bakhit's more important point was that the caliph represented both the Prophet *and* the Muslim community (*niyaba 'an al-nabi [. . .] niyaba 'an al-muslimin*) as the highest power. In essence, Bakhit wrote, "there is no difference between the political *mulk* and the caliphate."[96] A caliph is the representative of the Prophet and his *mulk* is *mulk siyasi shar'i*. If this is the function of the office, it does not matter whether the officer is named a caliph, imam, sultan, or king: "the meaning is important and not the titles."[97] What is critical is that the imamate is based on a contractual agreement "between the one who fulfills this position and the leaders (*ahl al-'aqd wa-l-hall*) of the Islamic community." This contract is valid even if the people recognize someone as caliph because they are afraid of him. Bakhit argued that the power (*quwwa*) of the caliph derived from the Muslim community (*al-umma al-islamiyya*), which is "represented by" the leaders of society. The imam, in turn, delegates this representative power (*sultan*) to governors, bureaucrats, and judges. The administrative-legal authority (*wilaya*) of all these people is his authority also as the simple consequence of his position as a representative of the community.[98]

The new element in Bakhit's theory was the idea that the imam is a transformer who converts virtual Muslim communal power (*quwwa*) into legislative authority (*sultan*). (This new idea may have come to him while serving on the constitutional drafting committee in 1922.) The guarantee of this change is the contract between representatives of community and the imam *qua* person of executive authority (*wali al-amr*). The character of the imam's office is open: it can be dynastic or elective; it can even be attained by violent means. Bakhit focused on the need for a process to translate the potential of the *umma* to an actual legal concept. He theorized the community as the source of authority, but he saw the imam's social contract as not directly with the community, but rather with the community's elite representatives, which is to say with Muslim jurists.

Upon King Fuad's suspension of the constitution in 1928, 'Abd al-Razzaq al-Sanhuri, a young lawyer freshly-arrived back in Cairo from Paris, further developed this new doctrine. His second French dissertation on the caliphate, published in 1926, has curious resemblances to Bakhit's 1925 book.[99] Some claim that al-Sanhuri's theory "differed from the accepted religious perception."[100] It is also presumed that al-Sanhuri's theory about the nature of the caliphate was translated into Arabic only much later.[101] Yet in a 1929 article published in the *shari'a* lawyers' journal, al-Sanhuri summarizes and refines his French theory to communicate it to the *shari'a* apparatus in Arabic. In my interpretation, this was a suggestion to reject absolute monarchy in Islamic terms.

The new royalist constitution gave extensive powers to the king (article 24: "the king and the houses of the shaykhs and representatives share legislative authority"; article 25: "laws can be only issued by the decision of the parliament and the king's agreement"; article 28: "consultation over the financial laws belong to the king alone"; article 29: "executive authority belongs to the king within the limits of the constitution"; article 49: "the king appoints the ministers").[102] Monarchical authority as defined here was not far removed from what Ottoman *shari'a* assigned to the sultan, though lacking of course the *shari'a* itself and the Ottoman Empire.[103]

Al-Sanhuri's 1929 article offered a response to the threat of absolutism by proposing a structural reconfiguration of *shari'a* norms. He began this exercise in legal spoliation by stating that the Prophet established an Islamic government with authority (*wilaya*) over all worldly issues. He made a distinction, however, between religion—a constant, unchanging relationship between the creator and the creation—and the state. The state is 1) subject to the rule of reason, with the consequence that even the Prophet had to seek consultation on issues of government; and 2) subject to place and time, meaning that worldly laws can change and evolve. Al-Sanhuri remarks that the Prophet, in his role as the chief executive of the government, can be rightly called king (*malik*). He defines "Islamic law" (*al-qanun al-islami*) as applicable only to transactions (*mu'amalat*) of two kinds: those between individuals (private, *khassa*) and those between people and government (public, *'amma*), this latter category including the laws about government itself. He acknowledges that this is a "new division" within Islamic thought but argues that it is nevertheless useful, allowing one to situate both the civil code and constitutional law within Islamic legal theory. This structural innovation, subsequently widely adopted by many Muslim jurists, enabled the rethinking of constitutional matters in a new way.

Al-Sanhuri argues that only God has legislative power (*sultan*), and that God's legislation is available to humans from three sources: the Koran, the *sunna* of the Prophet, and, after the death of the Prophet, the consensus of the community (*ijma'*). The latter is expressed not by the community as a whole but by its learned representatives, who embody the community through their knowledge—just as Bakhit had previously affirmed in 1925. Thus, al-Sanhuri reaches the unsurprising conclusion that Islamic government is government by Muslim jurists. There is thus no room in Islam for an absolute ruler (*al-sayyid al-mutlaq*), because the caliph has no legislative power, and is entitled to participate in the legislative process only if he is a learned scholar. Legislative authority (*sultan*) lies with the community; in reality, therefore, "the community is the caliph of God on his Earth."

In al-Sanhuri's view, the caliphate as an institution is thus a very special form of government; the caliph as a person 1) has executive authority over all Muslims (*wali umur al-muslimin*) within the boundaries of the Koran and the *sunna*; and 2) is the leader (*imam*) in the ethical sense of being the human core of community rituals such as the Friday prayer and the pilgrimage. The caliph executes rules in consultation with scholars, and he can devise new principles in the revealed legal domain (*ahkam al-shariʻa*), based on the consensus of scholars, if they identify a particular interest of the community. Such executive authority is global in its reach, because Muslim unity is based on the unity of the caliphate, even if there are many governments. This, he argued, would be possible only in a League of Muslim Governments, an organization which, properly speaking, would itself constitute the caliphate, for the caliph would transfer authority to the *shariʻa* judges in all new Muslim countries even though the judges were independent.[104]

Al-Sanhuri's idea, in essence a late reincarnation of anti-Ottoman utopian federalism, marked a profound normative shift within Muslim legal-political theory. It was an ideology for a new imperial project without an imperial state. He stands on the shoulders of Rida and Bakhit in formulating this new recognition of the community as the basis of caliphal authority (he makes no mention of violence as another, unjust but legally acceptable, source of Muslim government). Yet he goes further than Rida and Bakhit when he identifies what Bakhit only termed "power" with the Christian, Hobbesian idea of sovereignty (law-making authority) based on delegated representation. The power of the virtual *umma* as popular sovereignty remained an invisible cornerstone in al-Sanhuri's later work in 1930s and 40s Egypt, Syria, and Iraq.[105]

By the 1930s, the Egyptian *shariʻa* apparatus came around to the revived consensus that the Muslim community was the main source of authority. For instance, one prominent judge, ʻAbd al-Wahhab Khallaf, a graduate of the *Shariʻa* Law School, promoted the idea that an Islamic government, by definition, is always constitutional and Muslim jurists (*ahl al-hall wa-l-ʻaqd*) represent the community. In his eyes, the supreme leadership (*al-riyasa al-ʻulya*) of an Islamic government is not the exclusive prerogative of the Quraysh tribe: rather, Muslims rightly should be able to elect anyone to such a position. Legislative powers belong to advanced scholars (*mujtahidun* and *ahl al-fataya*) for the reason that only they can interpret the law of the Islamic state, which God gave in the form of the Koran via the tongue of the Prophet. In Khallaf's eyes, all Islamic states must be theocracies: "The grand imamate, the caliphate, the leadership of the believers are all various expressions of one meaning whose form is the *'ulama*."[106] In a popular 1935 book, he declared of the caliphate: "The community (*umma*) is the source of all power"—which had been indeed the central principle also of the 1923 constitution.[107]

Such was the *shari'a* apparatus's offer, first to King Fuad and then to his son Faruq when he was crowned in the late 1930s. This new ideology now confirmed to Western epistemology and vocabularies of constitutionalism. The *shari'a*-men could recognize government of any type, even those established through violence, so long as it enforced revealed law. But unlike the ruler of the Ottoman Empire, a non-imperial Muslim ruler must accept that his power derives from the Muslim community, and must yield ground to legislation by *shari'a* jurists. This idea of a local dynast cooperating with a clergy-like group of Muslim scholars was new, and it offered a fresh doctrine by which to preserve the relevance of Islam without empire.

Conclusion

Let us take a look at a ceremony that was held in the sovereign local state of Egypt on 29 July 1937. We see the Society of Muslim Brothers setting off, flags waving, on a long, majestic march that will take them from Shubra to 'Abdin, the royal palace in Cairo. When they arrive, they raise the shout "Allahu Akbar, Grace to God!" Next, they pledge their loyalty to the young king Faruq, loudly proclaiming "Islam is the savior of humanity, the Koran is the constitution of the world, those who make a law without the Koran shall fail, we pledge ourselves to you based on the Koran and the Sunna of the Prophet."[108]

This episode, related in the 1950 first edition of Hasan al-Banna's collected writings, was carefully edited out of all subsequent versions of this work by the founder of the Brotherhood. After the 1952 military coup d'état, it was embarrassing to the Muslim Brothers that they had once pledged themselves to the hated king. But it is also possible that it was expurgated because the story it told was not exactly what happened.[109]

From January to July 1937, all of Egypt had been preparing for the celebration of young Faruq's coming of age and accession to the throne. Behind the scenes, however, there was a struggle underway, between a number of Egyptian parties that hoped to take advantage of Faruq's minority by abolishing the monarchy altogether. The British ambassador intervened, fearing that a regnal crisis would enable the spread of Italian Fascist influence.[110] The Arab uprising in mandate Palestine at that same time made the British authorities particularly anxious to retain stability. In Egypt, the Palace and monarchist notables were constantly "parading" Faruq, the young prince, before cheering masses. Their efforts led to what Matthew Ellis calls "the repackaging of the Egyptian monarchy."[111] The renewed Shaykh of al-Azhar, Muhammad Mustafa al-Maraghi—who in 1915 had requested that the

British authorities proclaim the Egyptian sultan as caliph—championed the young Faruq as a pious, Muslim prince. In the late 1930s Shaykh al-Maraghi advocated for the monarchy and a coronation, and even for making Faruq the caliph.[112] For Faruq's accession, many Muslim organizations together planned a "general Islamic ceremonial procession." The organizational committee decided that the participants should proclaim the *takbir* (Allahu Akbar!) and shout "for his Majesty the king." Sandwiched between the Muslim Youth organization and the Society for Preserving the Qur'an, the Muslim Brothers also participated.[113]

The pledge and the staged Islamic processions in 1937 testify to a renewed effort to associate kingship with Islam. For many in the late 1930s, preserving Islam meant preserving the dynasty. Yet by that time the new ideology of Islamic constitutionalism also allowed the concept of *wali al-amr* to be identified not with a person but with a composite body, such as the government. Bakhit, al-Sanhuri, and Khallaf quite clearly outlined the idea of a Sunni Islamic republic—led by jurists. Hence the *shari'a* apparatus split into two opposing political camps (a monarchist and a non-monarchist one).

It thus required no great theological-legal shift for Muslim jurists to accept the establishment of a republican government in Egypt in the 1950s. The foundations were laid in the 1920s when the Ottoman imperial ideology of Muslim government was recycled into the ideology of the representative imamate. Indeed, after the 1952 military coup d'état, the Grand Mufti opined that the republican government was now the *wali al-amr*. This has remained to date the official doctrine of all Egyptian Grand Muftis.[114] The Brotherhood, for their part, put forward a constitution in September 1952, which specified that no one was above the law, but proposed a life-long presidency. In their plan, the people (*umma*) would exercise their power (*sultan*) through elected representatives.[115] However, unlike the monarchical regime of the interwar period, the Egyptian military officers now in charge no longer considered revelation a source of legislation and thus abolished the *shari'a* courts and the private pious endowments. The legal genealogy of *wali al-amr* that I quoted from Grand Mufti Jad al-Haqq in the 1980s was, in fact, a retroactive validation of the military government's decision to abolish private pious endowments in 1950s Egypt.[116] The military found both monarchical-imperial constitutionalism and Muslim authority unacceptable and sought a new ideology to protect the *umma* from itself. At that point, a new chasm opened between those in the *shari'a* apparatus who accepted a yet again reconfigured Islamic law and those who preferred to follow the new caliphate utopia toward a new light.

PART IV

Paths of Extrication

CHAPTER EIGHT

The Syrian Making of the Arab Saudi Kingdom

IN SEPTEMBER 1932, 'ABD al-'Aziz ("Ibn Saud"), King of the Hijaz and the Najd and Its Dependencies, announced the establishment of a new country, *al-mamlaka al-'arabiyya al-su'udiyya*. It was an act that many Saudi and non-Saudi historians have called "unification." The new polity's name has been translated as the "Kingdom of Saudi Arabia" ever since, though the correct English translation is the "Arab Su'udi Kingdom," or, following standard English transliteration, the "Arab Saudi Kingdom." To point out this discrepancy is, as we shall see, more than an assertion of philological exactitude.

Most historians begin the history of this polity with the story of Islamic puritanism in the Najd, an oasis-dotted desert territory in Eastern Arabia. Popular histories tell of an eighteenth-century alliance between the puritan scholar Muhammad b. 'Abd al-Wahhab and the emir Muhammad b. Su'ud (the first "Ibn Saud"), the ruler of an oasis-city in this remote place, whose desert economy relied on trade with the Gulf and, further on, with the Indian Ocean. Next, we are told of their conquest of Ottoman Mecca in the Hijaz on the other side of Arabia, of the Ottoman-Egyptian countercampaign, and of the break-up of this "first Saudi state" in the 1810s. Then comes the "second Saudi state," and finally 'Abd al-'Aziz appears, the legendary "Ibn Saud," and we hear of his conquests from 1902, which led to the "third Saudi state" in 1932. Islam is the force that drives this heroic narrative, whose purpose is most often to build a kind of royal cult around the figure of 'Abd al-'Aziz.[1]

There have been sceptics. Scholars have provided different explanations to explain "Saudi state formation" between the 1920s and the 1950s.

Causal explanations include tribal "chieftaincy," instead of religion, as the main political force; biopolitical practices in the occupied Hijaz; British imperial design and foreign policy; the United States as the "sole protector" of the kingdom from the 1940s; and "radical popular mobilizations" in the 1950s.[2] For the 1932 unification itself, the economic explanation is the most convincing, namely, that only the assumption of control over merchants along the Red Sea coast and the creation of a single economy enabled the survival of the new polity.[3] The argument that conquest brought together a hitherto divided economy is actually an old one: a Saudi author in the 1970s proudly noted that the conquest of the Hijaz made it possible to create Arabia as "a resource for development."[4] However, the common element in these diverse approaches is that they look at the emergence of the Saudi polity in almost complete isolation from other post-Ottoman Arab regimes and from international law.

In this chapter, looking beyond Islam and the economy, I explore the making of the new Saudi polity as part of the grand operation of recycling the Ottoman Empire in the age of the League of Nations. In this global history framework, the name "Arab Saudi Kingdom" calls our attention to a larger issue. In 1932, the official Saudi gazette announced this new name as just "the first step in realizing the unity of Arabs."[5] Taking this propaganda statement seriously, I propose two connected arguments in this chapter.

First, I argue that the logic of composite polities dictated state-formation in the post-Ottoman Red Sea region in the mid-1920s. A new Saudi-led association of polities was to replace a sharifian confederation. In the late 1920s, this collection of subordinated polities (the Saudi Kingdom of the Hijaz and the Najd and Its Dependencies) flirted also with the remaking of some Ottoman institutions. For the British, this polity was quite convenient, a ready-made subordinated confederation that fit neatly with imperial interest. For the early Saudi government, however, the legal sovereignty of the Kingdom of the Hijaz was crucial—for Islam, for international relations, and for economic contracts. Alongside Afghanistan, the Kingdom of the Hijaz was one of only two acknowledged sovereign Muslim polities in the 1920s.[6] The Najdi conquerors hence avoided declaring a conquest and instead relied on the sovereignty of the earlier Kingdom of the Hijaz, the recycled Ottoman emirate of Mecca, while struggling to make the Najdi polity similarly recognized. The Hijaz's incorporation in 1932 into the Arab Saudi Kingdom aimed at a flattening of the uneven legal and fiscal landscape.

The importance of the Hijazi-Saudi story between 1919 and 1932 for the history of international law is that it represents a period and location in which the British Empire, the Allied Powers as a virtual body, and the League of Nations were competing sources of sovereignty. Under these unique circumstances, the new Saudi local polity exemplified the coexistence of imperial ("interpolity") and inter-sovereign regimes.[7]

Second, I will look at this early Saudi government as a cosmopolitan, somewhat pan-Arab (especially Syrian) and even global enterprise. Global because the Saudi-led effort at replacing the sharifian empire was the work of various groups in addition to the Najdi fighters and the Hijazi merchants and guilds. Diaspora Syrians, Egyptians, and some Iraqis; and Americans, such as Amin al-Rihani and the anti-mandate millionaire Charles Crane also contributed to Saudi state-formation in its early stage.[8] At the core of this eclectic state-making enterprise was 'Abd al-'Aziz's partnership with Syrian anti-mandate activists, especially a group called the "Independence Party" (*Hizb al-Istiqlal*) in the late 1920s. I call them the "*Istiqlali* activists."

Priya Satia has argued that an informal British intelligence community managed Arabian affairs during WWI.[9] In the late 1920s, we see a somewhat similar external presence, but this time an inter-Arab one. The *Istiqlali* activists were in search of a source of power that would enable them to achieve their various goals: to regain French Damascus, to protect Mecca and Medina, to sustain Islam as a source of authority in post-Ottoman polities, to find employment, and to realize what remained of pre-war Ottoman utopian federalism. Their wanderings in the scorched post-Ottoman lands contributed to the establishment of the Hijazi Kingdom, its subordinate emirate of Transjordan, and the Saudi polity. In the final analysis, for these exiled Syrian activists, the Arab Saudi Kingdom was their revenge on both the League's mandate and the *ashraf* of Mecca, in whom they had been utterly disappointed. As we shall see in the next chapter, some *Istiqlali* activists even considered incorporating the State of Syria into a new Saudi-led association. Their activities are evidence that the British and French were not alone in creating the modern Middle East.

My focus on the *Istiqlali* activists is not to deny the considerable tact of 'Abd al-'Aziz and his clever secretary of finance, 'Abd Allah b. Sulayman al-Hamdan. After all, both men were seasoned merchants in oasis cities along the Gulf.[10] Scholars have already pointed out that in the post–1925 period, 'Abd al-'Aziz's policy was compromise, importantly with the Hijazi merchant communities, alongside the violent suppression of the tribes.[11]

However, the *Istiqlali* Syrian activists helped 'Abd al-'Aziz to use Hijazi sovereignty fully and to gain acceptance among post-Ottoman Arabs. Instead of Riyadh or London, therefore, we must begin the story of the Saudi project at the nexus between Damascus and Mecca, along the Hijazi railway.

The Istiqlali *Network in the Empire of* Ashraf: *Making Transjordan*

Three men shared a good joke in Mecca in January 1921: Sharif Zayd, the youngest son of King al-Husayn, Yusuf Yasin, and Khayr al-Din al-Zirikli. The last two had recently fled from Damascus after its occupation by the French. Both were devoted campaigners for Syrian independence and belonged to the loose grouping of *Istiqlali* Syrians. Sharif Zayd told the two Syrians that he thought them "the only *ikhwan* in Mecca," to which al-Zirikli answered jokingly, "But what do you say your Highness?!" All three of them burst into laughter because the Arabic word *ikhwan*, "brothers," also had a secondary meaning, referring to the *Ikhwan* of 'Abd al-'Aziz, the imam and sultan of Najd at the time. This puritan military force posed the biggest threat to sharifian rule in Mecca in 1921. None of them could know that Yasin and al-Zirikli, and in general the *Istiqlal* network, would soon switch their loyalties to 'Abd al-'Aziz.[12]

Mecca in 1921 was the capital of the Kingdom of the Hijaz, the first sovereign post-Ottoman polity. In January 1919, the Supreme Council of the Allied Powers had recognized this polity as the Kingdom of the Hijaz and as a belligerent power.[13] This was why a "Hijazi" delegation could participate in the Paris peace conference.[14] Its ruler, the old Sharif al-Husayn, initially loved the idea of the League, which he understood as a "charitable society" (*jam'iyya khayriyya*) acting to advance peace around the world. Citing the Koran verse 49:9, which speaks of the importance of peace and equity, his official journal *al-Qibla* argued that such an organization was legitimate according to Islam, adding that the United States of America was acting in the spirit of the words of God.[15] His representatives (the "Hijazi party") signed the Covenant of the League in June 1919 and thus the Kingdom of the Hijaz became a forgotten founder of the new world order.[16] However, in the end al-Husayn did not ratify the Covenant because of Article 22 (the mandates), and he also denied the very existence of his own polity by sticking to his claim to be the king of all Arabs.

The old *sharif* intended to rule over a sovereign amorphous association of local, non-sovereign polities—Syria, Iraq, and the Hijaz, possibly Iraq. In 1920, his representative in Cairo told his son Faysal that his fatal mistake was to claim sovereignty in Damascus, instead of acting only as the representative of his father, one of the "Treaty Allies."[17] The material core of this imperial formation was, as we have seen, the Hijaz railway, stretching between Damascus and Medina. The empire of *ashraf* after the expulsion of Faysal from Damascus, however, became reduced to the Hijaz and Transjordan, with some possible Iraqi connections where the British administrators had crowned Faysal in 1921. In the space between Mecca and Damascus, the ruined Hijazi trainline still represented a material, coal-based land route. The "Arab government" even printed stamps to sustain the railway (see frontispiece).

The story of the post-1920 *ashraf* regional federation up to about 1925 offers us a unique glimpse into how post-Ottoman and British modular state-making came together in Transjordan and into the formation of the *Istiqlali* "brotherhood." The Hijazi kingdom *as* a local government had been a small military polity, which recycled the earlier Ottoman infrastructure in the Hijaz into a sharifian, genealogical Muslim regime. Whereas under Ottoman rule the Hijaz had been exempted from imperial conscription, by 1917 al-Husayn had an army of some 30,000 men, in addition to his own bodyguards and the British-Egyptian and French military missions. This mixed army was largely financed from the British subsidy. New military barracks, army factories, and a disciplinary system of schooling to create "righteous men" (*rijal salihun*) were established in Mecca, Jidda, and Ta'if. There were regular military parades in Mecca. The king obtained machinery, cars, and airplanes from the Allied Powers; and new telegraph lines were installed alongside the old Ottoman line. There was a telephone connection between Mecca and Jidda. The journal *al-Qibla* praised the military industrialization of the Hijaz and compared al-Husayn to Mehmed Ali, the founder of the khedivial dynasty and the creator of Egypt's army.[18] Islamic laws were trumpeted as the best and only possible social laws. Al-Husayn ordered the use of *hudud*, punishments for crimes prescribed by the Koran. He also considered local education crucial. In 1921, he forbade sending Hijazi children to foreign schools, even to Iraq.[19]

The political construction of this local polity as a center of a post-Ottoman composite federation was partly the work of Syrians. In 1916, British headquarters had sent two journalists to found a propaganda journal in Mecca, aimed at a global Arabic-reading public.[20] One of the two, Fu'ad al-Khatib, soon became an important foreign affairs advisor. The other was Muhibb al-Din al-Khatib (no family relation between the two Khatibs), the activist and former student of Sheikh Rashid Rida in Cairo (see Chapter Five). Captured Ottoman Syrian and Iraqi soldiers enlisted in the sharifian army, including the young Nuri al-Sa'id who had joined the Arab utopian federalists in 1914. Rashid Rida—whom High Commissioner Wingate considered to be a "very useful man"—was also allowed to visit the Hijaz in the winter of 1916, but he immediately fell out with al-Husayn because of a clash of personalities.[21] Yet his friend, Shaykh Muhammad Kamil al-Qassab, another Muslim educator whom we have already met, joined the *ashraf.* In early 1918, he distributed money on behalf of the "Arab Government" in Cairo.[22]

By 1920, the activists had gradually fallen out with the sharifian governments both in Mecca and in Damascus. Al-Qassab was among the first Syrians to enter into open conflict with Faysal. Upon arrival in occupied Damascus, he advocated resistance to the French, and possibly even to the Meccan *ashraf,* speaking in the terminology of jihad. Faysal sought to exile him as early as 1919.[23] Muhibb al-Din al-Khatib also left Mecca for Damascus to establish yet another official journal and in the hope of transforming Syria into a constitutional polity "within its natural limits." In an interview with a French officer he claimed that al-Husayn wanted the Koran to be the sole constitution in the Hijaz, whereas he, Muhibb al-Din, knew that in Syria this would not work.[24] Al-Khatib, Sheikh al-Qassab, al-Zirikli, and others created an organization that called for armed resistance against the French. Al-Qassab also headed a committee that advocated for taking a large loan in June 1920. They fled after the French invasion in July, fearing French punishment. Not without reason. Among other measures, a French military court sentenced al-Qassab to death and confiscated his property in his absence.[25]

Modular state-making continued with a new unit in the sharifian imperial project. In 1921, the Emirate of Transjordan was established, the last sharifian local polity to be built on Ottoman infrastructure and genealogical politics. At the same time, this legacy also helped shape the emerging Syrian *Istiqlali* ("Independence") activist network. Exiled activists like al-Qassab, lower rank Arab military officers, and *ashraf* were commuting up and down along the Hijaz railway for shorter and shorter distances. When Sharif 'Abd Allah Bey arrived at Ma'an station from Arabia, ostensibly to liberate Damascus, a delegation of activists from Jerusalem, with

British encouragement, called upon him. Sheikh al-Qassab, leader of the delegation, invited the emir to the Amman station. He also summoned other activists such as Yasin and al-Zirikli, who were similarly committed to independence, hoping to create a base from which to liberate Damascus. Aware of their goals, the French and British secret services and Arab observers started to call their loose grouping the "Independence Party." The activists called each other "brothers" (*ikhwan*), as a gesture towards an "ethical promise of fraternity."[26] In Amman, the mostly bourgeois ex-Ottomans had to stay in tents and rooms at the train station, at some distance from Amman proper, because 'Abd Allah did not want to enter the city.[27]

The classic Jordanian national narrative explains 'Abd Allah's arrival in Ma'an as resulting from a number of accidents: his father claimed that the region (and the train station) of Ma'an belonged to the Hijaz instead of the Palestine mandate, that Syrian notables had sent telegraphs to Mecca to ask one of his sons to help "the national movement against the French," and that 'Abd Allah was the only Meccan sharif available at the time, adding even that he actually had come to ask the British for his promised Iraqi kingship.[28]

In this story, Sheikh Kamil al-Qassab appears as one of the local "free men," the activists propagating resistance to the French (*ahrar*, referring to the Syrian *Istiqlali* grouping) to whom 'Abd Allah had promised political assistance in the liberating of Damascus.[29] However, alongside religious activists and soldiers, we also find scions of the Ottoman Damascene bourgeoisie among the Istiqlalis, such as the al-'Azmah brothers and Khayr al-Din al-Zirikli. Plus, about two hundred ex-Faysali Syrian soldiers joined as well, took over important positions in the new emirate, and instead of supporting the *sharif*, listened rather to the *Istiqlali* activists. (See Figure 8.1)

Writing in 1925, al-Zirikli, now a disgruntled *Istiqlali*, described the foundational episode quite differently: 'Abd Allah arrived in Amman in March 1921 to a warm welcome. Sheikh al-Qassab, we read, during a large gathering of local notables and activists, asked the *sharif* to establish an agreement (*'ahd*) with those present. The sheikh swore loyalty in the name of the community (*bi-lisan al-jam'*) to 'Abd Allah as their emir and in return asked the new emir also to swear loyalty to the *umma* and promise to fight for independence—that is, to fight against the French occupation of Damascus. 'Abd Allah did not exactly swear, but he did assure Sheikh al-Qassab that he was ready to fight. After this somewhat theatrical gathering, the emir retired to sleep in his house at the train station.[30] Instead

FIGURE 8.1. The *Istiqlali* group (in the middle Sheikh Kamil al-Qassab) in Amman, 1922. *Source*: Al-Madi and Musa, *Tarikh al-Urdun* (1959) (Amman: Maktabat al-Muhtasib, 1988), 247, with permission.

of fighting, he soon sent an emissary to the British High Commission with a letter of friendship and agreed to Churchill's terms over a nice lunch in Jerusalem.[31] Al-Qassab, for his part, travelled to Yemen in 1922 to talk to the ruler Imam Yahya about a possible new association of Muslim emirs.[32]

Hence the Emirate of Transjordan, the last sharifian local polity, was established from below and from above at the same time in a modular logic. Eugene Rogan has advanced the convincing argument that in late Ottoman times, local changes in the administration and the economy, as well and the Hijazi railway, had created the "preconditions" for 'Abd Allah's experiment to succeed.[33] In the eyes of Syrian utopian federalists, this polity was to be one element in the post-Ottoman association of emirates fighting for Damascus. It was also useful for British interests as a frontier polity, an Arab princely state, a buffer between the sovereign Hijaz, French Syria, and soon to be colonized British Palestine. Its imperial recognition—and the acknowledgement of its existence separate from Palestine—was only a question of time. (Figure 8.2).

But Transjordan was not created to be a nation-state. At this time, both the *ashraf* and local activists, and the British officials, still entertained

FIGURE 8.2. T. E. Lawrence greets Sharif 'Abd Allah, 17 April 1921, Amman. *Source:* American Colony. *Sir Herbert Samuel's second visit to Transjordan, etc. Col. T. E. Lawrence and Emir Abdullah. Jordan, 1921.* LC-M34-1947 [P&P], LoC.

composite visions of new imperial projects. Rida and al-Qassab still hoped for the utopian federalist idea of a post-Ottoman association of Muslim emirs. In fact, in November 1921, 'Abd Allah himself proposed to surprised British administrators a constitutional text in which his authority derived from his father—a would-be sharifian emperor and caliph—and not from the British Empire or the local nation.[34] In 1922, the first treaty between 'Abd Allah and the British Empire would be ratified by King al-Husayn and King George, indicating that even the British recognized the new emirate as somehow part of a sharifian commonwealth.

We get a glimpse into the complexities of Muslim monarchical territoriality during a famous visit that King al-Husayn paid to Transjordan in January–March 1924. He arrived for an inter-sharifian meeting and, as usual, for a British treaty negotiation, but he left as the newly-declared caliph of Muslims. This aging Hamidian *sharif* was received as the true ruler in Transjordan by some local delegations who submitted petitions against 'Abd Allah and organized demonstrations in mosques. Al-Husayn gave some thought to "annexing" Transjordan and possibly greater Palestine to the Hijaz.[35] A bourgeois Palestinian delegation, fearing a possible extension of the sharifian regime to Palestine, emphasized that they want complete freedom for their region, meaning freedom also in deciding their regime form without regard to the descendants of the Prophet. Another Palestinian faction, included Amin al-Husayni, the mufti of Jerusalem, visited al-Husayn's camp in Transjordan and conditionally accepted the declaration of the *sharif*'s caliphate after the Turkish assembly's decision in March 1924. Imams in mandate Palestine again started the symbolic Friday prayers in the name of al-Husayn, as they had done in 1919, while the French authorities prohibited this in their regions.[36] Behind the scenes of the caliphate issue, there remained a struggle over whether the *ashraf* would extend their rule to mandate Palestine or the British High Commission would again assume direct rule in Transjordan, thereby cancelling its "independence."

The *Istiqlali* party in search for an anti-French emirate did not know the extent of 'Abd Allah's pragmatism and his prior track-record of cooperating with the British Empire in 1914, which we saw in Chapter Five. Rida and al-Qassab were utterly disappointed when in the summer of 1924 'Abd Allah quickly got rid of the *Istiqlali* activists and soldiers because their militancy against the French mandate administration, which went as far as targeted assassinations, became a source of inconvenience for the British administration. The new emir never allowed the Jordanian notables to question the British connection, and, as Avi Shlaim has demonstrated, he regularly negotiated with Zionists.[37] In 1924, the *Istiqlali* party yet again had to flee, some to Egypt. Others went to Mecca, the traditional place of Muslim exile and the heart of the crumbling Kingdom of the Hijaz, while yet others decamped to Eastern Arabia.[38]

From the Sharifian Project to the Saudi Hijazi Kingdom, 1924–28

While some Syrian *ikhwan* were on their way to Mecca, another group of *ikhwan* were also making their way to the Holy City. Now we can understand the joke Sharif Zayd told in 1921. The imam and emir of Najd, ʿAbd al-ʿAziz, who had promoted himself to the position of Sultan of Najd, led the *Ikhwan*, his Muslim tribal force, against the sovereign Kingdom of the Hijaz. It was the meeting of these two post-Ottoman groups, the urban *Istiqlali* Syrians and the Najdi fighters, two very different types of Muslim brothers, that came to define the direction of the early Saudi polity.

AN OTTOMAN TWILIGHT IN ARABIA?

The logic of modular state-making and the idea of an association of emirates were familiar to ʿAbd al-ʿAziz. His relationship with Ottoman Arabs critical of CUP politics dated back to pre-war times. Rashid Rida from Cairo was in touch with this young emir. In 1912, when ʿAbd al-ʿAziz conquered the Ottoman region of al-Ahsa in Eastern Arabia, the imperial government offered him an appointment as governor (*vali*) of al-Ahsa (the British agents called this position the "ruler of Hasa"), with autonomy, his own flag(!), a monthly stipend, and rights to tax collection. This was an attempt by the Ottoman authorities to maintain their positions in the Gulf in the face of British advances.[39] In 1914 Rashid Rida in Egypt reported to Khedive Abbas Hilmi II that the emir of Najd cursed the Ottoman delegation yet extracted 4,000 lira in annual support.[40] In fact, ʿAbd al-ʿAziz, now an Ottoman governor, assumed full domestic sovereignty as imam in terms of Islamic law in al-Ahsa; thus, for instance, British reports confirm that he exercised such sovereignty by confiscating land from owners in 1913 and by direct taxation.[41] After the outbreak of war, in 1915 he entered into a new agreement with the British Empire as an "independent Ruler" of his "countries," the treaty stipulating only that his foreign relations should be conducted through the British Empire.[42] His family came to understand the British Empire: his second son Faysal visited London in 1919 where he was entertained by the British officer

Harry St. John Philby; and his first son Saud once called England *wilaya* (the "authority" [?]).[43]

The diary of Sayyid Siddiq Hasan, a British Indian Muslim officer stationed in Bahrain, provides a fascinating insight into the life of post-Ottoman Arabia. Siddiq Hasan and his Arab assistant Farhan Bey al-Ramah were entrusted with negotiating a peace treaty of some sort between King al-Husayn of Mecca and Emir ʿAbd al-ʿAziz of Riyadh during the pilgrimage season in 1920. This mission—in fact a *hajj*—took Siddiq Hasan on a desert journey from Bahrain to Riyadh to Mecca in July and August that year. Unlike the British Orientalists who crossed this same desert, this Indian Muslim officer did not achieve world fame, but his diary does testify to excellent intelligence gathering skills and the extraordinary strength that enabled this demanding journey.[44] To achieve *Pax Britannica* in the Arab peninsula, the empire mobilized Indian Muslim loyalties.

In 1920, Arabia was still full with the debris of the Ottoman Empire. Before departing with the emir's delegation to Mecca, Siddiq Hasan received a trenchant gift from the emir: an Ottoman rifle (with a date of 1912, possibly from the conquest of al-Ahsa).[45] Ahmad Al Thunayan, a cousin of ʿAbd al-ʿAziz, was the leader of their delegation. Yet another Ottomanized Arab (he had been born and educated in Istanbul) and a product of Hamidian politics, he had been in the entourage of ʿAbd al-ʿAziz since the early 1910s, although his position there occasioned some unease (his father had competed for the Najdi emirate before fleeing to Istanbul). Fluent in Turkish and French, Ahmad Al Thunayn was also part of the Saudi delegation in London in 1919. Even during the 1920 desert journey to Mecca, he read French newspapers and translated the news to Najdi Arabs in camps.[46] Although the puritan Najdis looked down on British Muslim officers as "servants of the English" and even "unbelievers," Siddiq Hasan and Ahmad Al Thunayan gradually warmed to each other during the journey, and the British-Indian officer attempted to convince his ex-Ottoman-Najdi colleague that achieving peace would be a great service to both his master in Riyadh and the British government.[47]

In fact, when the *ashraf* of Mecca saw the Najdi delegation in August 1920, that was pretty much how they saw them: a delegation from a subordinated British emir, exactly when the French army was taking Damascus. Once arrived in Mecca, the Najdi delegation was surprised to find that ʿAbd Allah (at this time, still before his trip to Amman) had a copy of the 1915 British-Najdi agreement. The young *sharif* recognized ʿAbd al-ʿAziz only as a British subordinate while they themselves were the sovereign Kingdom of the Hijaz. The Meccans wanted to fix the line of the Hijaz-Najd frontier (drawing on information contained in an Ottoman Hijaz province register of tribal leaders' salaries), but Ahmad Al Thunayan had no authorization from 'Abd al-'Aziz to proceed with such a scheme. In a typical act of the post-Ottoman world, Ahmad Al Thunayan and 'Abd Allah at one point conversed with one another in Turkish, so as to exclude Siddiq who belonged to the British world. Finally, they did sign a treaty of peace and friendship, which however did not last long.[48] Between Riyadh and Mecca in 1920, the Ottoman cultural and political legacy was still alive, ready to be reforged in new British imperial and League-oriented worlds.

AVOIDING CONQUEST

A history of wars in twentieth-century Arabia is yet to be written. In the course of the years 1924–25, 'Abd al-'Aziz, now the Sultan of Najd, easily conquered the technologically more advanced polity of the Hijaz. He owed his success in large part to tacit British imperial support and to the fact that al-Husayn and his eldest son and successor 'Ali had no significant loyal forces—the thousands of fighters brought together on British money during the war had dispersed quickly after 1918; Hijazi merchants formed a constitutional party and forced al-Husayn to step down in favor of his first-born 'Ali, and they initiated secret negotiations with the Najdi ruler in 1924.

Sandwiched between British officials and Syrian activists, the *ashraf* could not deliver to either of these parties. The League of Nations refrained from intervention because al-Husayn had refused to ratify the Covenant and thus the Hijaz did not become a member state.[49] In 1923, when the old *sharif* changed his mind, the legal chief Joost Van Hammel deliberately obstructed the Hijaz's membership in Geneva. Van Hammel advised the League leadership not to inform al-Husayn that, legally, he could still ratify the Covenant and that the Kingdom of the Hijaz could thus become a protected member. Van Hammel wrote a sternly worded note stating that "the Secretary General could give no other indication than to refer to the applicability of Article I."[50] It was convenient for all concerned to consider the Saudi conquest of the sharifian Hijaz a conflict between two non-League members, associated only with the British Empire.

One way this new empire over Arabia hoped to solve the dispute was through what we might term "genealogical solidarity," similar to that of Ottoman times. In 1924, the new king 'Ali gathered an eclectic group of advisors: the British officer St. John Philby, the writer Amin al-Rihani, and Sayyid Talib al-Naqib; the latter we met already. Sayyid Talib was the Hamidian Basra notable who wanted to become a monarch in Baghdad, or at least an autonomous emir in Basra. All arrived to mediate between the parties in Jidda. British officials considered Sayyid Talib an especially good negotiator because he had known ʿAbd al-ʿAziz well in the past, when both were Ottoman subordinated local strongmen in the Gulf. In any case, the occasion of the war for the holy cities was a good excuse to delay the return of this troublesome *sayyid* to Iraq. To great surprise, the only mediator who received a promising reply from ʿAbd al-ʿAziz was the American Amin al-Rihani.[51]

After a year of siege, Sharif ʿAli left Jidda under the provisions of a treaty in December 1925. The chief articles of the treaty stipulated that ʿAbd al-ʿAziz provide safety for the populations of Jidda and Yanbuʿ; that the *ashraf* might retain possession of personal properties in the Hijaz; and that the three steamers of the kingdom should become the "private property" (*milk*) of ʿAbd al-ʿAziz. ʿAli left Jidda by a steamer, and the provisional Jidda government, in company with the British consul, surrendered to the sultan of Najd on 21 December 1925. The following day, the local municipal council began to govern Jidda in ʿAbd al-ʿAziz's name. Thus ended sharifian rule in the Hijaz.[52]

It was initially unclear what the consequences of Sultan ʿAbd al-ʿAziz's accession to the Hijazi region would be. Would the puritan Najdi forces embark upon a full-scale campaign of destruction, or would they be satisfied with the obliteration of a few Muslim shrines? Would they stay or would they leave? They had no means to govern the holy cities and the coast. They needed the cooperation of Hijazi merchants and guilds, if only on account the long distance and lack of communication between Riyadh and Mecca.

For this reason, ʿAbd al-ʿAziz soon set up a new governing council, consisting mostly of local merchants. The arrangement in January 1926 was that this Hijaz council would pay 140,000 (Egyptian?) pounds to ʿAbd al-ʿAziz for maintaining the army and security, and an additional 60,000 as his allowance as the King of the Hijaz (see below).[53] A month later an additional 21,000 pounds was granted for the maintenance of captured Hijazi airplanes.[54] Like his predecessor al-Husayn, the new ruler of the Kingdom of Hijaz was an admirer of Western military technology and used machine guns in many of his later wars of consolidation.[55]

Though Sultan ʿAbd al-ʿAziz avoided declaring the Hijaz his own domain, there can be no doubt that upon entering Mecca he considered himself the city's ruler in Muslim terms. He minted coins in his own name as early as March 1925, on the Ottoman model and with a *tuğra* featuring his name on one side—a classic act of spoliation *in re*.[56] He embarked also on a program of land reform. Some claim that he declared all pastoral land government property (*miri*) in 1925; whether or not this is indeed the case, 'Abd al-'Aziz's fighters certainly received usufruct rights (*iqta'*) to the lands in question.[57]

The new Saudi regime also recycled the legal institutions established by the previous sharifian administration and, in an unmistakable act of legal spoliation, even promised to follow the Ottoman *Mecelle*. In the early days, the new government accepted claims to property if claimants had certificates registered in *qadi* courts attesting their valid, full ownership under the Ottoman government (and presumably under the sharifian government, too).[58] There was also a proposal for a new civil law code, a new *Majalla* in Arabic, put forward by the judge Ahmad b. 'Abd Allah al-Qari. 'Abd al-'Aziz and his advisors in fact endorsed the plan for this new code as a restoration of Ottoman legality (after the *ashraf*'s alleged misrule) in 1927; however, the code was never issued.[59] But despite these practices of sovereignty there was no declaration of conquest and annexation. Instead, the new Saudi power embarked, or was forced to embark, on a composite project.

Avoiding the declaration of conquest was a tactic to obfuscate the status of the holy cities, an issue of global concern to European empires, including the new Soviet Union, now ruling over millions of Muslims. Take as an example the representatives of the Indian Khilafat Committee who visited Jidda, ostensibly to help establish "peace," but also to find out whether the British government intended to intervene in this territory. They sent three delegations in rapid successions over the course of 1925–26, known as the "Servants of the Two Holy Cities" (*Khuddam al-Haramayn*) delegations. The Indians' goal was to set up a Muslim, republican government in the Hijaz to be overseen by the global community of Islam, a move that researchers today read as an "ethical space" initiative.[60] They appear to have distributed money to foment intrigue against 'Abd al-'Aziz's new regime, going so far as to "order" him and his army to leave the Hijaz. The third Indian delegation, unsurprisingly, was politely asked to leave.[61] The leading members of the Khilafat movement next argued for a republic in a hastily organized caliphate conference held in Mecca in June-July 1926, and they continued this effort in the Hijaz in the coming years. The Soviet delegation of Muslims, however, supported 'Abd al-'Aziz's takeover. Even more importantly, Rashid Rida, and the *Istiqlali* Syrians, saw the republican idea as a "disaster," since they equated "republican" government with the "Turkish" way, that is, nationalist secularization.[62] 'Abd al-'Aziz had three personal meetings with the Indian Khilafat activists to discuss the ethical-republican idea and his assumption of the Hijazi kingship, but the meetings were tension-filled.[63]

Next, a deeper constitutional issue arose regarding conquest in Islamic law. Ever since the early Muslim conquests there had been a debate about the status of Mecca, this latter interpreted variously as either the Hijaz or the whole of the Arabian Peninsula (*bilad al-'Arab*). Early Sunni and Shi'i jurists agreed that the Prophet had occupied Mecca without treaty ("by force," *'anwatan*) and that the land was therefore the common property of Muslims, over which the imam had distributive authority and authority to collect the large *kharaj* tax. Later, however, many Sunni jurists re-interpreted the Prophet's conquest of Mecca as a "capture by treaty," and therefore claimed that it remained privately owned land, which the imam could tax only with the tithe (*'ushr*).[64] This reinterpretation was rejected by Hanbali jurists—of which 'Abd al-'Aziz was ostensibly a follower—who held that Mecca was the common property of all Muslims, and that as part of the "land of the Arabs" it was liable to pay *kharaj*.[65] Rashid Rida, in 1909, had interpreted the Ottoman Hijaz metaphorically "as a mosque for Muslims," and declared that Mecca "is God's endowment for the Muslims" (*waqf Allah 'ala al-muslimin*), noting that the special places of pilgrimage were to be "shared among the people."[66] In the light of these discussions, it seems that if 'Abd al-'Aziz had followed the logical implication of his conquest in 1925, he would have declared Mecca under King al-Husayn to be a land of infidels, upon conquest would have collected the *kharaj*, and next would have dissolved the Kingdom of the Hijaz. He could have given the region to the Indian Muslim republicans or to local Hijazi merchants to whom he did make promises of independence.[67]

This is the background that explains the new composite polity that was born between 1925 and 1928: the Kingdom of the Hijaz and Najd and Its Dependencies. First, 'Abd al-'Aziz publicly took the title "King of the Hijaz" on 8 January 1926. As early as November 1925 he had already used this title in a treaty demarcating the Hijaz-Jordan border. It was his way of indicating that he recognized and upheld the continuity of this sovereign polity. *Umm al-Qura* portrayed his assumption of the regnal title as an election, enacted through the Hijazi notables' oath of loyalty. The British consul, on the other hand, remarked to his superiors that the Hijazi people were quite surprised to hear the announcement as there had been much talk about an independent Hijazi government, with the Indians and some locals preferring a republic.[68]

'Abd al-'Aziz's adoption of the royal title made the British officials anxious, particularly with regard to India. Sir Arthur Hirtzel from the India Office warned against entering into too close a treaty-relationship with the new Hijazi ruler, because he feared that for Britain to establish any sort of mediated authority over the Hijaz would occasion immense resistance from Indian Muslims.[69] One member of the Indian Khilafat Committee in the Hijaz noted that "the Syrians around Ibn Saud and the Ahl-i Hadees of India were working for his kingship here [. . .]. Ibn Saud got himself proclaimed King of Hijaz yesterday [. . .] but all this is bunkum. It was a pre-arranged plan. The Hijazis do not want him."[70] As noted above, the delegation wanted to create a republic with a caliph, *à la* Kawakibi's Arab caliphate, in the Hijaz. Let us meet now with the Syrian activists of utopian federalism, who instead of an ethical Muslim republic preferred a Saudi composite monarchy.

ISTIQLALIS ASSEMBLED

In addition to merchants' money, clever and determined activists around 'Abd al-'Aziz—called "advisors" in today's Saudi historiography—assisted in the creation of the composite state. Some of these Syrians came to the Najdi sultan through the good offices of Rashid Rida.[71] Importantly, individuals born in the Ottoman Syrian provinces had been part of the merchant community of the Hijaz, and Syrian scholars and exiled individuals also had an established present in cosmopolitan Mecca and Medina.[72] The assembling of activists in the Saudi Hijaz was a significant turning point in the history of Muslim utopian federalism, for it replaced an *ashraf*-led empire (that they now considered a British creation) with a Saudi-led composite polity.

One of the first non-Najdi Arab advisors to Emir 'Abd al-'Aziz had been 'Abd Allah al-Damluji (1890–1970), not a Syrian but an Iraqi Ottoman officer. His career exemplifies in miniature the spoliation of the Ottoman political order. He had been a member of "The Covenant," the Arab nationalist Ottoman military club in Istanbul, whose leader 'Aziz al-Misri was exiled to Cairo, along with two Iraqis (Damluji and Nuri al-Sa'id, whom we have already met), in the spring of 1914. From Cairo, al-Damluji travelled to Basra and to Riyadh, attracted by the lure of Rashid Rida's utopia of a post-Ottoman federation.[73] Some sources suggest that al-Damluji was not a soldier but a doctor, a medical student, and that he was employed in this capacity by 'Abd al-'Aziz in 1915.[74] In either case, all sources agree that he was of Mosuli origin and connected to activists in Istanbul and Cairo. He became very influential in the entourage of 'Abd al-'Aziz after 1922, and he played an important role in preparations for the conquest of the Hijaz. In later years, al-Damluji served as Foreign Minister in sharifian Iraq; thus, having participated in negotiations over Iraqi borders as the Najdi representative in the 1920s, he did so once again as the Iraqi representative in the 1930s. The ease with which he fit himself to Ottoman, Najdi, Najdi-Hijazi, or Iraqi contexts, is typical of Syrian activists as well, in their search for position and influence.

Beginning in 1924, 'Abd al-'Aziz called upon able Syrians to help him in the Hijazi government, sending an envoy to mandate Palestine and Syria to select appropriate individuals.[75] An important, perhaps even vital, Syrian for state-making was Yusuf Yasin.[76] Yasin was born in Latakia and studied in Cairo with Rashid Rida before the war. After the war, he was attracted to the *Istiqlali* group, and like many other independence activists he circulated in the early 1920s between Mecca, Amman, Jerusalem, and Damascus.[77] In 1921 he edited a newspaper, *al-Sabah*, in British Jerusalem, and studied law in the new Law Institute in French Damascus. He initially entertained high hopes for the Meccan *ashraf*, only to be disappointed by the collapse of sharifian rule in Syria in 1920 and the *Istiqlali* expulsion from Transjordan.[78] In 1924, just before the Najdi conquest of the Hijaz, he travelled to Riyadh to join 'Abd al-'Aziz, possibly through the good offices of Rashid Rida.[79] It appears that he and 'Abd al-'Aziz struck up a rapport. (There are anecdotes suggesting that Yasin's services to the Najdi sultan extended to the procuring of female slaves.) In any case, when 'Abd al-'Aziz entered Mecca in late 1924 he already had al-Damluji and Yasin in his entourage, two individuals connected to Rashid Rida.

Yasin founded the new official journal in Mecca, *Umm al-Qura*, which portrayed 'Abd al-'Aziz's conquest of the Hijaz in December 1924 as an act of liberation, in a very similar fashion to the Arabic Allied propaganda during the war and in the fall of 1918. In the journal's words, 'Abd al-'Aziz came to "return the Hijaz to the Arab world."[80] He was the "Caesar of the Arabs" (*qaysar al-'arab*).[81]

Another prominent *Istiqlali* Syrian in Saudi service was Sheikh Kamil al-Qassab, who became the Director of Public Education in the Saudi Hijaz in 1926. Perhaps not incidentally, nearly forty Syrian teachers were hired for the new teacher training school in Mecca in the same year. Al-Qassab apparently had a political conflict with 'Abd al-'Aziz, who acknowledged the League's mandate system in 1927 or, possibly, he was simply a victim of a purge of Syrians that took place in the new Saudi polity in the same year. Whatever the cause, the sheikh was soon appointed to look into what one official called "the press issue in Egypt," and in September 1927 departed on a British passport to Haifa, his earlier place of exile. As we shall see, he remained in contact with the Saudi ruler for many years.[82]

A third Syrian-Saudi *Istiqlali* was Fu'ad Hamza, a Syrian Druze (who may have turned Sunni in his later years). A teacher of English, he taught in his village in 'Ayba in Lebanon, then in Damascus, and finally in British Jerusalem in the early 1920s. Hamza arrived in the Hijaz in December 1926 to join the new Saudi government, perhaps as a translator for 'Abd al-'Aziz. He had been in Egypt since early 1925 and had established contact there with 'Abd al-'Aziz's local representative. It appears that Hamza was actively recruited into 'Abd al-'Aziz's service, and that his Druze origin was no obstacle to his recruitment. Like Yasin and al-Qassab, he was a devoted anti-mandate activist. Hamza became the right hand of Yasin and, although they had frequent quarrels, he remained in Mecca and Jidda to help build a new Muslim bureaucracy and to lay the basis for the establishment of Saudi foreign relations.[83] He was appointed in 1928 to the "executive committee" of royal orders in the Hijaz, and in 1930 to a "permanent committee" in the royal diwan. He was required to meet with Yusuf Yasin every night to discuss administrative matters.[84] Hamza published the first Arabic book to propagate the new, united kingdom in 1933.[85] In the late 1920s, this Syrian was the most important member of the *Istiqlali* network connecting Yasin in Riyadh, al-Qassab in Haifa, the al-Husaynis in Jerusalem, and Rashid Rida in Cairo. We shall look into their not-so-secret activity in regard to French Syria in the next chapter.[86]

Hamza's arrival provides a window into the Syrian milieu of the occupied Hijaz at a time when a fierce uprising was also underway in the French mandate.[87] In the winter of 1926, new king 'Abd al-'Aziz himself greeted Hamza, first in Medina. Then there occurred a second, unexpected meeting in December 1926, when many exiled Syrians from mandate Damascus—Shukri Quwwatli, Sabri al-'Asali, Khalid al-Hakim—were in the city. One evening, they went together to 'Abd al-'Aziz's audience (*majlis*), and there Yusuf Yasin read aloud part of the latest book by the American-Lebanese writer Amin al-Rihani. In January 1927, the Syrian group together travelled from Medina to Jidda in a car-caravan.[88]

The book they read aloud must have been *The Kings of the Arabs*, which had just been published in Beirut. Rihani had visited 'Abd al-'Aziz in person in 1922 in his grand tour of Arab polities, and again in 1924, and he had remained in close touch with him during his conquest. His ideas

FIGURE 8.3. Sultan of Najd and King of the Hijaz 'Abd al-'Aziz greets Amin Rihani (just arrived by plane). Also present are Shaikh Hafiz Wahba and Shaikh Yusuf Yasin, c.1926. *Source*: Middle East Center Archive, Saint Antony's College, Oxford. GB165–0201, Norman Mayers 1/40, with permission.

were clearly influential at 'Abd al-'Aziz's court. In both his English and Arabic writings, Rihani portrayed the new king favorably (with a touch of Arab Orientalism); and soon, in 1926, he again visited him, travelling this time on an airplane (Figure 8.3). Small wonder then that this American writer-activist received a horse from Arabia as a token of gratitude for his support.[89]

The gathering in Medina in December 1926 marks a moment when Syrians looking to bring an end to the French mandate, or simply to employment, turned their hopes to the new Saudi project. 'Abd al-'Aziz, for his part, needed able men to run his new domains and to help secure recognition of his authority both within the region and internationally, and he found a good number of them among the Syrians.[90] The king's personal doctor Midhat Shaykh al-Ard, the director of the Mecca health system Mahmud Hamdi Hamuda, the editor of the Meccan paper Rushdi Milhis, and Nabih al-'Azma and Fawzi al-Qawuqji, the officers temporarily in charge of training the new Saudi army, were all Syrians in search of employment.[91] The French army's suppression had also forced many Druze fighters to seek protection in Transjordan and in northern Arabia.

According to one statistic, there were 1,254 such Syrian fighters (together with their families) in northern Arabia in 1929.[92] Even the verifier of the descendants of the Prophet Muhammad (the *naqib al-ashraf*) in Damascus visited Mecca in 1926.[93] Some exiled Damascene notables in the *Istiqlali* group, such as Shukri al-Quwwatli, also turned to 'Abd al-'Aziz for material support, including weapons. Al-Quwwatli and Khalid al-Hakim, for example, organized a caravan full of weapons destined for the remaining Druze fighting groups in Syria in December 1926.[94]

As for the constitutional convictions of the *Istiqlali* activists, Yasin and Hamza appear to have regarded monarchy as the only regime form proper to a Muslim polity. Hamsa's edited memoirs include a remark he is said to have made in the 1920s that we may consider a piece of retroactive monarchical propaganda

> I am among those who studied the democratic and parliamentary order, and I was among those who warned about its disadvantages. It does not serve the needs of the people because it is based on the system of election in which the winner is not always the most honest person. Sometimes the winner of the election is the one who lies and deceives and misleads the most [. . .]. I rather approved the regime of one individual's government (*nizam al-hukuma al-fardiyya*), the just kind which confirms to the law of divine revelation that binds the head of government if he wants to oppress the people. That is: I would rather secure the freedoms of the people using divine obstruction and emotional inspiration [. . .]. I was of this opinion already at the time when I saw the problems of parliamentary order and its disadvantages and I still was far away from [living actually under] the rule of one individual's [monarchical] regime.[95]

Perceptions of these individuals differ. Writing in summer 1926, a British consul called 'Abd al-'Aziz's new hires "the Syrian parasites."[96] As to non-Saudi Syrians, many entertained a certain admiration towards the distant conqueror of the late 1920s, whom they, like the Europeans, called "Ibn Saud." Even Christians, such as the Palestinian historian 'Arif al-'Arif mentions how the new emir of Transjordan, 'Abd Allah, hated the conqueror from the Najd, but recounts that he himself in the summer of 1926 saw 'Abd al-'Aziz as a pure Arab leader.[97] A Saudi composite project, propelled by Syrian anti-mandate nationalism, was on its way to replacing the sharifian empire in the post-Ottoman Arabist imagination.

INTERNATIONAL LAW AND THE "KINGDOM OF THE HIJAZ AND THE NAJD AND ITS DEPENDENCIES"

The Istiqlalis, and especially Yusuf Yasin, were keen to help 'Abd al-'Aziz create what they considered a fully independent polity. They sought recognition both from the British Empire and the League of Nations. However, the League norms increasingly denied conquest as a legitimate means of territorial acquisition (as we have seen in Chapter Three). I propose in this section that the wartime title "King of the Hijaz" and its Allied recognition became what we may call a "sovereignty resource" for the new Saudi regime in international law. In other words, the Kingdom of the Hijaz was the Najdi occupiers' oxygen line to independence, because it averted the danger of the British government's continued control over their foreign relations. The final result was the new composite polity, officially called the "Kingdom of the Hijaz and the Kingdom of the Najd and Its Dependencies" in 1927.

The new government had to be careful because the 1915 treaty with the British Empire had subordinated the Najdi emirate to the British Empire. The *Istiqlali* activist Yusuf Yasin was aware that a Najdi annexation of the Hijaz would result in the Hijaz, too, being subordinated to British imperial authority. Instead, therefore, he reversed the situation and claimed not that 'Abd al-'Aziz had appended the Hijaz to the Najd, but rather that he had appended the Najd to the Hijaz, and thereby enjoyed sovereign authority by dint of the Allied Powers' 1919 recognition of Hijazi sovereignty.

Yasin had studied in the new Law Faculty in Damascus and knew the language of international law. As one of his first assignments, he seconded the Egyptian advisor Hafiz Wahba in October 1925 in the negotiations over the Iraqi border troubles with the British. The "Najdi party" in this negotiation thus comprised a Syrian and an Egyptian. Yasin came well prepared. He presented detailed lists and tables of Najdi casualties in the British air bombings over the Iraqi borderlands, raising such uncomfortable questions that British officials sought to remove him from negotiations.[98] Before long, he was the central figure in 'Abd al-'Aziz's foreign policy task force.

The cornerstone of Yusuf Yasin's policy was Hijazi international (what political scientists call "Westphalian") sovereignty. During the conquest period, the new Saudi official journal several times explained to the Arabic-reading public the "political status" of the Hijaz. Its second issue (December 1924) published, in Arabic, the joint letter of foreign consuls in Jidda stating their neutrality in the conflict (and warning that the Najdi army had no jurisdiction over their subjects). The journal also printed a message from 'Abd al-'Aziz to the effect that the Hijaz remained an independent country but that Muslims could participate in its governance, and calling for a conference to discuss its future (it became known eventually as the second caliphate conference).[99]

Yasin himself wrote in an article in *Umm al-Qura* that scholars of international law held that a "spot of land" was a "state" (*dawla*) if 1) if there existed a power with political authority to execute its will; 2) there was a population on that spot; and 3) the population possessed lands with known borders. If any of these conditions were not met, then the plot of land in question was not a state. Yasin added that, in his opinion, there was a fourth condition: recognition by other states. He concluded that the Hijaz satisfied all four conditions because many European states recognized it when it announced its independence from the Ottoman "Sultanate." He emphasized that neither changes in regime form nor revolts alter the international obligations of a state, and therefore they do not change the already existing recognition of a state. An example was Kemalist Turkey which, despite dethroning the Ottoman "king" (! *al-malik*), became the recognized successor of the Ottoman Empire. Thus, argued the author, the dethronement of the Hashemite dynasty and the establishment of an Islamic local government (*hukuma islamiyya ahliyya*) did not annul the recognized statehood of the Hijaz. In the same issue, Yasin explained again the consuls' letter, arguing that the consuls recognized the Hijaz and the Najd as two independent states and they affirmed that "the victor would be granted the land of the other."[100]

Recognition was indeed the crucial condition for the international legitimacy of the Najdi conquest, just as Yasin acutely highlighted. And this was a problem for, despite his efforts, Yasin was unable at first to secure inter-imperial recognition of the new regime. In the joint letter dated 2 December 1924, foreign consuls in the Hijaz made no acknowledgement of any transfer of sovereignty, but merely called 'Abd al-'Aziz's attention to the fact that protection of their "nationals" should be consistent with the "international law applicable to war time" and asserted full neutrality in the conflict.[101] 'Abd al-'Aziz responded that protection of foreign nationals in Mecca was founded on "the respect due to people of the Muslim lands."[102]

Adopting the earlier rationale of imperial inter-polity relations, foreign governments held off from recognizing a Saudi Kingdom of the Hijaz and waited instead for the British Empire first to make the first move. By a calculated coincidence, the French government did acknowledge, indirectly, that the Najd was an independent state when it stated that 'Abd al-'Aziz's representative in Damascus could no longer work under the supervision of the British consul in 1925. 'Abd al-'Aziz's ambiguous status also prompted the newly enthroned Reza Shah of Iran to send his consul in Damascus to the Hijaz to thank 'Abd al-'Aziz for his greetings—and of course to enquire, on behalf of his own Shi'i subjects, about the future of the holy cities.[103] The Soviets tacitly recognized 'Abd al-'Aziz, but they requested that he should not advertise this fact until the British publicly followed suit.[104] The British Government of India, however, asked the imperial government in London to postpone their recognition to discourage Indian Muslims whom, they feared, might understand it as a British plan for a new caliphate.[105]

The status of the sacred cities after the Saudi occupation was, certainly, a hot potato for British officials. In addition to the League-recognized sovereignty of the Kingdom of the Hijaz, the Indian Khilafat movement, the many caliphate conferences, and the now-forgotten Egyptian claims on the holy cities also complicated imperial recognition. And there was yet another conflict between the Foreign Office and the India Office. The imperial government was reluctant to upgrade 'Abd al-'Aziz from the status of a subordinated frontier sultan in the Gulf to a sovereign ruler in the Red Sea region. In January 1926, the Jidda consul was still addressing 'Abd al-'Aziz as "His Highness the Sultan" rather than "His Majesty."[106]

The Saudi government did not want a mere *de facto* recognition of the title. It insisted on British *de jure* recognition. Foreign Office officials doubted whether 'Abd al-'Aziz himself understood the legal niceties at stake: "It is impossible," wrote one with a touch of racist Orientalism, "that Ibn Saud in his own mind drew the distinction suggested."[107]

Discussion among British officials during February and March of 1926 underscores their fear that Islam might incite an uprising in India. L. D. Wakely of the Foreign Office recalled that the Allied Powers in 1916 designated al-Husayn "King of the Hijaz" as the title least freighted with religious significance. He explained that it would be better for a Muslim state to recognize 'Abd al-'Aziz's title first, because Muslims attached some sense of a "guardianship of the Holy Places" to this title. He also remarked that the British government in fact had not acknowledged 'Ali as king after al-Husayn's abdication in 1924.[108] Foreign Secretary Chamberlain strongly opined that they should not wait to recognize the "temporal" power of 'Abd al-'Aziz over the Hijaz, and that if Indian Muslims enquired into the "why" of the matter, it should be explained to them that this had nothing to do with the caliphate. He also emphasized that 'Abd al-'Aziz should not be enlightened about the difference between *de jure* and *de facto* recognition (as we have seen, either he or Yasin clearly knew the difference already).[109] Lord Birkenhead in India opposed a formal recognition of 'Abd al-'Aziz "as rightful king of the Hijaz" (*de jure*), but he had no objection to the simple symbolic recognition of him as "His Majesty" (*de facto*).[110] When India Office officials discovered that the Saudi assumption of kingship provoked less outrage among Muslims in India than Khilafat delegates had predicted, they dismissed fears that British recognition of 'Abd al-'Aziz's Hijazi kingship, whatever form it might take, would result in mass public disorder.[111]

London accordingly authorized the consul in Jidda to address 'Abd al-'Aziz as "His Majesty," thus giving their stamp of official recognition. There was one caveat, however: that despite said recognition Britain remained neutral as regarded "the regime in the Holy Places of Islam."[112] This was the British government's message that they were not opposed to the idea of an eventual Hijazi republic. Consul Jordan thereupon sent a telegraph to 'Abd al-'Aziz, informing him that the British government "now recognize[s] your Majesty as King of the Hijaz."[113] 'Abd al-'Aziz replied with a message of thanks, expressing the hope that he would be able to safeguard the "independence" of "this holy country."[114]

The British de facto recognition of 'Abd al-'Aziz's authority did not automatically entail recognition by Arab polities under British administration. For instance, there was no reaction from sharifian Iraq and Transjordan, nor from the occupied kingdom of Egypt. British officials, despite their best efforts, failed at convincing King Fuad of Egypt to recognize yet another Muslim Arab king as his equal. In addition, Fuad claimed the Hijaz as part of Egypt's Red Sea project.[115]

The new Saudi Syrians also had to accept that empire remained a source of sovereignty. They attempted to extend Hijazi League-sovereignty to the Najd, and 'Abd al-'Aziz began styling himself "King of the Hijaz and the Najd" instead of merely the (newly-recognized) King of the Hijaz. The British government vetoed the title as they still considered the Najd a subordinate polity.[116] The new king thus announced that once he returned to Riyadh the "necessary formalities, in the shape of the usual Bayat" would ensue.[117] And that is just what happened. Yusuf Yasin wrote to the British consul, explaining that "deputations" in Riyadh had decided "to constitute the Sultanate of Najd and Its Dependencies a kingdom" on 29 January 1927. Soon, in April 1927, "Abd al-'Aziz's new title "King of the Najd" was announced and communicated to the British government, which recognized it immediately.[118]

Thus, the "Kingdom of the Hijaz and the Kingdom of the Najd and Its Dependencies" was born as a new composite imperial project in April 1927.

One part (Hijaz) was a sovereign polity based on the Allied Powers' 1919 decision, whereas the other (Najd) remained merely a British-recognized kingdom; the territorial status of the "dependencies" (especially al-Ahsa) was unclear.

The Flattening of Sovereignty, 1932: From Composite Monarchy to the Arab Saudi Kingdom

There was a problem with a Saudi composite polity in which the parts were unequal. It carried the potential that the Hijaz's Allied-given recognition might be revoked and the Hijaz restored to the realm of British inter-polity relations. So long as this subtle threat persisted, the central control of Hijazi revenue, including the *hajj* dues, was impossible, not to speak of the debris of the uneven Ottoman and sharifian property regimes. Finally, the uncertainty also made it impossible to contract for much needed loans with sovereign actors and overseas companies. A flattening of sovereignty was needed.

As early as 1925, 'Abd al-'Aziz and Yasin had requested a new treaty with the British Empire. 'Abd al-'Aziz explained to the British consul in December of 1925 that three issues were at stake: the recognition of the Najd as an independent state, the right to import arms to the Najd, and financial assistance, because he had to pay the tribes who otherwise would venture into Iraq and Transjordan. He also warned the British consul of Bolshevik influence in Arabia and noted that he had received several financial offers from the Soviets.[119] Pointedly, the new government—possibly Yusuf Yasin or Fu'ad Hamza, acting on his behalf—continued to push for a new treaty in the name of the "Arab nation."[120]

Where does imperial law stop and where does international law start? At a series of inter-departmental conferences in London from March to November 1926, British officials from the Foreign Office, the Colonial Office, and the Government of India devoted minute attention to the question of exactly how a new treaty should be worded. British policy was shaped by a handful of guiding principles, such as the avoidance of any defense commitment, the recognition of the mandates, and the maintenance of the authority of consular officials to manumit slaves. On other points it was flexible, and indeed changed significantly during the conferences. These included the question as to who were the actual contractual parties to the treaty (the two governments or the two kings), whether the Foreign Office or the Colonial Office would communicate with the new Hijazi government (British officials noted Arab leaders' fear of the connotations evoked by the name of the Colonial Office, so agreed that instead the Foreign Office would conduct communication), and whether the Ottoman Capitulations could be enforced—this latter question ulti- mately being answered in the negative.[121]

The British officials also prepared to face the new professional Syrian- Saudi internationalism, in the person of Yusuf Yasin and others. Some suggested that George Antonius, "a first-class Arabist scholar," should be attached to the consul to negotiate the revised drafts that Yasin and others would counter-propose in Arabic.[122] Antonius, a trusted British official in mandate Palestine, was hoping for a promotion. He requested an up-grade in status from mere translator to delegate, and his wish was granted.[123] He would go on to write *The Arab Awakening* (financed by the anti-mandate American entrepreneur Charles Crane), the most important work on the Hashemite-inflected Arab nationalism of the interwar period.

What became known as the Treaty of Jidda in 1927 marked the tran- sition from intra-imperial to League-relations. It was also a diplomatic juncture, being the point at which the new Arabism emerged as an unof- ficial ideology in international relations; George Antonius helped the British officials—and it appears also the Saudi ones, too. The final text of the treaty, a product of long negotiations, differed greatly from the one the government officials had debated in London in 1926. Signed in Jidda on 20 May 1927, its first point stated that "His Britannic Majesty recognizes the complete and absolute independence of the domains of His Majesty the King of the Hejaz and of Nejd and Its Dependencies." The Arabic ver- sion mirrored this wording, referring to "complete and absolute indepen- dence" (*al-istiqlal al-tamm al-mutlaq*), terms familiar since late Ottoman times now in new meanings. Article 10 carefully underlined that the 1915 treaty, which subordinated the Najd to British representation abroad, would be void once this new treaty was signed. The English and Arabic versions were both deposited at the League of Nations, and the Arabic text (!) was published also in the League's *Treaty Series* as treaty N. 1658, as well as in Yasin's *Umm al-Qura*. It should be noted that that the "full independence" mentioned in the text still a somewhat murky issue. For instance, the British king recognized separate (!) Najdi and Hijazi "nation- ality" (*jinsiyya*) and promised "protection" to these individuals in British territories (possibly, for lack of a Saudi ambassy in Britain).[124]

Public recognition by the British Empire and the League was still not sufficient for business purposes. The United States of America, for exam- ple was not part of either organization, so when Jidda-based ex-officer- turned-businessman Harry St. John Philby wanted desperately to do

business with American companies, he had to wait until diplomatic relations with the US were properly established. By this time, Philby was an
agent in the Hijaz for a number of American companies (including Singer
Sewing Machines). In 1929, he begged the millionaire Charles Crane to
use his "influence in the right quarters" to help secure American recognition of the new polity.[125] (Crane also sent his engineer Karl Twitchell to
look for water in the Hijaz and then for oil in Eastern Arabia between
1928 and 1931, which led to the great oil finds there.[126]) But it was not
until May 1931 that the US recognized the Kingdom of the Hijaz and the
Kingdom of the Najd and Its Dependencies.

The new Saudi composite polity was independent, poor, and unstable.
The federated government was not able to fully control the Hijazi merchants and the domestic market, so that the years of the Great Depression
were particularly difficult. The economy reached a particular low in 1931,
when unidentified men stole gasoline from foreign companies in the
Hijaz, allegedly to fill the beloved cars of the king.[127] And in the summer
of 1932, exiled Hijazis with sharifian support attempted an uprising.[128]
In the same summer, the *Istiqlali* brother Fu'ad Hamza and Emir Faysal's
undertook a Euro-Asian tour seeking loans and offered as collateral con-
cessions for hydrocarbons in al-Ahsa. It was unsuccessful.[129] This dire
state of affairs demanded a solution.

The September 1932 unification was the answer. It made possible the
complete control over the "Dependencies" such as oil-rich al-Ahsa. When
in the next year the American company Standard Oil acquired the concession to drill for Arabian oil in the Eastern Province the terms of the contract specified that, in return for the concession, the company would issue
a multi-installment loan to the Saudi government. The Saudi government
saw American Standard Oil first and foremost as a source of private credit.
This was so important that Article Three in the contract specified the
financial conditions of the first installment of the loan in minute details.[130]

After 1932, the flattening of sovereignty in the Saudi polity also formalized the transformation of property relations, slowly replacing a
qadi-centered legal apparatus with a centralized state bureaucracy, and
placing the Hijazi economy under government control.[131] The new Hijazi
property law of 1934 authorized only subjects (*ra'aya*) of the government
to own real estate in the Hijaz. "In keeping with the practice of previous
governments," foreigners had no right to own real estate. The law thus
entailed the enforced dispossession of the large number of non-Saudi
Muslims in the Hijaz. Those who had possessed real estate in the Hijaz
before 1932 became foreigners "by the change of sovereignty (*hakimiyya*)

or citizenship" and had to sell or endow their property. These conditions entailed a legal distinction between non-Saudi and Saudi Muslims, because for the former category pious endowments were henceforth the only form of real-estate "ownership" that they were permitted in the Hijaz.[132] After some confusion over this law, Yasin's journal communicated again that it was valid only within the Hijazi region (*bilad al-Hijaz*), whose borders were given "in the noble revelation." Finally, the government had to announce that those who owned property in the Hijaz in the time of Ottoman and sharifian governments but had since legally become foreigners, might "enjoy" their properties if these were returned to them in a legally valid way.[133] Thus ended the decentralized polity known as the "Kingdom of the Hejaz and of Nejd and Its Dependencies" and a new era opened for the new Arab Saudi Kingdom.

Conclusion

I have argued that the logic of modular state-making directed the transition from a sharifian imperial formation to a Saudi-led polity in the late 1920s. Due to the inability of the Najdi invaders to control the Hijaz and the British fear of Muslim reaction in India, the right of conquest was not enforced. The Istiqlali Syrian activists also preferred the composite logic at the time, if only to re-use the sovereignty of Hijazi kingship in British negotiations. All their available private and public discourses suggest that these Syrians were driven by an anti-French nationalist ideology. The new Saudi polity was their revenge on the League of Nations.

Positive international law, emerging between empire (organizing inter-polity relations) and the League (organizing inter-sovereign relations), was their instrument. From the very beginning, the Saudi government did not consider Islamic laws of conquest in its takeover of the Hijaz. The act of "unification" in 1932 then enabled the government to intervene in both customary and Islamic laws of property in the Hijaz and al-Ahsa. The flattening of sovereignty certainly served the Saudi ruling elite. But did this Arab polity fulfill the hopes of the anti-mandate activists? In order to answer this question, we now turn to the connected and parallel origins of the State of Syria.

CHAPTER NINE

The Throne of Damascus, 1925–1939

IN OCTOBER 1928, Fu'ad Hamza sent a secret letter from Mecca to Sheikh al-Qassab in British Haifa. These two members of the not-so-secret Independence Party (*Hizb al-Istiqlal*), a loose network of Syrian activists dispersed around the Mediterranean and the Red Sea, were disappointed by the outcome of the constitutional process in the new State of Syria under French administration, which had been in existence now for about three years, beginning in 1925. The French High Commission had just suspended the constituent assembly in Damascus because the draft constitution contained six articles that denied the validity of the partitions agreed upon by the Allied Powers. But this was not the main reason for Hamza's and al-Qassab's disappointment. They objected to the draft because it created a republic with a Muslim president, while they had instead advocated for a monarchy with a Saudi emir. Hamza took the view that the struggle between the Syrians and the French would continue endlessly because the two parties differed as to their preferred "forms of constitutional regime" (*al-ashkal al-dusturiyya*). The *Istiqlali* group now needed a new, "nationalist strategy": they would need to organize and mobilize, and they would need to collect money if they were going to bring their imagined monarchy into being. In order to test the waters, Fu'ad Hamza asked al-Qassab to canvass the other *Istiqlali* "brothers."[1]

Historians often interpret this and the various other monarchical plans that circulated in mandate Syria, as deliberate maneuvers on the part of the French High Commission to obstruct national unity during the constitutional process in 1928 and later.[2] The story of the 1928 Syrian constitution is an element in the larger story about nationalist struggle against the French. In this narrative, both parties—and there are only two, the French and the republican Syrians—understood the constitution as a declaration of freedom. Hence, we learn, the French authorities wanted to prevent the party of the Syrian secular, republican nationalists (the Syrian National Bloc) from such an act as they feared they would have to provide independence. Accordingly, a number of studies critique the French manipulations and, on the other hand, what they call the Syrian National Bloc's "paternal republicanism," while others interpret the 1928 constitution as a foundational text in republican history.[3]

I argue in this chapter that, instead of unity, a disagreement about Syria's political nature occurred among Syrians during the making of the new local state. The story of the 1928 constitution I present is not a story of national unity marshalled against a colonizing power, but rather a bundle of narratives about disagreement among secularist nationalists, Muslim activists, successor diasporic groups, and former Ottoman patricians over Syria as a political idea. The story of this constituent moment is also about how the advocates of a genealogical, sharifian association confronted with the advocates of a Saudi-led Muslim federation over Syria. Secondly, this argument also emphasizes the uncertainty of the French officials over how to use the new League-instruments available through international administrative law to perpetuate their domination.

The first issue directs our attention to monarchist individuals and groups, who have been largely left outside of the republican narrative. There is a significant literature on the "Syrian throne" question in the interwar period, most of which sees it as an element in the pan-Arab nationalist discourse.[4] But viewed from the perspective of new imperial history, the idea of Syria-as-a-princely-state was a post-Ottoman feature. Successor societies and successor diasporas competed in state-making. In the late 1920s, in addition to the *Istiqlali* activists, there were at least two other groups: a sharifian-Hashemite group (which had its origin in the 1918–1920 period of Faysal's reign over OETA East) and post-Ottoman patricians, including other *ashraf*, who were in search of new dominions. The survey of this teeming post-imperial world in the 1920s and 1930s Eastern Mediterranean, including successor diasporas debating the making of a new external homeland in Syria, provides us a fascinating view of the difficulty of post-imperial state-making.[5]

This second issue is the easiest to understand. From the French point of view, the Syrian constitution was part of the "organic law" (*statut organique*) prescribed by the class A mandate, a legal instrument to be composed by the mandatory power and submitted to the League of Nations, "in agreement with the native authorities."[6] French bureaucrats, who considered the mandate a prestige region in the interwar French Empire, saw the organic law of mandated regions not as a declaration of independence, but rather as an administrative document that fulfilled the conditions for continued French domination and the partition imposed by the Covenant of the League, as I have explained in Chapter Three. Due to leftist pressure in Paris and public condemnation after the brutal suppression of the 1925 uprising, they had to accept local elections and an assembly as the means to the creation of the constitutional text, but nevertheless held it to be strictly an element in the organic law. Their strategy therefore ended in a constituent act in 1930, namely, the declaration by Henri Ponsot, the French High Commissioner, of a slightly modified 1928 republican constitution.[7]

The post-Ottoman monarchists and the French administrators operated through ideas what scholars call "imperial constitutionalism." "Imperial constitutionalism" in the twentieth century was a counterrevolutionary, cosmopolitan legal imaginary, the advocacy for a system of segmented, subordinated, and often unelected sovereignty, quite unlike the theoretically homogenous and democratic order of a nation-state.[8] We can see the 1930 French declaration of the Syrian constitution as an imperial constituent act from above and the monarchical ambitions of individuals— sheiks, intellectuals, post-Ottoman grandees, emirs, and tribal leaders—as imperial constitutionalism from below. All shared the view that the constitution was not an expression of the people's will but rather a changeable symbol of popular consent to an unelected form of domination.

Instead of the secular-nationalist focus, imperial constitutionalism about Syria recenters our attention on Islam as an important element in Syrian state-making. The Islamic component was so strong that finally even the 1928 republican constitution had to include the condition that the president be a Muslim. (We must note that, unlike the situation in Cold War religious republics like Pakistan and Israel, religion was not a defining mark of nationality in Syria.)[9] This is why, after Ponsot's appointment of an unmistakenly Muslim president (Shaykh Taj al-Din, the ex-*qadi* of Damascus), in 1932 a man who was perhaps the last Arab-Ottoman Hamidian, Muhammad 'Ali 'Abid (his father had been a close confident of Sultan Abdülhamid II before 1908) was elected to preside over the republican polity.[10] Using Islam in state-making testifies to the lingering shadow that Sultan Abdülhamid II cast over Syria, right down to the time of the Second World War.

Recycling Empire in Syria: The Last Hamidian State?

We'll begin with two vignettes from the archives. Both show groups of Syrians and lingering Hamidian patricians contemplating the establishment of a Syrian monarchy well after the collapse of the sharifian polity in 1920. In these visions, recycling Ottoman authority in Syria translated into the search for a Muslim individual to manage local diversity, to ensure the continued relevance of Islam, and to preserve the new French imperial connection.

The first vignette takes us to December 1926. Henri Ponsot the powerful but somewhat colorless French High Commissioner to Mandate Lebanon and Syria sends a letter to the French Ministry of Foreign Affairs. The letter has an Arab genealogical tree attached. Ponsot informs the ministry of the claims of a certain ʿAli Haydar to "the throne of Syria." As we saw him in the previous chapters, Haydar was an Ottomanized *sharif*, a descendant of the Prophet Muhammad, who ended up as the last Ottoman Emir of Mecca during the final years of the First World War. In 1926, now as a refugee in Beirut, his son ʿAbd al-Majid—the one who got his portrait painted by Abdülmecid Efendi, the last caliph—had submitted their family tree to the High Commission, along with a detailed explanation in French. Should the new State of Syria become a Franco-Arab monarchy, this young *sharif* suggested to the High Commission and, consequently, Ponsot to the ministry, ʿAli Haydar had the best credentials to rule.[11]

The second vignette is set a few years later. In September 1931, Abbas Hilmi II, the ex-khedive of Egypt, received an exciting letter while in his Swiss exile. Ahmed Hamdi Zeza Pasha, an ex-Ottoman army general, wrote from Constantza, Romania, that Abbas Hilmi should become the ruler of the new State of Syria. The general attached another letter written by a certain Dr. Arif Hikmet (Quluji) of Aleppo. Hikmet had written to Abbas Hilmi that "now that your rights to rule in Egypt have been abolished, you should look for another place to rule. In Syria, the political parties considered neither ʿAli, the king of the Hijaz, nor Sharif ʿAli Haydar, nor Ahmed Nami, nor Zayd b. al-Husayn acceptable as a ruler."[12] Both the general and the Aleppine doctor viewed the ex-khedive positively as a remnant of the Ottoman world. Their letters were written in ceremonial Ottoman Turkish in 1931, well after the Kemalist reforms had abolished this script and language in the new Turkish republic. In a strange but not at the time an unusual turn of events, despite its denial of the imperial past, Turkey's own preferred regnal candidate for Syria was also ex-khedive Abbas Hilmi II.[13]

These two vignettes are about ex-Ottoman patricians, once powerful Muslim aristocrats in the old Hamidian regime. Years after the dissolution of their empire they and some luminaries still cherished hopes of creating a Muslim monarchy in the new State of Syria. Given the many post-imperial local monarchies of the 1920s, from Hungary to Afghanistan, the prospect of a political spoliation of imperial rule was not an anachronistic dream. The first plan with 'Ali Haydar as king of Syria would have created a small Franco-sharifian genealogical monarchy, similar to British-sharifian Transjordan. The second would have transplanted the ex-khedive of Egypt to a place where he could create an even more "Ottoman," and perhaps Turkey-friendly polity.

The aborted plans for monarchical state-making represent paths of extrication from the imperial Ottoman context into the League-world. Their significance lies first in understanding the importance of the old-style monarchical emancipation of subordinated regions in the interwar period (see Chapter Two) as a form of integration through empire into the League. Second, the fact that they never came to realization does not mean they did not survive in transmuted and clandestine forms. As we shall see, some of these plans and their central goal of making Islam a part of the political order evidence a concern to plan societies in which the politics of diversity and inequality from above and from below would persist. Let us now survey more fully the catalog of ex-imperial Muslim grandees who presented their candidatures before the somewhat surprised Syrian people and the calculating French administrators.

A FRANCO-OTTOMAN PRINCELY STATE

Until the summer of 1928, it looked likely that Syria's future would take the form of a Franco-Ottoman princely state. This would require the appointment of a Muslim patrician—possibly ethnically non-Arab and Turkish-speaking—as a monarch in Damascus, who would function in the same way as Faysal did in Baghdad and 'Abd Allah in Amman, simultaneously catering to both local and imperial interests while representing a light Islamic politics.

This prospect had emerged immediately after the 1920 occupation of Damascus, when the French authorities considered Ahmad Nami (1879–1962), a Francophone and Francophile ex-Ottoman patrician; Abbas Hilmi II, the ex-khedive of Egypt; Emir Sa'id al-Jaza'irli, from the famous localized pro-French Moroccan notable family in Damascus; and Sharif 'Ali Haydar, whom we have already met more than once, as possible candidates to create such a political order.

A rich Circassian Muslim patrician whose family had moved to Syria in the nineteenth century, Ahmad Nami had studied in the Military College in Istanbul, and later received high-level appointments in Ottoman army units in Beirut and Izmir. He married one of the last Ottoman princesses (Hamide Ayşe, a daughter of Abdülhamid II), hence his nickname "the

Damad" (the son-in-law of the sultan).[14] He spent the war years comfortably in Geneva. (Coincidentally, he was a freemason and the president of a freemasonic lodge in Beirut.)[15] In 1920, Nami had been quick to offer himself as the new king when the French forced Faysal out of Damascus. He was judged suitable by those French officials who lobbied for a strictly "non-Arab" monarch. But the High Commission judged it too early to install a "prince" at the head of their new Federation of the States of the Levant. At the time, they actually considered that the political form of this federation should be left to the Syrians.[16] In a move paradigmatic of spoliation, the president of the States of the Levant became Subhi Barakat, an Ottoman and French loyalist, who did not speak Arabic well and thus his council meetings were often conducted in Turkish.[17] Nami, staying in Beirut, waited throughout the 1920s for the post-Ottoman Syrian throne.

In the early 1920s, the swirl of monarchical ideas and rumors in the postwar political underworld was a correlate to the emerging Anglo-French rivalry and the confusion among the Allied Powers over how to quiet the post-Ottoman tumult. Beirut, a Franco-Ottoman city of exile, was a microcosm of the larger scene, awash with rumors and uncertainties. It was where both Nami and Haydar stayed in the mid-1920s, and it enabled them to be in direct discussions with the French High Commission (whose headquarters were in Lebanon and not in Damascus).

For his part, the ex-khedive Abbas Hilmi, now circulating between the new Turkey and an old Switzerland, wanted to take revenge on the British Empire. An opportunity presented itself as early as 1922. By presenting his candidacy for a kingship in the occupied Syrian regions, the ex-khedive was able to spark an outbreak of Anglo-French rivalry. The British authorities evaluated a possible khedivial monarchy in Syria as a French attempt at "retaliation" for Britain's making Faysal king in Iraq. And it indeed may have been the product of a bit of diplomatic scheming on behalf of General Gouraud or his staff through their representative, Comte de Cardes, in Egypt. The latter wanted to see "iron despotism on oriental lines" in occupied Syria. Upon being challenged by British diplomats, however, French Prime Minister Poincaré denied any knowledge of such a scheme. The rumors briefly abated when the announcement of the Federation of the Levant in 1922 ended the immediate possibility of any Franco-Ottoman Syrian monarchy.[18] But in 1924 they began to resurface, now from below: a French agent reported that the Ottoman-Syrian activist Shakib Arslan had offered "the throne of Syria" to Abbas Hilmi II at a meeting in Lausanne, in anticipation of a future French evacuation of Syria after the peace treaty.[19]

After the French High Commission created the State of Syria in 1925, the League of Nations and Socialist representatives in the French parliament together forced the High Commission to begin the *political* construction of the new state through elections and thus involve to local assemblies in the making of the mandate's "organic law." Now the French administrators and resident Syrians would have to fashion the mandate's organic law *together*, an essentially imperial instrument, using democratic institutions, but without freedom. While this task was relatively easily accomplished in Lebanon where the notables opted for French rule, in the more complex and disorderly State of Syria (and the still autonomous, federated small governments of Jebel Druze and the Alawites) all parties resorted to secret deals, negotiations, and spying.[20]

First, the French High Commission devised a plan to create a dynastic state. It was thereby following the imperial constitutional logic familiar from nineteenth-century Europe and twentieth-century British India. In 1926, in the midst of the Druze revolt, the journalist High Commissioner Henry de Jouvenel appointed none other than Ahmad Nami, the ex-Ottoman patrician dubbed "the Damad" whose career we outlined above, as the head of the new Syrian government. His appointment was the first step towards the construction of a Franco-Ottoman Syrian princely state. In the opinion of High Commissioner de Jouvenel, "the Damad" was the perfect monarchical candidate, ideally suited to facilitating an easy French exit from Syria. The High Commissioner and Nami achieved what Syrians called "the Damad–de Jouvenel Agreement": a road map to independence, involving the establishment of a constitutional assembly, a bilateral treaty, and dynastic rule.

The timing seemed perfect. 1926 was a year when the modular Muslim dimension of the French empire was already on full display, as Yusuf, the reigning sultan of Morocco, was visiting Paris to inaugurate the city's new Grand Mosque. At precisely that moment, in July 1926, de Jouvenel started to lobby the foreign ministry for the establishment of a "throne in Syria" and for the careful choice of a Muslim monarch whose instructions would be to achieve independence. Informally, even the League of Nations heard of his plan. Throughout 1927, Nami spent large sums on propaganda, sponsoring tribal petitions in his favor, establishing lobbying groups in cities, and employing the *Qadi* of Beirut to champion him in communications with the diaspora.[21] The head of French intelligence, Colonel Catroux, liked or at least trusted Nami.[22] De Jouvenel's preferred candidate was clearly Nami. And not only his. During a tour Nami made in Northern Syria, village people in Alexandretta and Aleppo greeted him

FIGURE 9.1. Ahmad Nami and his government, 1926. *Source*: private archive of a Syrian family, with permission.

in Turkish with the traditional Ottoman greeting: "Long live my sultan (*padişahım çok yaşa*)!"[23] It would be difficult to cite a clearer example of empire recycled from below. (Figure 9.1)

But De Jouvenel did not understand that his superiors in the French Foreign Ministry (most of whom belonged to the infamous *parti colonial*) considered the mandate a permanent form of control over what was for France a strategic asset. In addition, learning of Nami's scheming, more than two hundred Damascene notables sent a telegram to the Foreign Ministry, requesting the fulfillment of de Jouvenel's promise that "the form of government should be left to a national assembly, which should be elected."[24]

The new High Commissioner Henri Ponsot forced Nami to step down in January 1928, but the ex-Ottoman patrician continued to nurture monarchical aspirations. For instance, in 1929, Nami's friend Musa Tawil, a rich merchant, sent a clear message to the High Commission: he requested that Ponsot should declare the *loi organique*, set aside the 1928 constitution, and, by placing his trust only in the country's rich, bring about economic prosperity in the country.[25] In December 1928, Ponsot received several, suspiciously artful supporting telegrams from Aleppo, the North of Syria and the "tribes of Syria" asking him to appoint "the

Damad" as king for this was the only hope for unity.[26] In late February and early March 1929, petitions, mostly from Aleppo, flooded the ministry and the High Commission, again applauding "the Damad" as *l'homme du jour* (*rajul al-yawm* in some of the Arabic originals, in others "a man free from faults," *al-shakhs al-munazzah 'an al-ghabat*).[27] The Lebanese journal *Hurriya* asked where had all the rival candidate "princes" been when Syria was in difficult circumstances (undoubtedly a reference to the 1925–26 French violence), and followed up with its own support for "the Damad." A reporter of the journal *al-'Ahd al-Jadid* visited Aleppo, the city where Nami enjoyed his strongest backing, and described his supporters: among them, he noted, "Turks."[28] Nami seems thus to have been a veritable "imperial" candidate, in the sense that his ethnicity was less important than his social status, even as late as 1929.

Ponsot's own preferred candidate was 'Ali Haydar, who as we have seen in previous chapters was a truly Hamidian *sharif* left behind after the partition of the Ottoman Empire. The High Commissioner was influenced here by Damascene notables who considered Nami too much of an alien (and perhaps an instrument of Aleppo merchants). Why Ponsot preferred Haydar, who was almost as much a foreigner to Damascus as Nami, remains a question for future research. Ponsot certainly understood the value of a descendent of the Prophet Muhammad, and possibly reckoned that the best weapon to counteract the British establishment of sharifian power from Transjordan to Iraq was the establishment of a similar French genealogical sub-empire.

By 1928, 'Ali Haydar was humiliated, poor, old, and tired. After shuttling back and forth between the Hijaz and Damascus during the war, he had stayed put for a year or so in Mount Lebanon, after his short tenure in besieged Medina. He was recalled to Istanbul by the imperial government in 1918. From that point onwards this Ottoman Arab patrician watched his world quite literally falling apart. He was obliged to remain in Istanbul until 1926(!); only his sons could leave the city. The sultan in 1919 withdrew his appointment as Emir of Mecca to ease agreements with the Allied Powers, and the splintering Ottoman government recognized Sharif al-Husayn as the King of the Hijaz.[29] Haydar was devastated. The Allied Powers and especially the British government had no intention of exchanging al-Husayn for Haydar but, for a fleeing moment in 1920, the imperial planners considered this *sharif* as a candidate also for the throne of Iraq. Haydar also proposed himself to the French authorities sometime during 1920 or in 1921 as the successor of Faysal in Damascus. His eldest son 'Abd al-Majid was particularly invested in his father's claims.

'Abd al-Majid was, as we have learned, also a *damad* since he had married Rukiya, a lesser princess from the sultanic family. He did not scruple to advance the rights he perceived as emanating from their relations with the vanquished Ottomans: in the moment of the Saudi occupation of Mecca in 1925 he and Haydar requested the throne of the Hijaz from the British government, or at least the remaking of the sharifian emirate of Mecca under the new Saudi reign. In 1926, they finally left Istanbul. The French High Commission invited them to Beirut, and after a futile and humiliating attempt to disembark in Jidda, where the new king 'Abd al-'Aziz did not allow them to step on shore, the impoverished Ottoman *ashraf* found refuge in Beirut.[30]

Ponsot thus had some individuals at hand with whom to create a Franco-sharifian polity, an anti-British genealogical monarchy in Syria. He allowed Haydar and his son 'Abd al-Majid to drum up support for their cause in Damascus, Aleppo, and the countryside, and the Haydars began to gain a following among the tribes of Syria as well. Ponsot met other possible candidates, but Haydar was his firm choice as founder for a new local dynasty.[31] In December 1926, as we have seen, Ponsot sent a letter to the foreign ministry about the candidates "well known to you" for the Syrian throne, but of these he described only 'Ali Haydar and attached the latter's extensive genealogy to the letter.[32] With Ponsot's approval, 'Abd al-Majid travelled to Damascus in the summer of 1927 to drum up support for his father's candidacy, this time among prominent merchants. Of all the potential regnal candidates, 'Abd al-Majid was perhaps the most bitter following the July 1928 decision on the establishment of a Syrian republic. On the very day of the assembly's meeting in August 1928, he wrote a long and angry letter in which he sought to persuade Ponsot and the French Foreign Ministry of the need for a royal government in Syria.[33]

Rumors about a vacant throne in Damascus in 1928 also attracted a number of random fortune-seeking aristocrats. One was "Prince" 'Adil b. Ayad (or Ben-Aïad, as he spelled his name in French), a completely unexpected Tunisian-Egyptian Frenchman. He sought to win support for his candidacy on the grounds that he was a "real French Muslim by education," which would enable him to serve as France's "auxiliary" in Syria.[34]

Others continued to lobby for Abbas Hilmi II, the ex-khedive of Egypt. After French officials had already considered and rejected his candidacy in the early 1920s, in 1926 he received in his Swiss exile a note about the Syrian throne and Haydar's candidature.[35] This strategically savvy ex-Ottoman notable, however, waited a few years until the more powerful candidates had played their cards. As it turned out, he waited too long.

As we have seen, in late 1931, with the support of the Turkish Republic, his supporters restarted a propaganda campaign in support of his candidature.[36] Hasan Khalid Abu al-Huda, prime minister in Transjordan, regularly updated the ex-khedive about events in Syria.[37] Abbas Hilmi's shadow remained over Syria. In June 1933, Sheikh Taj al-Din, the first president of the Syrian Republic, was questioned yet again about the candidature of the ex-khedive Abbas Hilmi II for the Syrian throne. In sad desperation, he replied: "Why Abbas Hilmi and why not me?"[38]

A SHARIFIAN PRINCELY STATE OF SYRIA?

The local vision that most unsettled the French High Commission was the prospect of a king from among the sons of Sharif al-Husayn. Historians have already shown how the neighboring Hashemite rulers, Faysal in Iraq and 'Abd Allah in Transjordan, presented their own claims to authority over the State of Syria and even to Palestine, premising these on their Arab and Muslim backgrounds.[39] The last of these took the form of the Greater Jordan project of 'Abd Allah in 1948, when the West Bank in Palestine became administered by Jordan.

In the 1920s, Faysal and 'Abd Allah, the Anglo-Ottoman *ashraf*, competed with each other for the throne of Damascus. They were not the only Hashemite candidates: their brothers Zayd and 'Ali—this latter briefly king of the Hijaz in 1925—were also competing, because Faysal often supported 'Ali's candidature instead of his own. A forgotten episode in this story saw a clash between these Hashemites and the new Saudi ruler, with the *Istiqlali* group advocating the candidacy of another Faysal, the second son of King 'Abd al-'Aziz, as king of Syria. The episode is an instructive one, and worthy of attention. I shall first focus on the sharifian story and then proceed to consider the Saudi-Istiqlali side.

The sharifian option began with diplomacy. French-Iraqi (Faysali) relations after the 1920 expulsion of Faysal took the form of a gradual rapprochement. In 1925, Faysal visited Paris once again. The chief diplomats, Berthelot and de Caix, asked advice informally from their former enemy, now the king in Baghdad, about the political order in the State of Syria, in hopes that this might help them in composing the League's organic law. Not surprisingly, Faysal advised them to look for a "native leader" to pacify and unite these Syrian lands.[40]

The idea of a new sharifian king, especially a son of King al-Husayn, did have local supporters in the major Syrian cities. The enthronement of a *sharif* presented also the possibility of realizing a composite Arab project based on ethnicity, language, and blood—and Islam. In the spring of 1928, this prospect revitalized the ex-Hijazi (ex-Ottoman) retired military officers 'Arif Idlibi and Tahsin Fakir, who began actively lobbying for an Arab Muslim and, if possible, Hashemite king.[41] Rida Bey al-Abad and others, also ex-Hijazi officers, expressed as well their preference for establishing a Hashemite sharifian monarchy.[42] A certain Ahmad Ratib seems to have been the main organizing force, as he established a number of Hashemite monarchist groups and parties. According to French secret service reports, he was the head of the *Watan* ("Homeland") party, which had its center in Aleppo, led by the Turkish doctor Aref Hikmet, and branches also in Homs, Tripoli, and Hama.[43] These were perhaps the best organized of the regional monarchist operations.

Excited also were intellectuals and notables who had held a position in the short-lived Faysalian government in 1920, or who believed in the benefits of a monarchy, or were enticed by hopes of their own promotion under a new monarchical regime. The Damascene journal *Alif Ba'*, which supported the Hashemites, in early May of 1928 republished, in Arabic, an originally French study on the regnal question. Its Christian editor Yusuf al-'Isa had served in Faysal's cabinet in 1920. In this article, two urban notables proclaimed their belief that "the Syrians are imbued with the spirit of republicanism." Another notable, Sa'id al-Ghazzi, expressed his republican views by observing that all of Syria's diverse communities could be represented by a president, whereas any king would have to be Muslim. Editor Yusuf al-'Isa published his own, fervently monarchical opinion two days later. He argued that "a king means independence. A king cannot be treated as a president [. . .], he cannot be impeached [. . .]; with a king, the laws of the High Commissioner would end soon." Another Christian notable, the legal scholar Faris al-Khuri, objected that a king would, on the contrary, be better placed than a parliament to serve the interests of the High Commissioner. To this argument al-'Isa answered that a constitutional king would be bound by a parliament. The notable Ata al-Ayyub in the next issue declared that the people seemed to be ready for a republic. Finally, *Alif Ba'* proposed a referendum on what type of regime should be adopted.[44] In May 1928, the Hashemite-partisan 'Arif Idlibi and others went to the *Alif Ba'* office to express their support and congratulations for the pro-monarchist articles. Idlibi's party had grown substantially and now included among its numbers the verifier of the descendants of the Prophet Muhammad (*naqib al-ashraf*), who had in fact been restored to this title by Faysal in 1919, and the al-Khatibs, a very influential local family of Muslim jurists. Importantly, the monarchists were mostly aged

60 or older, much older than the republican group, representing the Hamidian political generation.[45]

Faysal, the king in Baghdad, was angry when he heard that some were considering the candidacy of another Faysal, the Saudi emir, a son of his rival. He told the French consul that appointing a "fanatic prince would be a grave danger," and recommended his older brother 'Ali as the Hashemite candidate.[46] Faysal's main goal was not necessarily to install a Hashemite prince, but he certainly wanted to exclude the possibility of a rival prince. He took the matter seriously. In June of 1928, his five-man delegation arrived in Damascus, where the Hashemites had a strong base. The leader of the delegation, Nuri al-Sa'id, told Ponsot that "his main goal was to explain the dangers of the candidature of a Wahhabite prince." He added that a Hashemite ruler would be best placed to establish close, "friendly" relations between Iraq and Syria. Ponsot replied that a Hashemite candidate would anger the "Wahhabites," and vice versa. Arguments aside, Ponsot firmly underlined that he would not tolerate divisive propaganda.[47] Nuri al-Sa'id then attended a session of the Constitutional Assembly, where he received a cold reception from both the National Bloc and the High Commission. Soon thereafter the Iraqi delegation left Damascus.

The local pro-Hashemite groups did not, however, cease their activity, and neither did Faysal, Zayd, and 'Abd Allah give up their claims to the throne of Syria. In July 1928, the important royalist Jabiri family organized evening gatherings in Aleppo.[48] A petition (*mazbata*) for a monarchy was signed by 1,500 individuals and sent to Ihsan Jabiri and Riyad al-Sulh, two Syrian elite activists who would later testify about the Syrian question at the League of Nations in Geneva.[49] On 1 August 1928, a monarchist meeting was held in the home of Ahmad Ratib. The attendees selected a committee, which visited Hashim al-Atassi, leader of the National Bloc, to present their demands for a monarchy.[50] As late as 4 August, as the republican constitution was getting accepted, the ex-sharifian, retired officers continued to pressure merchants into signing a petition for a monarchy in hopes of forcing the constituent assembly to change the proposed republican draft.[51]

The French suspension of the assembly caused a split among the sharifian monarchists. In a strange reenactment of the nineteenth century, the two Meccan *ashraf* clans—the Zayd and the 'Awn clans (see Chapter Four)—had a skirmish over Syria in the fall of 1928. The monarchists interpreted the suspension in a way that still left some hope for a monarchy—but the question now presented itself, whose monarchy would this be? In the fall of 1928, some felt that Sharif Haydar would be more acceptable to High Commissioner Ponsot than the sons of al-Husayn. In November, the French secret service noted that 'Arif Idlibi had quarreled with Ahmad Ratib in Aleppo and now had founded his own party. The reason for the split was that Ratib had shifted his loyalty and was now lending support to a monarchical program with 'Ali Haydar as its royal candidate.[52] Idlibi thus formed a new nexus of power with other two parties, whose leaders agreed that a constitutional monarchy should be formed in Syria with a king from "a noble Arab family," that is to say, a son of al-Husayn. In December 1928, Idlibi argued to the High Commission that Islam required a monarchy, thus identifying Islam with this regime form. He called his group the "Monarchist National Bloc" (*al-Kutla al-Malakiyya al-Wataniyya*).[53]

Sharifian monarchist propaganda, much like the propaganda for "the Damad" Ahmed Nami, intensified in 1929, long after the decision had been made to adopt a republican constitution. Ratib wrote to Arif Hikmet and others in Aleppo urging them to step up their campaign for a monarchy.[54] On 21 January 1929, he organized a large gathering of monarchists, including once again 'Arif Idlibi.[55] On 16 August 1929, ten "chiefs of the Syrian tribes" submitted a telegram to the Foreign Ministry expressing their disappointment with the present government and asking "to change the mentioned government into a kingship (*royauté*)."[56] The same day some members of the Reform, National Unity, and the Monarchist parties (the latter comprising the factions of Khayri Jaza'irli, 'Arif Idlibi, and Tahsin al-Fakhir) also sent a telegram, welcoming unfounded rumors that the French Foreign Minister had decided to create a monarchy in Syria.[57] As we shall see in the last section of this chapter, the Hashemites themselves did not abandon their attempts to create a modular polity through a monarchy in the State of Syria until the 1940s.

The Istiqlali *plan: A Saudi Emirate of Syria?*

I return now to Fu'ad Hamza and Sheikh Kamil al-Qassab, and the dispersed *Istiqlali* brothers' search for an anti-mandate power. Back in 1917, 'Abd al-'Aziz, at the time the ruler of Najd in Eastern Arabia, had told a British officer that he had a dream: to conquer and destroy Ottoman Damascus. In the midst of war, the officer thought this an excellent idea.[58] A different dream about a Saudi Syria was born in 1925, and it appears that on this occasion the dreamer was not 'Abd al-'Aziz, but rather the *Istiqlali* network. They found their anti-mandate pole of power in this Najdi conqueror.

I have argued in the previous chapter that we should situate the making of Saudi Arabia and the making of the State of Syria within one regional framework of social-political history. 'Abd al-'Aziz needed able men to run his new domains and to promote his acceptance in the region and internationally; he seized the opportunity during the global financial crisis to acquire well-trained Syrians with excellent connections.[59] I have described a group of Syrians in the service of 'Abd al-'Aziz in Mecca and Riyadh, who were interested and invested in the future of Syria. There was constant traffic between Mecca, Damascus, Cairo, and Jerusalem. Syrian intellectuals of all kinds, seeking a new core of resistance, mobilized notions of ethical solidarity and used Mecca in its traditional role as a Muslim place of asylum. Fu'ad Hamza and Yusuf Yasin, employees of 'Abd al-'Aziz, played a major role in organizing and receiving these visitors.

One such individual who travelled to Mecca regularly was Shukri al-Quwwatli. He was from one of the richest Ottoman landowning families in Damascus, and a graduate of the Mekteb-i Mülkiye, the School of Civil Administration in Istanbul in Istanbul, where he had studied in the same class as the 1920s defining Syrian politicians Fawzi al-Ghazzi and Sa'd Allah al-Jabiri.[60] A highly engaged independence activist during the Faysali government, he was exiled from the French mandate and lived in Cairo until 1930. His family had business ties to 'Abd al-'Aziz, and some even claim that it was he who sent Yusuf Yasin to advise 'Abd al-'Aziz in 1924.[61] Quwwatli was also an important figure connecting the Syrian-Palestinian committees and 'Abd al-'Aziz, especially during the Syrian uprising of 1925–27.[62] He was to become the first president of independent Syria in 1943.

In the Hijaz, the Syrians Hamza, Yasin, Milhis, and Shaykh al-Ard formed a loose grouping—one letter written to al-Qassab referred to them as "our center here."[63] Anxious French consular reports also testify to the existence of this grouping. [64] These Saudi Syrians were regularly in touch—Hamza writing the most often—with al-Qassab in Haifa, who in turn was in close communication with Rashid Rida and Shukri al-Quwwatli in Cairo, and Amin al-Husayni in Jerusalem. (We should not forget that Yusuf Yasin was Rida's student before the war.[65]) Al-Qassab and Rida also appear to have been friends. In his letters, Rida regularly adds greetings from his mother and requests that al-Qassab send spices from Palestine. Unless this is coded language, the two sheikhs were quite close.[66]

Let us follow Sheikh al-Qassab during the 1928 constituent process. He is generally omitted from Syrian nationalist narratives because he was a Muslim activist and had to remain outside of the French mandate until 1933.[67] He is also an unusual champion of Arab monarchism, as the master narrative is still the Hashemite version: ex-military officers and some intellectuals supporting a pan-Arab regime under the aegis of the Hashemite family.[68] Al-Qassab's story and his Saudi relations are thus missing from the canonical narratives, nor do recent global histories of Islamic thought mention him.[69] He is remembered only as one among those Syrian Muslim sheikhs who organized resistance, were somewhat puritan, and are described today as "Salafi."[70]

The al-Qassab of the 1920s was a figure still quite familiar in today's world: an exiled educator in search of money and influence so as to realize his own vision in the Middle East, or at least in his external homeland. In March 1928, Fu'ad Hamza informed al-Qassab that King 'Abd al-'Aziz made his final decision about 2,000 (perhaps British) pounds, which he was sending to the mufti Amin al-Husayni in Jerusalem through Rida. The purpose of this money is not specified (in Hamza's diary, it is mentioned in connection with buying rifles and munition).[71] Hamza wrote to al-Qassab that this money should be used economically, because he feared that they would receive no more from the king in the future. Finally, he sent best regards from "brother Yusuf" and asked al-Qassab to find out "the truth about the Syrian situation."[72] The French secret service suspected that Rida and al-Husayni would use the money for propaganda to support a Saudi candidate for a Syrian monarchy.[73]

The Istiqlali-network was an inter-regional post-Ottoman successor diaspora which came into being as the result of French political decisions and not through the chase for economic opportunities, the standard way of diaspora-making before the Great War. Importantly, High Commissioner Ponsot did not include al-Qassab and Quwwatli in the general amnesty he issued for Syria in the spring of 1928; they would not be permitted to return and run in the elections for the constituent assembly in the new State of Syria. The French secret services dubbed them "nationalist-extremist-monarchists."[74] Hence, the *Istiqlali* activists would have only external means to intervene in the constituent process in 1928.

The core *Istiqlali* activists' priority was to secure a political order in Syria that included Islamic laws. They regarded the new Saudi power as the likeliest means of securing this goal. To this end, al-Qassab embarked on a propaganda campaign aimed at supporting Faysal b. 'Abd al-'Aziz, the second son of the new king, as a candidate for the Syrian throne. He sent pamphlets to Damascus, but the police confiscated them.[75] His ally, the Haifa-based newspaper *al-Karmil* started a propaganda campaign in support of Faysal;[76] and al-Qassab soon attempted to finance *al-Yarmuk*, another Haifa-based paper as well.[77] The influential *al-Jami'a al-'Arabiyya* in Jerusalem, edited by an al-Husayni, was also supportive of the establishment of a Saudi prince in Syria.[78] In opposition to this group, there were many republican Palestinians; for instance, the journal *Filastin* disdainfully reported that monarchists and republicans were fighting amongst themselves, and that the only people supporting the Saudi option were Independence Party members led by Shaykh Kamil al-Qassab.[79]

In June 1928, Rashid Rida's Cairo-based journal with global reach *al-Manar* argued for a Muslim monarchy in Syria. Its special monarchist issue began with a defense of the Saudi government against the leaders of the Indian Khilafa movement, the very same republican Muslim group who sent their representatives to the Saudi-occupied Hijaz in 1925–26. In this mini-debate, the Indians claimed that kingship was intrusive to Islam and an abuse of "God's sovereignty." Rashid Rida ridiculed this idea. He argued that 'Abd al-'Aziz protected the pilgrimage and, referring to the composite state-making practices, allowed the Hijazis to rule themselves (thus following the rightly-guided caliphs), and that a Hijaz governed by a global Muslim council would be impractical. There then followed a long article titled "The New Syrian Government: Kingdom or Republic?" in which Rida asserted that Syrian public opinion was strongly in favor of a kingdom, and that in his opinion Faysal, the Saudi prince, would be the ideal ruler. He indicated, in fact, that his support for Faysal was stronger than his support for the monarchical institution itself: if Faysal were not chosen to rule, he wrote, then Syria would be better served by a republic. Rida singled out some "secularists," who were arguing against a Muslim king, emphasizing that a Muslim religious (*mutadayyin*) king would be better than an atheist for both Christians and Muslims, because such a king would not restrict religious practices, Christian or Muslim. Apart from being an honest Muslim, Rida added, Faysal, like his father, would be able to control the Bedouins. He closed his essay by accusing the American Amin al-Rihani, who favored a republic and a Christian president in Syria (but who meanwhile supported the new Saudi Muslim monarchy in Arabia) of sectarianism.[80]

The Qassab-Rida-Quwwatli group argued in favor of a Muslim constitutional monarchy as the form of government best placed to enable the effective administration of a country as diverse as Syria. In June 1928, they sent a letter to all deputies in the Constituent Assembly in Damascus. Rather than confiscating the letter, the police carefully read it. The letter argued that "Ibn Saud" had become the head of the Arab cause and that a

constitutional king drawn from his family would thus be best for the Syrians. The authors acknowledged that "the republic is the form of progress,"
but they argued that the imposition of a republic would cause chaos in
Syria. Their main argument was that "kingship is the guaranty of neutrality in the country." A republic could not survive in a religiously diverse
country like Syria: elections would be dangerously divisive, and thus only
a king could spare the country from anarchy. The final argument was that
a truly constitutional king would not be able to rule, only to reign, and that
thus no one should be afraid of tyranny.[81] (The deputies may have taken
these arguments with a pinch of salt, given that the very same month King
Fuad of Egypt—a Muslim, constitutional ruler—suspended the Egyptian
constitution). A mass demonstration in support of establishing a monarchy was organized but suppressed by the police in Damascus.

There is no evidence that al-Qassab and Rida's argument in favor of
monarchy was motivated by deference to any Islamic monarchical norms.
Other monarchist groups tried to acquire a legal opinion (*fatwa*) from
Muslim jurists in favor of the monarchical form in general. Yet even the
question they posed was delicately crafted: "It is known to your Eminences
that the basis of government in Islam is consultative government which
rests on a king who collects opinions and executes laws. Is it possible to
replace this regime form [. . .] with the civil republican form?"[82] In contrast, the pro-Saudi activists—being well aware of the revived argument
about the imam as a contractual representative of the Muslims in the
Egyptian *shariʿa* apparatus—appear to have advanced a practical argument against secularism in Syria. To their way of thinking, Islam followed
monarchy, especially a constitutional Saudi monarchy, rather than the
other way around.

A Suspended Republic

In the midst of all this debate and agitation, the new National Bloc and its
core of young secularist republicans in Damascus faced a challenge. How
could they establish a republic in the midst of such a cacophony of monarchists? This question was closely related to another: How could they create
a constitution without Islamic laws? First, they consulted with the *Istiqlali*
network—that is, al-Qassab, Rida, and al-Quwwatli. In early June 1928,
Fawzi al-Ghazzi, a young nationalist law professor in charge of oversee-
ing the drafting committee, travelled, with fellow republican Saʿd Allah
al-Jabiri and others, to Baalbek for a holiday. The French secret service
noted that they met with two agents of the exiled Shukri Quwwatli, yet

another of al-Ghazzi's former classmates from pre-war Istanbul. After this meeting there were rumors that they had agreed on elevating a Saudi prince for Syria, but the secret service advised that this was not the case.[83] Following these negotiations, al-Ghazzi had to be sure that when he presented the republican draft everyone—or at least the majority—in the Constituent Assembly would be in line. He regularly invited the local monarchists— both Damascene and Alepine pro-Hashemites and pro-Saudis—to his house, in the hope that they might reconcile their views with the republicans.[84] At one point, al-Qassab accused al-Ghazzi of aspiring to the presidency of the new republic.[85] High Commissioner Ponsot finally also came out in support of a republic. He harbored a fear, typical of high French officials, that a new Arab king in Syria, of whatever kind, would be dangerous for their rule in North Africa.

Al-Ghazzi could not prevent his fellow nationalists from inserting in the final republican draft a statement denying the validity of the territorial divisions legalized by the League of Nations. In contrast to his fellows in the National Bloc, al-Ghazzi was highly strategic in his legal thinking. His guiding principle was that the constitution was an instrument to be voted on at the present time, but to be applied fully only later.[86] He understood that, at bottom, constitution-making was also part of a French racial-civilizational discourse. Syrians had to "prove" to the League that they were capable of composing basic laws. In fact, al-Ghazzi considered that it would be most effective to negotiate an agreement with the High Commission behind the scenes. This was in keeping with the instincts of a small sub-group in the National Bloc, to which al-Ghazzi belonged, who had set their sights only on what they might realistically hope to gain from the French.[87] When in August 1928 Ponsot asked the assembly to delete the articles in question, al-Ghazzi remarked in a speech: "I preached a week ago that [territorial] unity should not be part of the constitution [. . .] because I saw already the clouds in the sky gathering," but he still persisted with the suggestion that the assembly should "vote about not suppressing the six articles."[88] The High Commission suspended the sessions on 9 August 1928. A few months later al-Ghazzi urged his fellow nationalists to reach an agreement, but in vain.[89] The following year, in summer 1929, he died, poisoned by his wife who had been conducting a love affair. With al-Ghazzi's death, a powerful pragmatic voice in Syrian politics was silenced.

In the end, High Commissioner Ponsot either reworded or removed the problematic articles from the constitutional draft and moved on. In May 1930, he promulgated the republican Syrian constitution together with the other French mandate constitutions. But this constituent act was not the final word. Pro-Sharifian and pro-Nami monarchist groups remained active; and the *Istiqlal* group also prepared for the future. They took the view that the National Bloc's aim was at achieving only what was convenient for French interests. This chapter began with Hamza's scheming, but there were other intrigues afoot after the suspension of the Syrian Assembly. The later controversial mufti Amin al-Husayni from Jerusalem got in touch with the American millionaire Charles Crane about a project relating to "the big society of Islam." As he dared not put it in writing, his messengers delivered the details in person.[90] Crane soon sent a "handsome donation" for the renovation of the Haram mosque.[91] In Mecca, Yasin also invited even more *Istiqlali* brothers to join the Saudi government.[92] And so a new chapter began in the story of the Syrian-Saudi network.

A Royal Pipeline: French Diplomatic Uses of the Syrian Throne, 1930s

And not only did the Syrian Muslim activists continue to agitate for Islam as the ultimate fount of the new order. Competition for the throne of Damascus also continued: many *ashraf*, the ex-khedive, and other post-imperial patricians regularly posed their own candidates. This uneasy background murmur was a constant reminder of the Hamidian nature of the post-Ottoman Arab political landscape under the iron umbrella of the League mandate. It enabled the French Foreign Ministry to use the throne-question cynically, as an important diplomatic card, up to the Second World War. In the story that follows, I conclude with how infrastructure and the question of the regime form once again meet in Syrian lands.

In late 1930, negotiations over the Mediterranean end-point of the oil pipeline from Kirkuk reached a critical phase. International agreements between the Allied Powers defined the structure and activity of the Iraq Petroleum Company (IPC), a conglomerate. (Upon the US government's pressuring the British and French governments, American companies had been also allowed to join in the concession following the 1927 discovery of the Kirkuk oil field.) In 1930, the IPC considered two routes for bringing the Kirkuk (Mosul) oil to the Mediterranean: one short and economic through French Syria to Tripoli, the other long and expensive through British Transjordan to Haifa.[93]

The French group on the company's board lobbied for a Tripoli pipeline against the British group's plan for a Haifa pipeline. Both the French and the British groups planned a railway line next to their own proposed pipeline; the Iraqi government and King Faysal in Baghdad supported the establishment of a railway to Haifa because this would connect Baghdad directly to the Mediterranean through the continuous British mandate territory. At this point, the French Foreign Ministry intervened in London to lobby for the Tripoli pipeline. The British government declared that their recent treaty (June 1930) with Iraq transferred the international obligations earlier taken by the mandatory to the Iraqi government, and that therefore they could not intervene. Only King Faysal and the Iraqi government could pressure the company's board (despite the fact that the IPC contained only non-Iraqi shareholders).

At London's advice, the French government turned to King Faysal in 1930. They indirectly learned of his three conditions: payment to Iraq of a share of Tripoli's customs receipts, the establishment of bilateral Syrian-Iraqi economic and military agreements, and assurances that France would not install 'Ali Haydar or Faysal b. 'Abd al-'Aziz in Syria. A little later, Faysal expressed his wish, yet again, that France should actually enthrone his brother 'Ali in Damascus (although this was not made into an explicit condition). The IPC convention in January 1931 decided to split the pipeline at Rutbah. The French wanted a more favorable bifurcation point at Haditha, over which they had control. Faysal soon offered 50 percent of the Tripoli pipeline oil to France and his support for the Haditha bifurcation, if France would accept his demands and also support Iraq in joining the League of Nations.[94]

These negotiations in January 1931 coincided with a quick visit of ex-king 'Ali in Syria and Lebanon, a visit that has been generally overlooked by historians.[95] Indeed, Ponsot deliberately organized 'Ali's visit with minimal publicity. It was a half-hearted preparation for another possible bid at establishing a sharifian monarchy. 'Ali met with the monarchist leaders, such as 'Arif Idlibi, and stopped his car symbolically in Maysalun to greet retired members of the Hashemite Arab army. The French officer in charge observed that, despite 150 people celebrating at his hotel and President Shaykh Taj al-Din visiting, the people of Damascus remained "completely indifferent" during the whole of 'Ali's one-night stay. 'Ali expressed to the officer that he was "ready to be the friend of France." As a true imperial patrician, he was of the opinion that "the social elite," rather than those who had no wealth and cultural capital, should represent the country. Pointedly, 'Ali mentioned the pipeline in conversations about the future of Syria.[96]

The High Commissioner noted that 'Ali's visit recreated three camps of opinion in Syria: a Hashemite monarchical camp, a Saudi monarchical camp, and a republican grouping. Yet Ponsot declared to his superiors that any arbitrary change in the republican constitution would mean "ignoring the country's wish." Accordingly, the foreign minister instructed the French consul in Baghdad to give assurances to Faysal only in very vague terms, and furthermore strictly orally, to the effect that the French mandatory did not intend to change the republican regime.[97]

Although the decisions had already been made in Paris and London, Faysal nonetheless mobilized his government. The rival dynastic heads, 'Abd al-'Aziz in Riyadh and Fuad in Cairo, grew nervous on account of rumors foretelling the establishment of a new Hashemite monarchy in French Syria in exchange for oil. Taking advantage of their anxiety, the French Foreign Ministry sent instructions to its representatives in Cairo and Jidda, and soon globally, that they should *not* "categorically" deny the rumors. French agents could only state that the present constitution was republican and that the French government respected this state of affairs. This strategy was principally aimed at, as the diplomats put it, "managing" King Faysal.[98]

Once again, the Arabic journals picked up and published the rumors that were circulating. Some took the view that this putative new scheme was the work of the French Orientalist Louis Massignon.[99] Massignon did have some lobbying power because he was on good terms with the French High Commission and with Ponsot personally, and also because he worked for the League of Nations as reviewer of the monthly Arabic press. Massignon's 1931 July press review for the League indeed favorably emphasized 'Ali's candidature in Damascus.[100] The Iraqi parliament voted in favor of the Haditha bifurcation in April 1931. Faysal visited Paris in the summer and misinterpreted his warm reception as a step towards securing the throne of Syria.[101] Nothing could have been further from the French Foreign Ministry's intentions. In February 1932 the French consul in Baghdad was finally allowed to make it categorically clear to Faysal that he would not receive the throne of Syria.[102] In December 1932 Berthelot, the chief diplomat, instructed all French agents that until such time as Syria should to be admitted to the League the League of Nations the throne question should not be addressed.[103] Arab journalists judged that the Hashemites had been tricked.[104] (Both end stations in Haifa and Tripoli were inaugurated in January 1935.)[105]

This story about oil infrastructure and politics not only confirms that Orientalists such as Massignon were not as influential in decision-making as it is often supposed, but also that infrastructural bargaining chips did not cancel out pragmatic political considerations. In 1932, the French interest was to retain the Syrian republican constitution against the imperial projects of the post-Ottoman *ashraf.*

The only time in the late 1930s when France seriously considered a royal candidate was when they suspended the Syrian constitution on 8 July 1939. On the eve of the Second World War, a new constituent arrangement looked appealing. In June 1939, 'Abd al-Rahman Shahbandar, a famous Syrian activist and, back in 1928, a staunch republican, had visited Amman with the intention of enthroning Emir 'Abd Allah as the king of Syria.[106] Now, on the eve of war, Fascist Italian journals announced that King 'Abd al-'Aziz of the Saudi polity was protesting yet another attempt by the English government to secure the elevation of a Hashemite king in Syria.[107] Certain Arab journalists speculated that Lebanon and Syria would be united under one monarch.[108] The French High Commissioner at the time, Gabriel Puaux, favored setting up an emir from the Saudi family as a Syrian monarch. In the end, the French Foreign Minister repeated the old argument: "pan-Arabism" threatened their North African possessions, and thus an Arab king in Syria—whether Saudi or Hashemite—would threaten the interests of France.[109]

Conclusion: Islam in Local State-Formation

My exploration of monarchical designs on the State of Syria has highlighted the post-Ottoman underworld of transregional connections. The making of the State of Syria in the French mandate relates in a horizontal way to the emerging Arab Saudi Kingdom. The spoliation of patricians who once belonged to the Ottoman world and their persistent hunger for a throne in Damascus sharply highlight the fact, that instead of bringing about a break with the past, the class A mandates sharpened conflicting Ottoman views of the political order in Syrian lands.

Yet the League of Nations also represented something new. The ex-Ottoman patricians could not compete with the League norms of elected representation and ethnic nationalism. Nami, Haydar, Abbas Hilmi, Faysal, 'Abd Allah, and many others belonged to the monarchical-territorial model of imperial constitutionalism. Republican-secularist Syrians, who advocated the new League norms instead of the imperial ones, had to make a series of compromises with the *Istiqlali* activists and the French High Commission. Instead of a secular republic, they therefore declared a

Muslim one, the first in world history. It was a post-Ottoman republic in which religion retained its place as a source of authority in elected political institutions: in 1932, Muhammad 'Ali al-'Abid, perhaps the last Hamidian patrician in French Damascus, was elected president.[110]

The story about constituting a subordinated sovereign order in the State of Syria showed us the various uses of Islam as a discursive argument for managing a diverse successor society. The recasting of the imperial political order, with its multiple sources of authority, into a local one did not entail the secularization of social life. Rather, both Allied officials and local-regional activists wanted to create a framework which would provide institutional guarantees for Muslim ethical-legal norms. The coproduction of such a framework, and its accidental and contested outcome of a local republic, hinged upon their unintended alliance and upon the new Allied method of governing without sovereignty. The end of the League-mandate after the Second World War thus posed new questions about the sources of authority in an environment of sovereign local polities without empire.

Subordinated Sovereignty
in the Twentieth Century

IN THIS BOOK, I have examined the political transition from the late Ottoman imperial order to that of the successor Arab governments. My goal has been to provide an analytical vocabulary of transformation in the twentieth century which can describe once imperial ideas, acts, and visions in the enforced making of successor societies. This goal has necessitated a general theory about the transformation of large political organizations. I have suggested that at the heart of such historical junctures we find, instead of radical revolutionary or colonial eradication, the spoliation and recycling of previous political, social, and economic institutions.

This historical method provides conceptual tools which can be used in other contexts and periods as well. For instance, the post-Habsburg successor societies in Eastern Europe, the "small kings" of republican and civil-war China, and the Central Asian new polities all represent local states with recycled imperial institutions, with or without sovereignty. Another temporal terrain where this conceptual toolbox might be used is what is often called "decolonization." We know well that in the 1960s some post-French African countries struggled to retain their previous politics of diversity and inequality, while, for instance, the birth of the United Arab Emirates by 1971 created a sovereign federation of emirates. Finally, we can follow pioneering sociologists and political scientists and turn our attention to how post-Soviet societies in the 1990s and 2000s retained elements of the previous regime and to what imperial continuities and returns mean for the future.

Some may argue that the "sovereign local state" is an empty and evasive concept. It evades the moral content in the adjectives of "national" and "colonial," and so it is a rhetorical maneuver to over-write the Allied subjugation of post-Ottoman Arabs with a different narrative. I must confess that I agree that it is an empty concept, and I myself remain somewhat unsatisfied. Perhaps this is not where the main contribution of this book lies. Perhaps the operations of recycling, repurposing, spoliation of the imperial political order and theme of the "successor society" are the important contribution to current debates. Perhaps refocusing the role of Islam and modular logic in postwar state-making is the main contribution. But the concept of a "local state" is a necessary theoretical maneuver, because it serves to distinguish the political construction of post-imperial, non-revolutionary societies at an abstract level from nation-state rhetoric. I emphasize again that by this term I mean not only the post-Ottoman Arab cases, but also most successor polities of the 1920s, from the Kingdom of Yugoslavia and the kingless Kingdom of Hungary to the Kingdom of the Hijaz to the Kingdom of Afghanistan. The adjective "local" has allowed a critique of static political science categories, and it has eased our approach to the uses of religion in state-making in the early twentieth century. Following others, I insist that the empire/nation-state paradigm is over. Again, to be clear, the 1850s–1950s was a hundred years of reconfiguring empire. I can only hope that my suggestion of a world of local states and imperial formations in the 1920s at the threshold of our contemporary world order will further the conversation about large transformations in the past and future of human societies.

Let me address one more issue. Many may find this book and my characterization of Arab local states as "sovereign" problematic. Despite considerable nostalgia among contemporary elites for Ottoman times, Arabs in the interwar period did not see themselves as living in successor societies under sovereign governments. Post-Ottoman peoples, especially Arabs, unlike the post-Habsburg peoples, did not suffer only the trauma of losing the war and the empire. Arabs also endured decade-long Franco-British control through military occupation and the League, the interwar European racialization of Arabs and Islam, and the Zionist settlement in Palestine, with the ultimate establishment of the State of Israel. For many Arab historians, and some others, these double traumas make it almost impossible to see the post-Ottoman dimension as the defining feature of the period. And any talk of interwar sovereignty might well strike them as an affront.

My goal in thematizing League-sovereignty as a bureaucratic quality was not to suggest that Arab governments were free. On the contrary, my research has demonstrated that national sovereignty was something of a trap in the age of the League of Nations. For Arabs, the only legal basis for opposing the Allied decisions should have been their Ottoman imperial belonging. League-sovereignty did not mean freedom. In this regard, there are two key insights here of value to historians, legal scholars, and anthropologists.

First, governing without sovereignty as the principal form of Allied Powers domination highlights sharply the importance of administrative law. After 1919, imperial formations typically have recognized the bureaucratic sense of sovereignty (that practices such as property title registration, adjudication, and elections belong to the purview of local governments without or with international contractual ability and representation), and hence they have sought to rule through non-sovereign means, such as contracts (hence the importance of treaties) and military occupations. Today, jurists and politicians increasingly discuss global administrative law as a regulatory tool for managing the unprecedented expansion of global companies. Hence, the historical uses of administrative law for political subordination should be a crucial field of future research.[1]

The subordination of sovereigns through contracts (treaties) was characteristic of the twentieth century. The interwar British Hashemite-bloc and the French States of the Levant are early examples of sovereign governments grouped in sub-federative blocs. The USSR, a federal polity itself, was especially drawn to this type of territorial organization.[2] Instead of embodiments of colonialism, we should see the League class A British and French mandates at large as capitalist versions of the interwar Soviet association. After the Second World War, the new Soviet bloc in Eastern Europe was a grouping of sovereign governments linked and subordinated through military occupations and contracts. The Allied Powers, especially the United States of America (the "West" during the Cold War) also transited to governing without sovereignty overseas, for instance, in Latin America and South-East Asia. Some commentators have called the American method "non-territorial domination."[3] This is imprecise. Like the communist version, capitalist domination in the later twentieth century has been also territorial *and* without legal sovereignty, often relying on economic-contractual means of control. The logic of non-sovereign federations (for instance the EU) and blocs continued after 1989 and persists to this day.

Secondly, *Modern Arab Kingship* has highlighted the use of religion and the dynastic realm in the construction of Arab successor societies in the 1920s. Perhaps the intellectual domain where my method provides the most useful new directions is in rethinking Islam's role in state-making in the twentieth century, and with it, the significance of monarchy as a fragile form of managing diverse societies and territorial autonomy. The "monarchical emancipation of colonies," as Talleyrand once formulated it, was both a European and local method for transforming empire in the interwar Middle East, and in some places (for instance, post-Italian Libya) it remained an actual practice up to the 1970s. I have proposed that the idea of the *imperial political order* can usefully serve as a framework of inquiry for the study of religion in successor polities. The legal codifications of religion as a principle of representation in Arab polities, driven from below and from above, translated the imperial politics of difference into a locally institutionalized form.[4] The uses of religion and the dynastic realm at the genesis of the modern international system highlights sharply the inadequacy of political science categories and forces us to rethink the so-far privileged role of nationalism in modern state-making.

An empire-based theory of post-WWI state-making provides a new historical basis for thinking about our contemporary diversity. From the 1920s to the 1970s Western thinkers tended to connect the idea of modernity with the process of disenchantment in the grand narrative of secularization.[5] In the last fifty years, a new wave of intellectuals has questioned whether this normative, Eurocentric theory accurately describes the historical trajectory of the entire world. They have proposed alternate concepts, such as "multiple modernities," "the deprivatization of world religions," and "nonmodern worlds"; and they have questioned categories of European provenance.[6] Beyond the normative debates about modernity, religion, and the state, the genealogical approach that takes empire as the foundation of successor polities can help to develop more refined categories to delineate the relationship between the remaking of religious norms, representation, and practices of administration, and the differing varieties of this relationship in imperial and local contexts.[7]

Today, we can find occasional debates around the world over whether monarchy is a useful regime form in that it preserves identity and promotes political stability. In Africa, people are finding new ways to claim authenticity through coronation rituals. In Europe one hears bizarre suggestions about creating a new European Union–wide imperial dynasty, such as might provide a way to secure the loyalty of various newly settled communities. In November 2022, a far-right monarchist group in Germany was arrested because they were preparing for a violent takeover. The post-Ottoman experiments a hundred years ago teach two lessons that bear on this issue.

First, modern monarchies indeed continued the imperial logic of managing diversity. But, secondly, the post-Ottoman monarchical polities all existed in some sort of subordination. The Allied prohibition of a new, composite Arab empire necessitated a constant military presence to maintain their partitions. Therefore, the monarchical political institutions relied on both imperial and local military violence. The monarchs could only stabilize the new, small polities as long as the imperial and local armies accepted the ruler as a useful constituent fiction in their order.

I hope that I have made it clear that this book is not an argument for empire, and certainly not for dynastic rule. A non-national form of political authority that can accommodate various religious ways of life need not be a monarchical-imperial one. It would be enough if that authority, whatever its form, acknowledged segmented communal-regional autonomies in some sort of composite government; and that this form of authority be institutionalized in order to maintain its temporal continuity. This would require relinquishing the normative idea of 1919 that sovereignty belongs only to the nation. Jurists, philosophers, and politicians should continue to reflect on whether composite forms of sovereignty might better serve our world.

The Multi-Time of Twentieth-Century World History

Finally, let me conclude with an important problem that faces the guild of historians: chronology. There is a tension between European, American, and Arab timelines in twentieth-century world history. How does "the age of recycling empire" in the post-Ottoman regions relate to the "age of extremes," the "age of crisis" and the "Deluge" in interwar Europe and the New Deal in the US? Often, at the heart of Euro- and US-centric narratives there is an effort to make sense of how and why the Second World war and the Holocaust were possible, driven by racial nationalisms and the Great Depression, the global economic crisis.[8] I have suggested that the Allied ban on empire among the defeated peoples of the Central Powers was possibly more important than historians have hitherto acknowledged. The revolt against this ban in the form of the expanding racist empires of Nazi Germany, Fascist Italy, and Arrow-Cross Hungary is all too familiar.

The post-Ottoman Arab regions in the period also exemplify what Christopher Bayly has called the "Third Age of Imperialism."[9] Sociologist Jonathan Wyrtzen has proposed a new period, the "Long Great War" that from a Middle Eastern perspective characterized the years between 1911 and 1934.[10] Adopting a genealogical-historical approach to imperial projects, we can demarcate an even longer period. Here I must call on my usual source of authority: a taxi driver in Cairo once told me that he thinks that Ottoman rule only ended in Egypt when Nasser and the Free Officers quashed the monarchy in 1953. I believe that he was right. The postwar "age of recycling empire" in the Arab regions was longer than the age of extremes and the Second World War; violence and border-making did not end in the early 1930s; the joining of Allied and Hamidian projects extended the politics of difference into the 1950s and in some places until today.

In world history, the chronological disjunctions between regions—the short and deadly age of extremes in Central and Eastern Europe and Japan-Korea versus the long, almost as deadly third age of empire in the Middle East—still sync at the higher level of the story of the defeated Central Powers. Historical sociologists argue that we can only speak of national polities after the Second World War and connect this "nationalism" to the Keynesian economic practices. It follows that we might ask how the Arab local polities, created for some type of layered existence (both in political and in economic terms) faced the difficult task of national independence in the age of the atomic bomb. Cold War Arab social engineering projects all problematized the fractured economy, elite property-holding, social hybridity, and the persistence of religion. How did polities *not* created for self-sustained independence enter a new world divided between the US and the USSR, two global imperial projects in the 1950s? In what way can the categories of composite economies and of regional blocs help in rethinking our contemporary world?

ACKNOWLEDGMENTS

IT DOES TAKE A VILLAGE. I am grateful to many colleagues who helped with conversations, research hints, materials, and criticism: Abhishek Kaicker, Cyrus Schayegh, Aziz Al-Azmeh, David Armitage, ʿAdnan Bakhit, Eugene Rogan, Bruce Hall, Prasenjit Duara, Malachi Hacohen, Till Grallert, Hyeju Janice Jeong, Intisar Rabb, Michael Provence, Adam Sabra, Michael Clinton, Rachel Simon, James Gelvin, Jennifer Commins, Ali Yaycıoğlu, Fred Cooper, miriam cooke, Laura F. Edwards, Engseng Ho, John French, Phil Stern, Natasha Wheatley, Bernard Haykel, Mona Hassan, Cemil Aydin, Sarah Shields, Penny Sinanoglu, Jehangir Malegam, Mercedes Volait, Nicolas Michel, Edhem Eldem, Philippe Pétriat, Nadirah Mansour, Ellen McLarney, Ranjana Khanna, Noah Feldmann, Mostafa Minawi, Aimee Genell, Alp Yenen, John Willis, Ali Ekber Cinar, Fethi Gedikli, Nadia Von Maltzahn, Léda Mansour, Milinda Banerjee, Frances Hasso, Daniel Foliard, Timur Kuran, Jennifer Pitts, Dina Rizk Khoury, Charles Kurzman, Faisal Devji, Bilen Işıktaş, Ulrike Freitag, Camille Cole, and Fred Cooper once again. I would like to express my gratitude to Sumathi Ramaswamy, Chair of the History Department at Duke University while this book was in the making, who generously allowed a reduced teaching load so that I could rewrite the first draft in the late pandemic spring of 2021, and to my colleagues, who provided numerous opportunities to discuss parts of the book. Kim Greenwell copy-edited some chapters; Thomas Welsford edited, criticized, and refined the whole manuscript; and Eva Jaunzems hammered it into a readable text. Fred Appel, James Collier, and Jill Harris shepherded it to publication.

I thank patient graduate students: Mohammed Ali, Whitney Wilkinson Arreche, Grazina Bielousova, Yooseong Heo, Sam Horewood, Rob Elliott, Abram Smith, and Holly Sentowski; and the brilliant undergraduates in Hist 469S in the spring of 2022: Steph Zempolich, Tyler Donovan, Joseph Laster, and Dominic Van Cleave-Schottland. I learned much from the participants at the conference "The Modern Invention of Dynasty: A Global Intellectual History, 1500–2000" at the Birmingham Research Institute for History and Cultures in September 2017; and from those at the symposium, organized by Prasenjit Daura and myself, "Monarchy and Sovereignty in Twentieth-Century Asia" at Duke University in April 2017. I also immensely benefitted from the following conferences in 2019: on the history of the Carnegie Endowment for International Peace, organized by Nadine Akhund-Lange and Jean-Michel Guieu in the Maison Heinrich Heine; on "Global Islam in the Interwar Period," organized by Amr Ryad at Leuven University; and "What Is a Treaty?" organized by David Armitage at the Wissenschaftskolleg zu Berlin.

I am grateful to the staff and the 2018–19 cohort at the Paris Institute of Advanced Studies (IEA). This book benefitted from their fellowship, and from the financial support of the French State program "Investissements d'avenir," managed by the Agence Nationale de la Recherche (ANR-11-LABX-0027–01 Labex RFIEA+). I am also indebted to the Josiah Charles Trent Memorial Foundation Endowment Fund at Duke University; to the Arts and Sciences Council Committee on Faculty Research at Duke University; to the Duke University Middle East Center; and to the Institute of Constitutional Law at the New York Historical Society. Some early (and very bad!) draft chapters were presented at the International History seminar at Columbia University, at the Comparative Law seminar at Harvard Law School, at the Middle East Historiography seminar at UCLA, and at the Faculty Seminar in the History Department of Duke University. I received fantastic feedback during the Franklin Humanities Institute's book manuscript workshop in December 2020, thanks to Sylvia Miller. A special thank you goes to Attila Szvétek, the director of the Balassi (Hungarian) Cultural Institute in Cairo, and to the staff of the Hungarian Embassy in Egypt, especially H.E. Ambassador Imre András Kovács at the time of research.

This book would have been impossible without the help of Sean Swanick, the Islamic and Middle East Librarian at Duke University Library. It is a pleasure to thank Sean. I also thank Prof. 'Adnan Bakhit for allowing me to do research in his center at the University of Jordan, and for tea and excellent conversations, and Dr. Nishrawan Taha, the Director of the University of Jordan Library (at the time of research) for all her help. I am indebted to Ibrahim 'Asi for his most generous help in Mu'assasat al-Mahfuzat al-Lubnaniyya in Beirut. I owe huge gratitude to Mr. Jacques Oberson at the League of Nations Archive at the UN in Geneva, who introduced me to interwar history in the most effective way in this symbolic space. In Egypt, my outstanding debts are many: I thank Yasmine El Dorghamy for showing me the Abbas Hilmi jewelry; Mr. 'Ali Faraj in Dar al-Ifta'; the staff of Maktabat al-Azhar; the Dar al-Hilal Library, the libraries and librarians of Dar al-Kutub, Dar al-Hilal, IDEO, IFAO, and NVIC in Cairo. In France, I express my sincere thanks to Mr. Clement Noual at CADC for allowing me to have access to the personal papers of

Henri Ponsot; Emmanuel Roy, Éric Lechevallier, and the friendly staff of CADN; and in England, as usual, to the Mohamed Ali Foundation and archivist Francis Gotto for helping me in the Abbas Hilmi II Papers and the Sudan Archive in the Special Collections at Durham University. In Türkiye, I would like to thank the staff of İSAM, especially Nuray Urkaç Güler, and the staff of BOA, especially Meliha Nur Gereçinli (even though in the end I did not ask for publication permission). It is a pleasure to thank the staff of KFCRIS in Riyadh, especially Majed Binkhunein at the time, and Shahad Turkistani who helped so much during my stay, and also Kamel Al-Ahmed, Dr. ʿAbdullah bin Khalid Al-Saud, Dr. Fahad L. Alghalib Alsharif; and Dr. Mohammed A. AlTuwaijri in Darat Al Faysal. In DMAA, the "Darah," I thank Dr. Fahd al-Sammari for allowing me to read computerized, carefully selected images of documents. In the UK, I had great help from Juliette Desplat in NAUK and Debbie Usher in MECA for her great assistance with images and permissions. This book is dedicated to the memory of Alföldi Lajos, my grandfather, perhaps the last Socialist in Hungary. Finally, I thank the patience of my girls Ya-Wen—who introduced me to political sociology—and Ning-Er, our pride and joy, and the only truly clever person in our family. After so many names, I must confess that all mistakes are mine alone.

Chapter 1. Recycling Empire

1. A short-lived discussion about post-empire began in the 1990s; see Brown, *Imperial Legacy*; Barkey, *After Empire*.

2. Burbank, "Empire and Transformation;" Halperin, "Imperial City States," 80–83.

3. Two opposing views about the imperial making of modernity are Hardt and Negri, *Empire* and Ferguson, *Empire*.

4. Maier, *Among Empires*; Darwin, *After Tamerlane*; Laurens, *L'empire*; Burbank and Cooper, *Empires*; Halperin and Palan, *Legacies of Empire*; Kumar, *Visions of Empire*; Burbank and Cooper, "Empires after 1919."

5. Weitz, "From the Vienna to the Paris System;" Mazower, *No Enchanted Palace*; Darwin, *After Tamerlane*, 402–403; Pedersen, *The Guardians*; Wempe, "A League to Preserve Empires."

6. Reynolds, *Shattering Empires*; Rogan, *The Fall of the Ottomans*; Motyl, *Imperial Ends*; Provence, *The Last Ottoman Generation*; Kayalı, *Imperial Resilience*.

7. Mikhail and Philliou, "The Ottoman Empire," 721.

8. For post-Habsburg states as "small empires," see Judson, *The Habsburg Empire*, 448; Reill, *The Fiume Crisis*, 229.

9. I was inspired by Fischel, *Local States in an Imperial World*; I learned from Americanist colleagues that some communities prefer the word "native" (and demand "native sovereignty") over "indigenous," "aboriginal," and "American Indian." One must note that the term "native states" would possibly work quite well in Arabic (*al-duwal al-ahliyya*); the term "ethnic state" in which "the state serves the national goals of one ethnic group only" is reserved for Israel in Middle East Studies (Rouhana and Ghanem, "The Crisis of Minorities," 321); the term "ethnographic state" characterizes the French colonial re-invention of "Moroccan Islam" and its monarchy to justify French rule (Burke, *The Ethnographic State*, 12); "quasi-state" and "failed state" reflect the deviation from a norm (Dodge, *Inventing Iraq*, 10, 19–21); while the term "minor state" is often preferred by specialists of British India (Beverley, *Hyderabad*, 19–21) and indeed it was used in interwar legal Arabic (Al-Ghazzi, *Al-Huquq al-Duwaliyya*, 1: 131–34) but I concluded that its use would reproduce the very interwar evolutionary-racist discourse. Schad, "Competing Forms of Globalization," was close to the use of "locality," but finally the nation state took over his narrative. For critiques of Eurocentric theories of nationalism, see Chatterjee, "Whose Imagined Community?," 217; Duara, *Rescuing History*.

10. Knox, "Haiti at the League," 256–57.

11. Krasner, *Sovereignty*, 14; Lawson, *Constructing International Relations*, 13.

12. Steinmetz, "The Colonial State as a Social Field," 592.

13. Latest is Todd, *Velvet Empire*.

14. Burbank, "Eurasian Sovereignty," 15.

15. My descriptive identification of this legalistic use of sovereignty by British and French administrators and some local actors in a historical period is neither endorsement, nor acceptance of this use.

16. Al-Muti'i, *Haqiqat al-Islam*, 8.

17. Barkey, "Thinking about Consequences of Empire," 101.

18. Biersteker and Weber, *State Sovereignty as Social Construct*; Khuen, "Bringing the Imperial Back In"; Burbank, "Eurasian Sovereignty," 3.

19. Barkey, *Empire of Difference*, 9–13; Maier, *Among Empires*, 31; Darwin, *After Tamerlane*, 22–25; Laurens, *L'empire*, 15, 33; Burbank and Cooper, *Empires*, 8–9; Pitts, "Political Theory of Empire," 213; Kumar, *Visions of Empire*, 13–15.

20. Gerwarth and Manela, "The Great War as a Global War."

21. Makdisi, *The Age of Co-Existence*, 7–8. By referring to modern Ottoman Muslim imperial authority I reject the essentialist, pseudo-historical idea of a timeless "Islamic imperialism" advocated by Karsh, *Islamic Imperialism*, 9.

22. Salaymeh, *The Beginnings of Islamic Law*, 12, uses the concept of "recycling" in the Late Antique-Islamic legal context.

23. *Spolia* research started with the work of Salvatore Setti; quotes are from Brilliant and Kinney, *Reuse Value*, 1–3; I was inspired by Volait, *Antique Dealing*, 2, 12, 122.

24. Brilliant, "I piedistalli del giardino di Boboli," 12.

25. Edgerton, *Shock of the Old*, xi.

26. Hobsbawm, "Introduction: Inventing Traditions."

27. Stoler, "Imperial Debris," 194.

28. Brubaker, *Nationalism Reframed*; Stark and Bruszt, *Postsocialist Pathways*, 7–8; 18–19; 103–104.

29. Payk and Pergher, *Beyond Versailles*; Miller and Morelon, *Embers of Empire*; the quote is from Egry, "Negotiating Post-Imperial Transitions," 15; Hacohen, *Jacob & Esau*, 343–44; Reill, *The Fiume Crisis*; Becker and Wheatly, *Remaking Central Europe*; Zahra, "Against the World;" Greble, *Muslims and the Making of Modern Europe*. An early work engaging with the idea of remaking is Maier, *Recasting Bourgeois Europe*, focusing on "stabilization" through "corporatism;" a recent one about continuity is Rigó, *Capitalism in Chaos*.

30. Al-Azmeh, *Islams and Modernities*, 51, 128.

31. Cooper, *Challenging Colonialism*; Burbank and Cooper, 11–13.

32. Antonius, *The Arab Awakening*; Rogan, *The Fall of the Ottomans*; Thompson, *How the West Stole Democracy*; latest in Arabic is Barut, *Al-Hukuma al-'Arabiyya*.

33. Owen, *State, Power, Politics*, 14–18; Thompson, *Colonial Citizens*; Neep, *Occupying Syria*; McDougall, "The British and French Empires," 48–50.

34. Darwin, *Britain, Egypt, and the Middle East*; Sayyid-Marsot, *Egypt's Liberal Experiment*; Hourani, *Arabic Thought*; Fitzsimons, *Empire by Treaty*; Fieldhouse, *Western Imperialism*; Fromkin, *A Peace*; Ouhaes, *Syria and Lebanon under the French Mandate*; Mizrahi, *Genèse de l'État Mandataire*; Khoury, *Syria and the French Mandate*.

35. Anscombe, "The Ottoman Legacy," 153.

36. Wyrtzen, *Worldmaking*, 47.

37. Lewis, "Malik," 109; Ayalon, "*Malik* in Modern Middle Eastern Titulature," 317.

38. Lawson, *Constructing International Relations*; Cummings and Hinnebusch, *Sovereignty After Empire*, 13–15.

39. Méouchy and Sluglett, *The British and French Mandates*; Schayegh and Arsan, *The Routledge Handbook*.

40. Fromkin, *A Peace*, 563.

41. Adelman, *Sovereignty and Revolution*.

42. Yenen, "Envisioning;" Polat, *Türk-Arap İlişkileri*; Bayat, "Al-Hukuma al-'Arabiyya;" Mestyan, "A Muslim Dualism?"; Kayalı, *Imperial Resilience*.

43. Recent studies include Wyrtzen, *Worldmaking*; Robson, *The Politics of Mass Violence*; Provence, *The Last Ottoman Generation*; see more in the later chapters.

44. For interwar royal aesthetics, Ellis, "Repackaging"; Whidden, *Monarchy and Modernity*, Wien, *Arab Nationalism*.

45. Ahmed, *Afghanistan Rising*.

46. Nasif, *Madi al-Hijaz*, 132–70; Freitag, *A History of Jeddah*, 287–91; Willis, "Burying Muhammad 'Ali Jauhar"; Devji, *Muslim Zion*, 4.

47. Okan, "Coping with Transitions."

48. Stoler, "Imperial Debris," 204.

49. Sinanouglu, *Partitioning Palestine*, 34; Khalidi, *The Hundred Years*, 71–76; Kattan, *From Coexistence to Conquest*, 81–83; Erakat, *Justice for Some*, Chapter One.

50. Kanafani, *Al-Dirasat al-Siyasiyya*, 5: 413; I learned about the existence of this poem from Rogan, *The Arabs*, Chapter Seven.

51. Getachew, *Worldmaking After Empire*, 2–4.

52. Armitage, *The Ideological Origins*; Benton, *Law and Colonial Cultures*; idem, *A Search for Sovereignty*; Burbank and Cooper, *Empires*; Can et al., *Subjects of Ottoman International Law*; Duve, "What is Global Legal History?" 96.

53. Feldman, "Imposed Constitutionalism"; Bhuta, "The Antinomies of Transformative Occupation"; Stirk, *The Politics of Military Occupation*; Arato, *Constitution-Making under Occupation*; Jackson and Moses, "Transformative Occupations."

54. Tate et al., *Global Legal History*.

55. Ghobrial, "The Secret Life of Elias."

56. Pomeranz, *The Great Divergence*, 8–9; Conrad, *What Is Global History?* 154–58; Bayly, *Remaking the Modern World*, 7.

57. Elliott, "A Europe of Composite Monarchies"; Burbank and Cooper, *Empires in World History*, 358–61; Nexon, *The Struggle for Power*, 67–98; Keene, "The Treaty-Making Revolution"; see references to early modern Ottoman history in Chapter Five.

58. Elliott, "A Europe of Composite Monarchies."

59. Cooper, "Routes Out of Empire."

60. An argument for the post-1919 nation-state order is in Manela, *The Wilsonian Moment*, 5, 63–75, 141–57.

61. Porath, *In Search of Arab Unity*; Podeh, *The Decline of Arab Unity*; Mufti, *Sovereign Creations*.

62. For Islam, see Aydin, *The Idea of the Muslim World*.

63. Dawn, *From Ottomanism to Arabism*, 53.

64. Moyn, "Fantasies of Federalism"; Goebel, *Anti-Imperial Metropolis*, 251, against Cooper, *Citizenship*; Wilder, *Freedom Time*. The importance of this debate became clear to me from Berndt, "Descendants of Zabarkan."

65. Brubaker, *Nationalism Reframed*, 55–59.

66. Duara, *Sovereignty and Authenticity*.

67. The quote is from Nassar, "From Ottomans"; Khalidi, *Palestinian Identity*, Chapter Seven; Bashkin, *The Other Iraq*, 19–51.

68. Darwin, *After Tamerlane*, 414.

69. Wigen, "Post-Ottoman Studies," 314.

70. Zürcher, *Turkey*, 4, 91–218; a critique of contemporary Hamidism is Eldem, "Sultan Abdülhamid II."

71. Fortna, *The Circassian*, 6; Ekmekçioğlu, *Recovering Armenia*, 106–110; Shissler, *Ahmet Ağaoğlu*; Hassan, *Longing*, 153–54; Philliou, *A Past Against History*, 60; Greble, *Muslims and the Making of Modern Europe*, 11–12.

72. Deringil, "The Ottoman Twilight Zone"; Nielsen, *Religion, Ethnicity and Contested Nationhood*; Halliday, *The Middle East in International Relations*, 81.

73. Schlaepfer, Bourmaud, and Hassan, "Fantômes d'Empire."

74. Watenpaugh, *Being Modern*.

75. Provence, *The Last Ottoman Generation*, 6–7; Kurt, "Osmanlı İmparatorluğu'ndan Irak Devletine."

76. Schayegh, *The Middle East*, 199–200.

77. Bryant, "Introduction," 16; Meeker, *A Nation of Empire*, 376–77. The Ottoman past even continued in Cold War US as a "useable past," a reference and justification for development economists. Citino, "The Ottoman Legacy."

78. Meiton, *Electrical Palestine*, 5–7, 15.

79. Chakrabarty, *The Climate of History in a Planetary Age*, 18–19; quote from Charbonnier, *Affluence and Freedom*, 3.

Chapter 2. The Imperial Origin of Successor Political Orders

1. Anderson, *Imagined Communities*, 22–25.

2. Chatterjee, "Whose Imagined Community?;" Duara, *Rescuing History*, 4; Barak, *On Time*, 83.

3. In this sense Wyrtzen writes about the "Middle East's political order," *Worldmaking*, 6, 241. American historian Gary Gerstle curiously claims to have introduced the term "political order" in 1989 (!) with Steven Fraser. He means by it "the constellation of ideologies, policies, and constituencies that shape American politics." Gerstle, *The Rise and Fall*, 2–3.

4. Weber, *The Theory of Social and Economic Organization*, 328–63.

5. Weber, *Gesamtausgabe*, II/10.2; Mommsen, "Max Weber's 'Grand Sociology,'" 376; Adams and Steinmetz, "Sovereignty and Sociology," 273–74; for an interpretation of Weber as a German imperialist, see Mommsen, *The Age of Capitalism and Bureaucracy*.

6. Google Books Ngram Viewer search "political order," 25 July 2022.

7. Huntington, *Political Order in Changing Societies*, 8–31.

8. Shapiro and Hardin, *Political Order*, 1–15.

9. Arendt, *Between Past and Future*, 97, 100, 106.

10. Alatas, *What Is Religious Authority?* 4–5; Li, *The Universal Enemy*, 82–85.

11. Duara, *Rescuing History*; Kaicker, *The King and the People*.

12. A good summary is Müller, "Assemblages and Actor-Networks"; Mitchell, "The Limits of the State."

13. Sewell, "Historical Events as Transformations of Structures"; Sewell, *Logics of History*, 10.

14. Armitage, *The Ideological Origins*, 4–5; Bell, "Ideologies of Empire," 537.

15. Pitts, "Political Theory of Empire," 225–26 enumerates fluidity, stratification, zones of ambiguity, capacities of imperial power, historical models, and discursive practices as part of such a theory. Benton and Ford, *Rage for Order*, 4, describe the imperial constitution as a "fluid vernacular."

16. Burbank and Cooper, *Empires*, 3–4; Benton and Ford, *Rage for Order*, 21–24; Colley, *The Gun, the Ship, and the Pen*, 8; Ford, *The King's Peace*, 9.

17. Maier, *Among Empires*, 21–22, 34.

18. Anderson, *Lineages*, 50; Bell, "Ideologies of Empire," 539–40.

19. Legal scholars in Britain call these unwritten, inexpressible ideas a "political constitution" as opposed to "legal constitutions." Griffith, "The Political Constitution."

20. Schulz, *Normen und Praxis*, 14–15; Dicey, *Introduction*, 277–79; Sager, "Fair Measure"; Azari and Smith, "Unwritten Rules."

21. Dworkin, *Law's Empire*.

22. Kelsen, *General Theory*, 116.

23. Hart, *The Concept of Law*, 100.

24. Kelsen, *General Theory*, 131–32.

25. I suspect this is one argument in Wheatley's forthcoming, *The Life and Death of States*.

26. Armitage, *Ideological Origins*, 14.

27. Anderson, *Imagined Communities*, 22. There is also an argument that the republican idea was not as hegemonic as it now appears in the eighteenth-century American revolt against the British. Nelson, *The Royalist Revolution*.

28. In the 1920s, sovereign local states with a monarchy included Romania, Yugoslavia, Albania, Greece, Hungary (kingdom without a king), Egypt, Transjordan, Iraq, the Saudi polity, Iran, Afghanistan, Nepal, Thailand, Italy, Sweden, Norway, Denmark, the Netherlands. Non-sovereign monarchies include Tunis, Morocco, the many dynasts in African colonies, the Gulf sheikhdoms, the Princely States of India, and warlords in Chinese regions. Some polities, such as Greece, oscillated between monarchy and republic.

29. The quote is from Milinda Banerjee, "Monarchic Idioms in Modern Indian Thinking about Sovereignty: European Challenges, Asian Solidarities, and Subaltern Militancy," unpublished paper for the conference "Monarchy and Sovereignty in Twentieth-Century Asia," 13 April 2018, Duke University, quoted with permission. Laursen, Simonutti, and Blom, "Introduction," in idem, *Monarchisms in the Age of Enlightenment*, 5; Fancy, "Of Sovereigns," 68.

30. Kroll, "Modernity of the Outmoded?"; for instance, see Gilbert, "The Person of the King: Ritual and Power in a Ghanian State," 313; Geertz, *Negara*; Duindam, *Dynasties*.

31. Mayer, *The Persistence of the Old Regime*, 10 and Chapter One.

32. Huntington, *Political Order in Changing Societies*, 177–92; and challenging him, Anderson, "Absolutism and the Resilience of Monarchy."

33. Anderson, *Imagined Communities*, 19.

34. Dirks, *The Hollow Crown*; Burke, *The Ethnographic State*; a somewhat critical view is in Hansen and Stepputat, "Sovereignty Revisited," 304; and a powerful critique is in Kaicker, *The King and the People*.

35. Al-Azmeh, *Muslim Kingship*, xvi, 90–96; Moin, *The Millenial Sovereign*; Yılmaz, *Caliphate Redefined*; Kaicker, *The King and the People*.

36. Ibn Khaldun emphasizes the materiality of the authority (*mulk*) of non-caliphal rulership, Ibn Khaldun, *Muqaddima*, 1: 308 ("it consists of all worldly *khayrat*"); Kantorowicz (*The King's Two Bodies*, 3–4) defines kingship as "physiological fiction"; also Anderson, *Lineages*, 53.

37. Al-Azmeh, "Monotheistic Kingship," 267; Kaicker, *The King and the People*, 56–65.

38. Sometimes objects (a tree, a crown, a building, a space) can also carry constituent fictions.

39. Foucault, *"Society Must Be Defended,"* 151–53.

40. Anderson, *Lineages*, 27.

41. Anderson, "Absolutism and the Resilience of Monarchy," 3.

42. Pillai, "Fragmenting the Nation," 745.

43. Quote from Sluga, *The Invention of International Order*, 188.

44. Talleyrand, *Mémoires*, 2:155–61; Schulz, *Normen und Praxis*, 585.

45. Holbraad, *The Concert of Europe*, 8, 16–34, 119–21; Von Knorrig, "Konservatives Staatsdenken"; Kwan, "The Congress of Vienna, 1814–1815"; Burbank and Cooper, *Empires*, 333; Zamoyski, *Rites of Peace*, 312–13; Schulz, *Normen und Praxis*, 584–91; Sluga, *The Invention of International Order*, Chapter 12.

46. Pirenne, *Histoire de Belgique*, 7: 11–30; Schroeder, *The Transformation*, 680–84.

47. The Holy Alliance Treaty (1815), the Congress of Troppeau Protocol (1820), and the Congress of Laibach (Ljubljana, 1821); in 1820, this principle was a counter-measure against Italian uprisings, Schroeder, *The Transformation*, 610–14. For methodologies to study "the culture of peace," Schulz, *Normen und Praxis*, 5–20; for the declaration of an imperial right to intervene, see "Circular of the Austrian, Russian, and Prussian Sovereigns . . ." 8 December 1820 (Troppeau conference), in Hertslet, *Map of Europe*, 1:658–61; De Graaf, "Bringing Sense."

48. Quoted in Mazower, *Governing the World*, 5.

49. Hertslet, *The Map of Europe*, 2: 894.

50. Hertslet, *The Map of Europe*, 2: 895; Schroeder, *The Transformation*, 710.

51. Political scientists point to the theory of "native society in dissolution" by Henry Maine (1822–1888) as the intellectual origin of British indirect rule. Mantena, *Alibis of Empire*, Chapter Five, cited at 152; Mamdani, *Define and Rule*, Chapter One.

52. Buckler, "The Political Theory," 73–74. We know now that the Company regarded itself practically as a sovereign polity, Stern, *The Company-State*, 49, 51.

53. Burke, *The Ethnographic State*, 111.

54. Shawcross, *France, Mexico*, 81.

55. Laurens, *Le Royaume impossible*; Murray-Miller, "A Conflicted Sense of Nationality"; Todd, *Velvet Empire*, 111–19.

56. Quoted in Mazower, *Governing the World*, 49.

57. Marx, "Letter to Ruse, May 1843."

58. Rivet, *Lyautey et l'institution du protectorat français*, 2: 130–40.

59. Lugard, *The Dual Mandate*, 203–204.

60. Lugard, *The Dual Mandate*, 210.

61. *Bulletin Officiel* 1, 1 (1912): 6–7.

62. Benton and Clulow, "Empires and Protection."

63. Galison, *Einstein's Clocks*; Ogle, *Global Transformation of Time*; Wishnitzer, *Reading Clocks*; Barak, *On Time*; Stolz, *The Lighthouse*.

64. I use "local time" in a rather different sense than Ogle, *Global Transformation of Time*, 18, where it is a synonym of solar time as opposed to newly introduced country-wide mean times.

65. Wishnitzer, *Reading Clocks*, 7.

66. EI2, "Tarikh" (F. C. de Bois); Rose, "The Ottoman Fiscal Calendar;" Georgeon, "Changes of Time," 189–90; Türesay, "Les temps des almanachs ottomanes," 141–146; Grallert, "To Whom Belong the Streets?", 27–28.

67. Georgeon, "Changes of Time," 185.

68. The Syrian use is confusing because Istanbul-based Turkish-speaking intellectuals used the term *rumi* to denote any solar months and the term *efrenci* ("Frankish") to denote specifically the solar Gregorian dates. Türesay, "Les temps des almanachs ottomanes," 144, cites Abüzziya Tevfik, the late Ottoman calendar-maker, who states that the term *rumi* is to be used for solar months, regardless of the calendar. Therefore Rose ("The Ottoman Fiscal Calendar," 158), Georgeon ("Changes of Time," 182), and Grallert ("To Whom Belong the Streets?" 26) are not entirely correct when they state that the Ottomans used the term *rumi* for the Julian calendar. For instance, Georgeon elsewhere cites the example of the Istanbul-based journal *Sabah*, which consistently indicated the *fiscal* dates as *rumi*. Georgeon adds that these are "Julian" dates but this is clearly not the case, because the years are dated from the *hijra*. Georgeon, "Temps de la réforme," 268–69.

69. *Al-Taqaddum*, 8 August 1913, 1.

70. For instance, DS-K 30, İSAM.

71. Ekinci, *Osmanlı Mahkemeleri*, 234.

72. DS-I 117, 239–40, İSAM.

73. Examples include DS-I 126; DS-T 124; DS-T 149; all in İSAM.

74. DS-I 117, 241, İSAM.

75. For instance, DS-I 117, 279; DS-I 125, 131; both in İSAM.

76. *Al-Tawfiq* (Hama), 1 Kanun al-Thani (January) 1919 / 29 Rabi' al-Awwal 1337, 1; *Al-'Uqab* (Damascus) 14 Shubat (February) 1919 / 13 Jumada al-Awwal 1337, 1.

77. *Al-'Asima*, 17 Jumada al-Ula 1337 / 17 Shubat 1919, 1; *Al-Istiqlal al-'Arabi*, 28 Ramadan 1337 / 27 Haziran 1919, 1; *Al-Mufid*, 8 Muharram 1338 / 3 Tishrin Awwal 1919, 1.

78. *Suriya al-Jadida*, 22 Nisan gh[arbi] 1921 (one day less than the Gregorian date) / 14 Sha'ban 1339 / 9 Nisan 1921.

79. "Hilafetin Ilgha ve Handan Osmaniyenin Türkiye Cumhuriyeti Mamaliki Haricine Cikarilmasina Dair Kanun—Kanun 341," *Resmi Ceride*, 6 Mart 1340 (6 March 1924), 6–7.

Chapter 3. Governing Without Sovereignty

1. Weitz, "From the Vienna to the Paris System"; Mazower, *No Enchanted Palace*; Pedersen, *The Guardians*; Wempe, "A League to Preserve Empires."

2. Anghie, *Imperialism, Sovereignty*, 146.

3. Fitzmaurice, *Sovereignty, Property and Empire*, 18.

4. The relationship between the emergence of governing without sovereignty and the emergence of "a sensibility about matters international in the late nineteenth century as an inextricable part of the liberal and cosmopolitan movements of the day," which according to Martti Koskenniemi motivated the making of international law between 1870 and 1960, should be the subject of a separate investigation, Koskenniemi, *The Gentle Civilizer of Nations*, 2–3.

5. Governing without sovereignty had occurred in world history before the nineteenth century, as in the British East India Company's control over Indian regions, for which see Stern, *The Company-State*. Informal imperialism through trade and debt is also often called "empire without sovereignty." Todd, *Velvet Empire*, Chapter One.

6. Even in such cases, as in French Tunisia, the trajectory of domination was slow from indirect to direct, from divided to "undivided" rule in the long run. Lewis, *Divided Rule*, 4, 13.

7. Korman, *The Right of Conquest*, 8; Sharma, *Territorial Acquisition*, 143–46; Benvenisti, *The International Law of Occupation*, 25–40; Arai-Takahashi, *The Law of Occupation*. My definition of this historical situation is close to Roberts' indications of occupation in today's public international law, Roberts, "Termination of Military Occupation."

8. This is as valid today (Kahlert, "Pioneers in International Administration") as in the 1950s (see Sharp's 1958 review of four books, "The Study of International Administration").

9. Petit, "Essay d'étude du régime juridique des pays placées sous mandate." 189PO/1/75, CADN.

10. Wright, *Mandates*, Chapter One; Chowdhuri, *International Mandates*, 230–36; Anghie, *Imperialism, Sovereignty*, 115–95; Pedersen, *The Guardians*, 400–401.

11. See more on Egypt's Islamic legal architecture in Chapter Six. For the 1900s British ideology about material wealth and its relation to the new Egyptian economic nationalism, Jakes, *Egypt's Occupation*, Chapter Four.

12. Genell, "The End of Egypt's Occupation."

13. Texts of proclamations and the explanation are cited in McIlwraith, "The Declaration of a Protectorate;" for Lugard's native ruler theory see Chapter One.

14. Qanun n. 8, 9 February 1915 (*'Amal al-sultat al-qada'iyya al-istithna'iyya fi al-qutr al-misri tamdidan mu'aqqatan*), published in *Al-Mahakim*, 24 February 1915, 1 (5900).

15. Darwin, *Britain, Egypt, and the Middle East*, 130; Long, *British Pro-Consuls in Egypt*, 10–13; quote from Innes, "In Egyptian Service," 93, 104.

16. High Commissioner to FO, 10 October 1917, FO 141/620/3, NAUK.

17. *Journal Officiel*, 10 October 1917, 1.

18. Wingate to Balfour, 20 October 1917, FO 141/620/3, NAUK.

19. "The Capitulations in Egypt and the Mixed Tribunals." Annex of letter by Crabitès to Senator Ransdell, 8 March 1918, FO 141/620/5, NAUK.

20. Ireland, *'Iraq*, 136 quotes Wilson.

21. "Interview with Sarwat," Diary of Milner, 13 December 1919, 15–17; "Conversation between Sir Cecil Hurst and Abdul Aziz Bey Fahmy," (n. 36) 199–200, both in FO 848/5, NAUK.

22. Milner to Cecil, 1 November 1919 from, 1/1970/1970, R13, LNA; Pedersen, *The Guardians*, 31–34.

23. Correspondence between 22 and 28 March 1922, in FO 371/7732, NAUK.

24. "Memorandum by Sir Gilbert Clayton, Advisor to Egyptian Ministry of Interior," 8 October 1921, in FO 800/153, NAUK; and Article One in *Treaty of Alliance*, 4.

25. Benvenisti, "Occupation, Belligerent."

26. Roberts, "Termination of Military Occupation."

27. Benvenisti, "Occupation, Pacific."

28. Benvenisti, *The International Law of Occupation*, 25–40; the 1907 agreement was signed but not ratified by the Ottoman Empire.

29. Article 55 is identical in Annex II of the 1899 Convention with Article 55 in Annex IV of the 1907 Convention, "1899—Annex to the Convention," in Schindler and Toman, *The Laws of Armed Conflicts*, 91.

30. Korman, *The Right of Conquest*, 8.

31. Benvenisti, *The International Law of Occupation*, 347–351; Arai-Takahashi, *The Law of Occupation*.

32. Tanenbaum, "France and the Arab Middle East;" Blatt, "France and Italy," 28; Smith, *Sovereignty*, 21–23.

33. Fromkin quoting Balfour in a War Cabinet meeting, 3 October 1918, *A Peace*, 364–365.

34. The close connection between the idea of right and right in property originates in Roman law. Fitzmaurice, *Sovereignty, Property, and Empire*, 33.

35. All quotes are from Jensis, "The Memel Territory."

36. Wright, "Sovereignty of the Mandates."

37. Memorandum by Mr. Balfour, 2 August 1921, 1/5959/161, R1, LNA.

38. Lindley, *The Acquisition and Government*, 267–68.

39. Chowdhuri, *International Mandates*; Pedersen, *The Guardians*, 205–207; also 1/51732/48622, R78, LNA.

40. Gerwarth and Manela, "The Great War as a Global War"; Gerwarth, *The Vanquished*.

41. Memorandum by Eric Drummond, 22 July 1920, 1/5690/4284, R21, LNA.

42. "Communication from the King of the Hedjaz," adapted 5 August 1920, 20/41/45, R21, LNA.

43. Answer to Victor Bérard, Commission des Affaires Extérieures du Sénat, 19 December 1920, 50CPCOM/55, CADC.

44. MAE to Lord Hardinge, 12 February 1921, 1SL/250/45, CADN.

45. Meinertzhagen, *Report on Middle East Conference*, 21–22; 62–68.

46. "Note sur le projet d'organisation du contrôle administratif à exercer par la France en vertu du mandat qui sera lui confié sur la Syrie," Copin, Contrôle Administratif, 30 April 1920, 50CPCOM/55, CADC.

47. Sheehan, "The Problem of Sovereignty;" Cooper, *Colonialism in Question*, 153; Darwin, *After Tamerlane*; Burbank and Cooper, *Empires in World History*.

48. *Correspondance de Napoléon Ier*, 10: 128.

49. *Protestation du Comité national polonais*, 3.

50. Genell, "Autonomous Provinces;" Fujinami, "Between Sovereignty and Suzerainty;" Rodogno, "European Legal Doctrines."

51. Milovanowitch, *Les Traités de garantie*, 383.

52. *Affaires de Tunisie*, 36. For the ambivalence, see the title of the French translation: *Loi Organique ou Code Politique et Administratif du Royaume Tunisien*.

53. Lamba, *Code administratif égyptien.*

54. Twenty-fifth Congress (1839), Session Three, Chapter XC, 356.

55. For instance, *The Revised Codes of the Territory of Dakota.*

56. Hoijer, *Le pacte de la Société des nations*, 207.

57. *The League of Nations Starts*, 109.

58. "American Draft"—"Class A Mandate," undated (1919 fall?) R1, 1/1224/161, LNA, perhaps by G. L. Beer; see also letter of Eric Forbes Adam to Drummond, 7 November 1919, R13, 1/1834/161, LNA; an undated "Projet du Colonel House— Mandat de la catégorie 'A'" also contains the organic law in 1SL/250/45, and drafts during 1920 and 1921, 1SL/1V/1563, CADN.

59. "Draft of the Mandate for Mesopotamia," appendix of letter by Balfour to Drummond, 6 December 1920, R2, 1/10533/161, LNA; *Final Drafts of the Mandates*, CAB 30/30, NAUK.

60. "Recommendations to the Council," Annex V, 3QO/64, CADC.

61. "Mandate for Syria and the Lebanon," 177.

62. Khadduri, "Constitutional Development," 140; Khoury, *Syria and the French Mandate*, 142, 246–47; Fieldhouse, *Western Imperialism*, 256, 263; Mizrahi, "La France et sa politique," 35–71; Sabbagh, *Sijill al-Dustur al-Suri*, 141; Atassi, *Syria, the Strength of an Idea*, 99.

63. Lapierre, *Le mandat français en Syrie*, 84–85.

64. *Treaty of Alliance*; Wilks, "The 1922 Anglo-Iraq Treaty."

65. Bentwich, "XIII. Palestine," 190; Kassim, "Legal Systems," 23–24.

66. Ministre des Affaires Étrangères (MAE) to Weygand, 19 December 1923, 143PAAP/175, CADC. For a Syrian evaluation of this federation, see Moubayed, *Tarikh Dimashq al-Mansi*, 99–122, especially at 120.

67. "Statut Organique," undated, 143PAAP/175, CADC.

68. Provence, *The Great Syrian Revolt*, 82–83.

69. Mestyan, "From Administrative to Political Order?"

70. Moumtaz, *God's Property*, 16–17; Williams, "Mapping the Cadastre," 170; for the French preparations for economic colonization see Jackson, "What is Syria Worth?" Rappas introduces the notion of "material sovereignty" to characterize the French goals in his "Three Murders," 3, 22; however, it is analytically better to restrict the use of the term "sovereignty" to the legal content and develop new terms for the new mode of domination.

71. Decision of Council of Ministers in Damascus, 24 April 1920, translation attached in Cousse to HC, 25 April 1920, 1SL-1-V-2347, CADN.

72. *Rapport général* (1921); Cardon, *Le régime*, 120–28; correspondence in 1SL/251/17, translated land register page in 1SL/250/8, CADN. Williams, "Mapping," 173. For the idea of land administration, see Mestyan, "Seeing Like a Khedivate."

73. Puech's undated lecture is in 189PO/1/75, the note is dated January 1926, 1SL/250/45, both in CADN.

74. Duraffaurd, "Note sur le service technique," undated (1928?), 1AE/118/11; contracts in 1AE/118/23; undated (1926 ?) note by Duraffaurd about the decision for privatization, and correspondence in 1AE/118/25, Grand Livre 1923–24 (account book) 1AE/118/138, all in CADN. I explore this company in greater detail in another project.

75. Bodin, *On Sovereignty*, 14, 35–36.

76. Burbank, "Eurasian Sovereignty," 15.

77. Pedersen, "Settler Colonialism," 125; Seikaly, *Men of Capital*, 4–5.

78. Pedersen, "Getting Out of Iraq."

Chapter 4. Ottoman Genealogical Politics

1. For more on this office, see Mayeur-Jaouen, "Vérification des généalogies." Scholars usually translate *naqib al-ashraf* into English as "marshal of the Prophet's descendants" or "syndic of the Prophet's descendants." However, I prefer the translation "verifier" based on both the actual meaning of the word *naqib* and the activity of this officer.

2. Morimoto, "Introduction," 1–2.

3. Al-Amir, "Hajat al-Muluk wa-l-Umara' li-'Ilm al-Nasab," 30 Jumada al-Akhira 1442 (13 February 2021). Ibrahim b. Mansur is a well-published genealogist in Mecca.

4. 'Abd Allah to Khedive Abbas Hilmi II, 17 February 1914, HIL 63/321, AHP.

5. *Al-Ahram*, 9 July 1914, 5.

6. Dawn, *From Ottomanism*, 3; Abu-Manneh, "Sultan Abdulhamid II;" Deringil, *The Well-Protected Domains*, 11, 14; Tauber, "Sayyid Talib and the Young Turks."

7. Hobsbawm, "Introduction: Inventing Traditions," 6.

8. Makdisi, "Ottoman Orientalism."

9. Deringil, *The Well-Protected Domains*, 10–11, 26–35, 43.

10. Berger and Miller, *Nationalizing Empires*.

11. Uzunçarşili, *Ashraf Makka*; Freitag, *A History of Jidda*; Low, *Imperial Mecca*; and further literature in the following notes.

12. Haykel, "Western Arabia," 436.

13. Low, *Imperial Mecca*; Barak, *Powering Empire*; for the relationship between Muslim politics and technology, see Gelvin and Green, *Global Muslims*; Kozma et al., *A Global Middle East*; Mestyan, "Domestic Sovereignty."

14. See for instance the book of the Aleppo *naqib*, Taj al-Din al-Husayni, *Ghayat al-Ikhtisar*, printed in Egypt in the official press in 1892 and edited by one al-Husayni.

15. Morimoto, "Toward the Formation of Sayyido-Sharifology," 93.

16. Goldziher, "A Nemzetiségi Kérdés"; Savant and de Felipe, *Genealogy and Knowledge in Muslim Societies*; Mayeur-Jaouen, "Vérification des généalogies."

17. Pernau, *Ashraf into Middle Classes*, 63.

18. Shryock, *Nationalism and the Genealogical Imagination*; Ho, *The Graves of Tarim*.

19. Koran 3:61, 33:33, 42:23; etc; for sayings, Sarijik, *Niqabat al-Ashraf*, 42–48.

20. The changing uses of the title of *sharif* and *sayyid* and the differences between them in various ages are summarized in C. van Arendonk and W. A. Graham, "Sharif," EI2; for early Ottoman Egypt see, Winter, *Egyptian Society*, 179–92; Kılıç, "The Reflection," 129; for the Mughal context, see Pernau, *Ashraf into Middle Classes*, 59–66.

21. Morimoto, ed, *Sayyids and Sharifs*; Meriwether, *The Kin Who Count*, 46; Hathaway and Barbir, *The Arab Lands*.

22. Sarijik, *Niqabat al-Ashraf*, 126–54 (127, critique of Uzunçarşili), 281–92; Kılıç, *Osmanlıda Seyyidler ve Şerifler*, 79–110; idem, "The Reflection;" Winter, *Egyptian Society*, 179–92; idem, "The *Ashraf*;" Yaycıoğlu, *Partners of Empire*, 13.

23. Yılmaz, *Caliphate Redefined*.

24. Freitag, *Indian Ocean Migrants*, 208–13.

25. Jacob, *For God or Empire*, 65.

26. Laffan, *Under Empire*, 249.

27. Abu-Manneh, "Sultan Abdülhamid and the Sharifs"; Commins, *Islamic Reform*; Weismann, *Taste of Modernity*; Eich, *Abu L-Huda L-Sayyadi*; idem, "The Forgotten Salafi"; see the debate between Weismann, "Abu L-Huda L-Sayyadi" and Eich, "Abu l-Huda l-Sayyadi"; for Ho's argument, *Graves of Tarim*.

28. Rıfaat, *Devhat ün-Nükaba*.

29. Abu-Manneh, "Sultan Abdulhamid II and Shaikh," 139–40; Deringil, *The Well-Protected Domains*, 65–66; Eich, *Abu L-Huda L-Sayyadi*, 52–53, 56–62; Jacob, *For God or Empire*, 128–139.

30. For instance, his 1889 little book: Al-Sayyadi, *Dhakirat al-Ma'ad*.

31. Al-Sayyadi, *Da'i al-Rashad*, 10.

32. Al-Sayyadi, *Da'i al-Rashad*, 17.

33. Sarıcık does not mention Abu al-Huda's name, but it is obvious that the appointments he describes are about Abu al-Huda's appointees, in his *Niqabat al-Ashraf*, 274–77.

34. Faydi, *Fi Ghamrat al-Nidal*; Yusufzade, *Asna Matalib al-Arib*, 8–17; Tauber, "Sayyid Talib and the Young Turks;" Tauber, "Sayyid Talib and the Throne;" Shalah, *Talib Basha al-Naqib*; Visser, *Basra, the Failed Gulf State*; Schlaepfer, "Between Ruler and Rogue;" Laffan, *Under Empire*.

35. Letter of the Grand Vizier for appointments, 28 August 1312 (*maliye*) (9 September 1896), İ.TAL. 104/25, BOA.

36. *Mirmiran* title appointment, along with others, in letter dated 19 Dhu al-Qa'ada 1316, İ.TAL. 170/34, BOA.

37. Decorations ordered on 17 Rabi'a al-Awwal 1320 (24 June 1902), İ.TAL. 280/16; later there were more decorations to even more family members, Yusufzade, *Asna Matalib al-Arib*, 13–14; correspondence about the Qatif incident is in Y.A.RES 119/58 and Y.A.RES 120/92, BOA; especially see the Ottoman translation of local *muhtars'* undated French telegraph accusing Sayyid Talib of taking money from 'Abd al-Husayni, Mansur Pasha's brother, and oppressing them; Tauber, "Sayyid Talib and the Young Turks," 4, used only British sources. For a local (al-Ahsa) view, see Al-Muslim, *Sahil al-Dhahab*, 191.

38. Tauber, "Sayyid Talib and the Young Turks;" Yusufzade, *Asna Matalib al-Arib*, 12–14; Faydi, *Fi Ghamrat al-Nidal*, 65–66, 78–80, 93–94, 96–98; Schlaepfer, "Between Ruler and Rogue," 243.

39. Letter of Basra's governor describing Sayyid Talib's activity to the sultan, 21 Rabi' al-Thani 1323 (5 June 1905), Y.A.HUS 491/31, BOA. The two books are Antaki, *'Urf al-Tib* and Yusufzade, *Asna Matalib al-Arib*. The image is from Yusufzade, *Asna Matalib al-Arib*. Antaki was the owner of the journal *al-'Umran* in Egypt.

40. Yusufzade, *Asna Matalib al-Arib*, 4, 12–13.

41. Sarijik, *Niqabat al-Ashraf*, 270–77; Winter, *Egyptian Society*, 139; 186–90; Meriwether, *The Kin Who Count*; Lemire, *Jerusalem 1900*, 106.

42. Mughazy and Sabra, *Manaqib al-Sada al-Bakriyya*, 7–12; Mestyan, "Tawfiq Muhammad al-Bakri," *EI3*.

43. Khoury and Kennedy, "Comparing Empires."

44. Kéchichian, *'Iffat Al Thunayan*, 20–21.

45. Deringil, *The Well-Protected Domains*, 65; Khuri-Makdisi, "Ottoman Arabs in Istanbul;" At the time of writing, Minawi (*Losing Istanbul*) was not yet available to me.

46. Dahlan, *Khulasat al-Kalam*, 16–21.

47. Dahlan, *Khulasat al-Kalam*, for the Ottoman takeover of Egypt and the Hijaz, 50; for the sultanic telegraph, 329. For Sharif 'Awn al-Rafiq, see Minawi, *The Ottoman Scramble*, 135–37 and Low, *Imperial Mecca*, 264–69.

48. Freitag, *Indian Ocean Migrants*, 201–208.

49. Al-Siba'i, *Tarikh Makka*.

50. Al-Ghazi, *Ifadat al-Anam*, 1: 4.

51. Together with the available Ottoman and other sources, and in the critical light of the works of Uzunçarşili, Buzpinar, Minawi, Freitag, and Low, al-Ghazi's text in particular provides a valuable entryway to the modern history of Mecca and the Hijaz. For various memory politics see Matthesian, "Shi'i Historians"; Bsheer, *Archive Wars*, 63–67.

52. Mortel, "Zaydi Shi'ism"; Peskes, "Western Arabia," 286–87; Faroqhi, *Pilgrims*, 79–80; Haykel, "Western Arabia," 439–40, 445–46; "Hashimis of Mecca" (G. Rentz, updated by William Ochsenwald), EI3.

53. Mubarak, *Al-Khitat al-Tawfiqiyya*, 12:79, al-Ghazi, *Ifadat al-Anam*, 4:52. It appears that the original letter was published by the French Orientalist Silvestre de Sacy and 'Ali Mubarak copied him; and a printed version was in the possession of De Sacy. Compare the amounts with the Egyptian payments in the sixteenth-seventeenth centuries, Faroqhi, *Pilgrims*, 79–82.

54. Al-Jabarti, *'Aja'ib*, 4:164ff; Peters, *Mecca*, 304–28.

55. The story of Mecca and 'Abd al-Muttalib in the age of Mehmed Ali awaits academic research. Al-Ghazi, *Ifadat al-Anam*, 4: 66–83; Uzunçarşili, *Ashraf Makka*, 205–14.

56. Uzunçarşili, *Ashraf Makka*, 210; al-Ghazi, *Ifadat al-Anam*, 4: 87.

57. Onley, *The Arabian Frontier*, 37; Crouzet, *Genèses du Moyen-Orient*, 119–20 ; Hanioğlu, *A Brief History*, 134–35; Motadel, "Introduction," in idem, *Islam and the European Empires*; Ryad, *The Hajj and Europe in the Age of Empire*; Barak, *Powering Empire*, 157; Low, *Imperial Mecca*; Can, *Spiritual Subjects*.

58. Pétriat, *Le Négoce des lieux saints*, Chapters One, Two, and Three.

59. Buzpinar, "The Hijaz, Abdulhamid II"; idem, "Vying for Power"; idem, "Opposition to the Ottoman Caliphate."

60. Uzunçarşili, *Ashraf Makka*; Ochsenwald, *Religion, Society*, 6–8, 14–15, 211–18; Buzpinar, "The Hijaz"; for a description of the 1905 pilgrimage, see Chantre, ed., *Un administrateur colonial*; for the Ottoman social/infrastructural policy, Kedouri, *In the Anglo-Arab Labyrinth*, 6; Rogan, "Abdulhamid II's School"; Akpınar, *Osmanlı Devleti'nde Aşiret Mektebi*, 20–28; Deringil, "'They Live in a State of Nomadism'"; Deringil, *The Well-Protected Domains*, 59–60; Minawi, *The Ottoman Scramble*, 99–115; Low, "Ottoman Infrastructures," 946–47; Bsheer, *Archive Wars*, 67–70; Low, *Imperial Mecca*.

61. Uzuncarsili, *Ashraf Makka*, 206, 222; Stitt, *A Prince of Arabia*, 49–50.

62. Stitt, *A Prince of Arabia*, 57–58, 67–69, 83.

63. Işıktaş, *Şerif Muhiddin*, 131–16.

64. 16 Safar 1304 (14 November 1886), I.DH 1135/88576, BOA.

65. 3 Ramadan 1306 (4 May 1889), I.DH 1135/88576; 9 Rabi'a al-Akhar 1311 (20 October 1893), BEO 299/22366, all in BOA.

66. Işıktaş, *Şerif Muhiddin*, 134.

67. 17 Dhu al-Qa'da 1316 (29 March 1899), I.DH 1362/48, BOA.

68. 25 Rabi' al-Thani 1318 I.ML. 39/35; 28 Rabi' al-Thani 1318 (25 August 1900), BEO 1524/114247; both in BOA.

69. Sarıcık/Sarijik, *Niqabat al-Ashraf*, 199–213, at 211. One must add that the restructuring of the modern pious finances of the empire awaits its researchers.

70. In fact, it would have been the case since 1891; Maliye to Defterhane, 25 Rabi' al-Akhar 1311 (5 November 1893), BEO 309/23111, BOA. For the sixteenth-century origins of the *sürre*, see Faroqhi, *Pilgrims*, 54–56.

71. Finance Minister to sultan, 4 Dhu al-Hijja 1330 (14 November 1912), BEO 4323/324151, BOA.

72. Finance Minister to sultan, 22 Ramadan 1318 (13 January 1901), BEO 1614/1120976, BOA.

73. Finance Ministry to Meclis-i Vukala, 25 Safar 1335 (21 December 1916), MV 205/13, BOA.

74. Göreli, *Devlet Şurası*; Özdeş, "Danıştay'ın Tarihçesi"; Shaw and Shaw, *The History of the Ottoman Empire*, 2: 79–81; Eraslan, *Şura'yı Devletten Danıştaya*; Gedikli, *Şura-yı Devlet*.

75. Although it is known to researchers, the social history of this important institution has not yet been properly studied.

76. Appointment to Council of State is 1 Rabi' al-Awwal 1310 (23 September 1892), ŞD 3191/60; his request for missing payments on 3 Dhu al-Qa'da 1311 (8 May 1894), BEO 405/30360, BOA.

77. Draft dated 24 Safar 1310 (17 September 1892), BEO 72/5345, and later more correspondence about the rent in BEO, long-term rent in letter dated 18 Rabi' al-Awwal 1314 (23 August 1896), BEO 845/63360; all in BOA.

78. 9 Rajab 1323 (9 September 1905), DH.MKT 1004/59, BOA.

79. Zürcher, *Turkey*, 93–110; Kayalı, *Arabs and Young Turks*; Philliou, *A Past*, 6, 13, 60.

80. Tauber, "Sayyid Talib and the Young Turks"; Schlaepfer, "Between Ruler and Rogue," 242–45; for the 1913 trial about a conspiracy against Basra's governor and the *mutasarrif* of the Muntafiq region, see the correspondence in BEO 4385/328871, BOA. An interesting wartime British portrayal of Sayyid Talib is in IOR/L/PS/10/586/2 (File 705/1916), BL, QDL.

81. Draft dated 10 Sha'ban 1326 (7 September 1908), BEO 3391/254286, BOA.

82. The Meclis-i 'Ayan appointment, 29 Nisan 1330 (*maliye*) (18 February 1912), BEO 4284/321256, BOA; Uzuncarsili, *Ashraf Makka*, 233–35; Stitt, *A Prince of Arabia*, 93–95, 103–105, 108, 118–22; Işıktaş, *Şerif Muhiddin*, 136–40.

Chapter 5. Utopian Federalism: Post-Ottoman Empires

1. *Al-Qibla*, 3 Muharram 1335 (30 October 1916), 1–2; also letter dated 5 November 1916, Wilson to McMahon, IOR/L/PS/10/637, BL, QDL; Al-Husayn ('Abd Allah b.), *Mudhakkirati*, 135–37; Ayalon, "*Malik*," 306; Wilson, *King Abdullah*, 31; Teitelbaum, *The Rise and Fall*, 107–11.

2. French reaction: telegram from Jidda dated 31 October 1916, 1CPCOM/1687, CADC; British one: "Memorandum on British Commitments to King Husein," p. 14, IOR/L/PS/18/B292, BL, QDL.

3. From Antonius to Rogan; even Tauber, *The Emergence*, an amazing piece of research, engages these ideas as proto-nationalist ones.

4. Adelman, *Sovereignty and Revolution*, 281; Cooper, *Citizenship between Empire and Nation*, 7, 9; Wilder, *Freedom Time*, 2–3, 139; Collins, "Decolonization," 22; Pillai, "Fragmenting the Nation," 765; Prendergast, "The Sociological Idea."

5. Salzmann, *Tocqueville in the Ottoman Empire*, 19–21; Mikhail and Philliou, "The Ottoman Empire"; Matossian, *Shattered Dreams*; Kostopoulou, "Autonomy and Federation"; Yenen, "Envisioning"; for cases in the Arab provinces, see Toledano, "The Emergence"; Minawi, *The Ottoman Scramble for Africa*; Mestyan, *Arab Patriotism*; Mestyan, "A Muslim Dualism?" Low, *Imperial Mecca*; and references later in this chapter.

6. Ersoy, Górny and Kechriotis, *Modernism: The Creation of Nation-States*, Chapter 4.

7. Matossian, *Shattered Dreams of Revolution*; Sohrabi, *Revolution and Constitutionalism*; Hajdarpašić, "Out of the Ruins"; Georgeon and Lévy, *The Young Turk Revolution*.

8. Aydin, *The Idea of the Muslim World*, 108–115.

9. Hillis, *Utopia's Discontents*, 4.

10. Arsan, "'This age is the age of associations'".

11. Cooper, "Routes Out of Empire."

12. Hassan, *Longing for the Lost Caliphate*; March, *The Caliphate of Man*.

13. Dawn, *From Ottomanism to Arabism*, 53.

14. Kedourie, *In the Anglo-Arab Labyrinth*, 7–11, quoting R. Storrs' report about the offer, with reference to a note by R. Storrs, 19 April 1914, FO 371/1973, 87396, NAUK; also Wilson, *King Abdullah*, 23, 26.

15. Visser, *The Failed Gulf State*, 46–50.

16. Kołodziejczyk, "What is Inside and What is Outside?" 428; Faroqhi, *The Ottoman Empire and the World*, 97; Philliou, "Communities on the Verge."

17. Barkey, *Empire of Difference*, 226–27; Yaycioğlu, *Partners of Empire*, 118.

18. Two excellent texts about centralized reform are Davison, *Reform in the Ottoman Empire*; Hanioğlu, *A Brief History of the Late Ottoman Empire*.

19. Anscombe, *The Ottoman Gulf*, 3–4; Benton, *A Search for Sovereignty*, 298; Elliot, "A Europe of Composite Monarchies"; Goffman and Stroop, "Empire as Composite"; Onley, *The Arabian Frontier*; Sheehan, "The Problem of Sovereignty"; Burbank and Cooper, *Empires in World History*, 306; Minawi, *The Ottoman Scramble*, 34–39; Toledano, "The Arabic-Speaking World," 464; Masters, *The Arabs*, Chapter Six; Anscombe, *State, Faith, and Nation*, Chapters 3 and 4.

20. 'Ammun, *Al-Amani al-Lubnaniyya*, 4.

21. Makdisi, *The Culture of Sectarianism*.

22. Can and Genell, "On Empire and Exception."

23. Belgradi, *Tarih-i Vak'a-i Heyret-nüma Belgrad*, 1:242–43.

24. Minawi, *The Ottoman Scramble*, 55–57, 73–78.

25. The titles were not imperial administrative grades. The civil grades like *vizir*, imperial honorific nobility titles like *mirmiran*, or military grade like *ferik*, all came with the official title "pasha," see Bouquet, *Les Pachas du Sultan*, 108–27; though some of these leaders received a grade in addition to their local-Ottoman title. Ambitious pashas carved out an exceptional status for themselves with an exceptional title. For instance, the reformer Midhat Pasha as governor of Damascus in 1879–1880

required that the title "khedive" be used in addressing him, similar to the privileged title of the Egyptian governor. Shamir, "Midhat Pasha," 123; Haim, *Arab Nationalism*, 5, n.2.

26. Ceylan, *Osmanlı Taşra İdarı*, 20–22, 27–33; Genell, "Autonomous Provinces."

27. Fujinami, "Between Sovereignty and Suzerainty," 56; the changing list of *eyalat-i mümtaze* is summarized in Ceylan, *Osmanlı Taşra İdarı*, 28, fn 57.

28. Hakkı, *Hukuk-i Idare*, 1: 54.

29. Privileged provinces and some princely regions did not send representatives to the 1877 Ottoman parliament, Hanioğlu, *A Brief History*, 118–19.

30. Genell, "Autonomous Provinces," 541.

31. Schayegh, *The Middle East*, 20.

32. Arts. "Khitta" (P. Crone); "Khitat" (Claude Cahen), EI2; Genell, "Empire by Law," 98, fn. 17; Hanioğlu, *A Brief History*, 9, fn. 8, 10, figure 10.

33. Crouzet, *Genèses du Moyen-Orient*, Chapters 3 and 4.

34. Ates, *Ottoman-Iranian Borderlands*, 18–20 for Ottoman imperial border-terminology; Maier, *Once within Borders*, Chapter 3; Ellis, *Desert Borderland*.

35. Report of emir of the *mahmal* in year 1331, HIL 77/1–6, AHP.

36. Rashid Rida, "Ara' al-Khawwas fi al-Masa'la al-'Arabiyya," *al-Manar*, 19, 3 (29 August 1916), 144–69, at 146.

37. Benton, *A Search for Sovereignty*, 13.

38. Moalla, *The Regency of Tunis*; Brown, *Tunisia of Ahmad Bey*; Oualdi, *Esclaves et maîtres*; Toledano, *State and Society*; Mestyan, *Arab Patriotism*.

39. *Hatt-i Hümayun-i Sharif ve Kanun-i Esasi*, 8–10; Ubicini, *Constitution Ottomane*, 19–20, 22, n.3.

40. The idea that the Sunni caliphate should belong to an ethnically Arab individual was different from what Cemil Aydin calls "the racialization of Muslim-ness." Aydin, *The Idea of the Muslim World*, 6–7, 37, 63.

41. Mouline, *The Clerics*, 87.

42. Teitelbaum, "Sharif Husayn," 104.

43. Buzpinar, "The Hijaz," 120; Low, *Imperial Mecca*, 99–100.

44. Buzpinar, "Opposition," 65–69, 84–88; Blunt, *The Future*, 95–131; Charmes, *L'avenir*, 182–194; Hanioğlu, *Young Turks in Opposition*, 253–54, n. 315, suggests that Blunt got the idea of the Arab caliph from the Egyptian sheikh Muhammad 'Abduh (d. 1905), but I have found no evidence for this.

45. Pickthall quoted in Haim, *Arab Nationalism*, 28.

46. Hanioğlu, *Young Turks in Opposition*, 48.

47. Commins, *Islamic Reform*, 109.

48. Low, *Imperial Mecca*, 20.

49. The Yeğen family, as its name shows ("cousin" in Turkish), was a relative of the khedive. This paragraph is based on an Arabic letter dated 25 September 1895 from 'Abd Allah Nadim to Abbas Hilmi II, HIL/9/30–37; undated Arabic letter 'Abd Allah Nadim to Abbas Hilmi II, HIL/9/44; French letter dated 29 May 1896, Mohamed Vali Eddin Yackan [Yeğen] to Lord Cromer, HIL/35/321–324; undated "Note sur l'Ile de Thasos," HIL 48/4–12, all in AHP. For later khedivial-CUP relations, Hanioğlu, *Young Turks in Opposition*, 162–164.

50. Commins, *Islamic Reform*, 109.

51. Arabic letter dated 25 December 1895, from 'Abd Allah Nadim to Abbas Hilmi II, HIL/9/59–61; Arabic letter dated 22 Jumada al-Thaniyya 1313, from 'Abd Allah Nadim to Abbas Hilmi II, HIL/9/65, all in AHP.

52. Undated treatises in Ottoman Turkish, HIL 24/7–54, AHP. Some scholars assume that Abbas Hilmi II had his own plans to gain the caliphate at the time: Kedourie, "The Politics of Political Literature," 107–109; Weismann, *Abd al-Rahman al-Kawakibi*, 62–63.

53. Letter dated 28 Dhu al-Qa'da 1330, from Yamani *a'yan* to Abbas Hilmi II, HIL 56/157, AHP.

54. Letter dated 1896 Aug 27, from ? to Nazir al-Khassa, HIL 161/38, AHP.

55. Haim, *Arab Nationalism*, 19–27; Haddad, "Arab Religious Nationalism," 257.

56. Lauzière, *The Making of Salafism;* Rock-Singer, *In the Shade of the Sunna.*

57. Zeine, *The Emergence*, 70–71.

58. Ryad, *Islamic Reformism*; Halevi, *Modern Things on Trial*, Chapter One; 161.

59. Weismann, *Abd al-Rahman*, 67–68. First al-Kawakibi's *Taba'i' al-Istibdad* (The Characteristics of Oppression) was serialized in the journal *al-Mu'ayyad* in 1898. Haim, *Arab Nationalism* (28–29) and Kedourie, "The Politics of Political Literature," (107–110), suspect that *Umm al-Qura* was a piece of khedivial propaganda; Weismann, *Abd al-Rahman*, 62, writes that al-Kawakibi declined Abbas Hilmi II's offer. In 1902, Rida added a note at the end of the serialized edition to the effect that he had agreed with the deceased author to publish it *without* the accusations against the Ottoman Empire. Rida also omitted one sentence. The deleted sentence states that an imaginary association "has chosen to establish its temporary center in Egypt [. . .] as he [the khedive] is the best young ruler raised on religious zeal and Arab fervor." "Lahiqat Sijill Jam'iyyat Umm al-Qura," *al-Manar* 5, n. 23, 28 February 1903, 910; and Weismann, *Abd al-Rahman*, 93.

60. Haim, "Alfieri" and also in "Blunt" (142), argues that Blunt "has exercised [. . .] a crucial influence on the doctrine of *Umm al-Qura.*"

61. Quoted in Haddad, "Arab Religious Nationalism," 256; Deringil, *The Well-Protected Domains.*

62. "Al-Islah al-Dini—Al-Muqtarah 'ala Maqam al-Khilafa al-Islamiyya," *al-Manar* 1, n. 39—n. 40 (1898): 764–71 and 788–93 respectively; Haddad, "Religious Arab Nationalism," 254–56.

63. Al-Kawakibi, *Umm al-Qura*, 197. For background: Tauber, "Three Approaches"; Pellitteri, "'Abd al-Rahman al-Kawakibi"; Sheehi, "Al-Kawakibi"; Commins, *Islamic Reform*, 89–115.

64. Al-Kawakibi, *Umm al-Qura*, 201, 203, 207–209. It is not impossible that the supplement was written after al-Kawakibi arrived in Egypt. He uses the word *amir* to describe the prince, and in the 1890s this word was the one intellectuals used to describe young Abbas Hilmi II.

65. Document without date, attached to Adana British Vice-Consul's letter to FO, dated 1 February 1905, in Burdett, *Arab Dissident Movements*, 1:3–9.

66. 'Azm, ed., *Majmu'at Athar Rafiq Bik al-'Azm*, 122.

67. Al-'Allaf, *Dimashq*, 289.

68. Stoler, "Considerations on Imperial Comparisons," 47.

69. Genell, "Autonomous Provinces"; Jankowski, "Ottomanism and Arabism"; Mestyan, *Arab Patriotism*, 286–88.

70. Abkariyus, *Qatf al-Zuhur*, 573; *Al-Jinan*, 15 Jan. 1876, 5–6; Al-Bustani, *Da'irat al-Ma'arif*, 1: 76; Al-Bustani, 'al-Nimsa', *al-Jinan*, 15 March 1876, 188–205; al-Tuwayrani, *'Awamil al-Mustaqbal*, 9.

71. Interview in *al-Liwa'*, 10 and 20 Sept. 1908, quoted in full in Fahmi, *Muhammad Tawfiq al-Bakri*, 81; a modified version is in al-Shubaki, *Muhammad Tawfiq al-Bakri*, 135–39.

72. Al-Bakri, "Bahth al-istiqlal al-tamm," *al-Liwa'*, 4 Oct. 1908, 5.

73. Mahmud Salim, "Al-Bab al-Maftuh fi Dar al-Sa'ada," *al-Liwa'*, 5 Oct. 1908, 1.

74. Sa'id Bey Suqayr's poem in *al-Muqtataf*, Nov. 1, 1908, 912–15.

75. Gershoni and Jankowski, *Egypt, Islam, and the Arabs*, 18–19.

76. Judson, *The Habsburg Empire*, Chapter 5 and 378–79.

77. Bozarslan, "Le prince Sabaheddin"; Fujinami, "Decentralizing Centralists."

78. Moroni, "Continuity and Change."

79. Sabeheddin, "A Second Account"; Hanioğlu, *A Brief History*, 144, 146; Taglia, *Intellectuals and Reform in the Ottoman Empire*, 85–103; EI3, "Sabah al-Din," Kayalı, *Arabs and Young Turks*, chapters 3 and 4; Fujinami, "Decentralizing Centralists." The liberal party in late 1912 initiated a coup but was overthrown by the CUP within a few months.

80. For Emrullah's letter, see Yenen, "Envisioning," 84; for Syrian discussions, Hartmann, *Reisebriefe aus Syrien*, 13–15; 35–39: for the Beiruti reform committee's demands, 40–42, 98; and for Aleppins' opinion about the Cairo Decentralization Party, 91–95.

81. Arslan, *Ila al-'Arab: Bayan al-Umma al-'Arabiyya*, 29–30, quotations from 34, 52; Atçıl, "Decentralization, Imperialism," 27, 35.

82. Al-Rihawi, "Tatawwur mafhum al-La-markaziyya"; Tauber, *The Emergence*, 285; for the meagre membership of the pre-1914 Arabist societies, see Dawn, "The Rise of Arabism in Syria."

83. Kayalı, *Arabs and Young Turks*, 136–37; Freiherr v. d. Goltz, "Die Türkei nach dem Frieden," *Neue Freie Presse*, 18 May 1913, 1–3. Yenen, "Envisioning," 86.

84. Shumsky, *Beyond the Nation-State*, 144–48.

85. Tauber, *The Emergence*, 369–70.

86. *Sadrazam ve Harbiye Nazırı*, 7–8.

87. Ibid., 53, 93.

88. Ibid., 184.

89. Kayalı, *Young Turks*, 137.

90. Yenen, "Envisioning," 89–90.

91. *İdare-i Umumiye-i Vilayat Kanun-ı Muvakkatı*.

92. Tauber, *The Emergence*, 221; I have slightly modified his translation.

93. Djemal Pasha, *Memoirs*, 58–60.

94. Tauber, *The Emergence*, 369.

95. Faydi, *Fi Ghamrat al-Nidal*, 87–88.

96. Honvault, "World War I;" Visser, *The Failed Gulf State*.

97. Al-'Allaf, *Dimashq*, 252.

98. Djemal, *Memoirs*, 58–60; Tauber, *The Emergence*, 115, 221; report dated 13 August 1914, FO 882/15/1, NAUK; Burj, *Muhibb al-Din al-Khatib*, 96–118, 171–76.

99. *Al-Muqtabas*, 13 Eylul (September) 1909, 3 ("Shukr al-Shaykh Muhammad Kamil al-Qassab ʿala Najahihi fi al-Madrasa al-ʿUthmaniyya"); copied in Al-Hafiz, *Hawadith Dimashq al-Yawmiyya*, 219, also 112–13, n.1; Al-Hafiz, *Jamʿiyyat al-ʿUlamaʾ*, 13–15.

100. Rogan, *The Fall of the Ottomans*, 230–35.

101. I could not locate the Arabic original, the English translation is an appendix of Storrs to Clayton, 5 December 1915, FO/882/15/1, NAUK; there is a copy also in the Sudan Collection among the Wingate Papers at Durham University, which was the basis of Halevi's analysis, *Modern Things on Trial*, 187–90.

102. Rashid Rida, "Al-Balagh al-Inklizi fi Shaʾn al-ʿArab wa-l-Sulta al-Diniyya," *Al-Manar*, 19, 3 (29 August 1916), 188–89.

103. Al-Husayn to McMahon, 2 Ramadan 1333 (14 July 1915), in Antonius, *The Arab Awakening*, appendix, 414–15.

104. *Al-Qibla*, 3 Muharram 1335 (30 October 1916), 1–2.

105. "Statement on the Hedjaz taken from Fuad Eff. El Khatib," ? January 1917, FO 882/3, NAUK.

106. "Telephone message by Emir Abdulla," dated 1 November 1916 and "Telephone," dated 1 November 1916; "Telephone—by the Sherif of Mecca himself," 2 November 1916, both in IOR/L/PS/10/637, BL, QDL.

107. "Statement on the Hedjaz taken from Fuad Eff. El Khatib," January 1917, FO 882/3, NAUK.

108. Al-Rihani, *Muluk al-ʿArab*, 1: 8–11; the English version (*Rihani, Around the Coasts of Arabia*) does not contain the nationalist introduction. The Alhambra visit likely occurred between 1916 and 1917, based on al-Rihani's letters and images in ARC-MKC; I thank Edhem Eldem for his unfortunately futile attempt to trace the signature of Rihani in the Alhambra guest books.

109. Appadurai, "Sovereignty without Territoriality," 41; Li, *The Universal Enemy*, 82.

110. Talk by Aimee Genell, MESA, 5 Oct. 2020, quoted with permission; Philliou, *Turkey*, Chapter 4.

111. Quoted in *al-Manar*, 20, 1 (30 July 1917), 60–1.

112. Karsh and Karsh, *Empires of the Sand*, 196–97.

113. Yenen, "Envisioning," 102–110; Polat, *Türk-Arap İlişkileri*, 236–308, Bayat, "Al-Hukuma al-ʿArabiyya," 351–89.

114. Quoted in Burj, *Muhibb al-Din al-Khatib*, 92.

Chapter 6. Occupying Authority: The King of OETA East

1. Case dated 15 Muharram 1337 (21 October 1918), page 2, DS-K 96, İSAM.

2. Tucker, *In the House of Law*, 42–43; "nafaqa," EI2 (R. Peters); Yazbak, "Muslim Orphans."

3. Falls and Becke, *Military Operations* 2: 563–67, sketch 38; Allenby to War Office, 2 March 1918, T 1/12278; report by Sir Walter Lawrence, 13 May 1919, T 1/12372, both in NAUK; and Allenby's article, 10191; FO to Cambon, 25 October 1918, MSS Eur F 112/277, BL-C; Zamir, "Faisal and the Lebanese Question"; Khoury, *Urban*

Notables, 82–83; *Al-Qibla*, 15 Rabiʻ al-Awwal 1337 (19 December 1918), 2; Rogan, *The Fall of Ottomans*, 377–79.

4. The identification as "Arab" did not occur in all cases. For instance in DS-K 33, İSAM, on page 128, the last case under Ottoman rule registers a female litigant's "Ottoman census-identification document" (*tadhkarat nufusiha al-ʻuthmaniyya*) number (case dated 24 Dhu al-Hujja 1336 [30 September 1918]), but after the occupation the first case on the same page, dated 26 Muharram 1337 (1 November 1918), omits mention of any legal or ethnic identification. See more on this below. For *dawla* in Arabic, see Al-Azmeh, *Islams and Modernities*, 129; Mestyan, *Primordial History*, 57–63.

5. Saʻid, *Al-Thawra al-ʻArabiyya al-Kubra*, vol. 2; Qasimiyya, *Al-Hukuma al-ʻArabiyya*; Arnaʼut, *Min al-Hukuma*; Barut, ed., *Al-Hukuma al-ʻArabiyya*; Allawi, *Faisal I.*

6. Thompson, *How the West*.

7. Russell, *The First Modern Arab State*, 42; Gelvin, *Divided Loyalties*.

8. Watenpaugh, *Being Modern*, 136.

9. Al-Husni, *Muntakhabat*, 2: 742–43; the full speech is in Saʻid, *Al-Thawra al-ʻArabiyya al-Kubra*, 2: 25–31. Other critical perspectives: Kurd ʻAli, *Khitat al-Sham* 3: 161–80; Al-ʻAzmah, *Mirʼat al-Sham*, 241–49; Al-Ustuwani, *Al-ʻArab*, 24–26; Al-Ghazzi, *Nahr al-Dhahab*, 3:610, 645–63; perhaps al-Qawuqji, *Mudhakkirat*, 74–75.

10. Letter to military governor, 7 Tashrin Thani (November) 1918, p. 242, DS-I 117, İSAM; al-Qawuqji, *Mudhakkirat*, 76.

11. For instance, DS-I 117 starts in Ottoman Turkish and ends in Arabic.

12. Al-ʻAzmah, *Mirʼat al-Sham*, 243.

13. Al-Hakim, *Suriyya wa-l-ʻAhd al-Faysali*, 42–43.

14. Falls and Becke, *Military Operations* 2: 563–67, sketch 38.

15. Hughes, "The Evolution of Large Technological Systems"; Mitchell, "Infrastructures Work on Time"; Anand et al, *The Promise of Infrastructure*.

16. Elyachar, "Next Practices," 120–21.

17. Low, *Imperial Mecca*, 44–45; 298–302, 320–25; Özyüksel, *The Hijaz Railway*, 136–37.

18. Özyüksel, *The Hijaz Railway*, 123, 220.

19. Rogan, *The Fall of the Ottomans*, 294–95.

20. Qadri, *Mudhakkirat*, 124–126.

21. Billings, "A Piece of Railway History."

22. Barak, *Empowering Empire*, 218–21.

23. Fortna, *The Circassian*, 179–204.

24. Qadri, *Mudhakkirat*, 126; Rogan, *The Fall of the Ottomans*, 300; for memories about the siege of Medina, see Murshid, *Tayba*; El Bakri, "Memories of the Beloved;" Işıktaş, *Şerif Muhiddin*, 140–43.

25. Falls and Becke, *Military Operations* 1: 239, 2: 396–98; Rogan, *The Fall of the Ottomans*.

26. Note by Major Gabriel, 13 November 1915, FO/882/2, and "Result of the second meeting of the Committee to discuss the Arab question in Syria," 23 November 1915, FO 882/2, both in NAUK.

27. Minutes, Eastern Committee meeting, 8 August 1918; FO 371/3381, NAUK. See works of Darwin; Paris, "British Middle East Policy-Making."

28. "Memorandum by the Emir Faysal," 16 January 1919, FO 608/80/5, NAUK.

29. Matar, *Al-'Uqud al-Durriyya*; Choueiri, "Two Histories of Syria"; Emerit, "La crise syrienne," 216, 218, 221; Buzpinar, "Opposition to the Ottoman Caliphate," 69–71; Dawn, "The Rise of Arabism."

30. Sa'id, *Al-Thawra al-'Arabiyya al-Kubra*, 2: 30; al-Husni, *Muntakhabat*, 2: 742–48.

31. *Al-'Asima*, 12 May 1919, 1–2; 17 May 1919, 1–3.

32. Undated document, RG 2/6, box 128, folder 5, OCA-KCC. A French translation (*Chartre Constitutionelle des Etats Unis de Syrie*) is in 50CPCOM/43, CADC ; "Report of American Section," VII.

33. "Report of American Section," V.

34. Handwritten Arabic petition, 27 signatures, 9 July 1919, Box 128, Folder 5, OCA-KCC.

35. For instance, see his visit to Damascus in 1922, Moubayed, *The Makers*, 18–23; for his role in the making of Saudi Arabia, see Chapter Eight.

36. *Al-'Asima*, 9 March 1920, 1.

37. *Al-'Asima* published this speech as "the throne speech" (*khutbat al-'arsh*) although it could not yet be such. *Al-'Asima*, 18 Jumada al-Thaniyya 1338 / 9 March 1920, 1–2. The speech justified the demand for Syria's complete independence on the grounds of the Arabs' fight for freedom together with the Allies, although no members of the congress actually fought together with the forces of al-Husayn. They may have found these words even more curious coming from the mouth of 'Abd al-Hadi, Faysal's new secretary, who had spent the war in Paris. In the congress' answer to the speech, they claimed that the Arab nation fought politically (*siyasiyyan*) against the Turks for complete independence.

38. "Bab al-Tarikh: Istiqlal Suriyya wa-l-Iraq," *Al-Manar* 21, 8 (17 June 1920), 434–447, at 438.

39. Thompson, "Rashid Rida," 249.

40. See Gertrude Bell's letter (11 October 1919) quoted in "Note by Sir A. Hirtzel," 3 November 1919, in "The Future Constitution of Mesopotamia," IOR/L/PS/18/B335, BL, QDL.

41. Wilson, *King Abdullah*, 41; "Bab al-Tarikh: Istiqlal Suriyya wa-l-Iraq," *Al-Manar* 21, 8 (17 June 1920), 434–47, here 446–47.

42. For the infrastructure argument, see Meiton, *Electrical Palestine*, 6. I thank Daniel Foliard for generously sharing this map with me. Foliard, "'More than One Palestine.'"

43. Weber, *The Theory of Economy and Society*, 347.

44. In 1910s provincial administrative registers, the *nizamiye* courts were also called *'adliye* ("justice") in the sense of "belonging to the Ministry of Justice."

45. Rafeq, "Les registres des tribuneaux"; Marino and Okawara, *Catalogue*; Akiba, "From Kadı to Naib"; Zürcher, *Turkey*, 122.

46. Ekinci, *Osmanlı Mahkemeleri*, 241–45; Rubin, *Ottoman Nizamiye Courts*; Akiba, "The Practice of Writing"; Ayoub, "The *Mecelle*"; Barakat, "Underwriting the Empire"; Akiba, "Shari'a Judges in Nizamiye Courts."

47. Ayoub, *Law, Empire*, 5, 8.

48. Skovgaard, "Levantine State Muftis," 277.

49. Al-Himsi, *al-Muftun al-'Ammun*.

50. Çiçek, *War and State Formation*, 49; the abolishment of the privileged status of the Lebanon mountain during the war resulted in the full introduction of *nizamiye* courts, 97.

51. Al-Husni, *Muntakhabat*, 1: 288–90.

52. This paragraph is based on a survey of *shari'a* and *nizamiye* court registers between 1914 and 1918; and *Salname-i Devlet-i 'Aliye* (for *maliye* years 1333–1334), 628–39; for Süleyman Ruşdi, see the personnel record questionnaire dated 1 Dhu al-Hijja 1311 in MŞH.SAID 19, BOA (that I saw in a scanned copy in the Ulema Sicil Dosyalari computer system of İSAM) as *naib* of Damascus (this office in the Arabic registers is always indicated as *qadi* of Damascus); for mufti Abu al-Khayr 'Abidin, see Al-Husni, *Muntakhabat*, 2:703; al-Sawwaf, *Sham Sharif*, 410–11 (imprecise dates); Taymur, *A'lam al-Islam*, 297–99.

53. War Office, *Manual of Military Law*, 288.

54. For Allenby's article sent as a "dispatch," see *The London Gazette*, Third Supplement, 11 August 1919, 10189–10196, at 10191.

55. Conference of Chief Administrators, 12 May 1919, FO/141/783, NAUK.

56. "Note," Charles Puech, 25 December 1919, 50CPCOM/102; "Note sur la réorganisation des services de la justice civile et criminelle en Syrie," 31 March 1919, 50CPCOM/98, both in CADC.

57. Gouraud to MAE, 7 April 1920, SHD/GR 4 H 43/1, AFL-MHMA.

58. Puech cited in "Mesures provisoires concernant la fonctionnement de la justice en Syrie," 30 January 1920, 50CPCOM/98, CADC.

59. Undated (around 1923) lecture, 189PO/1/75, CADN. This was a very generous interpretation because article 43 says: "The authority of the legitimate power having in fact passed into the hands of the occupant, the latter shall take all the measures in his power to restore, and ensure, as far as possible, public order and safety, while respecting, unless absolutely prevented, the laws in force in the country."

60. MAE to High Commissioner, 10 April 1920, 50CPCOM/98, CADC.

61. Bentwich, "The Legal Administration of Palestine"; for Bentwich as a Zionist, see Money to Clayton, 7 June 1919; FO 608/100/1, NAUK.

62. Al-Husni, *Muntakhabat*, 1: 291; Russell, *The First Arab State*, 45–47; Malaji, *'Ali Rida al-Rikabi*, 30–31.

63. Note dated 27 Dhu al-Hijja 1336 (3 October 1918), DS-I 117, İSAM.

64. Note dated 17 Tashrin al-Awwal (October) 1918, 212, DS-I 124, İSAM.

65. Draft to all branches, dated 20 Tashrin al-Awwal (October) 1918, 241 DS-I 117, İSAM.

66. Al-Hakim, *Suriyya wa-l-'Ahd Faysali*, 38–39.

67. *Al-'Asima*, 3 Nisan 1919, 4–8; Qasimiyya, *al-Hukuma al-'Arabiyya*, 251–253.

68. Qasimiyya, *Al-Hukuma al-'Arabiyya*, 63.

69. February-March 1919 correspondence between Foreign Office and Treasury, especially Note by G. K. dated 10 February 1919, and Montague's letter dated 19 February 1919, in T 1/12372; Treasury to Foreign Office and War Office, 19 March 1919, FO 608/100, all in NAUK.

70. Picot to MAE, 8 March 1919, 45CPCOM/3, CADC.

71. Draft dated 9 Nisan (April) 1919 to Aleppo Appeal Court, DS-MA 5, İSAM.

72. Shuqayr to Colonel, 12 April 1920, SAD/493/10, SA; Russell, *The First Arab Modern State*, 56–61.

73. Letter dated 11 November 1918, 1/9, Allenby Papers, LHCMA; Russell, *The First Modern Arab State*, 43.

74. Draft dated 1 January 1919, DS-MA 5, İSAM.

75. Draft dated ?, n. 1331, DS-MA 5, İSAM.

76. Draft dated 8 Shubat 1919, n. 1342, DS-MA 5, İSAM.

77. Draft dated 19 Shubat (February) 1919 DS-MA 5, İSAM.

78. The usual Arabic title of al-Rikabi was *al-hakim al-'askari al-'amm* although he referred to himself in more civilian terms in public as "general director" (*mudir 'amm*). For instance, his order prohibiting antiquity sales, *al-'Asima*, 9 June 1919, 6 starts "Because I am 'Ali Rida al-Rikabi, based on the authority that is given to me as general director. . . ."

79. Qasimiyya and others state that Faysal as Hijazi military leader was under the orders of Allenby (Qasimiyya, *al-Hukuma al-'Arabiyya*, 52–55), but this was clearly not the case.

80. Russell, *The First Modern Arab State*, 15.

81. Allenby to War Office, 21 October 1918, MSS Eur F 112/277, BL-C.

82. Examples in 45CPCOM/3, CADC.

83. Note, 30 January 1919, 45CPCOM/3, CADC.

84. For instance, drafts dated 29 Kanun Thani 1919 to 'Abd al-'Aziz Efendi al-Khayat; and 10 Shubat 1919 to al-Mudda'i al-'Amm bi-l-Markaz, DS-MA 5, İSAM.

85. Based on the analysis of 192 draft letters in DS-MA 5, İSAM.

86. Al-Hakim, *Suriyya wa-l-'Ahd al-Faysali*, 41–42; draft dated 13 Mart (March) 1919, DS-MA 5, İSAM.

87. DS-I 118, İSAM.

88. DS-MA 15, İSAM.

89. DS-MA 10, İSAM.

90. The first such notice with Faysal's name is dated 19 Adhar (March) 1919, on pages 134–35, DS-MA 10, İSAM.

91. Session 6 Adhar (March) 1920, p. 22, session 15 Adhar (March)1920, p. 30; session 26 Adhar (March) 1920, p. 327–28, DS-MA 16, İSAM.

92. Rida arrived in Damascus only in early 1920, because first he had visited his hometown of Tripoli to transfer the income of a pious endowment to himself and settle inheritance debates; and while in Tripoli he was briefly arrested and thus delayed by the French occupation army. HC to Col. Nieger, 16 December 1919, 1SL-1V-2319, CADN.

93. See Faysal's letter dated Ghurrat Sha'ban 1335 (23 May 1917) to the Druze in *Al-Ahram*, 14 August 1925, 1.

94. *Al-Qibla*, 4 Muharram 1337, 2.

95. Russell, *The First Modern Arab State*, 16.

96. *'Ulama'* protest with 63 signatures, 10 August 1919, 50CPCOM/43, CADC. For the Aleppo events, see Al-Ghazzi, *Nahr al-Dhahab*, 655–64.

97. Al-Mahasini is missing from almost all *'ulama'* biographies of Damascus, except Al-Husni, *Muntakhabat*, 2: 839. For al-Kasm, see al-Sawwaf, *Sham Sharif*,

316–18; Al-Himsi, *Al-Muftun al-ʿAmmun*, 27–19. The exact date of his appointment is unclear.

98. Case dated 9 Muharram 1337, DS 1530, İSAM.

99. Case dated 9 Muharram 1337, DS-K 93, İSAM.

100. Pages 2–8, DS-K 96, İSAM.

101. 9? Muharram 1337, DS-K 32, İSAM.

102. Case dated 11 Muharram 1337, DS-1517, İSAM.

103. Case dated 11 Muharram 1337, DS-K 32, İSAM.

104. *Al-ʿUqab*, 13 Jumada al-Ula 1337 (14 February 1919), 1; Gelvin, *Divided Loyalties*, 141–195.

105. *Al-ʿAsima*, 17 Jumada al-Ula 1337 (18 February 1919), 2.

106. Letter dated 19 February 1919, 45CPCOM/3, CADC.

107. *Al-ʿAsima*, 10 Ramadan 1337 (9 June 1919), 1.

108. Letter dated 3 Shubat (February) 1919, to Wilaya, DS-MA 5, İSAM.

109. For instance, *al-ʿAsima*, 27 Jumada al-Awwal 1337 (28 February 1919), 4.

110. *Al-ʿAsima*, 2 Rajab 1337 (3 April 1919), 8.

111. 17 and 29 January 1918, Wingate to FO, FO 371/3395, NAUK.

112. *Al-Qibla*, 5 Rabiʿ Awwal 1337 / 9 December 1918, 1.

113. "Political, Baghdad" to Cairo High Commissioner, 19 June 1918, FO 371/3395, NAUK.

114. Others report that Faysal dismissed ʿAbidin because the mufti issued a fatwa allowing smoking. Al-Sawwaf, *Sham al-Sharif*, 410, 417–18.

115. See declaration in *Al-Ahram*, 14 August 1925, 1. It is perhaps no coincidence that this declaration about Druze independence was published in August 1925, when the Druze uprising started.

116. Watenpaugh, *Being Modern*, 168.

117. Al-Qawuqji, *Mudhakkirat*, 86–87.

Chapter 7. Authority and the Shariʿa Apparatus in Post-Ottoman Egypt

1. *Al-Ahram*, 22 December 1914, 5; Yunan Labib Rizq, "Azmat al-Sultan," *Al-Ahram*, 20 August 1998, 17; *L'Égypte contemporaine* 6 (November 1914–January 1915): 345–50 with an explanatory note by the Ministry of Justice.

2. Hallaq, *Shariʿa*, 549.

3. Krämer, *Gottes Staat*, 258–60; Feldman, *The Fall and Rise*, 14.

4. March, *The Caliphate of Man*, 39. Legal authority in Muslim countries remains an important problem. Brown, "Wali al-Amr?"

5. Maghraoui, *Liberalism without Democracy*, 13.

6. Scott, *Recasting Islamic Law*, 5.

7. Important studies include al-Rafiʿi, *Fi Aʿqab al-Thawra*, vols. 2 and 3; Deeb, *Party Politics*; Darwin, *Britain, Egypt*; Gershoni and Jankowski, *Redefining the Egyptian Nation*; Sharkey, *Living With Colonialism*; Mitchell, *Rule of Experts*; Ryzova, *The Age of Efendiya*.

8. Al-Azmeh, *Islams and Modernisms*, 51.

9. Gershoni and Jankowski, *Egypt, Islam, and the Arabs*, 73.

10. Mestyan, *Arab Patriotism*, 292; Jakes, "Peaceful Wars."

11. Al-Azmeh, *Islams and Modernities*, 43–48.

12. Quadri, *Transformations of Tradition*; Bechor, *The Sanhuri Code*. A selection of Bakhit's *fatawa* are in the two editions of *al-Fatawa al-Islamiyya* by Dar al-Ifta'; another selection is published by Abu 'Asi, ed., *al-Fatawa*; and idem, ed., *al-Fatawa*, 2 vols.

13. Fahmi, *Hadhihi Hayati*, 64–66.

14. Al-Rafi'i, *Fi A'qab al-Thawra al-Misriyya*, 1: 227.

15. Wizarat al-Maliyya, *Mizaniyyat al-Hukuma al-Misriyya li-Sanat 1922–1923*, 15.

16. Lord Milner, Private Diary, 20, 22–23, FO 848/5, NAUK.

17. Lord Milner, Private Diary, 42, FO 848/5, NAUK.

18. Lefevre-Pontalis to MAE, 27 May 1919, 65CPCOM/37, CADC.

19. *Journal Officiel*, 17 April 1920, 1.

20. Tusun's offer in note dated 10 May 1920 from Consul general in Monaco; Protest by Central Committee of the Egyptian Delegation, signed Mahmud Sulayman, 5 May 1920, both in 65CPCOM/37, CADC.

21. Protest by National Party, signed Aly J. Kamel, 8 May 1920, 65CPCOM/37, CADC.

22. Pillai, "Fragmenting the Nation," 762.

23. Minutes on file E/2431/1/16, 4 March 1922, FO 371/7732, NAUK.

24. Minutes on file E/2543/16, 7 March 1922, FO 371/7732, NAUK.

25. Memorandum by Mr. Bentinck, 10 March 1922, FO 371/7732, NAUK.

26. Gershoni and Jankowski, *Egypt*, 53; *Al-Siyasa*, 31 January 1923, 6; 8 February 1923, 5.

27. For example, Ibrahim Hilmi, Fuad's brother, in March 1921 made an embarrassing argument in *The Times* against the independence of Egypt ("The Needs of Egypt," *The Times*, March 14, 1921, 13–16; Issue 42668), to which all princes of the family reacted; Tusun, *Mudhakkira bi-ma Sadara*, 37; or some princes asked for a constitution and free elections in March 1922, idem, 49–51. Fuad aimed at restricting especially 'Umar Tusun, Fahmi, *Hadhihi Hayati*, 82.

28. "Mudhakkira tafsiriyya," in *Majmu'at al-Awamir wa-l-Qawanin*, 13–15.

29. "'Amr Malaki Raqm 63 li-Sanat 1922 bi-Isdar La'ihat Ijra'at Majlis Balat al-Malaki," in *Majmu'at al-Awamir wa-l-Qawanin*, 27–37.

30. "Al-Dustur al-Misri, al-Sadir sanat 1923," in *Watha'iq wa-Nusus*, 1: 368–92.

31. Sayyid-Marsot, *Egypt's Liberal Experiment*, 64; Haridi, *Al-Haraka al-Dusturiyya fi Misr*, 11–18.

32. Fahmi, *Hadhihi Hayati*, 138; Van den Bosch, *Vingt Années D'Égypte*, 54–68.

33. Sayyid-Marsot, *Egypt's Liberal Experiment*, 100; Deeb, *Party Politics*, 58–61, Abu al-Nur, *Dawr al-Qasr*, 72–82.

34. *Lajnat al-Dustur*, 12–14 (Fifth Session, 4 June 1922); 41 and 43–44 (Eleventh Session, 19 19 June 1922); the discussion continued through several sessions, 41–55.

35. "Al-Dustur al-Misri, al-Sadir sanat 1923," in *Watha'iq wa-Nusus*, 1: 368–92.

36. Abu al-Nur, *Dawr al-Qasr*, 83; Sabry, *Le Pouvoir législatif*, 28–40.

37. Gershoni and Jankowski, *Egypt*, 24; I thank Yasmin Dorghamy for the image of an earring.

38. *Berliner Lokalanziger*, 27 July 1918, in 65CPCOM/35, CADC.

39. Gaillard to MAE, 1 June 1922, 65CPCOM/35, CADC.

40. Gaillard to MAE, 20 July 1922, 65CPCOM/35, CADC, and decree (Law 28; 17 July 1922) attached from *Journal Officiel*.

41. Renseignements, 17 October 1923, 65CPCOM/35, CADC.

42. Jessé-Marely to MAE, ? (June 1924?), 65CPCOM/36, CADC.

43. Declaration signed by Abbas Hilmi, 4 February 1925, 65CPCOM/36, CADC.

44. Sharkey, *American Evangelicals*; Culang, "'The Shari'a Must Go.'"

45. The following summary is largely based on Zaghlul, *Al-Muhama*, 209- 19, 243–45, 301; EI2 art. "mahkama" (Schacht et al.); Fahmy, *In Quest of Justice*, Chapter Two; Cheta, "A Prehistory"; Hilal, *Al-Ifta' al-Misri*; *La'ihat Tartib al-Mahakim*.

46. In addition, there were Coptic and Jewish courts for personal matters. For consular courts before 1914, see Hanley, *Identifying with Nationality*.

47. Baldwin, *Islamic Law and Empire*, Chapter Two.

48. Zaghlul, *Al-Muhama*, 209–11, 233–34; "Al-Qada' al-Shar'i fi Misr," *Majallat al-Ahkam al-Shar'iyya* 1 (1902 April), 3–5.

49. The 1880 Code of Shari'a Courts formulated the courts *as* shari'a courts, separate from other judicial administrative bodies (the Mixed and Native Courts); an 1883 law reorganized the courts; the government issued in 1897 a general procedural code, followed by amendments and laws in 1909–10, 1920, 1929, 1931, and later.

50. Verdict dated 3 August 1885, *Al-Huquq*, 20 March 1886, 30–33.

51. Public prosecutor vs. Hasan al-Sayyid Salama (26 December 1914), *Al-Mahakim*, 11 April 1915, 2.

52. In addition to the titles above, Peters, "Administrators and Magistrates"; Khanki, *Al-Mahakim al-Mukhtalita wa-l-Mahakim al-Ahliyya*.

53. Hilal, *Al-Ifta' al-Misri*; Zaghlul, *Al-Muhama*, 209–11, 233–34; "Al-Qada' al-Shar'i fi Misr," *Majallat al-Ahkam al-Shar'iyya* 1 (1902 April), 3–5.

54. Hilal, *Al-Ifta' al-Misri*, 3: 1226, 1242, 1303.

55. Hallaq, *The Origins*, 99.

56. A summary of the critiques of Hallaq is in Baldwin, *Islamic Law and Empire*, 55–57.

57. Skovgaard-Petersen, *Defining Islam*, 387 (Appendix A).

58. Peters, "Muhammad al-'Abbasi al-Mahdi"; Skovgaard, *Defining Islam*, 102–103.

59. Ziadeh, *Lawyers*, 55–61.

60. Al-Gharib, *Al-Dalil al-Murshid*, 28.

61. Al-Jami'i, *Madrasat al-Qada' al-Shar'i*, 20–21, 40–41.

62. Kupferschmidt, *The Supreme Muslim Council*, 22–26, 81, Appendix 1.

63. EI2, waqf 78–79; EI1, wakf, 1101; Order 753, in *Recueil des Actes Administratifs* 2 (1921), 53–64; Reiter, *Islamic Awqaf in Jerusalem*.

64. Weiss, *In the Shadow of Sectarianism*, Chapter 4.

65. *Al-Qanun al-Waqti li-l-Murafa'at al-Shar'iyya*, 1 January 1921, in *Qa'idat al-Tashri'at al-'Iraqiyya* (*http://iraqld.hjc.iq:8080/LoadLawBook.aspx?page=1&SC =&BookID=4208*).

66. Qanun al-Mahakim al-Shar'iyya, 30 June 1923, in *Qa'idat al-Tashri'at al-'Iraqiyya* (http://iraqld.hjc.iq:8080/LoadLawBook.aspx?page=1&SC=&BookID=42).

67. Ahmed, *What Is Islam*, 323.

68. The main sources of this section is Sherman Jackson's *Islamic Law and the State* and the works of Rudolph Peters, Baber Johansen, Colin Imber, 'Imad Hilal, Hüseyin Yılmaz, Guy Burak, James Baldwin, and Samy Ayoub cited in the following footnotes.

69. Imber, *Ebu's-su'ud*, 66–67; Baldwin, *Islamic Law and Empire*, Chapter Four.

70. Imber, *Ebu's-su'ud*, 100–110.

71. Ayoub, *Law, Empire*, 4, 22.

72. Imber, *Ebu's-su'ud*, 110.

73. Imber, *Ebu's-su'ud*, 95, 244–46; Ayoub, *Law, Empire*, 74, 118–19.

74. Al-Haqq refers to the work of Ibn Nujaym (a Hanafi like Jad al-Haqq) and al-Suyuti's work (who, one must add, was Shafi'i, but his authorship is now questioned; the important issue, however is that the work is Shafi'i). Al-Haqq adds that Ibn Nujaym refers to Abu Yusuf, *al-Fatawa al-Islamiyya*, 3481–3490 at 3488.

75. Hanna, *Kitab Nizam al-Hukuma*, 15; Debs, *Islamic Law and Civil Code*, 58.

76. Krawietz, "Cut and Paste in Legal Rules."

77. Al-Gharib, *Al-Dalil al-Murshid*, 29.

78. Ayoub, *Law, Empire*, 73–75.

79. Quadri, *Transformations of Tradition*, 19; original is Rida, *Maqalat al-Shaykh Rashid Rida al-Siyasiyya*, 3: 1268.

80. Abu 'Asri, ed., *Al-Fatawa* (2012), 46–47.

81. Kedourie, "Egypt and the Caliphate," 210–14.

82. Lord Milner, "Private Diary," 27, FO 848/5, NAUK.

83. The discursive invention of a pre-1914 Egyptian sovereign state to claim independence in the 1910s and 1920s deserves a separate study.

84. Consul to Ambassador, 6, 18 March 1922; Ambassador to Ministry, 16, 17, 20 March 1922, all in 65CPCOM, CADC.

85. See Gallini Pasha's opinion in Lord Milner, Private Diary, 27–29, FO 848/5, NAUK.

86. A. H., "al-Malik wa-l-Khilafa wa-l-Imama," *Majallat al-Qada' al-Shar'i* 1 (Muharram 1341/August 1922), 127–32.

87. Ahmad Ibrahim, "Al-Khilafa al-Islamiyya," *Majallat al-Qada' al-Shar'i* 5–6 (Rabi' I and II 1341/November–October 1922), 201–209, 252–59; Adams, *Islam and Modernism in Egypt*, 214; Shubayr, *Ahmad Ibrahim Bik*.

88. Al-Muti'i, *Mudhakkiru*, 2–4.

89. Rida, *Al-Khilafa*, 10, 13–15.

90. Abu al-Kalam Azad, "Kitab al-Khilafa al-Islamiyya," *Al-Manar*, 23)1922), 1: 45–56, 2: 102–106; 3: 193–201, etc; quote from 1: 48.

91. Rida, *Al-Khilafa*, 14, 52–57.

92. Ahmad Ibrahim, "Al-Khilafa al-Islamiyya," *Majallat al-Qada' al-Shar'i* 5–6 (Rabi' I and II 1341/November–October 1922), 201–209, 252–259.

93. 'Afifi 'Umar, "Al-Khilafa wa-l-Saltana," *Majallat al-Qada' al-Shar'i* 7 (Jumada I 1341/December 1922), 289–297.

94. "Qarar," *Nur al-Islam* 2, 8 (1931): 590–91.

95. The issue peaked with two inconclusive caliphate conferences in Cairo and Mecca, and the manipulations by King Fuad from 1925–1926 to get the caliphate for himself. On top of everything, the old ex-king of the Hijaz Sharif al-Husayn assumed

the caliphate in Amman in 1924. Kedourie, "Egypt and the Caliphate," 215–17; 223; 226–27; Hassan, *Longing for the Lost Caliphate*; Pankhurst, *The Inevitable Caliphate?*

96. Al-Muti'i, *Haqiqat al-Islam*, 7.

97. Al-Muti'i, *Haqiqat al-Islam*, 8.

98. Al-Muti'i, *Haqiqat al-Islam*, 24.

99. Hill, "Al-Sanhuri and Islamic Law," 46–47.

100. Bechor, *The Sanhuri Code*, 46.

101. March, *The Caliphate of Man*, 68.

102. Hammad, *Qissat al-Dustur*, 205–206.

103. One may even see Khallaf's and others' idea about *al-siyasa al-shar'iyya* in this period as they are offering Islamic law instead of the secular constitution.

104. 'Abd al-Razzaq al-Sanhuri, "Al-Din wa-l-Dawla fi al-Islam," *Al-Muhama al-Shar'iyya* 1, 1 (1929): 8–14. (In the next issue of the *shari'a* lawyers' journal, the old ex-mufti Bakhit also joined the discussion with a few corrections.)

105. Later in the 1940s, the shari'a jurists vehemently opposed al-Sanhuri's *shari'a*-inspired Civil Code (implemented in 1949) in Egypt but that opposition was not related to his constitutional theory. Hill, "Al-Sanhuri."

106. *Al-Muhama al-Shar'iyya* 2, 3 (1930), 199–201; *Al-Muhama al-Shar'iyya* 2, 4 (1931), 192–93, 197.

107. Khallaf, *Al-Siyasa al-Shar'iyya*, 28.

108. Al-Banna, *Mudhakkirat*, 252–55.

109. For the end of the Egyptian monarchy, Salim, *Faruq wa-Suqut al-Malakiyya*; Gayffier-Bonneville, *L'Échec de la monarchie*.

110. Al-Zawahiri, *Al-Siyasa wa-l-Azhar*, 322–25; Thornhill, "Informal Empire," 286–287.

111. Ellis, "Repackaging," 184; Whidden, *Monarchy and Modernity*, 35–36.

112. Ellis, "Repackaging," 198; Salim, *Faruq wa-Suqut al-Malakiyya*, 736–43.

113. *Al-Ahram*, 29 July 1937, 12.

114. *Al-Fatawa al-Islamiyya*, 3250–51.

115. Cited from Hammad, *Qissat al-Dustur*, 626–36.

116. *Al-Fatawa al-Islamiyya*, 3489.

Chapter 8. The Syrian Making of the Arab Saudi Kingdom

1. Al-Zirikli, *Shibh al-Jazira*, 1: 31–67; Vassil'ev, *The History of Saudi Arabia*; Commins, *The Wahhabi Mission*; Alangari, *The Struggle for Power: A History of Saudi Arabia*; Ochsenwald, "Islam and Loyalty," 9; Al-'Isa, *Arshif Mamlakat al-Hijaz*.

2. Kostiner, *The Making of Saudi Arabia*, 4; Vitalis, *America's Kingdom*, 6; El-Enazy, *The Creation of Saudi Arabia*; Willis, "Governing the Living and the Dead"; Bsheer, "A Counter-Revolutionary State," 238.

3. Chaudhry, *The Price of Wealth*, 58–76; Pétriat, *Le Négoce des lieux saints*, Chapter Six.

4. Hajrah, *Public Land Distribution*, 18.

5. *Umm al-Qura*, 23 September 1932, 1, 3.

6. Ahmed, *Afghanistan Rising*, 207–209.

7. For interpolity law, see Benton and Clulow, "Empires and Protection."

8. Crane to 'Abd al-'Aziz, 1 September 1931, CCP-CUL.

9. Satia, *Spies in Arabia*, Chapter Two.

10. That 'Abd al-'Aziz was a merchant-emir in his early years is confirmed by the correspondence in MW-DMW.

11. Sedgwick, "Saudi Sufis"; Ochsenwald, "Islam and Loyalty"; Freitag, *A History of Jeddah*, 80–82.

12. Al-Zirikli, *'Aman fi 'Amman*, 35. For Zirikli, see the works of al-'Alawina, especially *Khayr al-Din al-Zirikli: Biblughrafiya, Suwar wa-Watha'iq*.

13. Mazower, *Governing the World*, 261–64.

14. Letter dated 17 January 1919, 45CPCOM/3, CADC.

15. *Al-Qibla*, 19 Jumada al-Ula 1337 (20 February 1919), 1.

16. In their memoirs, the accidental Syrian members of the Hijazi delegation, do not mention that they signed the Covenant (Haydar, *Mudhakkirat*, 425, 'Abd al-Hadi, *Mudhakkirat*, 76). An authenticated copy of the Covanant, made for the Government of Australia in 1919, is available at https://www.foundingdocs.gov.au/item-sdid-94.html (last viewed 3 December 2018); signature page 8 shows Haydar and 'Abd al-Hadi's signatures.

17. "Conversation with Sheikh Abdul Malik el Khatib," 25 August 1920, in Priestland, *Records of Syria*, 2: 331–32.

18. *Al-Qibla*, 22 Dhu al-Qa'da 1336 (29 August 1918), 1.

19. Al-Khatib, *Wamadat*, 65; Nasif, *Madi al-Hijaz*, 3–4.

20. Al-Khatib to Wingate, 19 May 1916, SAD 101/17/1, WP; Handwritten note dated 19 July 1916 "Newspaper at Mecca"; Fu'ad al-Khatib to Arab Bureau, 19 July 1916; and telegram by Arhur (sic!) Clayton to Private Secretary, Khartoum, 25 July 1916, both in FO 882/14, NAUK; Çiçek, "Visions of Islamic Unity," 467; Fu'ad al-Khatib to Arab Bureau, 19 July 1916, FO 882/14, NAUK. Al-Husayn himself wrote many articles and censored those he did not like. At least this is what he told to a French agent in 1919. Letter dated 16 May 1919, Djedda, capitaine Depui to MAE, 45CPCOM/4, CADC.

21. Wingate to Clayton, letter dated 27 September 1916, SAD.130/4/63–66, WP.

22. Receipt, 'Abd al-Muhsin to al-Qassab, 24 January 1918, MKQ, MW-DMAA.

23. Gelvin, *Divided Loyalties*, 97–9, 107–14, 116, 120–21, 126, 132, 141–42, 166, 211 12, 247, 280; see also "Dispatch from Civil Commissioner, Mesopotamia, to Secretary of State for India," December 1919, IOR/L/PS/18/B337, BL, QDL.

24. Letter dated 16 May 1919, Djedda, capitaine Depui to MAE, 45CPCOM/4, CADC.

25. Cousse to HC, 5 June 1920, 1SL/1/V/2347, CADN; Ministry of Justice to Editor of *al-'Asima*, 22 August 1920, DS-M 21, İSAM; Sanagan, *Lightning*, 57, n. 21; Al-Hafiz, *Jam'iyyat al-'Ulama'*, 16–17.

26. The phrase is from Willis, "Burying Muhammad 'Ali Jauhar."

27. Darwaza, *Mudhakkirat*, 1: 484, 499–500, 503–504, 506–10; Matthews, *Confronting an Empire*, 76–77; a description of this period is al-Zirikli, *'Aman fi 'Amman*.

28. Al-Madi and Musa, *Tarikh al-Urdun*, 1: 132.

29. Al-Madi and Musa, *Tarikh al-Urdun*, 1: 145; Sa'id, *al-Thawra al-'Arabiyya al-Kubra*, 3:11–14.

30. Al-Zirikli, *'Aman fi 'Amman*, 66–67.

31. "Report of interview with Auni Abdul Hadi," Herbert Samuel to Curzon, 12 February 1921, CO 733/13/53, NAUK; Wilson, *King Abdullah*, 50.

32. Al-Hafiz, *Jam'iyyat al-'Ulama'*, 18.

33. Rogan, *Frontiers of the State*, 255.

34. 30 November 1921, Philby diary vol. 1, 1/5/3/1, GB165–0229, MECA.

35. 5–10 February 1924, Philby diary vol. 4, 1/5/3/4, GB165–0229, MECA.

36. 16 January 1924 and 1–5 March 1924, Philby diary vol. 4, 1/5/3/4, GB165–0229, MECA; Pankhurst, *The Inevitable Caliphate*, 49–52; Hasan, *Longing*, 171–183.

37. Shlaim, *Collusion Across the Jordan* and challenging him Bradshaw, *Britain and Jordan*.

38. Al-Madi and Musa, *Tarikh al-Urdun*, 1: 245–48; Shahin, *Khayr al-Din al-Zirikli*, 41.

39. Political Agent, Kuwait, to Political Resident, 6 May 1914; Political Agent, Bahrain, 16 June 1914; 26 June 1914, Political Agent, Kuwait to Cox, all in IOR/R/15/2/31, BL, QDL. Anscombe, *The Ottoman Gulf*, 161–65; Al-Muslim, *Sahil al-Dhahab*, 194–95; Matthesian, "Shi'i Historians."

40. Letter dated 9 Rajab 1332 (3 June 1914), from Rashid Rida to Abbas Hilmi II, HIL 9/81, AHP.

41. "Summary of News," July 1917, p. 4, IOR/L/PS/10/827, BL, QDL.

42. Text of the treaty in Troeller, *The Birth of Saudi Arabia*, 254–56.

43. "Diary of Journey," 29.

44. "Diary of Journey from Bahrein to Mecca," 1–58, File E-15, IOR/R/15/2/41, BL, QDL.

45. "Diary of Journey," 31.

46. "Diary of Journey," 41.

47. "Diary of Journey," 48.

48. "Sixth meeting" (page 202), File E-15, IOR/R/15/2/41, BL, QDL.

49. Note by Van Hamel, London, 3 June 1920, French delegation's note, dated 1 September 1920; Van Hamel to Secretary-General, 2 October 1920; Drummond to Spicer, 5 November 1920; Van Hamel to Secretary-General, 5 November 1920; all in R1219, LNA.

50. Minute Sheet signed by Van Hamel, 5 June 1925, 28/44377/29239, R1454, LNA.

51. See correspondence in IOR/L/PS/10/1115, BL, QDL; Schlaepfer, "Between Ruler and Rogue," 256.

52. Nasif, *Madi al-Hijaz*, 170–212; Rafi', *Makka*, 291–93; Freitag, *A History of Jidda*, 287–291; Report, attached to Consul (Jordan) to FO, 31 December 1925, IOR/L/PS/10/1165/1, BL, QDL.

53. Report, attached to Consul (Jordan) to FO, 4 February 1926, IOR/L/PS/10/1165/1, BL, QDL.

54. Report, attached to Consul (Jordan) to FO, 1 March 1926, IOR/L/PS/10/1165/1, BL, QDL.

55. Almana, *Arabia*, 140–41.

56. Report, attached to Consul (Bullard) to FO, 11 April 1925, IOR/R/15/5/37, BL, QDL; in 1928 January images of new coins were published in *Umm al-Qura*, 13 January 1928, 2.

57. Walpole, *Area Handbook*, 219.

58. Hajrah, *Public Land Distribution*, 16, 19.

59. Al-Qari, *Majallat al-Ahkam al-Shar'iyya*, 29.

60. *Umm al-Qura*, 6 February 1925, 1. Report, attached to Consul (Jordan) to FO, 8 January 1925; "Aims of the Indian Caliphate Committee," 13 January 1925, both in IOR/R/15/5/37, BL, QDL; see interpretation in Willis, "Burying Muhammad 'Ali Jauhar."

61. Report, attached to Consul (Jordan) to FO, 1 March 1926, IOR/L/PS/10/1165/1, BL, QDL.

62. Willis, "Burying Muhammad 'Ali Jauhar."

63. Willis, "Burying Muhammad 'Ali Jauhar."

64. Tabataba'i, *Kharaj in Islamic Law*, 135; Johansen, *The Islamic Law on Land*, 12; for a great interpretation of the origins of the *sulhan* and *'anwatan* distinction, see Noth, "Some Remarks."

65. Ibn Qudama, *Al-Mughni*, 11: 613–17; Tabataba'i, *Kharaj in Islamic Law*, 118, fn. 5. It happens that this is the Shi'i interpretation, too, Tabataba'i, *Kharaj in Islamic Law*, 119.

66. Rida, *Fatawa*, 2: 713–16 (n. 269).

67. Nasif, *Madi al-Hijaz*, 212–213; Willis, "Burying Muhammad 'Ali Jauhar";

68. Report attached to Consul (Jordan) to FO, 4 February 1926, IOR/R/15/5/37, BL, QDL.

69. Hirtzel to Secretary of State, 6 March 1926, IOR/L/PS/10/1165/1, BL, QDL.

70. Part of the report "Muhammadan Activities in Europe and the Near East," 18 February 1926, IOR/L/PS/10/1165/1, BL, QDL.

71. If non-Najdi Arabs are mentioned at all in the making of Saudi Arabia, they are usually part of its "expansion." Traboulsi, "The Saudi Expansion."

72. The importance of Syrian merchant networks in the Hijazi region is to be investigated. I thank Ulrike Freitag for this observation; more on merchants in Pétriat, *Le Négoce des Lieux saints*.

73. Tauber, *The Emergence*, 114–15, 232.

74. Vassil'ev, *The History of Saudi Arabia*, 610–11; Kostiner, *The Making*, 105.

75. Hamza, *Mudhakkirat*, 1:51.

76. The propagandist-historian of the Saudi dynasty Joseph Kéchichian wrote a biography of this man, possibly based on his private papers in DMAA. The publication has been constantly delayed. As of 15 April 2022, the book is not yet available.

77. Al-Zirikli, *'Aman fi 'Amman*, 35–36.

78. Lauzière, *The Making of Salafism*, 72, fn. 45.

79. Al-Zirikli, *Al-A'lam*, 8:253; Hamza, *Mudhakkirat*, 1:51; Tarrazi, *Tarikh al-Sihafa*, 4:68.

80. *Umm al-Qura*, 12 December 1924, 4.

81. *Umm al-Qura*, 10 February 1925, 4.

82. Hamza, *Mudhakkirat*, 1: 99; Ochsenwald, "The Transformation of Education"; French consulate (Ibrahim) Jedda to HC, 12 September 1927, 45CPCOM/310, CADC; al-Hafiz, *Jam'iyyat al-'Ulama'*, 18 writes that al-Qassab left the Hijaz because he became ill in Mecca.

83. Kostiner, *The Making*, 173–84.

84. Hamza, *Mudhakkirat*, 2:547, 2:561–2.

85. Hamza, Qalb Jazirat al-ʿArab.

86. The proper analysis of this network cannot begin until the relevant documents, including Rida's papers and Hamza's original diary, become available to researchers.

87. Provence, *The Great Syrian Revolt*.

88. Al-Zirikli, *Al-Aʿlam*, 5:159; Hamza, *Mudhakkirat*, 1:61, 69, 71–72 (Yasin's car broke down so he had to go back to Medina for another one).

89. Yasin al-Ruʾaf to Amin al-Rihani, 9 September 1928, ARC-MKC.

90. Hamza, *Mudhakkirat*, 1: 56–69; Qasimiyya, *Al-Raʿil al-ʿArabi*, 43–50.

91. Parsons, *Fawzi al-Qawuqji*, Chapter Two; Qasimiyya, *Jawanib*; Hamza, *Mudhakkirat*. Munir Zaki Shaykh al-Ard, from the important Shaykh al-Ard family, was also a doctor and an activist against the French mandate, see his letter to Charles Crane, ? April 1922, CCP-CUL.

92. Hamza, *Mudhakkirat*, 2:551.

93. Consul to FO, Munshi Ihsanullah's report, 17 April 1926, IOR/L/PS/10/1165/1, BL, QDL.

94. "Fiche de renseigements—Khaled Bey Hakim," January 1928, 50CPCOM/214, CADC.

95. Hamza, *Mudhakkirat*, 1: 77–8 (5 February 1927).

96. Jordan to FO, 24 August 1926, Enclosure 1, IOR/L/PS/10/1115, BL, QDL.

97. Entry 6 August 1926, GB65–0016, MECA.

98. ʿAbd al-ʿAziz to Clayton, 1 November 1925, IOR/L/PS/10/1165/1, BL, QDL; Almana, *Arabia Unified*, 171–177.

99. *Umm al-Qura*, 19 December 1924, 2.

100. *Umm al-Qura*, 2 January 1925, 2 (1924 is incorrectly printed).

101. The British, Italian, Dutch and Persian consuls' letter, 2 December 1924, IOR/R/15/5/37, BL, QDL.

102. ʿAbd al-ʿAziz to consuls, 5 December 1924, IOR/R/15/5/37, BL, QDL.

103. Smart to FO, 24 March 1926, IOR/L/PS/10/1165/1, BL, QDL.

104. Consul to FO, 29 March 1926, IOR/L/PS/10/1165/1, BL, QDL.

105. FO to India Office, 15 January 1926; India Office to FO, 27 January 1926; Viceroy to Secretary of State for India, 28 January 1926, IOR/L/PS/10/1165/1, BL, QDL.

106. Consul to FO, 11 February 1926, IOR/L/PS/10/1165/1, BL, QDL.

107. 13 January 1926, Handwritten note in IOR/L/PS/10/1165/1, BL, QDL.

108. Wakely to FO, 2 February 1926, IOR/L/PS/10/1165/1, BL, QDL.

109. Oliphant to India Office, 16 February 1926, IOR/L/PS/10/1165/1, BL, QDL.

110. India Office to FO, 23 February 1926, IOR/L/PS/10/1165/1, BL, QDL.

111. Handwritten Minutes, 18–19 February 1926, IOR/L/PS/10/1165/1, BL, QDL.

112. FO to Consul, 25 February 1926, IOR/L/PS/10/1165/1, BL, QDL.

113. Consul to ʿAbd al-ʿAziz, 1 March 1926, IOR/L/PS/10/1165/1, BL, QDL.

114. ʿAbd al-ʿAziz to Consul, 3 March 1926, IOR/L/PS/10/1165/1, BL, QDL.

115. FO to Lord Lloyd, 30 June 1926, IOR/L/PS/10/1165/1, BL, QDL.

116. Harding to FO, 21 March 1927, IOR/L/PS/10/1165/1, BL, QDL.

117. Oliphant to CO, 21 March 1927, IOR/L/PS/10/1165/1, BL, QDL.

118. Yusuf Yasin to Consul, 4 April 1927; Consul to FO, 4 April 1927; FO to Consul, 8 April 1927, Consul to FO, 9 April 192; CO to High Commissioners, 13 April 1927; all in IOR/L/PS/10/1165/1, BL, QDL.

119. Clayton to CO, 16 December 1925, IOR/L/PS/10/1165/1, BL, QDL.

120. 'Abd al-'Aziz to Consul, 10 April 1926, IOR/L/PS/10/1165/1, BL, QDL.

121. Minutes, 12 March 1926; Clayton to ?, 21 April 1926; Viceroy to Secretary of State, 12 July 1926; Minutes of conference, 11 August 1926; Minutes of Conference, 6 October 1926, and draft treaty, all IOR/L/PS/10/1165/1, BL, QDL.

122. Minutes of conference, 11 August 1926; IOR/L/PS/10/1165/1, BL, QDL.

123. Officer to Secretary of State for the Colonies, 11 September 1926, IOR/L/PS/10/1165/1, BL, QDL.

124. *League of Nations Treaty Series* 71, 1–4 (1928), 133–64.

125. Philby to Crane, 27 December 1929, CCP-CUL. Philby's own narrative is in *Arabian Oil Ventures.*

126. Twitchell, *Saudi Arabia*, 211–24; Longrigg, *Oil in the Middle East*, 106–108; historians do not investigate the details, Jones, *Desert Kingdom*, 39; Anderson, *Aramco, the United States*, ix; Fitzgerald, "The Iraq Petroleum Company," 444–45. Crane's letters to Twitchell and 'Abd al-'Aziz during 1929–1933 are in CCP-CUL.

127. Kostiner, *The Making of Saudi Arabia*, 144–151. For the introduction of paper money, see O'Sullivan, "Paper Currency."

128. Pétriat, *Le Négoce des Lieux saints*, Chapter Six.

129. Hamza, *Mudhakkirat*, 1:107–137.

130. *Umm al-Qura*, 14 July 1933, 1.

131. Haykel, "Oil in Saudi Arabian Culture," 135.

132. *Umm al-Qura*, 19 October 1934, 3. The reference to previous practice was correct. The Ottoman Empire from the early 1880s also prohibited non-Ottoman Muslims from acquiring property in Mecca, and it even paid attention to the case of non-Ottoman Muslim property acquisition by marriage. Low, *Imperial Mecca*, 131–140.

133. *Umm al-Qura*, 25 January 1935, 2.

Chapter 9. The Throne of Damascus, 1926–1939

1. Hamza to al-Qassab, 15 Jumada al-Awwal 1347 (30 October 1928), MKQ, MW-DMAA.

2. Khoury, *Syria and the French Mandate*, 351–352.

3. Thompson, *Colonial Citizens*, 53; Atassi, *Syria—The Strength of An Idea*, 101.

4. Rabinovich, "Inter-Arab Relations Foreshadowed;" Porath, *In Search of Arab Unity*, 1–57; Khoury, *Syria and the French Mandate*, 228–30, 337–40, 352–59, 586–87; Gomaa, "The Syrian Throne"; Shambrook, *French Imperialism in Syria*, 25–27, 55–60; Thomas, *The French Empire*, 218–26.

5. Brubaker, *Nationalism Reframed*, 6.

6. "Mandate for Syria and the Lebanon," 177.

7. Mestyan, "From Administrative to Political Order?"

8. Pillai, "Fragmenting the Nation," 769; Benton and Ford, *Rage for Order*, 21–24; Colley, *The Gun, the Ship, and the Pen*, 8. For studies of national constitutions, see

Edwards, *A Legal History of the Civil War*; Ahmed, *Afghanistan Rising*; and De, *A People's Constitution.*

9. Devji, *Muslim Zion*, 22.

10. Moubayed, "Syria's Forgotten First President."

11. Ponsot to MAE, with attachment, 29 December 1926, 50CPCOM/201, CADC.

12. Ahmed Hamdi to Abbas Hilmi, 10 September 1931 24/74–5; Arif Hikmet to Ahmed Hamdi, 29 July 1931, 24/78, both in AHP; see also Bein, *Kemalist Turkey*, 78–82.

13. Bein, *Kemalist Turkey*, 73–82.

14. Bouquet, "The Sultan's Sons-in-Law," 354.

15. BR 15 January 1929, 143PAAP/181, CADC.

16. Note, 29 April 1921 and Note, 7 May 1921, both in 1SL/1V/1563, CADN.

17. Moubayed, "Syria's Forgotten First President," 430.

18. Allenby to FO, 11 and 13 August 1922 and attachments; Beirut to FO, 16 August 1922; Hardinge to FO 24 August 1922; Notes 28 August 1922; Consul in Damascus to FO, 14 September 1922; all in FO 371/7852, NAUK.

19. Renseignement, 21 October 1924, 65CPCOM/36, CADC.

20. For more background, Mestyan, "From Administrative to Political Order."

21. Renseignements 260/DV, 2 February 1928, "306/DV", 4 February 1928; "N 543," 27 February 1928, 143PAAP/224, CADC.

22. Renseignmenets, 29 February 1928, 143PAAP/224, CADC.

23. Al-Hakim, *Suriya wa-l-Intidab*, 155; Khoury, *Syria and the French Mandate*, 197.

24. Telegram with signatures, 3 March 1927; Reffye to MAE, 5 March 1927, 50CPCOM/201, CADC.

25. "Moussa Taoul," 28 February 1929, 143PAAP/177, CADC.

26. Telegrams, 17 and 25 December 1928, 50CPCOM/205, CADC.

27. 27 February (Idlib notables), 1 March (Aleppo merchants), four undated (Aleppo notables, doctors, bankers), all 1928 and in 50CPCOM/206; the Arabic originals in 50CPCOM/207, CADC.

28. Revues de la presse Libanaise, 7–8, 8–10, Mars 1929, 50CPCOM/288, CADC.

29. Stitt, *A Prince of Arabia*, 239.

30. Stitt, *A Prince of Arabia*, 290–302.

31. Ponsot to H.C.P.I. Beyrouth, 23 February 1927; Reffye to Ponsot, 24 February 1927; both in 50CPCOM/201, CADC.

32. Ponsot to MAE, with attachment, 29 December 1926, 50CPCOM/201, CADC.

33. "Le Prince Abdul-Mejid Haidar" to Ponsot, 7 August 1928, and to MAE, 10 August 1928, 50CPCOM/226, CADC.

34. Adil Ben-Aïad to MAE, 13 October 1928, 50CPCOM/205, CADC.

35. Unsigned note, Lausanne, 10 December 1926, HIL 35/166–167, AHP.

36. Letter from Arif Hikmet (ex-Ottoman general; from Romania) to Abbas Hilmi, 29 July 1931, HIL/24/76; press cuts from 1931, HIL 35/302, both in AHP; Bein, *Kemalist Turkey*, 79–82.

37. 1931 correspondence in CO 732/54/4; CO 732/47/7, NA; Abu al-Huda's letters in HIL 2, AHP.

38. Conversation between M. Ruppel and Sheikh Taj, 1 June 1933, 50CPCOM/485, CADC; letters of Arif Hikmet and Ahmed Hamdi in 1932, HIL 24; Hasan Khalid Abu al-Huda to Abbas Hilmi, 9 June 1933, HIL 2/3–4, both in AHP.

39. Porath, *In Search of Arab Unity*; Gomaa, "The Syrian Throne."

40. Pedersen, *The Guardians*, 153.

41. Compte-rendu hebdomadaire, Colonel Tracol, 24 February 1929, 143PAAP/177, CADC.

42. S.R. Damas ville, 20 May 1928, 143PAAP/180, CADC.

43. "Le Docteur Ahmad Ratib," 27 February 1929, 143PAAP/177, CADC.

44. Analyse de presse arabe II, June 1928, 6A/10289/1474, R2328, LNA.

45. SR's list, 19 June 1928, and personal files, 143PAAP/180, CADC.

46. Extract from report, Maigret to Ponsot, undated, attachment to Ponsot to MAE, 20 June 1928, 50CPCOM/204, CADC.

47. Ponsot to MAE, 5 July 1928, 50CPCOM/204, CADC.

48. Police Alep, 20 July 1928, 143PAAP/180, CADC.

49. Police Alep, 22 July 1928, 143PAAP/180, CADC.

50. Renseignements, 143PAAP/179, CADC.

51. Renseignements, ? and 6 August 1928, 143PAAP/179, CADC.

52. Alep, 15 November 1929, , 143PAAP/234, CADC.

53. 'Arif Idlibi and *mazbata* to HC, 27 December 1928, original Arabic and French translation, 143PAAP/180, CADC.

54. "Police Alep," 26 January 1929, 143PAAP/181, CADC.

55. Extrait de BR, 24 January 1929, 143PAAP/181, CADC.

56. Telegram dated 16 August 1929, 50CPCOM/206, CADC.

57. Telegram dated 16 August 1929, 50CPCOM/206, CADC.

58. "Diary of Colonel Hamilton's Visit to Nejd 1918," 17–18, IOR/R/15/5/104, BL, QDL.

59. Hamza, *Mudhakkirat*, 1: 56–69; Qasimiyya, *Al-Ra'il al-'Arabi*, 43–50.

60. Blake, "Training Arab-Ottoman Bureaucrats," 269, 275.

61. Seale, *The Struggle*, 26; Khury, *Syria and the French Mandate*, 238.

62. Khoury, *Syria and the French Mandate*, 239.

63. Abu Tariq and Abu Samir (Fu'ad Hamza) to al-Qassab, 16 Jumada al-Awwal 1348 (20 October 1929), MKQ, MW-DMAA.

64. Hadj Hamdi to Briand, 6 September 1928, 45CPCOM/26, CADC.

65. Lauzière, *The Making of Salafism*, 72, fn. 45.

66. Rida to al-Qassab, 8 Dhu al-Qa'da 1347 (18 April 1929), MKQ, MW-DMAA.

67. White, "Addressing the State," 10.

68. Antonius, *The Arab Awakening*; Rabinovich, "Inter-Arab Relations Foreshadowed"; Porath, *In Search of Arab Unity*.

69. Lauzière, *The Making of Salafism*; Aydin, *The Idea of the Muslim World*.

70. Sanagan, *Lightning*, 57–58ff.

71. Hamza, *Mudhakkirat*, 1:102.

72. Hamza to al-Qassab, 9 Shawwal 1346 (31 March 1928), MKQ, MW-DMAA; the edited version of Hamza's memoirs is silent about this issue.

73. Gaillard to ?, 4 June 1928, 50PCOM/204, CADC.

74. Blacklist in the Syrian State Archive quoted in Khoury, "Factionalism," 469, fn. 83.

75. *Al-Karmil*, 20 May 1928, 7.

76. *Al-Karmil*, 4 June 1928, 4–5.

77. 'Ali Kusur to al-Qassab, 24 Safar 1347 (20 July 1928), MKQ, MW-DMAA.

78. *Al-Jami'a al-'Arabiyya*, 4 June 1928, 2; Khoury, *Syria and the French Mandate*, 337–40; *Filastin*, 5 June 1928, 2.

79. *Filastin*, articles against al-Qassab: 10 and 14 February 1928, both pages 2; candidates: 19 June 1928, 2.

80. *Al-Manar* 29, no. 3 (18 June 1928), 229–37; Willis, "Burying Muhammad 'Ali Jauhar."

81. "Police Damas," 15 June 1928, 143PAAP/180, CADC.

82. Qarqut quotes *al-Mirsad* journal (9 August 1928) in his *Tatawwur al-Haraka*, 234, fn. 33. Here the adjective "civic" (*al-madani*) could mean "secular."

83. "Au sujet de Baalback," 3 June 1928, 143PAAP/224, CADC.

84. "Renseignements," 12 July 1928, 143PAAP/179, CADC.

85. "Informations fn. 396," 12 July 1928, 1SL/1V/953, CADN.

86. Al-Yafi, *Al-Faqid al-'Azim*, 82–88.

87. "Renseignements," 29 June 1928, 143PAAP/177, CADC.

88. "Comptes-Rendus des Séances de l'Assemblée Syrienne, séance 9 August 1928," 143PAAP/177, CADC.

89. Bulletin de Renseignements, 2 February 1929; "Sûreté générale," 7 February 1929, both in 143PAAP/181, CADC.

90. Al-Husayni to Crane, 2 April 1929, CCP-CUL.

91. Al-Husayni's letter of thanks to Crane, 25 Muharram 1350 (12 June 1931), CCP-CUL.

92. Shahin, *Khayr al-Din al-Zirikli*, 43.

93. Bet-Shlimon, *City of Black Gold*, 79–88.

94. Note "Candidature hachemite du trône de Syrie" (13-page-long memo), 10 April 1934, in 50CPCOM/459, CADC.

95. Shambrook, *French Imperialism in Syria*, 56–57.

96. "Note sur le séjour en Syrie de l'Emir Ali, ex-Roi du Hedjaz (11 au 13 Janvier 1931)" 15 January 1931, 50CPCOM/480, CADC.

97. Telegrams quoted in note "Candidature hachemite du trône de Syrie" (13-page long memo), 10 April 1934, in 50CPCOM/459, CADC; Shambrook, *French Imperialism in Syria*, 58.

98. Dispatches 15–17 April 1931, 50CPCOM/480, CADC.

99. Analyse de presse arabe XXXIII, January 1931, 6A/10289/1474, R2329, LNA.

100. Analyse de presse arabe XXXIX, July 1931, 6A/10289/1474, R2329, LNA.

101. Note "Candidature hachemite du trône de Syrie" (13-page-long memo), 10 April 1934, in 50CPCOM/459, CADC; and *al-Ahrar* in Analyse de presse arabe XL, August 1931, 6A/10289/1474, R2329, LNA.

102. 17 February 1931, 50CPCOM/481, CADC.

103. Letter dated 20 December 1932, Berthelot to Ministre Français—Le Caire, 50CPCOM/482, CADC.

104. Nasib Shihab's article in *al-Ahrar*, 5 August 1931, also *Analyse de presse arabe* XL, August 1931, 6A/10289/1474, R2329, LNA.

105. *Le Génie Civil*, 9 March 1935, 221–27.

106. Khoury, *Syria and the French Mandate*, 586.

107. Francois-Poncet to MAE, 11 July 1939, 50CPCOM/496, CADC.

108. *Filastin*, 30 Nisan 1939, 3.

109. MAE to H-C, 11 July 1939, 50CPCOM/496, CADC.

110. Shambrook, *French Imperialism in Syria*, 63–76.

Afterword: Subordinated Sovereignty in the Twentieth Century

1. Krisch and Kingsbury, "Introduction: Global Governance."

2. Burbank, "Eurasian Sovereignty," 10.

3. D'Eramo, "American Decline."

4. Weiss, *In the Shadow of Sectarianism*, 106; White, *The Emergence of Minorities*, 29–31, 47–52; Makdisi, *The Age of Coexistence*, 163.

5. Gramsci, *Prison Notebooks*, 2: 33; Arendt, *Between Past and Future* 39–40, 54–56, 68–71.

6. Eisenstadt, "Multiple Modernities," 2; Asad, *Formations of the Secular*, 13; Casanova, *Public Religions in the Modern World*, 5–6; Latour, *We Have Never Been Modern*, 47–48; Chakrabarty, *Provincializing Europe*.

7. Today, historians also argue that transcendental cosmologies may prove invaluable in the face of impending ecological catastrophe. Duara, *The Crisis of Global Modernity*, 2–3.

8. Hobsbawm, *Age of Extremes*; Tooze, *The Deluge*.

9. Bayly, *Remaking*, 95.

10. Wyrtzen, *Worldmaking*, 35–36.

A Note on Sources

Modern Arab Kingship appears at an exciting moment in research on the late Ottoman Empire and the post-Ottoman and the post-Habsburg regions. I could not add books that were published after October 2022, when I ended my substantive work on the manuscript of this book. These include Mostafa Minawi's *Losing Istanbul*, Ryan Gringeras's *The Last Days of the Ottoman Empire*, Andrew Hammond's *Late Ottoman Origins of Modern Islamic Thought*, Elizabeth R. Williams's *States of Cultivation*, Natasha Wheatly's *Life and Death of States*, Jane Burbank and Fred Cooper's *Post-Imperial Possibilities,* and Aimee Genell's *Empire by Law.* No doubt further publications are in preparation.

I have conducted research in several archives for this book, but to spare space I cite documents only from a selected few. Official (state and non-state) archives in Jordan, Saudi Arabia, Iraq, Oman, and Egypt were constructed with the conscious aims of connecting nation and dynasty in history-writing. French and British archives preserve selected documents about military occupations and the mandates. I have drawn on private and state documents from a number of these archives in this book and it is important here to provide a note of caution.

The earliest attempt to assemble a modern royal archive based on selected documents took place in interwar Egypt.[1] As in the nineteenth century, interwar loyalist publications often connected kings, nationalism, and sovereignty. Consider this introduction about King Fuad of Egypt in a 1930 French booklet. Fuad "crowns the beautiful building to which his ancestors gave solid foundations and he gives to Egypt the rank with which she has the legitimate ambition to become among the great modern nations."[2] Recently assembled Saudi private archives have been created through a similar process of selection—especially in the somewhat guarded *Darat al-Malik ʿAbd al-ʿAziz*, a private foundation dedicated to fashioning the memory of King ʿAbd al-ʿAziz.[3]

In addition to problems of access, another challenge relates to the absence of archival materials. One might expect all official or semi-state Arab archives to contain documents from the Ottoman Empire or from the immediate post-Ottoman polities, but these materials are not always to be found. For instance, we know that when ʿAbd al-ʿAziz captured Mecca in 1925 he took possession of the archive of the Kingdom of the Hijaz, and "he was amused by it," but there is no trace of it today.[4] Similarly, in Jordan, there are surprisingly few materials about the 1920s and 1930s to be found in the Directorate of Documents within the *Daʾira* of the National Library; this appears to be the result of institutional decentralization and the rehousing of archival documents elsewhere, including—as I heard during my stays in Amman—in the royal palace.[5]

During my research, I benefited from the kind assistance of archivists and librarians wherever I went. Nevertheless, access to materials was frequently constrained by periodic archival closures for maintenance and curatorial work, and in 2020 by the COVID-19 pandemic, as well as by ongoing political and private restrictions on academic research. Nor, I should note, were my problems of securing access to materials confined to the Middle East: a number of colleagues in Western academia were perhaps not as liberal in sharing their own findings as they could have been.

An important note: I learned during this research that the *Darat al-Malik ʿAbd al-ʿAziz* in Riyadh has amassed perhaps the most important private collection about the interwar Arab Middle East in the past three decades. This is because King ʿAbd al-ʿAziz was in touch with a surprising number of non-Saudi Arabs. The private papers, especially those belonging to individuals that I identify in this book as the loose 1920s *Istiqlali* grouping, are important sources for the interwar political, intellectual, and social history of Egypt, Syria, Jordan, Lebanon, and Palestine.[6] It is only through a careful engagement with these sources that we can write a new history of Islam and empire in the twentieth century.

A similarly important issue is the unreliability of Arabic memoirs. For instance, the later Palestinian major of Jerusalem and celebrated "sheikh of Palestinian historians," ʿArif al-ʿArif's "diary" about his service in the Transjordan Emirate between 1926 and 1929 contains long odes about al-ʿArif's loyalty to Arab nationalism. This type-written Arabic document held in St Antony's College in Oxford is so ideologically charged that "a reader" (perhaps Albert Hourani?) cautioned that it may be "doctored."[7] Most edited collections of Arab personal papers and memoirs about the interwar period—often written in the 1950s-60s—are uncritical editions, lacking a scholarly apparatus. The American Lebanese Amin Rihani's private papers, available online, also have been altered to censure certain words and topics.[8] A more recent example are the memoirs of Fuʾad Hamza, an *Istiqlali* "brother," and key Syrian diplomat in the service of ʿAbd al-ʿAziz from 1926. The editor of the memoirs explains in the introduction that he agreed with Hamza's son to leave out "personal details" and "family information" from which "the reader would not benefit." However, the edition does not indicate what was deleted, and several years are missing. Hamza himself before his death wanted to publish the memoirs and returned to some issues to re- or over-write some passages but the edition, again, does not indicate which ones.[9] The editorial decisions in this and other memoirs and diaries are indicative of the unfortunate tendency of official and private actors to decide what would "benefit" researchers.

Notes

1. Di-Capua, *The Gatekeepers*, 102–22.

2. Herreros, *Sa Majesté le Roi Fouad Ier*, 7.

3. Bsheer, *Archive Wars*, 49–54, 108–23, 134–70.

4. British Agency Jidda to Mallet, 22 May 1925, IOR/R/15/1/574, BL, QDL.

5. For a good overview, which remained pertinent and up to date when I last visited in 2018, see Rogan, "Archival Resources and Research Institutions in Jordan."

6. The collections include the private papers of Rashid Rida, Kamil al-Qassab, Yusuf Yasin, Fu'ad Hamza, Khayr al-Din al-Zirikli, Muhibb al-Din al-Khatib, and others. DMAA allows only selected documents to be published, such as those from the Zirikli papers or the Hamza memoirs.

7. GB65–0016, MECA.

8. Note in the Khayrallah Center, Ameen Fares Rihani (1876–1940) Collection website, (https://lebanesestudies.omeka.chass.ncsu.edu/collections/show/104, last checked 25 April 2022).

9. Hamza, *Mudhakkirat*, 1: 33.

Unpublished Sources

ONLINE SOURCES

AFL-MHMA = Armées françaises au Levant (SHD/GR 4 H 1–269), Mémoire des Hommes, Ministère des Armées, Paris, https://www.memoiredeshommes.sga.defense.gouv.fr/.

ARC-MKC = Amin al-Rihani Collection, Moise A. Khayrallah Center for Lebanese Diaspora Studies Archive, North Carolina State University (https://lebanesestudies.ncsu.edu/).

BL = British Library.

QDL = Qatar Digital Library, https://www.qdl.qa.

LoC = Library of Congress.

Marx, Karl. "Letter to Ruse, May 1843," http://www.marxists.org/archive/marx/works/1843/letters/43_05.html.

MW-DMW = Mudiriyyat al-Watha'iq, Da'irat al-Maktaba al-Wataniyya, Amman (http://adlibweb.nl.gov.jo/adlibweb/default.aspx).

OCA-KCC = Oberlin College Archives, King-Crane Commission Digital Collection, http://www2.oberlin.edu/library/digital/king-crane/.

Qa'idat al-Tashri'at al-'Iraqiyya (Collection of Iraqi Legislative Acts, Supreme Judicial Council of Iraq), http://iraqld.hjc.iq:8080/main_ld.aspx.

Treaty of Peace between the Allied and Associated Powers with Germany (Treaty of Versailles) 28 June 1919. Museum of Australian Democracy, Documenting Democracy, Commonwealth, https://www.foundingdocs.gov.au/item-sdid-94.html.

Twenty-fifth Congress of the United States of America (1839), Session Three, Chapter XC, 356; Status at Large, Library of Congress, Law Library, https://www.loc.gov/law/help/statutes-at-large/25th-congress.php.

OFFLINE ARCHIVES

France

CADC = Centre des Archives Diplomatiques, La Courneuve, Ministère de l'Europe et des Affaires Étrangères, Paris.

CADN = Centre des Archives Diplomatiques, Nantes, Ministère de l'Europe et des Affaires Étrangères.

Jordan

MW-DMW = Mudiriyyat al-Watha'iq, Da'irat al-Maktaba al-Wataniyya, Amman.

MW-UJ = Markaz al-Watha'iq, University of Jordan, Amman.

Saudi Arabia

DMAA and MW-DMAA = Darat al-Malik 'Abd al-'Aziz, Markaz al-Watha'iq, Riyadh.

Switzerland

LNA = League of Nations Archive, United Nations International Organization, Geneva.

Türkiye

İSAM = İslam Araştırmları Merkezi, Istanbul.
    DS = Dımaşk (Şam) Siciller.
    DS-İ = İstinaf.
    DS-K = Kasrüladli.
    DS-MA = Muhtelita Arapça.
    DS-MF = Muhtelita Fransızca.
    DS-T = Ticari.
BOA = Başbakanlık Devlet Arşivleri Genel Müdürlüğü—Osmanlı Arşivi, Istanbul.
    İ.TAL. = İrade Taltifat.
    Y.A.HUS. = Yıldız Sadaret Hususi Maruzat Evrakı.
    BEO. = Bab-ı Ali Evrak Odası.
    DH.MKT. = Dahiliye Nezareti Mektubi Kalemi.
    İ.DH. = İrade Dahiliye.
    İ.ML. = İrade Maliye.
    ŞD. = Şura-yı Devlet Evrakı.
    Y.A.RES. = Yıldız Sadaret Resmi Maruzat Evrakı.

United Kingdom

AHP = Abbas Hilmi II Papers, Special Collections, Durham University.
BL = British Library, London.
BL-C = Curzon Papers, British Library, London.
BL-W = Wilson Papers, British Library, London.
LHCMA = Liddell Hart Centre for Military Archives, King's College, London.
MECA = Middle East Centre Archive, St Antony's College, Oxford.
NAUK = The National Archives of the UK Government, Kew.
SA = Sudan Archive, Special Collections, Durham University.
WP = Wingate Papers, Sudan Archive, Special Collections, Durham University.

United States of America

CCP-CUL = Charles Crane Papers, Columbia University Library, Rare Books Collection.
Rare Books Collection, Princeton University.
Timur Kuran Collection of Ottoman Revenue Documents, Durham, North Carolina.

DISSERTATIONS

Berndt, Nathaniel. "Descendants of Zabarkan, Citizens of the World: A History of Cosmopolitan Imagination in Decolonizing Niger, 1958–1974." PhD dissertation, Duke University, 2022.

Blake, Corinne. "Training Arab-Ottoman Bureaucrats: Syrian Graduates of the Mul-kiye Mektebi, 1890–1920." PhD dissertation, Princeton University, 1991.

Genell, Aimee M. "Empire by Law: Ottoman Sovereignty and the British Occupation of Egypt, 1882–1923." PhD dissertation, Columbia University, 2013.

Grallert, Till. "To Whom Belong the Streets? Property, Propriety, and Appropriation: The Production of Public Space in Late Ottoman Damascus, 1875–1914." PhD Dissertation, Freie University, 2014.

Innes, Mary. "In Egyptian Service: The Role of British Officials in Egypt." DPhil Dissertation, St Antony's College, University of Oxford, 1986.

Jensis, Donald F. "The Memel Territory, 1919–1924." MA thesis, Fordham University, 1958.

Okan, Orcun. "Coping with Transitions: The Connected Construction of Turkey, Syria, Lebanon, and Iraq, 1918–1928." PhD Dissertation. Columbia University, 2020.

Quadri, Syed Junaid A. "Transformations of Tradition: Modernity in the Thought of Muhammad Bakhit al-Muta'i." PhD. Dissertation, McGill University, 2013.

Rizvi, Sayyid Muhammad. "Portrait of a Salafi-Arabist, 1886–1969." MA thesis, Simon Fraser University, 1991.

Published Sources

PERIODICALS

Alif Ba' (Damascus), 1920–1921.

Al-Ahrar (Beirut), 1931.

Al-Ahram (Cairo), 1914–1945, 1998.

Al-'Asima (Damascus), 1919–1921.

Bulletin Officiel (Morocco), 1912.

L'Égypte contemporaine (Cairo), 1914.

Al-Fallah (Mecca), 1920–1921.

Filastin (Jaffa) 1925–1935.

Al-Balagh (Beirut), 1918–21, 1928.

Al-Bashir (Beirut), 1914, 1919–21, 1928.

Al-Huquq (Cairo), 1886.

Al-Istiqlal al-'Arabi (Damascus), 1919.

Al-Jami'a al-'Arabiyya (Jerusalem), 1928–1930.

Journal Officiel (Cairo), 1917.

Al-Karmil (Haifa), 1928–1930.

League of Nations Treaty Series, 1928.

Al-Liwa' (Cairo), 1908–1910, 1919.

The London Gazette, 1919.

Al-Mahakim (Cairo), 1914–1915.

Majallat al-Ahkam al-Shar'iyya (Cairo), 1902–1920.

Majallat al-Qada' al-Shar'i (Cairo), 1922–1931.

Al-Manar (Cairo), 1898–1933.

Al-Mufid (Damascus), 1919.

Al-Muhama (Cairo), 1920–1923.

Al-Muhama al-Shar'iyya (Cairo), 1929–1955.

Al-Muqtataf (Cairo), 1913.

Neue Freie Presse (Vienna), 1913.

Nur al-Islam (later *Majallat al-Azhar*, Cairo), 1931–34.

Al-Qibla (Mecca), 1916–1919.

Recueil des actes administratifs du Haut-commissariat de la République Française en Syrie et au Liban, 1921.

Resmi Ceride (Ankara), 1924.

Salname-i Hicaz, 1304.

Salname-I Hicaz, 1309.

Salname-i Devlet-i 'Aliye 'Uthmaniye, 1333–1334.

Al-Siyasa (Cairo), 1922–23.

Al-Siyasa al-Usbu'iyya (Cairo), 1927, 1937–38.

Suriya al-Jadida (Damascus), 1921.

Al-Taqaddum (Aleppo), 1913, 1919.

Al-Tawfiq (Hama), 1919.

Al-'Uqab (Damascus), 1919.

Umm al-Qura (Mecca), 1924–1939.

PUBLISHED MATERIAL WITHOUT AUTHOR OR EDITOR

Affaires de Tunisie: supplément, avril-mai 1881. Paris: Impr. Nationale, 1881.

Correspondance de Napoléon Ier. Vol. 10. Paris: H. Plon-J. Dumaine, 1862.

Al-Fatawa al-Islamiyya. 20 vols. Cairo: Wizarat al-Awqaf, 1980—.

Final Drafts of the Mandates for Mesopotamia and Palestine. London: His Majesty's Stationery Office, 1921.

Hatt-i Hümayun-i Şerif ve Kanun-i Esasi—Turki ve 'Arabi. Istanbul: Matba'at al-Jawa'ib, 1297 (1879/80).

İdare-i Umumiye-i Vilayat Kanun-ı Muvakkatı. Istanbul: [Jihan Matba'a, 1915].

La'ihat Tartib al-Mahakim al-Shar'iyya wa-l-Ujrat al-Muta'lliqa bi-ha. Cairo: Matba'at al-Hindiyya, 1897.

Lajnat al-Dustur—Majmu'at Mahadir al-Lajna al- 'Amma. Cairo: al-Matba'a al-Amiriyya, 1924.

The League of Nations Starts: An Outline by Its Organisers. London: MacMillan, 1920.

Loi Organique ou Code Politique et Administratif du Royaume Tunisien, Traduction d'Arabe. Gènes: Impremerie et Litografie Faziola, 1861.

Majmu'at al-Awamir wa-l-Qawanin al-Khassa bi-Nizam al-Usra al-Malika. Cairo: al-Matba'a al-Amiriyya, 1923.

"Mandate for Syria and the Lebanon." *American Journal of International Law* 17, 3 [Supplement] (1923): 177–82.

Protestation du Comité national polonais contre le statut organique & les oukases de Nicolas. [Paris]: H. Fournier, 1832.

Rapport général sur les études foncières effectuées en Syrie et au Liban. [Beirut]: Services Fonciers, 1921.

Recueil des actes administratifs du Haut-commissariat de la République française en Syrie et au Liban. Vol. 5. Beirut: Imp. Jeanne D'Arc, 1924.

"Report of American Section of Inter-Allied Commission on Mandates in Turkey." *Editors & Publishers*, 2 December 1922, IV-XX.

The Revised Codes of the Territory of Dakota. A.D. 1877. Comprising the Codes and General Statutes Passed at the Twelfth Session of the Legislative Assembly, and All Other General Laws Remaining in Force. To Which Is Prefixed the Organic Law and the Constitution of the United States, Second edition. Yankton: Bowen and Kingsbury, 1880.

Sadrazam ve Harbiye Nazırı Mahmut Şevket Paşa'nın Günlüğü. Istanbul: Arba, 1988.

Treaty of Alliance (Egypt). London: His Majesty's Stationery Office, 1937.

Treaty of Alliance (Iraq). London: His Majesty's Stationery Office, 1925.

"Treaty of Peace between Italy and Turkey." *American Journal of International Law* 7, no. 1 (1913): 58–62.

United States Department of State, *Papers relating to the foreign relations of the United States, The Paris Peace Conference, 1919,* vol. 12. Washington, DC: U.S. Government Printing Office, 1919.

Watha'iq wa-Nusus. vol.1: Dasatir al-Bilad al-'Arabiyya, Ma'had al-Dirasat al-'Arabiyya al-'Aliyya, ed. [Cairo]: Jami'at al-Duwal al-'Arabiyya, 1955.

PUBLISHED SOURCES WITH AUTHOR

Note: In the following entries, *'ayn* and *al-* are not considered as distinct letters, *de* and *von* are not considered [De Graaf is at G, Von Knorrig at K, Van den Bosch at B], Ibn is at I, Dj is at D.

'Abd al-Hadi, 'Awni. *Mudhakkirat 'Awni 'Abd al-Hadi.* Khayriyya Qasimiyya, ed. Beirut: Markaz Dirasat al-Wahda al-'Arabiyya, 2002.

Abkariyus, Yuhanna. *Qatf al-Zuhur fi Tarikh al-Duhur.* Beirut: n.p., 1873.

Abu 'Asi, Muhammad Salim, ed. *Al-Fatawa li-l-Imam al-'Allama Muhammad b. Bakhit al-Muti'i.* ['Akkar, Lebanon]: Dar al-Siddiq li-l-'Ulum, 2012.

———., ed. *Al-Fatawa li-l-Imam al-'Allama Muhammad b. Bakhit al-Muti'i,* 2 vols. Cairo: Maktabat Wahba, 2013; also e-book version.

Abu-Manneh, Butrus. "Sultan Abdulhamid II and the Sharifs of Mecca (1880–1900)." *Asian and African Studies* 9 no. 1 (1973): 1–21.

———. "Sultan Abdulhamid II and Shaikh Abulhuda Al-Sayyadi." *Middle Eastern Studies* 15, no. 2 (1979): 131–53.

Abu al-Nur, Sami. *Dawr al-Qasr fi al-Hayat al-Siyasiyya fi Misr, 1922–1936.* [Cairo]: Al-Hay'a al-Misriyya al-'Amma li-l-Kitab, 1985.

Adams, Charles C. *Islam and Modernism in Egypt: A Study of the Modern Reform Movement Inaugurated by Muhammad 'Abduh.* New York: Russell & Russell, 1968.

Adams, Julia, and George Steinmetz. "Sovereignty and Sociology: From State Theory to Theories of Empire." *Political Power and Social Theory* 28 (2015): 269–85.

Adelman, Jeremy. *Sovereignty and Revolution in the Iberian Atlantic.* Princeton: Princeton University Press, 2006.

Ahmed, Faiz. *Afghanistan Rising: Islamic Law and Statecraft between the Ottoman and British Empires.* Cambridge: Harvard University Press, 2017.

Ahmed, Shahab. *What Is Islam? The Importance of Being Islamic.* Princeton: Princeton University Press, 2015.

Akiba, Jun. "From Kadı to Naib: Reorganization of the Ottoman Sharia Judiciary in the Tanzimat Period." In *Frontiers of Ottoman Studies*, edited by Colin Imber and Keiko Kiyotaki, vol. 1: 43–60. London: I. B. Tauris, 2005.

———. "The Practice of Writing Curricula Vitae among the Lower Government Employees in the Late Ottoman Empire: Workers at the Şeyhülislâm's Office." *European Journal of Turkish Studies* 6 (2007), online, 30 April 2022, http://journals .openedition.org/ejts/1503; DOI: https://doi.org/10.4000/ejts.1503.

———. "Sharia Judges in the Ottoman Nizamiye Courts, 1864–1908." *Osmanlı Araştırmaları* 51 (2018): 209–37.

Akpınar, Alişan. *Osmanlı Devleti'nde Asiret Mektebi*. İstanbul: Göçebe Yayınları, 1997.

Alangari, Haifa. *The Struggle for Power in Arabia: Ibn Saud, Hussein and Great Britain, 1914–1924*. Reading: Ithaca Press, 1998.

Alatas, Ismail Fajrie. *What Is Religious Authority? Cultivating Islamic Community in Indonesia*. Princeton: Princeton University Press, 2021.

Al-'Alawina, Ahmad Ibrahim. *Khayr al-Din al-Zirikli, 1309–1396 H/1893–1976 M: al-Mu'arrikh al-Adib al-Sha'ir, Sahib Kitab al-A'lam*. Damascus: Dar al-Qalam, 2002.

———. *Khayr al-Din al-Zirikli: Dirasa wa-Tawthiq*. Riyad: Darat al-Malik 'Abd al-'Aziz, 1433 [2011–2012].

———. *Khayr al-Din al-Zirikli: Biblughrafiya, Suwar wa-Watha'iq*. Beirut: Dar al-Basha'ir al-Islamiyya, 2014.

Al-'Allaf, Ahmad Hilmi. *Dimashq fi Ma'la' al-Qarn al-'Ishrin*. Damascus: Wizarat al-Thaqafa wa-l-Irshad al-Qawmi, 1976.

Allawi, Ali A. *Faisal I of Iraq*. London: Yale University Press, 2014.

Almana, Mohammed. *Arabia Unified: A Portrait of Ibn Saud*. London: Hutchinson Benham Limited, 1982.

Al-Amir, Ibrahim b. Mansur al-Hashimi. "Hajat al-Muluk wa-l-Umara' li-'Ilm al-Nasab." 30 Jumada al-Akhira 1442 (13 February 2021), http://www.alamir.info /inf4/include/plugins/article/article.php?action=s&id=2080, last viewed 5 January 2022.

'Ammun, Iskandar. *Al-Amani al-Lubnaniyya*. Cairo: Matba'at al-Ahram, 1912.

Anand, Nikhil, Akhil Gupta, and Hannah Appel, eds. *The Promise of Infrastructure*. Durham: Duke University Press, 2018.

Anderson, Benedict. *Imagined Communities—Reflections on the Origin and Spread of Nationalism*, rev. ed. London: Verso, 2006.

Anderson, Irvine H. Jr. *Aramco, the United States, and Saudi Arabia: A Study of the Dynamics*. Princeton: Princeton University Press, 1981.

Anderson, Lisa. "Absolutism and the Resilience of Monarchy in the Middle East." *Political Science Quarterly* 106, no. 1 (1991): 1–15.

Anderson, Perry. *Lineages of the Absolutist State*. London: Verso, 1979.

Anghie, Antony. *Imperialism, Sovereignty, and the Making of International Law*. Cambridge: Cambridge University Press, 2005.

Anscombe, Frederick. *The Ottoman Gulf: The Creation of Kuwait, Saudi Arabia, and Qatar*. New York: Columbia University Press, 1997.

———. *State, Faith, and Nation in Ottoman and Post-Ottoman Lands*. New York: Cambridge University Press, 2014.

———. "The Ottoman Legacy to Post-Ottoman States." In *Imperial Lineages and Legacies in the Eastern Mediterranean: Recording the Imprint of Roman, Byzantine and Ottoman Rule*, Rhoads Murphey, ed., 143–55. London: Routledge, 2017.

Antaki, 'Abd al-Masih. *'Urf al-Tib fi Mada'ih al-Sayyid Talib Basha al-Naqib*. Cairo: Al-Matba'a al-Misriyya al-Akhawiyya, 1904.

Antonius, George. "Syria and the French Mandate." *International Affairs* 13, 4 (1934): 523–39.

———. *The Arab Awakening: The Story of the Arab National Movement*. London: H. Hamilton, 1938.

Appadurai, Arjun. "Sovereignty without Territoriality: Notes on a Postnational Geography." In *The Geography of Identity*, P. Yaeger, ed., 40–58. Ann Arbor, Michigan: University of Michigan Press, 1996.

Arai-Takahashi, Yutaka. *The Law of Occupation: Continuity and Change of International Humanitarian Law, and Its Interaction with International Human Rights Law*. Leiden: Martinus Nijhoff, 2009.

Arato, Andrew. *Constitution-Making under Occupation: The Politics of Imposed Revolution in Iraq*. New York: Columbia University Press, 2009.

Arendt, Hannah. *Between Past and Future: Eight Exercises in Political Thought*. New York: Viking Press, 1969.

Armitage, David. *The Ideological Origins of the British Empire*. Cambridge: Cambridge University Press, 2000.

Arna'ut, Muhammad Mufaku. *Min al-Hukuma ila al-Dawla—Tajrabat al-Hukuma al-'Arabiyya fi Dimashq (1918–1920)*. Amman: Al-An Nashirun wa-Muwazzi'un, 2020.

Arsan, Andrew. "'This Age is the Age of Associations'": Committees, Petitions, and the Roots of Interwar Middle Eastern Internationalism." *Journal of Global History* 7, no. 2 (2012), 166–88.

Arslan, Shakib. *Ila al-'Arab: Bayan al-Umma al-'Arabiyya 'an Hizb al-La-Markaziyya*. 1913; Beirut: Dar al-Taqaddumiyya, 2009.

Asad, Talal. *Formations of the Secular: Christianity, Islam, Modernity*. Stanford: Stanford University Press, 2003.

Atassi, Karim. *Syria, the Strength of an Idea: The Constitutional Architectures of Its Political Regimes*. Cambridge: Cambridge University Press, 2018.

Atçıl, Abdurrahman. "Decentralization, Imperialism, and Ottoman Sovereignty in the Arab Lands before 1914: Shakīb Arslān's Polemic Against the Decentralization Party." *Welt des Islams* 53, no. 1 (2013): 26–49.

Ateş, Sabri. *The Ottoman-Iranian Borderlands: Making a Boundary, 1843–1914*. Cambridge: Cambridge University Press, 2013.

Ayalon, Ami. "Malik in Modern Middle Eastern Titulature." *Die Welt des Islams*, New Series, 23–24 (1984): 306–19.

Aydin, Cemil. *The Idea of the Muslim World: A Global Intellectual History*. Cambridge: Harvard University Press, 2017.

Ayoub, Samy A. "The Mecelle, Sharia, and the Ottoman State: Fashioning and Refashioning of Islamic Law in the Nineteenth and Twentieth Centuries." *Journal of the Ottoman and Turkish Studies Association* 2, no. 1 (2015): 121–46.

———. *Law, Empire, and the Sultan: Ottoman Imperial Authority and Late Hanafi Jurisprudence*. New York: Oxford University Press, 2020.

Azari, Julia R., and Jennifer K. Smith. "Unwritten Rules: Informal Institutions in Established Democracies." *Perspectives on Politics* 10 (2012): 37–55.

Al-'Azm, 'Uthman, ed. *Majmu'at Athar Rafiq Bik al-'Azm*. Cairo: Matba'at al-Manar, 1925.

Al-'Azmah, 'Abd al-'Aziz. *Mira'at al-Sham*. London: Riad el-Rayyes Books, 1987.

Al-Azmeh, Aziz. *Islams and Modernities*, 2nd ed., London: Verso, 1996.

———. *Muslim Kingship: Power and the Sacred in Muslim, Christian and Pagan Polities*. London: I.B. Tauris, 1997.

———. "Monotheistic Kingship." In *Monotheistic Kingship: The Medieval Variants*, Aziz Al-Azmeh and János Bak, eds., 9–29. Budapest: CEU Press, 2004.

El Bakri, Alia. "'Memories of the Beloved': Oral Histories from the 1916–19 Siege of Medina." *International Journal of Middle East Studies*, 46 (2014): 703–18.

Baldwin, James E. *Islamic Law and Empire in Ottoman Cairo*. Edinburgh: Edinburgh University Press, 2017.

Al-Banna, Hasan. *Mudhakkirat al-Da'wa wa-l-Da'iyyin*. [Cairo]: Matabi' Dar al-Kitab al-'Arabi bi-Misr, Muhammad Hilmi al-Minyawi, 1950.

Barak, On. *On Time: Technology and Temporality in Modern Egypt*. Berkeley: University of California Press, 2013.

———. *Powering Empire: How Coal Made the Middle East and Sparked Global Carbonization*. Berkeley: University of California Press, 2020.

Barakat, Nora. "Underwriting the Empire: Nizamiye Courts, Tax Farming, and the Public Debt Administration in Ottoman Syria." *Islamic Law and Society* 26, no. 4 (2019): 374–404.

Barkey, Karen. "Thinking about Consequences of Empire." In *After Empire: Multiethnic Societies and Nation-building—The Soviet Union and the Russian, Ottoman, and Habsburg Empires*, Karen Barkey and Mark von Hagen, eds., 99–114. Boulder: Westview Press, 1997.

———. *Empire of Difference: The Ottomans in Comparative Perspective*. Cambridge: Cambridge University Press, 2008.

Barkey, Karen and Mark von Hagen, eds. *After Empire: Multiethnic Societies and Nation-building—The Soviet Union and the Russian, Ottoman, and Habsburg Empires*. Boulder: Westview Press, 1997.

Barut, Muhammad Jamal, ed. *Al-Hukuma al-'Arabiyya fi Dimashq: al-Tajraba al-Mubakkira li-l-Dawla al-'Arabiyya*. Doha: Arab Center for Research and Policy Studies, 2020.

Bashkin, Orit. *The Other Iraq: Pluralism and Culture in Hashemite Iraq*. Stanford: Stanford University Press, 2009.

Al-Batatuni, Muhammad Labib. *Al-Rihla al-Hijaziyya*. Cairo: al-Matba'a al-Jamaliyya, 1329.

Bayat, Fadil. "Al-Hukuma al-'Arabiyya." In *Al-Hukuma al-'Arabiyya fi Dimashq*, Muhammad Jamal Barut, ed., 351—89. Qatar: Al-Markaz al-'Arabi li-l-Abhath wa-Dirasat al-Siyasat, 2020.

Bayly, C. A. *Remaking the Modern World, 1900–2015: Global Connections and Comparisons*. Hoboken: John Wiley & Sons Ltd, 2018.

Bechor, Guy. *The Sanhuri Code and the Emergence of Modern Arab Civil Law (1932 to 1949)*. Leiden: Brill, 2007.

Becker, Peter and Natasha Wheatley, eds. *Remaking Central Europe: The League of Nations and the Former Habsburg Lands*. Oxford: Oxford University Press, 2020.

Bein, Amit. *Kemalist Turkey and the Middle East: International Relations in the Interwar Period*. Cambridge: Cambridge University Press, 2017.

Belgradi, Rashid. *Tarih-i Vak'a-i Hayret-nüma Belgrad ve Sırbistan*, 2 vols. Istanbul: Tatyos Dividjiyan Matba'ası, 1291 (1874).

Bell, Duncan. "Ideologies of Empire." In *The Oxford Handbook of Political Ideologies*, Michael Freeden, Lyman Tower Sargent, and Marc Stears, eds. 536–61. Oxford: Oxford University Press, 2013.

Benton, Lauren. *Law and Colonial Cultures: Legal Regimes in World History, 1400–1900*. Cambridge: Cambridge University Press, 2001.

———. *A Search for Sovereignty: Law and Geography in European Empires, 1400–1900*. Cambridge: Cambridge University Press, 2010.

Benton, Lauren, and Adam Clulow. "Empires and Protection: Making Interpolity Law in the Early Modern World." *Journal of Global History* 12, no. 1 (2017): 74–92.

Benton, Lauren, and Lisa Ford. *Rage for Order: The British Empire and the Origins of International Law, 1800–1850*. Cambridge, MA: Harvard University Press, 2017.

Bentwich, Norman. "The Legal Administration of Palestine under the British Military Occupation." *British Year Book of International Law* 1 (1920–1921): 139–48.

———. "XII. Palestine." *Journal of Comparative Legislation and International Law* 7, no. 3 (1925): 190–92.

Benvenisti, Eyal. *The International Law of Occupation*, 2nd ed. Oxford: Oxford University Press, 2012.

———. "Occupation, Belligerent." *Max Planck Encyclopedia of Public International Law*. New York: Oxford University Press, 2009.

———. "Occupation, Pacific." *Max Planck Encyclopedia of Public International Law*. New York: Oxford University Press, 2009.

Berger, Stefan, and Alexei Miller, eds. *Nationalizing Empires*. Budapest: CEU Press, 2015.

Bet-Shlimon, Arbella. *City of Black Gold: Oil, Ethnicity, and the Making of Modern Kirkuk*. Stanford: Stanford University Press, 2019.

Beverley, Eric Lewis. *Hyderabad, British India, and the World: Muslim Networks and Minor Sovereignty, c. 1850–1950*. Cambridge: Cambridge University Press, 2015.

Bhuta, Nehal. "The Antinomies of Transformative Occupation." *The European Journal of International Law* 16, no. 4 (2005): 721–40.

Biersteker, Thomas J. and Cynthia Weber, eds. *State Sovereignty as Social Construct*. Cambridge: Cambridge University Press, 1996.

Billings, Malcolm. "A Piece of Railway History," BBC, 14 January 2006, http://news.bbc.co.uk/2/hi/programmes/from_our_own_correspondent/4609450.stm, last viewed 1 June 2021.

Blatt, Joel. "France and Italy at the Paris Peace Conference." *The International History Review* 8, no. 1 (1986): 27–40.

Blunt, Wilfrid Scawen. *The Future of Islam*. London: Kegan Paul, Trench, 1882.

Bodin, Jean. *On Sovereignty: Four Chapters from the Six Books of the Commonwealth*, Julian H. Franklin, ed. and trans. Cambridge: Cambridge University Press, 1992.

Bosch, Firmin van den. *Vingt Années D'Égypte; Les Idées—les Hommes—les Faits—la Vie Politique—la Vie Judiciaire—la Vie Sociale et Mondaine—l'Art et l'Histoire.* Paris: Librairie Académique Perrin, 1932.

Bouquet, Olivier. *Les Pachas du Sultan: Essai sur les agents supérieurs de l'État ottoman (1839-1909).* Paris: Peeters, 2007.

———. "The Sultan's Sons-in-Law: Analysing Ottoman Imperial Damads." *JESHO* 58 (2015): 327–61.

Bowen Savant, Sarah, and Helena de Felipe, eds. *Genealogy and Knowledge in Muslim Societies.* Edinburgh: Edinburgh, 2014.

Bozarslan, Hamit. "Le prince Sabaheddin (1879–1948)." *Schweizerische Zeitschrift für Geschichte* 52, no. 3 (2002): 287–301.

Bradshaw, Tancred. *Britain and Jordan: Imperial Strategy, King Abdullah I and the Zionist Movement.* London: I.B. Tauris, 2012.

Brilliant, Richard, and Dale Kinney, eds. *Reuse Value: Spolia and Appropriation in Art and Architecture from Constantine to Sherrie Levine.* Farnham: Ashgate, 2011.

Brilliant, Richard. "I piedistalli del giardino di Boboli: spolia in se, spolia in re." *Prospettiva* 31 (1982): 2–17.

Brown, L. Carl. *The Tunisia of Ahmad Bey, 1837-1855.* Princeton: Princeton University Press, 1974.

———, ed. *Imperial Legacy—The Ottoman Imprint on the Balkans and the Middle East.* New York, NY: Columbia University Press, 1996.

Brown, Nathan J. "Who or What Is the Wali al-Amr: The Unposed Question." Forthcoming, Oñati Socio-Legal Series. Available at SSRN: https://ssrn.com/abstract=3346372.

Brubaker, Rogers. *Nationalism Reframed: Nationhood and the National Question in the New Europe.* Cambridge: Cambridge University Press, 1996.

Bryant, Rebecca. "Introduction." In *Post-Ottoman Coexistence: Sharing Space in the Shadow of Conflict*, Rebecca Bryant, ed., 1–38. New York: Berghahn Books, 2016.

Bsheer, Rosie. "A Counter-Revolutionary State: Popular Movements and the Making of Saudi Arabia." *Past & Present* 238, no. 1 (2018): 233–77.

———. *Archive Wars: The Politics of History in Saudi Arabia.* Stanford: Stanford University Press, 2020.

Buckler, F. W. "The Political Theory of the Indian Mutiny." *Transactions of the Royal Historical Society* 5 (1922): 71–100.

Burbank, Jane. "Eurasian Sovereignty: The Case of Kazan." *Problems of Post-Communism* 62, no. 1 (2015): 1–25.

———. "Empire and Transformation—The Politics of Difference." In *Comparing Modern Empires: Imperial Rule and Decolonization in the Changing World Order*, Tomohiko Uyama, ed., 11–33. [Tokyo?]: Sapporo Slavic Research Center, Hokkaido University, 2018.

Burbank, Jane and Frederick Cooper. *Empires in World History: Power and the Politics of Difference.* Princeton: Princeton University Press, 2010.

———. "Empires after 1919: Old, New, Transformed." *International Affairs* 95, no. 1 (2019): 81–100.

Burdett, A.L.P., ed. *Arab Dissident Movements, 1905-1955.* Vol. 1: 1905–1920. [London?]: Archive Editions, 1996.

Burj, Muhammad 'Abd al-Rahman. *Muhibb al-Din al-Khatib wa-Dawruhu fi al-Haraka al-'Arabiyya, 1906–1920*. Cairo: al-Hay'a al-Misriyya al-'Amma li-l-Kitab, 1990.

Burke, Edmund, III. *The Ethnographic State: France and the Invention of Moroccan Islam*. Berkeley: University of California Press, 2014.

al-Bustani, Butrus. *Da'irat al-Ma'arif*, vol. 1. Beirut: n. p., 1876.

Buzpinar, Tufan Ş. "The Hijaz, Abdulhamid II and Amir Hussein's Secret Dealings with the British, 1877–80." *Middle Eastern Studies* 31 (1995): 99–123.

———. "Opposition to the Ottoman Caliphate in the Early Years of Abdülhamid II, 1877–1882." *Die Welt des Islams* 36, no. 1 (1996): 59–89.

———. "Vying for Power and Influence in the Hijaz: Ottoman Rule, The Last Emirate of Abdulmuttalib and the British (1880–1882)." *The Muslim World* 95 (2005): 1–22.

Can, Lâle. *Spiritual Subjects: Central Asian Pilgrims and the Ottoman Hajj at the End of Empire*. Stanford: Stanford University Press, 2020.

Can, Lâle, Michael Christopher Low, Kent F. Schull, and Robert Zens, eds. *The Subjects of Ottoman International Law*. Bloomington: Indiana University Press, 2020.

Can, Lâle, and Aimee M. Genell. "On Empire and Exception: Genealogies of Sovereignty in the Ottoman World." *Comparative Studies of South Asia, Africa and the Middle East* 40, 3 (2020): 468–473.

Cardon, Louis. *Le régime de la propriété foncière en Syrie et au Liban*. Paris: Recueil Sirey, 1932.

Casanova, José. *Public Religions in the Modern World*. Chicago: University of Chicago Press, 1994.

Ceylan, Ayhan. *Osmanlı Taşra Idarî Tarzı Olarak Eyâlet-i Mümtaze ve Mısır Uygulaması*. Istanbul: Kitabevi, 2014.

Çiçek, M. Talha. "Visions of Islamic Unity: A Comparison of Djemal Pasha's Al-Sharq and Sharīf Ḥusayn's Al-Qibla Periodicals." *Welt Des Islams* 54 nos. 3–4 (2014): 460–82.

———. *War and State Formation in Syria: Cemal Pasha's Governorate during World War I, 1914–17*. Abingdon: Routledge, 2014.

Chakrabarty, Dipesh. *Provincializing Europe: Postcolonial Thought and Historical Difference*. Princeton: Princeton University Press, 2000.

———. *The Climate of History in a Planetary Age*. Chicago: University of Chicago Press, 2021.

Chantre, Luc, ed. *Un administrateur colonial au Cœur de l'islam: Rapport de Paul Gillotte sur le Pèlerinage des Algériens à la Mecque en 1905*. Aix-en-Provence: Presses universitaires de Provence, 2016.

Charbonnier, Pierre. *Affluence and Freedom: An Environmental History of Political Ideas*. Cambridge: Polity Press, 2021.

Charmes, Gabriel. *L'avenir de la Turquie: le Panislamisme*. Paris: Calmann Lévy, 1883.

Chatterjee, Partha. "Whose Imagined Community?" In *Mapping the Nation*, edited by Gopal Balakrishnan, 214–225. London: Verso, 1996.

Chaudhry, Kiren Aziz. *The Price of Wealth: Economies and Institutions in the Middle East*. Ithaca: Cornell University Press, 1997.

Cheta, Omar Youssef. "A Prehistory of the Modern Legal Profession in Egypt." *International Journal of Middle East Studies* 50 (2018), 649–68.

Choueiri, Yusuf. "Two Histories of Syria and the Demise of Syrian Patriotism." *Middle Eastern Studies* 23, no. 4 (1987): 496–511.

Chowdhuri, Ramendra Nath. *International Mandates and Trusteeship Systems: A Comparative Study.* Gravenhage: Martinus Nijhoff, 1955.

Citino, Nathan J. "The Ottoman Legacy in Cold War Modernization." *International Journal of Middle East Studies* 40, no. 4 (2008), 579–97.

Colley, Linda. *The Gun, the Ship, and the Pen: Warfare, Constitutions, and the Making of the Modern World.* New York: Liveright Publishing Corporation, a Division of W. W. Norton & Company, 2021.

Collins, Michael. "Decolonisation and the 'Federal Moment.'" *Diplomacy & Statecraft* 24 (2013): 21–40.

Commins, David Dean. *Islamic Reform: Politics and Social Change in Late Ottoman Syria.* New York: Oxford University Press, 1990.

———. *The Wahhabi Mission and Saudi Arabia.* London: I.B. Tauris, 2006.

Conrad, Sebastian. *What Is Global History?* Princeton: Princeton University Press, 2016.

Cooper, Frederick. *Colonialism in Question: Theory, Knowledge, History.* Berkeley: University of California Press, 2005.

———. *Citizenship between Empire and Nation: Remaking France and French Africa, 1945-1960.* Princeton: Princeton University Press, 2014.

———. "Routes Out of Empire." *Comparative Studies of South Asia, Africa and the Middle East* 37, no. 2 (2017): 406–11.

Crouzet, Guillemette. *Genèses du Moyen-Orient: Le Golfe persique à l'âge des imperialisms (vers 1800—vers 1914).* [Ceyzérieu (Ain)]: Champ Vallon, 2015.

Culang Jeffrey. "'The Shari'a Must Go': Seduction, Moral Injury, and Religious Freedom in Egypt's Liberal Age." *Comparative Studies in Society and History* 60, no. 2 (2018): 446–75.

Cummings, Sally N. and Raymond A. Hinnebusch, eds. *Sovereignty after Empire: Comparing the Middle East and Central Asia.* Edinburgh: Edinburgh University Press, 2011.

Dahlan, Ahmad Ibn Zayni. *Khulasat al-Kalam fi Bayan Umara' al-Balad al-Haram.* Cairo: Al-Matba'a al-Khayriyya, 1305.

Darwaza, Muhammad 'Izzat. *Mudhakkirat.* Beirut: Dar al-Gharb al-Islami, 1993.

Darwin, John. "An Undeclared Empire: The British in the Middle East, 1918–39." *Journal of Imperial and Commonwealth History* 27, no. 2 (1999): 159–76.

———. *Britain, Egypt, and the Middle East: Imperial Policy in the Aftermath of War, 1918-1922.* London: Macmillan Press, 1981.

———. *After Tamerlane: The Global History of Empire.* London: Allen Lane, 2007.

———. *The Empire Project: The Rise and Fall of the British World-system, 1830-1970.* Cambridge: Cambridge University Press, 2009.

Davison, Roderic H. *Reform in the Ottoman Empire, 1856-1876.* Princeton: Princeton University Press, 2015.

Dawn, C. Ernest. "The Rise of Arabism in Syria." *Middle East Journal,* 16, 2 (1962), 145–68.

———. *From Ottomanism to Arabism: Essays on the Origins of Arab Nationalism.* Urbana: University of Illinois Press, 1973.

De, Rohit. *A People's Constitution: The Everyday Life of Law in the Indian Republic*. Princeton: Princeton University Press, 2018.

Debs, Richard A. *Islamic Law and Civil Code: The Law of Property in Egypt*. New York: Columbia University Press, 2010.

Deeb, Marius. *Party Politics in Egypt: The Wafd & Its Rivals, 1919–1939*. London: Ithaca Press for the Middle East Centre, St Antony's College, Oxford, 1979.

Deringil, Selim. "The Ottoman Twilight Zone of the Middle East." In *Reluctant Neighbor: Turkey's Role in the Middle East*, Henry Barkey, ed., 13–22. Washington DC: US Institute of Peace, 1996.

——. *The Well-Protected Domains: Ideology and the Legitimation of Power in the Ottoman Empire, 1876–1909*. London: I.B. Tauris, 1998.

——. "'They Live in a State of Nomadism and Savagery': The Late Ottoman Empire and the Post-Colonial Debate." *Comparative Studies in Society and History* 45, no. 2 (2003): 311–42.

——. *The Ottoman Twilight in the Arab Lands: Turkish Memoirs and Testimonies of the Great War*. Brighton: Academic Studies Press, 2019.

Devji, Faisal. *Muslim Zion: Pakistan as a Political Idea*. Cambridge: Harvard University Press, 2013.

Di-Capua, Yoav. *Gatekeepers of the Arab Past: Historians and History Writing in Twentieth-Century Egypt*. Berkeley: University of California Press, 2009.

Dicey, A. V. *Introduction to the Study of the Law of the Constitution*. Reprint of 1915 (8th) Edition. Indianapolis: Liberty, 1982.

Dirks, Nicholas B. *The Hollow Crown: Ethnohistory of an Indian Kingdom*. Ann Arbor: University of Michigan Press, 1993.

Djemal Pasha. *Memoirs of a Turkish Statesman, 1913–1919*. London: Hutchinson & Co, 1922.

Dodge, Toby. *Inventing Iraq: The Failure of Nation Building and a History Denied*. New York: Columbia University Press, 2003.

Duara, Prasenjit. *Rescuing History from the Nation: Questioning Narratives of Modern China*. Chicago: University of Chicago Press, 1995.

——. *Sovereignty and Authenticity: Manchukuo and the East Asian Modern*. Lanham: Rowman & Littlefield Publishers, 2003.

——. *The Crisis of Global Modernity: Asian Traditions and a Sustainable Future*. Cambridge: Cambridge University Press, 2015.

Duindam, Jeroen. *Dynasties: A Global History of Power, 1300–1800*. Cambridge: Cambridge University Press, 2016.

Duve, Thomas. "What is Global Legal History?" *Comparative Legal History* 8, no. 2 (2020): 73–115.

Dworkin, Ronald. *Law's Empire*. Cambridge: Belknap Press, 1986.

Edgerton, David. *The Shock of the Old: Technology and Global History since 1900*. Oxford: Oxford University Press, 2007.

Edwards, Laura F. *A Legal History of the Civil War and Reconstruction: A Nation of Rights*. New York: Cambridge University Press, 2015.

Egry, Gábor. "Negotiating Post-Imperial Transitions." In *Embers of Empire: Continuity and Rupture in the Habsburg Successor States after 1918*, Paul B. Miller and Claire Morelon, eds., 15–42. New York: Berghahn Books, 2019.

Eich, Thomas. *Abū L-Hudā Aṣ-Ṣayyādī: Eine Studie Zur Instrumentalisierung Sufischer Netzwerke und Genealogischer Kontroversen im Spätosmanischen Reich.* Berlin: Klaus Schwarz, 2003.

———. "The Forgotten Salafi-Abu l-Huda as-Sayyadi." *Welt des Islams* 43, no. 1 (2003): 61–87.

———. "Abū L-Hudā L-Sayyādī—Still Such a Polarizing Figure (Response to Itzchak Weismann)." *Arabica* 55, no. 3 (2008): 433–44.

Eisenstadt, S. N. "Multiple Modernities." *Daedalus* 129, no. 1 (2000): 1–29.

Ekinci, Ekrem Buğra. *Osmanli Mahkemeleri: Tanzimat ve Sonrası* Istanbul: Ari Sanat, 2004.

Ekmekçioğlu, Lerna. *Recovering Armenia: The Limits of Belonging in Post-Genocide Turkey.* Stanford: Stanford University Press, 2016.

Eldem, Edhem. "Sultan Abdülhamid II: Founding Father of the Turkish State? (Keynote Address)." *Journal of the Ottoman and Turkish Studies Association* 5, no. 2 (2018): 25–46.

Elliott, J. H. "A Europe of Composite Monarchies." *Past & Present* 137 (1992): 48–71.

Ellis, Matthew H. "Repackaging the Egyptian Monarchy: King Faruq in the Public Spotlight, 1936–39." *History Compass* 7, no. 1 (2009): 181–213.

———. *Desert Borderland: The Making of Modern Egypt and Libya.* Stanford: Stanford University Press, 2018.

Elyachar, Julia. "Next Practices: Knowledge, Infrastructure, and Public Goods at the Bottom of the Pyramid." *Public Culture* 24, no. 1 (2012): 109–29.

Emerit, Marcel. "La crise syrienne et l'expansion économique française en 1860." *Revue Historique* 207, Fasc. 2 (1952): 211–32.

Al-Enazy, Askar H. *The Creation of Saudi Arabia: Ibn Saud and British Imperial Policy, 1914–1927.* Milton Park: Routledge, 2010.

Erakat, Noura. *Justice for Some: Law and the Question of Palestine.* Stanford: Stanford University Press, 2019.

D'Eramo, Marco. "American Decline." *New Left Review* 135 (May-June 2022): 5–21.

Eraslan, Zeki. *Şura'yı Devletten Danıştaya: Yapısal ve Fonksiyonel Dönüşüm (1868–1922).* Ankara: Türk Tarih Kurumu, 2018.

Ersoy, Ahmet, Maciej Górny, and Vangelis Kechriotis, eds. *Discourses of Collective Identity in Central and Southeast Europe (1770–1945): Texts and Commentaries, Vol. III:1, Modernism: The Creation of Nation-States.* Budapest: CEU Press, 2010.

Fahmi, 'Abd al-'Aziz. *Hadhihi Hayati.* [Cairo]: Dar al-Hilal, 1963.

Fahmi, Hasan. *Muhammad Tawfiq al-Bakri.* Cairo: Dar al-Kitab al-'Arabi, 1967.

Fahmy, Khaled. *In Quest of Justice: Islamic Law and Forensic Medicine in Modern Egypt.* Berkeley: University of California Press, 2018.

Fahrenthold, Stacy D. *Between the Ottomans and the Entente: The First World War in the Syrian and Lebanese Diaspora, 1908–1925.* New York: Oxford University Press, 2019.

Falls, Cyril and A. F. Becke, eds. *Military Operations—Egypt & Palestine,* vol. 2. London: His Majesty's Stationery Office, 1930.

Fancy, Hussein. "2. Of Sovereigns, Sacred Kings, And Polemics." *History and Theory* 56, no. 1 (2017): 61–70.

Faroqhi, Suraiya. *Pilgrims and Sultans: The Hajj under the Ottomans, 1517–1683*. London: I.B. Tauris, 1994.

———. *The Ottoman Empire and the World around It*. London: I.B. Tauris, 2004.

Faydi, Sulayman. *Fi Ghamrat al-Nidal: Mudhakkirat Sulayman Faydi*. Baghdad: ['Abd al-Hamid Sulaymān Faydi], 1952.

Feldman, Noah. "Imposed Constitutionalism." *Connecticut Law Review* 37, no. 4 (2005): 857–90.

———. *The Fall and Rise of the Islamic State*. Princeton: Princeton University Press, 2008.

Ferguson, Niall. *Empire: The Rise and Demise of the British World Order and the Lessons for Global Power*. New York: Basic Books, 2003.

Fieldhouse, D. K. *Western Imperialism in the Middle East, 1914–1958*. Oxford: Oxford University Press, 2006.

Fischel, Roy S. *Local States in an Imperial World*. Edinburgh: Edinburgh University Press, 2020.

Fitzgerald, Edward Peter. "The Iraq Petroleum Company, Standard Oil of California, and the Contest for Eastern Arabia, 1930–1933." *International History Review* 13, no. 3 (1991): 441–65.

Fitzmaurice, Andrew. *Sovereignty, Property, and Empire, 1500–2000*. Cambridge: Cambridge University Press, 2014.

Fitzsimons, M. A. *Empire by Treaty: Britain and the Middle East in the Twentieth Century*. London: Ernest Benn, 1965.

Foliard, Daniel. "'More than one Palestine': Nationalist Cartographies, the Middle East and the 1919 Peace Negotiations in Paris." In *Redrawing the World: 1919 and the History of Cartography*, Peter Nekola, ed. Chicago: University of Chicago Press, forthcoming.

Ford, Lisa. *The King's Peace: Law and Order in the British Empire*. Cambridge: Harvard University Press, 2021.

Fortna, Benjamin C. *The Circassian: A Life of Eşref Bey, Late Ottoman Insurgent and Special Agent*. Oxford: Oxford University Press, 2016.

Foucault, Michel. *"Society Must Be Defended": Lectures at the Collège de France, 1975–1976*. New York: Picador, 2003.

Freitag, Ulrike. *A History of Jeddah: The Gate to Mecca in the Nineteenth and Twentieth Centuries*. Cambridge: Cambridge University Press, 2020.

———. *Indian Ocean Migrants and State Formation in Hadhramaut: Reforming the Homeland*. Leiden, Boston: Brill, 2003.

Fromkin, David. *A Peace to End All Peace: Creating the Modern Middle East, 1914–1922*. London: A. Deutsch, 1989.

Fujinami, Nobuyoshi. "Decentralizing Centralists, or the Political Language on Provincial Administration in the Second Ottoman Constitutional Period." *Middle Eastern Studies* 49, no. 6 (2013): 880–900.

———. "Between Sovereignty and Suzerainty: History of the Ottoman Privileged Provinces." In *A World History of Suzerainty: A Modern History of East and West Asia and Translated Concepts*, by Takashi Okamoto, ed., 41–69. Tokyo: Toyo Bunko, 2019.

Galison, Peter. *Einstein's Clocks, Poincaré's Maps: Empires of Time*. New York: W.W. Norton, 2003.

Gayffier-Bonneville, Anne-Claire De. *L'Échec de la monarchie égyptienne, 1942–1952.* Cairo: Institut Français d'archéologie orientale, 2010.

Gedikli, Fethi. *Şura-yı Devlet: Belgeler, Biyografik Bilgiler ve Örnek Kararlarıyla.* Istanbul: On İki Levha Yayıncılık, 2018.

Geertz, Clifford. *Negara: The Theatre State in Nineteenth-Century Bali.* Princeton: Princeton University Press, 1980.

Gelvin, James L. "The Other Arab Nationalism: Syrian/Arab Populism in Its Historical and International Contexts." In *Rethinking Nationalism in the Arab Middle East*, James Jankowski and Israel Gershoni, eds., 231–48. New York: Columbia University Press, 1997.

———. *Divided Loyalties: Nationalism and Mass Politics in Syria at the Close of Empire.* Berkeley: University of California Press, 1998.

Gelvin, James L., and Nile Green, eds. *Global Muslims in the Age of Steam and Print.* Berkeley: University of California Press, 2013.

Genell, Aimee M. "Autonomous Provinces and the Problem of 'Semi-Sovereignty' in European International Law." *Journal of Balkan and Near Eastern Studies* 18, no. 6 (2016): 533–49.

———. "The End of Egypt's Occupation—Ottoman Sovereignty and the British Declaration of Protection." In *Beyond Versailles: Sovereignty, Legitimacy, and the Formation of New Polities after the Great War*, Marcus M. Payk and Roberta Pergher, eds., 77–98. Bloomington, Indiana: Indiana University Press, 2019.

Georgeon, François. "Changes of Time: An Aspect of Ottoman Modernization." *New Perspectives on Turkey* 44 (2011): 181–95.

———. "Temps de la réforme, réforme du temps. Les avatars de l'heure et du calendrier à la fin de l'Empire ottoman." In *Les Ottomans et le temps*, François Georgeon and Frédéric Hitzel, eds., 241–79. Leiden: Brill, 2012.

———and Noémi Lévy-Aksu, eds. *The Young Turk Revolution and the Ottoman Empire: The Aftermath of 1908.* New York: I.B. Tauris, 2017.

Gershoni, Israel, and James P. Jankowski. *Egypt, Islam, and the Arabs: The Search for Egyptian Nationhood, 1900–1930.* New York: Oxford University Press, 1986.

———. *Redefining the Egyptian Nation, 1930–1945.* New York: Cambridge University Press, 1995.

Gerstle, Gary. *The Rise and Fall of the Neoliberal Order: America and the World in the Free Market Era.* New York: Oxford University Press, 2022.

Gerwarth, Robert. *The Vanquished: Why the First World War Failed to End, 1917–1923.* London: Allen Lane, 2016.

Gerwarth, Robert, and Erez Manela. "The Great War as a Global War: Imperial Conflict and the Reconfiguration of World Order, 1911–1923." *Diplomatic History* 38, no. 4 (2014): 786–800.

Getachew, Adom. *Worldmaking after Empire: the Rise and Fall of Self-Determination.* Princeton: Princeton University Press, 2019.

Al-Gharib, Muhammad. *Al-Dalil al-Murshid fi Qawanin wa-l-Awamir wa-l-Manshurat li-l-Mahakim al-Shar'iyya wa-l-Majalis al-Hisbiyya.* Cairo: Matba'at al-Nasr, 1935.

Al-Ghazi, 'Abd Allah bin Muhammad. *Ifadat al-Anam bi-Dhikr Akhbar Balad Allah al-Haram.* Mecca: Maktabat al-Asadi li-l-Nashr wa-l-Tawzi', 2009.

Al-Ghazzi, Fawzi. *Al-Huquq al-Duwaliyya al-ʿAmma*. Vol. 1. Damascus: Matbaʿat Hukumat Dimashq, 1922.

Al-Ghazzi, Kamil. *Nahr al-Dhahab fi Tarikh Halab*. Vol. 3. Aleppo: al-Matbaʾa al-Maruniyya, 1926.

Ghobrial, John-Paul A. "The Secret Life of Elias of Babylon and the Uses of Global Microhistory." *Past & Present* 222 (2014): 51–93.

Gilbert, Michelle. "The Person of the King: Ritual and Power in a Ghanian State." In *Rituals of Royalty: Power and Ceremonial in Traditional Societies*, David Cannadine and S.R.F. Price, eds., 298–330. Cambridge: Cambridge University Press, 1992.

Goebel, Michael. Anti-Imperial Metropolis: Interwar Paris and the Seeds of Third World Nationalism. New York: Cambridge University Press, 2015.

Goffman, Daniel, and Christopher Stroop. "Empire as Composite: The Ottoman Polity and the Typology of Dominion." In *Imperialisms: Historical and Literary Investigations, 1500–1900*, E. Sauer and B. Rajan, eds., 129–45. New York: Palgrave Macmillan US, 2004.

Goldziher, Ignác. *A Nemzetiségi Kérdés az Araboknál*. Budapest: Eggenbergerféle M. Akadémiai Könyvkereskedés, 1873.

Gomaa, Ahmad M. "The Syrian Throne." In *The Great Powers in the Middle East, 1919–1939*, Uriel Dann, ed., 183–96. New York: Holmes & Meier, 1988.

Göreli, İsmail Hakkı. *Devlet Şûrası*. Ankara: Yeni Matbaa, 1953.

De Graaf, Beatrice. "Bringing Sense and Sensibility to the Continent: Vienna 1815 revisited." *Journal of Modern European History* 13, 4 (2015): 447–57.

Gramsci, Antonio. *Prison Notebooks*. Vol. 2. New York: Columbia University Press, 1996.

Greble, Emily. *Muslims and the Making of Modern Europe*. New York: Oxford University Press, 2021.

Griffith, J.A.G. "The Political Constitution." *The Modern Law Review* 42, no. 1 (1979): 1–21.

Hacohen, Malachi Haim. *Jacob & Esau: Jewish European History between Nation and Empire*. Cambridge: Cambridge University Press, 2019.

Haddad, Mahmoud. "Arab Religious Nationalism in the Colonial Era: Rereading Rashid Rida's Ideas on the Caliphate." *Journal of the American Oriental Society* 117, no. 2 (1997): 253–77.

Al-Hafiz, Muhammad Mutiʿ. *Jamʿiyyat al-ʿUlamaʾ bi-Dimashq min Sanat 1356 hatta 1360 Hijrī wa-1937 hatta 1941 Miladi*. Damascus: Dar Tayba, 2014.

———, ed. *Hawadith Dimashq al-Yawmiyya*. Damascus: Dar Tayba li-l-Tibaʿa wa-l-Nashr wa-l-Tawziʿ, 2017.

Haim, Sylvia G. "Alfieri and al-Kawakibi." *Oriente Moderno* 34, no. 7 (1954): 321–34.

———. "Blunt and al-Kawakibi." *Oriente Moderno* 35, no. 2 (1955): 132–43.

———. *Arab Nationalism: An Anthology*. Berkeley: University of California Press, 1976.

Hajdarpašić, Edin. "Out of the Ruins of the Ottoman Empire: Reflections on the Ottoman Legacy in South-Eastern Europe." *Middle Eastern Studies* 44, no. 5 (2008): 715–34.

Hajrah, Hassan Hamza. *Public Land Distribution in Saudi Arabia*. London: Longman, 1982.

Al-Hakim, Yusuf. *Suriya wa-l-ʿAhd al-Faysali*. Beirut: Dar al-Nahar, 1966.

Hakkı, Ibrahim. *Hukuk-i Idare*. 2 vols. Istanbul: Karabat Matbaʿası, 1312.

Halevi, Leor. *Modern Things on Trial: Islam's Global and Material Reformation in the Age of Rida, 1865–1935*. New York, NY: Columbia University Press, 2019.

Hallaq, Wael B. *The Origins and Evolution of Islamic Law*. Cambridge: Cambridge University Press, 2005.

——. *Shariʿa: Theory, Practice, Transformations*. Cambridge: Cambridge University Press, 2009.

Halliday, Fred. *The Middle East in International Relations: Power, Politics, and Ideology*. Cambridge: Cambridge University Press, 2005.

Halperin, Sandra. "Imperial City States, National States, and Post-National Spatialities." In *Legacies of Empire: Imperial Roots of the Contemporary Global Order*, Sandra Halperin and Ronen Palan, eds., 69–95. Cambridge: Cambridge University Press, 2015.

Halperin, Sandra, and Ronen Palan, eds. *Legacies of Empire: Imperial Roots of the Contemporary Global Order*. Cambridge: Cambridge University Press, 2015.

Hammad, Muhammad. *Qissat al-Dustur al-Misri—Maʿaruk wa-Watha'iq wa-Nusus*. Cairo: Maktabat Jazirat al-Ward, 2011.

Hamza, Fuʾad. *Qalb Jazirat al-ʿArab*. Cairo: Al-Matbaʿa al-Salafiyya, 1933.

——. *Al-Bilad al-ʿArabiyya al-Saʿudiyya*. Mecca: Matbaʿat Umm al-Qura, 1937.

——. *Mudhakkirat wa-Watha'iq*, 2 vols. [Riyadh]: Darat al-Malik ʿAbd al-ʿAziz, 2016.

Hanioğlu, M. Sükrü. *The Young Turks in Opposition*. Oxford: Oxford University Press, 1995.

——. *A Brief History of the Late Ottoman Empire*. Princeton: Princeton University Press, 2010.

Hanley, Will. *Identifying with Nationality: Europeans, Ottomans, and Egyptians in Alexandria*. New York: Columbia University Press, 2017.

Hanna, Murqus. *Kitab Nizam al-Hukuma al-Misriyya*. Cairo: Matbaʿat al-Tawfiq, 1896.

Hansen, Thomas Blom, and Finn Stepputat. "Sovereignty Revisited." *Annual Review of Anthropology* 35 (2006): 295–315.

Hardt, Michael, and Antonio Negri. *Empire*. Cambridge: Harvard University Press, 2000.

Haridi, Farghali ʿAli Tusun. *Al-Haraka al-Dusturiyya fi Misr, 1923–1952*. Alexandria: Dar al-Wafaʾ li-Dunya al-Tibaʿa wa-l-Nashr, 2012.

Hart, H.L.A. *The Concept of Law*, 2nd ed., Oxford: Calendron Press, 1994.

Hartmann, Martin. *Reisebriefe aus Syrien*. Berlin: Reimer, 1913.

Hassan, Mona. *Longing for the Lost Caliphate: A Transregional History*. Princeton: Princeton University Press, 2017.

Hathaway, Jane, and Karl K. Barbir. *The Arab Lands under Ottoman Rule, 1516–1800*. Harlow: Pearson Longman, 2008.

Haydar, Muhammad Rustum. *Mudhakkirat Rustum Haydar*, ed. Najda Fathi Safwa. Beirut: Al-Dar al-ʿArabiyya li-l-Mawsuʿat, 1988.

Haykel, Bernard. "Western Arabia and Yemen during the Ottoman Period." In *The New Cambridge History of Islam*, vol. 2, Maribel Fierro, ed., 436–50. Cambridge: Cambridge University Press, 2010.

——. "Oil in Saudi Arabian Culture and Politics." In *Saudi Arabia in Transition: Insights on Social, Political, Economic and Religious Change*, Bernard Haykel,

Thomas Hegghammer, and Stéphane Lacroix, eds., 125–47. Cambridge: Cambridge University Press, 2015.

Herreros, E. G. *Sa Majesté le Roi Fouad Ier*. Alexandria: Whitehead Morris Limited, 1930.

Hertslet, Edward. *The Map of Europe by Treaty: Showing the Various Political and Territorial Changes Which Have Taken Place since the General Peace of 1814.* 4 vols. London: Butterworths, 1875.

Hilal, 'Imad. *Al-Ifta' al-Misri: Min al-Sahabi 'Uqba Ibn 'Amir Ila al-Duktur 'Ali Jum'a.* 5 vols. Cairo: Matba'at Dar al-Kutub wa-l-Watha'iq al-Qawmiyya, 2010–2016.

Hill, Enid. "Al-Sanhuri and Islamic Law: The Place and Significance of Islamic Law in the Life and Work of 'Abd Al-Razzaq Ahmad Al-Sanhuri, Egyptian Jurist and Scholar, 1895 -1971." *Arab Law Quarterly* 3, no. 1 (1988): 33–64.

Hillis, Faith. *Utopia's Discontents: Russian Émigrés and the Quest for Freedom, 1830s-1930s.* New York: Oxford University Press, 2021.

Al-Himsi, Lina. *Al-Muftun al-'Ammun fi Suriyya: Mundhu Intiha' al-'Ahd al-'Uthmani wa-hatta al-Waqt al-Hadir wa-Ba'd Fatawahim al-Rasmiyya li-l-Umur al-Mustajadda.* Damascus: Dar al-'Asma', 1996.

Ho, Engseng. *The Graves of Tarim: Genealogy and Mobility across the Indian Ocean.* Berkeley: University of California Press, 2006.

Hobsbawm, Eric J. "Introduction: Inventing Traditions." In *The Invention of Tradition*, E. J. Hobsbawm and T. O. Ranger, eds., 1–14. Cambridge: Cambridge University Press, 2005.

———. *Age of Extremes: The Short Twentieth Century, 1914–1991.* London: Abacus, 1995.

Hoijer, Olof. *Le pacte de la Société des nations: commentaire théorique et pratique.* Paris: Editions Spes, 1926.

Holbraad, Carsten. *The Concert of Europe: A Study in German and British International Theory, 1815–1914.* New York: Barnes & Noble, 1971.

Honvault, Juliette. "World War I and the Perspective of a Hashemite Order in Yemen. Study of the Chronicle of Isma'il b. Muhammad al-Washali." In *The First World War from Tripoli to Addis Ababa (1911–1924)*, Shiferaw Bekele et al., eds., Electronic edition. Addis Abbeba: Centre français des études éthiopiennes, 2018, http://books.openedition.org/cfee/1341.

Hourani, Albert Habib. *Arabic Thought in the Liberal Age, 1798–1939.* Cambridge: Cambridge University Press, 1983.

Hughes, Thomas P. "The Evolution of Large Technological Systems." In *The Social Construction of Technological Systems*, edited by Wiebe Bijker, Thomas P. Hughes, and Trevor Pinch, eds., 45–46. Cambridge: MIT Press, 1987.

Huntington, Samuel P. *The Political Order in Changing Societies.* New Haven: Yale University Press, 1968.

Al-Husayn, 'Abd Allah b. *Mudhakkirati.* Amman: al-Ahliyya li-l-Nashar wa-l-Tawzi', 1989.

Al-Husayni, Taj al-Din ibn Muhammad. *Ghayat al-Ikhtisar fi Akhbar al-Buyatat al-'Alawiyya al-Mahfuza min al-Ghubar.* Cairo: Al-Matba'a al-Amiriyya, 1892.

Al-Husni, Muhammad Adib Al Taqi al-Din. *Kitab Muntakhabat al-Tawarikh li-Dimashq.* Damascus: al-Matba'a al-Haditha, 1927.

Ibn Khaldun, *Muqaddima*, 'Abd Allah Muhammad al-Darwish, ed., vol. 1. Damascus: Dar al-Ya'rab, 2004.

Ibn Qudama. *Al-Mughni*. 12 vols. Cairo: Matba'at al-Manar, 1921–1929/30.

Imber, Colin. *Ebu's-su'ud: The Islamic Legal Tradition*. Stanford: Stanford University Press, 1997.

Ireland, Philip Willard. *'Iraq: a Study in Political Development*. New York: Macmillan, 1938.

Al-'Isa, Abd al-'Aziz b. Muhammad al-Fahd. *Arshif Mamlakat al-Hijaz wa-Saltanat Najd wa-Mulhaqatihi*. Beirut: Jadawil, 2013.

Işıktaş, Bilen. *Şerif Muhiddin Targan: Modernleşme, Bireyselleşme, Virtüozite*. Istanbul: Bilgi Üniversitesi İktisadi İşletmesi, 2018.

Al-Jabarti, 'Abd al-Rahman. *'Aja'ib al-Athar fi al-Tarajim wa-l-Akhbar*, Shmuel Moreh, ed., 4 vols. Jerusalem: al-Jami'a al-'Ibriyya, 2013.

Jackson, Sherman A. *Islamic Law and the State: The Constitutional Jurisprudence of Shihāb Al-Dīn Al-Qarāfī*. Leiden: E.J. Brill, 1996.

Jackson, Simon. "What is Syria Worth?", *Monde(s)* 4, no. 2 (2013), 83–103.

Jackson, Simon and Dirk A. Moses. "Transformative Occupations in the Modern Middle East." *Humanity: An International Journal of Human Rights, Humanitarianism, and Development* 8, no. 2 (2017): 231–46.

Jacob, Wilson Chacko. *For God or Empire: Sayyid Fadl and the Indian Ocean World*. Stanford: Stanford University Press, 2019.

Jakes, Aaron. *Egypt's Occupation: Colonial Economism and the Crises of Capitalism*. Stanford: Stanford University Press, 2020.

———. "Peaceful Wars." *Comparative Studies in Society and History*. Forthcoming.

Al-Jami'i, 'Abd al-Mun'am Ibrahim al-Disuqi. *Madrasat al-Qada' al-Shar'i, 1907–1930*. Cairo: Matba'at al-Jiblawi, 1986.

Jankowski, James. "Ottomanism and Arabism in Egypt, 1860–1914." *The Muslim World* 70, no. 3–4 (1980): 226–59.

Johansen, Baber. *The Islamic Law on Land Tax and Rent: The Peasants' Loss of Property Rights as Interpreted in the Hanafite Legal Literature of the Mamluk and Ottoman Periods*. London: Croom Helm, 1988.

Jones, Toby C. *Desert Kingdom: How Oil and Water Forged Modern Saudi Arabia*. Cambridge: Harvard University Press, 2010.

Judson, Pieter M. *The Habsburg Empire: A New History*. Cambridge: Harvard University Press, 2016.

Kahlert, Torsten. "Pioneers in International Administration: A Prosopography of the Directors of the League of Nations Secretariat." *New Global Studies* 13, no. 2 (2019): 191–228.

Kaicker, Abhishek. *The King and the People: Sovereignty and Popular Politics in Mughal Delhi*. New York: Oxford University Press, 2020.

Kanafani, Ghassan. *Al-Dirasat al-Siyasiyya*. Vol. 5. Beirut: Dar Manshurat al-Rimal, 2015.

Kantorowicz, Ernst H. *The King's Two Bodies: A Study in Mediaeval Political Theology*. 1957; Princeton: Princeton University Press, 1997.

Karsh, Efraim. *Islamic Imperialism: A History*. New Haven: Yale University Press, 2006.

Karsh, Efraim, and Inari Karsh. *Empires of the Sand: The Struggle for Mastery in the Middle East, 1789–1923*. Cambridge: Harvard University Press, 1999.

Kassim, Anis F. "Legal Systems and Developments in Palestine." *The Palestine Yearbook of International Law* 1, no. 1 (1984): 19–35.

Kattan, Victor. *From Coexistence to Conquest: International Law and the Origins of the Arab-Israeli Conflict, 1891–1949*. London: Pluto Press, 2009.

Kayalı, Hasan. *Arabs and Young Turks: Ottomanism, Arabism, and Islamism in the Ottoman Empire, 1908–1918*. Berkeley: University of California Press, 1997.

———. *Imperial Resilience: The Great War's End, Ottoman Longevity, and Incidental Nations*. Berkeley: University of California Press, 2021.

[Al-Kawakibi, 'Abd al-Rahman] Al-Sayyid Furati. *Umm al-Qura*. Cairo: al-Matba'a al-Misriyya bi-l-Azhar, 1931.

Kéchichian, Joseph A. *'Iffat Al Thunayn: An Arabian Queen*. Brighton: Sussex Academic Press, 2015.

Kedourie, Elie. "Egypt and the Caliphate 1915–1946." *Journal of the Royal Asiatic Society of Great Britain and Ireland* 3–4 (1963): 208–48.

———. "The Politics of Political Literature: Kawakabi, Azouri, and Jung." *Middle Eastern Studies* 8, no. 2 (1972): 227–40.

———. *In the Anglo-Arab Labyrinth*. 2nd expanded ed. London: Taylor & Francis Group, 2000.

Keene, Edward. "The Treaty-Making Revolution of the Nineteenth Century." *International History Review* 34, 3 (2012): 475–500.

Kelsen, Hans. *General Theory of Law and State*. Cambridge: Harvard University Press, 1949.

Khadduri, Majid. "Constitutional Development in Syria." *Middle East Journal* 5, no. 2 (1951): 137–60.

Khalidi, Rashid. *Palestinian Identity: The Construction of Modern National Consciousness*. New York: Columbia University Press, 1997.

———. *The Hundred Years' War on Palestine: A History of Settler Colonialism and Resistance, 1917–2017*. New York: Metropolitan Books, 2020.

Khallaf, 'Abd al-Wahhab. *Al-Siyasa al-Shar'iyya aw Nizam al-Dawla al-Islamiyya fi al-Shu'un al-Dusturiyya wa-l-Kharijiyya wa-l-Maliyya*. Cairo: al-Matba'a al-Salafiyya, 1931.

Khanki, 'Aziz. *Al-Mahakim al-Muhtalita wa-l-Mahakim al-Ahliyya—Madiha, Hadiruha, Mustaqbaluha*. [Cairo]: Al-Matba'a al-'Asriyya, 1939.

Al-Khatib, Ihsan Fu'ad. *Wamadat min 'Umr al-Zaman*. [Beirut]: Dar al-'Ilm li-l-Malayin, 1994.

Khoury, Dina Rizk, and Dane Keith Kennedy. "Comparing Empires: The Ottoman Domains and the British Raj in the Long Nineteenth Century." *Comparative Studies of South Asia, Africa, and the Middle East* 27, no. 2 (2007): 233–44.

Khoury, Gérard D. *Une tutelle coloniale—Le mandat français en Syrie et au Liban, écrits politiques de Robert de Caix*. Paris: Belin, 2006.

Khoury, Philip S. "Factionalism among Syrian Nationalists during the French Mandate." *International Journal of Middle East Studies* 13, no. 4 (1981): 441–69.

———. *Urban Notables and Arab Nationalism*. Cambridge: Cambridge University Press, 1983.

———. *Syria and the French Mandate—The Politics of Arab Nationalism (1920–1945)*. Princeton: Princeton University Press, 1987.

Khuen, Thomas. "Bringing the Imperial Back In: Reconsidering Governance in the Late Ottoman Empire, 1839–1923 (Parts I-II)." *History Compass* 19, no. 8 (2021): without page numbers.

Khuri-Makdisi, Ilham. "Ottoman Arabs in Istanbul, 1860–1914: Perceptions of Empire, Experiences of the Metropole through the Writings of Aḥmad Fāris al-Shidyāq, Muḥammad Rashīd Riḍā, and Jirjī Zaydān." In *Imperial Geographies in Byzantine and Ottoman Space*, Sahar Bazzaz, Yota Batsaki, and Dimiter Angelov, eds., 254–96. Washington, DC: Center for Hellenic Studies, 2013.

Kılıç, Rüya. *Osmanlıda Seyyidler ve Şerifler*. Istanbul: Kitap Yayınevi, 2005.

———. "The Reflection of Islamic Tradition on Ottoman Social Structure: The Sayyids and Sharifs." In *Sayyids and Sharifs in Muslim Societies: The Living Links to the Prophet*, Kazuo Morimoto, ed.,123–38. London: Routledge, 2012.

Von Knorrig, Marc. "Konservatives Staatsdenken zwischen Beharrung und Wandel: Das 'monarchische Prinzip' bei Carl Ernst Jarcke und Friedrich Julius Stahl." In *Inszenierung oder Legitimation? Die Monarchie in Europa im 19. und 20. Jahrhundert*, Frank-Lothar Kroll and Dieter J. Weiss, eds., 77–94. Berlin: Duncker & Humblot, 2015.

Knox, Robert. "Haiti at the League of Nations: Racialisation, Accumulation, and Representation." *Melbourne Journal of International Law* 21, no. 2 (2020): 245–74.

Kołodziejczyk, Dariusz. "What Is Inside and What Is Outside? Tributary States in Ottoman Politics." In *The European Tributary States of the Ottoman Empire in the Sixteenth and Seventeenth Centuries*, Gábor Kármán and Lovro Kunčević, eds., 421–32. Leiden: Brill, 2013.

Korman, Sharon. *The Right of Conquest: The Acquisition of Territory by Force in International Law and Practice*. Oxford: Clarendon Press, 1996.

Koskenniemi, Martti. *The Gentle Civilizer of Nations: The Rise and Fall of International Law, 1870–1960*. Cambridge: Cambridge University Press, 2002.

Kostiner, Joseph. *The Making of Saudi Arabia, 1916–1936: From Chieftaincy to Monarchical State*. New York: Oxford University Press, 1993.

Kostopoulou, Elektra. "Autonomy and Federation within the Ottoman Empire: Introduction to the Special Issue." *Journal of Balkan and Near Eastern Studies* 18, no. 6 (2016): 525–32.

Kozma, Liat, Cyrus Schayegh, and Avner Wishnitzer. *A Global Middle East: Mobility, Materiality and Culture in the Modern Age, 1880–1940*. London: I.B. Tauris, 2015.

Krämer, Gudrun. *Gottes Staat als Republik: Reflexionen zeitgenössischer Muslime zu Islam, Menschenrechten und Demokratie*. Baden-Baden: Nomos, 1999.

Krasner, Stephen D. *Sovereignty: Organized Hypocrisy*. Princeton: Princeton University Press, 1999.

Krawietz, Birgit. "Cut and Paste in Legal Rules: Designing Islamic Norms with Talfiq." *Die Welt Des Islams* 42, no. 1 (2002): 3–40.

Krisch, Nico and Benedict Kingsbury. "Introduction: Global Governance and Global Administrative Law in the International Legal Order." *The European Journal of International Law* 17, no. 1 (2006): 1–13.

Kroll, Frank-Lothar. "Modernity of the Outmoded?" In *Inszenierung Oder Legitimation?: Die Monarchie in Europa Im 19. Und 20. Jahrhundert*, edited by Frank-Lothar Kroll and Dieter J. Weiss, 11–19. Berlin: Duncker & Humblot, 2015.

Kumar, Krishan. *Visions of Empire: How Five Imperial Regimes Shaped the World*. Princeton: Princeton University Press, 2017.

Kupferschmidt, Uri M. *The Supreme Muslim Council: Islam under the British Mandate for Palestine*. Leiden: E.J. Brill, 1987.

Kurd 'Ali, Muhammad. *Khitat al-Sham*. Beirut: Dar al-'Ilm li-l-Malayin, 1969.

Kurt, Burcu. "Osmanlı İmparatorluğu'ndan Irak Devletine: Bağdatlı Mülkiyelilerin Serencamı." In *Türkiye'nin Modernleşme Süreci ve Mekteb-i Mülkiye*, Orhan Çelik, Can Umut Çiner, and Abdullah Pekel, eds., 729–55. Ankara: Ankara Üniversitesi Yayınları, 2021.

Kwan, Jonathan. "The Congress of Vienna, 1814–1815: Diplomacy, Political Culture, and Sociability." *Historical Journal* 60, no. 4 (2017): 1125–46.

Laffan, Michael. *Under Empire: Muslim Lives and Loyalties Across across the Indian Ocean World, 1775–1945*. New York: Columbia University Press, 2022.

Lamba, Henri. *Code administratif égyptien, contenant les actes et lois organiques du Khédivat, les lois, décrets et règlements administratifs, annotés de la jurisprudence mixte et indigène, les lois financières*. Paris: L. Larose et L. Tenin, 1911.

Lapierre, Jean. *Le mandat français en Syrie: origines, doctrine, exécution*. Paris: Université de Paris, 1936.

Latour, Bruno. *We Have Never Been Modern*. Cambridge: Harvard University Press, 1993.

Laurens, Henry. *Le Royaume impossible: La France et la genèse du monde arabe*. Paris: Armand Colins, 1990.

———. *L'empire et ses ennemis: la question impériale dans l'histoire*. Paris: Seuil, 2009.

Laursen, John Christian, Luisa Simonutti, and H.W. Blom. "Introduction." In *Monarchisms in the Age of Enlightenment: Liberty, Patriotism, and the Common Good*, idem, eds., 3–16. Toronto: University of Toronto Press, 2007.

Lauzière, Henri. *The Making of Salafism: Islamic Reform in the Twentieth Century*. New York: Columbia University Press, 2016.

Lawson, Fred Haley. *Constructing International Relations in the Arab World*. Stanford: Stanford University Press, 2006.

Lemire, Vincent. *Jerusalem 1900: the Holy City in the Age of Possibilities*. Chicago: The University of Chicago Press, 2017.

Lewis, Bernard. "Malik." *Les Cahiers de Tunisie* 35 (1987): 101–109.

Lewis, Mary Dewhurst. *Divided Rule: Sovereignty and Empire in French Tunisia, 1881–1938*. Berkeley: University of California Press, 2014.

Li, Darryl. *The Universal Enemy: Jihad, Empire, and the Challenge of Solidarity*. Stanford: Stanford University Press, 2020.

Lindley, M. F. *The Acquisition and Government of Backward Territory in International Law, Being a Treatise on the Law and Practice Relating to Colonial Expansion*. London: Longmans, Green and Co., 1926.

Long, Richard. *British Pro-Consuls in Egypt, 1914–1929: the Challenge of Nationalism*. London: Routledge, 2005.

Longrigg, Stephen Hemsley. *Syria and Lebanon under French Mandate*. London: Oxford University Press, 1958.

———. *Oil in the Middle East: Its Discovery and Development*. London: Oxford University Press, 1968.

Low, Michael Christopher. "Ottoman Infrastructures of the Saudi Hydro-State: The Technopolitics of Pilgrimage and Potable Water in the Hijaz." *Comparative Studies in Society and History* 57, no. 4 (2015): 942–74.

———. *Imperial Mecca: Ottoman Arabia and the Indian Ocean Hajj*. New York: Columbia University Press, 2020.

Lugard, F. D. *The Dual Mandate in British Tropical Africa*. Edinburgh: W. Blackwood and Sons, 1922.

Al-Madi, Munib, and Sulayman Musa. *Tarikh al-Urdun fi al-Qarn al-'Ishrin*. 2 vols. Amman: Maktabat al-Muhtasab, 1988.

Maghraoui, Abdeslam. *Liberalism without Democracy: Nationhood and Citizenship in Egypt, 1922–1936*. Durham: Duke University Press, 2008.

Maier, Charles S. *Recasting Bourgeois Europe: Stabilization in France, Germany, and Italy in the Decade after World War I*. Princeton: Princeton University Press, 1975.

———. *Among Empires: American Ascendancy and Its Predecessors*. Cambridge: Harvard University Press, 2006.

———. *Once within Borders: Territories of Power, Wealth, and Belonging since 1500*. Cambridge: Harvard University Press, 2016.

Makdisi, Ussama Samir. "Ottoman Orientalism." *American Historical Review* 107, no. 3 (2002): 768–96.

———. *Age of Coexistence: The Ecumenical Frame and the Making of the Modern Arab World*. Berkeley: University of California Press, 2019.

Malaji, Ra'd Ahmad Salim. *'Ali Rida al-Rikabi wa Dawrahu al-Siyasi fi 'Ahd al-Hukuma al-'Arabiyya al-Faysaliyya wa Imarat Sharqi al-Urdun 1918–1926 M.* Amman: Wizarat al-Thaqafa al-Urduniyya, 2020.

Mamdani, Mahmood. *Define and Rule: Native as Political Identity*. Cambridge: Harvard University Press, 2012.

Manela, Erez. *The Wilsonian Moment: Self-determination and the International Origins of Anticolonial Nationalism*. Oxford: Oxford University Press, 2007.

Mantena, Karuna. *Alibis of Empire: Henry Maine and the Ends of Liberal Imperialism*. Princeton: Princeton University Press, 2010.

March, Andrew F. *The Caliphate of Man: Popular Sovereignty in Modern Islamic Thought*. Cambridge: Belknap Press, 2019.

Marino, Brigitte, T. Okawara, and Daad al-Hakim. *Catalogue des registres des tribunaux ottomans conservés au Centre des Archives de Damas*. Damascus: Institut Français de Damas, 1999.

Masters, Bruce Alan. *The Arabs of the Ottoman Empire, 1516–1918: A Social and Cultural History*. New York: Cambridge University Press, 2013.

Matar, Ilyas Dib. *Al-'Uqud al-Durriyya fi Tarikh al-Mamlaka al-Suriyya*. Beirut: Matba'at al-Ma'arif, 1874.

Matossian, Bedross Der. *Shattered Dreams of Revolution: From Liberty to Violence in the Late Ottoman Empire*. Stanford: Stanford University Press, 2014.

Matthesian, Toby. "Shi'i Historians In a Wahhabi State: Identity Entrepreneurs and the Politics of Local Historiography in Saudi Arabia." *IJMES* 47 (2015), 25–45.

Matthews, Weldon. *Confronting an Empire, Constructing a Nation*. London: I.B. Tauris, 2006.

Mayer, Arno. *The Persistence of the Old Regime: Europe to the Great War*. New York: Pantheon Books, 1981.

Mayeur-Jaouen, Catherine. "Vérification des généalogies (*taḥqīq al-ansāb*) et centralité égyptienne: Le Syndicat des descendants du Prophète (*niqābat al-ashrāf*) à l'époque contemporaine." In *The Presence of the Prophet in Early Modern and Contemporary Islam*. Vol. II: *Heirs of the Prophet: Authority and Power*, Rachida Chih, David Jordan and Stefan Reichmuth, eds., 172–207. Leiden: Brill, 2022.

Mazower, Mark. *No Enchanted Palace: The End of Empire and the Ideological Origins of the United Nations*. Princeton: Princeton University Press, 2009.

———. *Governing the World: The History of an Idea, 1815 to the Present*. New York: Penguin Books, 2013.

McDougall, James. "The British and French Empires in the Arab World: Some Problems of Colonial State-Formation and Its Legacy." In *Sovereignty after Empire: Comparing the Middle East and Central Asia*, Sally N. Cummings and Raymond A. Hinnebusch, eds., 44–65. Edinburgh: Edinburgh University Press, 2011.

McIlwraith, Malcolm. "The Declaration of a Protectorate in Egypt and Its Legal Effects." *Journal of the Society of Comparative Legislation* 17, no. 1–2 (1917): 238–59.

Meeker, Michael E. *A Nation of Empire: The Ottoman Legacy of Turkish Modernity*. Berkeley: University of California Press, 2002.

Meinertzhagen, Richard. *Report on Middle East Conference: held in Cairo and Jerusalem, March 12th to 30th, 1921*. [London]: [Colonial Office], 1921.

Meiton, Fredrik. *Electrical Palestine: Capital and Technology from Empire to Nation*. Berkeley: University of California Press, 2019.

Méouchy, Nadine, and Peter Sluglett, eds. *The British and French Mandates in Comparative Perspectives*. Leiden: Brill, 2004.

Meriwether, Margaret Lee. *The Kin Who Count: Family and Society in Ottoman Aleppo, 1770–1840*. Austin: University of Texas Press, 1999.

Mestyan, Adam. *Arab Patriotism: The Ideology and Culture of Power in Late Ottoman Egypt*. Princeton: Princeton University Press, 2017.

———. "Domestic Sovereignty, A'yan Developmentalism, and Global Microhistory in Modern Egypt." *Comparative Studies in Society and History* 60, 2 (2018): 415–45.

———. "Tawfiq Muhammad al-Bakri." *Encyclopaedia of Islam, Three* (Leiden: Brill, 2019), 6:19–21.

———. "Seeing Like a Khedivate: Taxing Endowed Agricultural Land, Proofs of Ownership, and the Land Administration in Egypt, 1869." *Journal of the Economic and Social History of the Orient* 63, no. 5–6 (2020): 744–88.

———. *Primordial History, Print Capitalism, and Egyptology in Nineteenth-Century Cairo: Mustafa Salama al-Naggari's "The Garden of Ismail's Praise."* Cairo: Institut français d'archéologie orientale, 2021.

———. "A Muslim Dualism? Inter-imperial History and Austria-Hungary in Ottoman Political Thought, 1867–1921." *Contemporary European History*, 30, no. 4 (2021): 478–96.

———. "From Administrative to Political Order? Global Legal History, the Organic Law, and the Constitution of Mandate Syria, 1925–1930." *Journal of Global History* 17, no. 2 (2022): 292–311.

Mikhail, Alan, and Christine M. Philliou. "The Ottoman Empire and the Imperial Turn." *Comparative Studies in Society and History* 54, no. 4 (2012): 721–45.

Miller, Paul B. and Claire Morelon, eds. *Embers of Empire: Continuity and Rupture in the Habsburg Successor States after 1918.* New York: Berghahn Books, 2019.

Milovanowitch, M. *Les Traités de garantie au XIXe siècle—étude de droit international et d'histoire diplomatique.* Paris: Arthur Rousseau, 1888.

Minawi, Mostafa. *The Ottoman Scramble for Africa: Empire and Diplomacy in the Sahara and the Hijaz.* Stanford: Stanford University Press, 2016.

Mitchell, Timothy. "The Limits of the State: Beyond Statist Approaches and Their Critics." *American Political Science Review* 85, no. 1 (1991): 77–96.

———. *Rule of Experts: Egypt, Techno-Politics, Modernity.* Berkeley: University of California Press, 2002.

———. "Infrastructures Work on Time." E-Flux Architecture, 2020, https://www.e-flux .com/architecture/new-silk-roads/312596/infrastructures-work-on-time/. Last viewed 29 April 2022.

Mizrahi, Jean-David. "La France et sa politique de mandat en Syrie et au Liban (1920–1939)." In *France, Syrie et Liban, 1918–1946 : les ambiguïtés et les dynamiques de la relation mandataire,* Nadine Méouchy, ed., 35–71. Damascus: Institut français d'études arabes de Damas, 2002.

———. *Genèse de l'État mandataire: Service des renseignements et bandes armées en Syrie et au Liban dans les années 1920.* Paris: Publications de la Sorbonne, 2003.

Moalla, Asma. *The Regency of Tunis and the Ottoman Porte, 1777–1814: Army and Government of a North-African Ottoman Eyâlet at the End of the Eighteenth Century.* London: Routledge, 2004.

Moin, A. Azfar. *The Millennial Sovereign: Sacred Kingship and Sainthood in Islam.* New York, NY: Columbia University Press, 2012.

Mommsen, Wolfgang J. "Max Weber's 'Grand Sociology': The Origins and Composition of *Wirtschaft und Gesellschaft: Soziologie.*" *History and Theory* 39, no. 3 (2000): 364–83.

———. *The Age of Capitalism and Bureaucracy: Perspectives on the Political Sociology of Max Weber.* New York: Berghahn Books, 2021.

Morimoto, Kazuo. "Toward the Formation of Sayyido-Sharifology: Questioning Accepted Fact." *Journal of Sophia Asian Studies* 22 (2004): 87–103.

———. "Introduction." In *Sayyids and Sharifs in Muslim Societies: The Living Links to the Prophet,* edited by Kazuo Morimoto, ed., 1–12. London: Routledge, 2017.

Moroni, Ileana. "Continuity and Change in the 1909 Constitutional Revision: An Ottoman Imperial Nation Claims Its Sovereignty." In *The Young Turk Revolution and the Ottoman Empire: The Aftermath of 1908,* François Georgeon and Noemi Lévy-Aksu, eds., 265–85. New York: I.B. Tauris, 2017.

Mortel, Richard T. "Zaydi Shiʿism and the Ḥasanid Sharifs of Mecca." *International Journal of Middle East Studies* 19, no. 4 (1987): 455–72.

Motadel, David, ed. *Islam and the European Empires.* Oxford: Oxford University Press, 2014.

Motyl, Alexander J. *Imperial Ends: The Decay, Collapse, and Revival of Empires.* New York: Columbia University Press, 2001.

Moubayed, Sami. "Syria's Forgotten First President Mohammad Ali al-Abed." *British Journal of Middle Eastern Studies* 41, no. 4 (2014): 419–41.

———. *Tarikh Dimashq al-Mansi: Arba' Hikayat, 1916–1936*. Beirut: Riad El-Rayyes Books, 2016.

———. *The Makers of Modern Syria: The Rise and Fall of Syrian Democracy, 1918–1958*. London: I.B. Tauris, 2018.

Mouline, Nabil. *The Clerics of Islam: Religious Authority and Political Power in Saudi Arabia*. New Haven: Yale University Press, 2014.

Moumtaz, Nada. *God's Property: Islam, Charity, and the Modern State*. Oakland: University of California Press, 2021.

Moyn, Samuel. "Fantasies of Federalism." *Dissent*, Winter 2015, https://www.dissentmagazine.org/article/fantasies-of-federalism.

Mubarak, 'Ali. *Al-Khitat al-Tawfiqiyya al-Jadida*. 20 vols. 1886–89; repr., Cairo: Dar al-Kutub wa-l-Watha'iq al-Qawmiyya, 1980–2007.

Mufti, Malik. *Sovereign Creations: Pan-Arabism and Political Order in Syria and Iraq*. Ithaca: Cornell University Press, 1996.

Mughazy, Mustafa, and Adam Abdelhamid Sabra, 2015. *Manaqib al-Sada al-Bakriyya: The Merits of the Bakri Lords*. Beirut: Dar al-Mashriq, 2015.

Müller, Martin. "Assemblages and Actor-Networks: Rethinking Socio-Material Power, Politics and Space." *Geography Compass* 9, no. 1 (2015): 27–41.

Murray-Miller, Gavin. "A Conflicted Sense of Nationality: Napoleon III's Arab Kingdom and the Paradoxes of French Multiculturalism." *French Colonial History* 15 (2014): 1–38.

Murshid, Ahmad Amin Salih. *Tayba wa-Dhikriyyat al-Ahibba*, vols. 1 and 2. [Medina?]: The Author, 1993.

Al-Muslim, Muhammad Sa'id. *Sahil al-Dhahab al-Aswad*. Beirut: Dar Maktabat al-Hayat, 1962.

Al-Muti'i, Muhammad Bakhit. *Mudhakkira . . . Muqaddima li-Majlis al-Shuyukh bi-Bayan 'an Wazifat al-Iftā' Wazifa Shar'iyya Diniyya Yajib 'ala Wali al-Amr an Yuwazzif fi-ha Man Yaliq La-ha*. Cairo: al-Matba'a al-Salafiyya, 1346.

———. *Haqiqat al-Islam wa-Usul al-Hukm*. Cairo: Al-Matba'a al-Salafiyya, 1925.

Nasif, Husayn b. Muhammad. *Madi al-Hijaz wa-Hadiruhu*. Cairo: Maktabat wa-Matba'at Khudayr, 1349 (1930).

Nasser, Issam. "From Ottomans to Arabs." In *The Storyteller of Jerusalem*, Issam Nasser and Salim Tamari, eds., 46–63. Northampton: Clockroot Books, 2013.

Neep, Daniel. *Occupying Syria under the French Mandate: Insurgency, Space and State Formation*. New York: Cambridge University Press, 2012.

Nelson, Eric. *The Royalist Revolution: Monarchy and the American Founding*. Cambridge: Harvard University Press, 2014.

Nexon, Daniel H. *The Struggle for Power in Early Modern Europe: Religious Conflict, Dynastic Empires, and International Change*. Princeton: Princeton University Press, 2009.

Nielsen, Jørgen S., ed. *Religion, Ethnicity and Contested Nationhood in the Former Ottoman Space*. Leiden: Brill, 2012.

Noth, Albrecht. "Some Remarks on the 'Nationalization' of Conquered Lands at the time of the Umayyads." In *Land Tenure and Social Transformation in the Middle East*, Tarif Khalidi, ed., 223–28. Beirut: American University of Beirut, 1984.

Ochsenwald, William. *Religion, Society, and the State in Arabia: The Hijaz under Ottoman Control, 1840–1908*. Columbus: Ohio State University Press, 1984.

———. "Ironic Origins: Arab Nationalism in the Hijaz, 1882–1914." In *The Origins of Arab Nationalism*, Rashid Khalidi et al., eds., 189–203. New York: Columbia University Press, 1991.

———. "Islam and Loyalty in the Saudi Hijaz, 1926–1939." *Die Welt des Islams* 47, no. 1 (2007): 7–32.

———. "The Transformation of Education in the Hijaz, 1925–1945." *Arabian Humanities* 12 (2019), online. http://journals.openedition.org/cy/4917.

Ogle, Vanessa. *The Global Transformation of Time: 1870–1950*. Cambridge: Harvard University Press, 2015.

Onley, James. *The Arabian Frontier of the British Raj: Merchants, Rulers, and the British in the Nineteenth-Century Gulf*. Oxford: Oxford University Press, 2007.

O'Sullivan, Michael. "Paper Currency, Banking, and Islamic Monetary Debates in Late Ottoman and Early Saudi Arabia." *Journal of the Economic and Social History of the Orient* 63, no. 3 (2020): 243–85.

Ouahes, Idir. *Syria and Lebanon under the French Mandate: Cultural Imperialism and the Workings of Empire*. London: I.B. Tauris, 2018.

Oualdi, M'Hamed. *Esclaves et Maîtres: Les Mamelouks des Beys de Tunis du XVIIe siècle aux années 1880*. Paris: Publications de la Sorbonne, 2011.

Owen, Roger. *State, Power and Politics in the Making of the Modern Middle East*. London: Routledge, 2004.

Özdeş, Orhan. "Danıştay'ın Tarihçesi." In *Yüzyıl boyunca Danıştay: 1868–1968*, 41–224. Ankara: Türk Tarih Kurumu Basımevi, 1968.

Özyüksel, Murat. *The Hejaz Railway and the Ottoman Empire*. Vol. 39. London: I. B. Tauris & Company, Limited, 2014.

Pankhurst, Reza. *The Inevitable Caliphate? A History of the Struggle for Global Islamic Union, 1924 to Present*. London: Hurst & Company, 2013.

Paris, Timothy J. "British Middle East Policy-Making after the First World War: The Lawrentian and Wilsonian Schools." *The Historical Journal* 41, no. 3 (1998): 773–93.

Parsons, Laila. *Fawzi al-Qawuqji*. London: Saqi Books, 2017.

Payk, Marcus M. and Roberta Pergher, eds. *Beyond Versailles: Sovereignty, Legitimacy, and the Formation of New Polities after the Great War*. Bloomington: Indiana University Press, 2019.

Pedersen, Susan. "Settler Colonialism at the Bar of the League of Nations." In *Settler Colonialism in the Twentieth Century: Projects, Practices, Legacies*, Caroline Elkins and Susan Pederson, eds., 113–34. London: Routledge, 2005.

———. "Getting Out of Iraq—in 1932: The League of Nations and the Road to Normative Statehood." *American Historical Review* 115, no. 4 (2010): 975–99.

———. *The Guardians: The League of Nations and the Crisis of Empire*. Oxford: Oxford University Press, 2015.

Pellitteri, Antonio. "'Abd Al-Rahman Al-Kawakibi (1853/54–1902): Nuovi Materiali Bio-Bibliografici." *Oriente Moderno* 15, no. 76 (1996): 1–69.

Pernau, Margrit. *Ashraf into Middle Classes: Muslims in Nineteenth-Century Delhi*. New Delhi: Oxford University Press, 2013.

Peskes, Esther. "Western Arabia and Yemen (Fifth/Eleventh Century to the Ottoman Conquest)." In *The New Cambridge History of Islam*, vol. 2, Maribel Fierro, ed., 285–98. Cambridge: Cambridge University Press, 2010.

Peters, F. E. *Mecca: A Literary History of the Muslim Holy Land*. Princeton: Princeton University Press, 1994.

Peters, Rudolph. "Muhammad al-'Abbasi al-Mahdi (d. 1897), Grand Mufti of Egypt, and His al-Fatawa al-Mahdiyya." *Islamic Law and Society* 1, no. 1 (1994): 66–82.

———. "Administrators and Magistrates: The Development of a Secular Judiciary in Egypt, 1842–1871." *Welt des Islams* 39, no. 3 (1999): 378–97.

Pétriat, Philippe. *Le Négoce des Lieux saints: Négociants hadramis de Djedda, 1850–1950*. Paris: Éditions de la Sorbonne, 2016.

Philby, H. St. J. B. *Arabian Oil Ventures*. Washington: Middle East Institute, 1964.

Philliou, Christine. "Communities on the Verge: Unraveling the Phanariot Ascendancy in Ottoman Governance." *Comparative Studies in Society and History* 51, no. 1 (2009): 151–81.

———. *Turkey: A Past Against History*. Berkeley: University of California Press, 2021.

Pillai, Sarath. "Fragmenting the Nation: Divisible Sovereignty and Travancore's Quest for Federal Independence." *Law and History Review* 34, no. 3 (2016): 743–82.

Pirenne, H. *Histoire de Belgique*, 2nd ed., vol. 7. Bruxelles: Maurice Lamertin, 1948.

Pitts, Jennifer. "Political Theory of Empire and Imperialism." *Annual Review of Political Science* 13, no. 1 (2010): 211–35.

Podeh, Elie. *The Decline of Arab Unity: The Rise and Fall of the United Arab Republic*. Brighton: Sussex Academic Press, 1999.

Polat, Ü. Gülsüm. *Türk-Arap İlişkileri—Eski Eyaletler Yeni Komşulara Dönüşürken (1914–1923)*. Istanbul: Kronik Kitab, 2019.

Pomeranz, Kenneth. *The Great Divergence: China, Europe, and the Making of the Modern World Economy*. Princeton: Princeton University Press, 2000.

Porath, Yehoshua. *In Search of Arab Unity, 1930–1945*. 1st ed. 1986, Abingdon: Routledge, 2013.

Prendergast, Thomas R. "The Sociological Idea of the State: Legal Education, Austrian Multinationalism, and the Future of Continental Empire, 1880–1914." *Comparative Studies in Society and History* 62, no. 2 (2020): 327–58.

Priestland, Jane, ed. *Records of Syria 1918–1973*, vol. 2. Archive Editions, 2005.

Provence, Michael. *The Great Syrian Revolt and the Rise of Arab Nationalism*. Austin: University of Texas Press, 2005.

———. *The Last Ottoman Generation and the Making of the Modern Middle East*. Cambridge: Cambridge University Press, 2017.

Qadri, Tahsin. *Mudhakkirat Tahsin Qadri*, Sayyar al-Jamil, ed. Amman: Al-Ahliyya li-l-Nashr wa-l-Tawzi', 2018.

———. *Transformations of Tradition: Islamic Law in Colonial Modernity*. New York: Oxford University Press, 2021.

Al-Qari, Ahmad b. 'Abd Allah. *Majallat al-Ahkam al-Shar'iyya*. Jidda: Tahama, 1981.

Qarqut, Dhuqan. *Tatawwur al-Haraka al-Wataniyya fi Suriyya, 1920–1939*. Beirut: Dar al-Tali'a, 1975.

Qasimiyya, Khayriyya. *Al-Hukuma al-ʿArabiyya fi Dimasq, 1918–1920.* Cairo: Dar al-Maʿarif, 1971.

——. *Al-Raʿil al-ʿArabi al-Awwal: Ḥayāt wa-Awrāq Nabīh wa-ʿĀdil al-ʿAzmah.* London: Riyad al-Rayyis, 1991.

——. *Jawanib min Siyasat al-Malik ʿAbd al-ʿAzīz Tujaha al-Qadaya al-ʿArabiyya: Dirasa Tahliliyya min Khilal Awraq Nabih al-ʿAzma* [Riyadh]: Darat al-Malik ʿAbd al-ʿAziz, 1999.

Al-Qawuqji, Fawzi. *Mudhakkirat Fawzi al-Qawuqji,* Khayriyya Qasimiyya, ed. Damascus: Dar al-Dabbas, 1995.

Quadri, Junaid. *Transformations of Tradition: Islamic Law in Colonial Modernity.* New York: Oxford University Press, 2021.

Rabinovich, Itamar. "Inter-Arab Relations Foreshadowed: The Question of the Syrian Throne in the 1920s and 1930s." In *Festschrift: In Honor of Dr. George S. Wise,* 237–50. [Tel Aviv]: Tel Aviv University, [1981].

Rafeq, Abdul-Karim. "Les registres des tribuneaux de Damas comme source pour l'histoire de la Syria." *Bulletin d'études Orientales* 26 (1973): 219–26.

Rafiʿ, Muhammad ʿUmar. *Makka fi al-Qarn al-RabiʿʿAshar al-Hijri.* Mecca: Manshurat Nadi Makka al-Thaqafi, 1981.

Al-Rafiʿi, ʿAbd al-Rahman. *Fi Aʿqab al-Thawra.* 3 vols. Cairo: Dar al-Maʿarif, 1987–88.

Rappas, Alexis. "Three Murders and a Mandate: On Property and French Sovereignty in Interwar Syria." *British Journal of Middle Eastern Studies* 48 no. 5 (2021): 850–72.

Al-Rasheed, Madawi. *A History of Saudi Arabia.* 2nd ed. New York: Cambridge University Press, 2010.

Reill, Dominique Kirchner. *The Fiume Crisis: Life in the Wake of the Habsburg Empire.* Cambridge: Harvard University Press, 2020.

Reiter, Yitzhak. *Islamic Awqaf in Jerusalem under British Mandate,* London: Taylor and Francis, 1996.

Reynolds, Michael A. *Shattering Empires: The Clash and Collapse of the Ottoman and Russian Empires, 1908–1918.* Cambridge: Cambridge University Press, 2011.

Rida, Rashid. *Al-Khilafa aw al-Imama al-ʿUzma.* Cairo: Matbaʿat al-Manar, 1922.

——. *Fatawa al-Imam Muhammad Rashid Rida.* 6 vols. Beirut: Dar al-Kitab al-Jadid, 1970.

——. *Maqalat al-Shaykh Rashid Rida al-Siyasiyya,* vol. 3. Beirut: Dar Ibn ʿArabi, 1994.

Rıfaat, Ahmet. *Devhat ün-Nükaba.* [Istanbul]: Karahisari Esad Efendi, 1866.

Rigó, Máté. *Capitalism in Chaos: How the Business Elites of Europe Prospered in the Era of the Great War.* Ithaca: Cornell University Press, 2022.

Al-Rihani, Amin. *Muluk al-ʿArab—Rihla fi al-Bilad al-ʿArabiyya tashtamil ʿala Muqaddima wa-Thamaniya Aqsam.* 2 vols. Beirut: al-Matbaʿa al-ʿIlmiyya li-Yusuf Sadir, 1924 and 1925.

Rihani, Ameen. *Around the Coasts of Arabia.* London: Constable and Co., 1930.

Al-Rihawi, Sahila. "Tatawwur mafhum al-La-markaziyya ʿinda al-ʿArab al-ʿUthmaniyyin." *Dirasat Tarikhiyya* 13–14 (1974): 138–83.

Rivet, Daniel. *Lyautey et l'institution du protectorat français au Maroc, 1912–1925,* 3 vols. Paris: L'Harmattan, 1996.

Roberts, Adam. "Termination of Military Occupation." *Max Planck Encyclopedia of Public International Law*. New York: Oxford University Press, 2009.

Robson, Laura. *The Politics of Mass Violence in the Middle East*. Oxford: Oxford University Press, 2020.

Rock-Singer, Aaron. *In the Shade of the Sunna: Salafi Piety in the Twentieth-Century Middle East*. Oakland: University of California Press, 2022.

Rodogno, Davide. "European Legal Doctrines on Intervention and the Status of the Ottoman Empire within the 'Family of Nations' throughout the Nineteenth Century." *Journal of the History of International Law* 18, no. 1 (2016): 5–41.

Rogan, Eugene L. "Archival Resources and Research Institutions in Jordan." *Middle East Studies Association Bulletin* 23, no. 2 (1989): 169–79.

———. "Abdulhamid II's School for Tribes (1892–1907)." *International Journal of Middle East Studies* 28, no. 1 (1996): 83–107.

———. *Frontiers of the State in the Late Ottoman Empire: Transjordan, 1850–1921*. Cambridge: Cambridge University Press, 1999.

———. *The Arabs: A History*. New York: Basic Books, 2009.

———. *The Fall of the Ottomans: The Great War in the Middle East*. New York: Basic Books, 2015.

Rose, Richard B. "The Ottoman Fiscal Calendar." *Middle East Studies Association Bulletin* 25, no. 2 (1991): 157–67.

Rouhana, Nadim and Asad Ghanem. "The Crisis of Minorities in Ethnic States: The Case of Palestinian Citizens in Israel." *International Journal of Middle East Studies* 30, no. 3 (1998): 321–46.

Rubin, Avi. *Ottoman Nizamiye Courts: Law and Modernity*. New York: Palgrave Macmillan, 2011.

Russell, Malcolm B. *The First Modern Arab State: Syria under Faysal, 1918–1920*. Minneapolis: Bibliotheca Islamica, 1985.

Ryad, Umar. *Islamic Reformism and Christianity: A Critical Reading of the Works of Muḥammad Rashid Rida and His Associates (1898–1935)*. Leiden: Brill, 2009.

———, ed. *The Hajj and Europe in the Age of Empire*. Leiden: Brill, 2016.

Ryzova, Lucie. *The Age of the Efendiyya: Passages to Modernity in National-Colonial Egypt*. Oxford: Oxford University Press, 2014.

Sabeheddin, (Prince). "A Second Account on Individual Initiative and Decentralization." In *Modernism: The Creation of Nation-States*, Ahmet Ersoy et al., eds., 331–37. Budapest: CEU Press, 2010.

Sabbagh, Mazin Yusuf. *Sijill al-Dustur al-Suri*. Damascus: Dar al-Sharq li-l-Tibaʻa wa-l-Nashr, 2010.

Sabry, El Sayed. *Le Pouvoir législatif et le pouvoir exécutif en Égypte*. Paris: Albert Mechelinck, 1930.

Salaymeh, Lena. *The Beginnings of Islamic Law: Late Antique Islamicate Legal Traditions*. Cambridge: Cambridge University Press, 2016.

Salim, Latifa Muhammad. *Faruq wa-Suqut al-Malakiyya fi Misr, 1936–1952*. Cairo: Maktabat Madbuli, 1989.

Salzmann, Ariel. *Tocqueville in the Ottoman Empire: Rival Paths to the Modern State*. Leiden: Brill, 2004.

Sager, Lawrence Gene. "Fair Measure: The Legal Status of Underenforced Constitutional Norms." *Harvard Law Review* 91 (1978): 1212–64.

Sanagan, Mark. *Lightning through the Clouds: 'Izz al-Din al-Qassam and the Making of the Modern Middle East.* Austin: University of Texas Press, 2020.

Sarıcık, Murat. *Osmanlı imparatorluğu'nda Nakîbü'l-Eşrâflık Müessesesi.* Ankara: Türk Tarih Kurumu Basımevi, 2003. (= Sarijik, Murad. *Niqabat al-Ashraf fi al-Dawla al-'Uthmaniyya.* Cairo: Dar al-Qahira, 2007.)

Sa'id, Amin. *al-Thawra al-'Arabiyya al-Kubra.* Vols. 2–3. Cairo: Matba'at 'Isa al-Babi al-Halabi & Co., 1934.

Satia, Priya. *Spies in Arabia: The Great War and the Cultural Foundations of Britain's Covert Empire in the Middle East.* Oxford: Oxford University Press, 2008.

Al-Sawwaf, Muhammad Sharif. *Sham Sharif: Dawr al-Fuqaha' fi al-Mujtama' al-Dimashqi fi al-'Ahd al-'Uthmani.* Damascus: Dar Afnan, 2014.

Al-Sayyadi, Muhammad Abu al-Huda. *Dhakhirat al-Ma'ad fi Dhikr al-Sada Bani al-Sayyad.* Matba'at Muhammad Efendi Mustafa, 1336 [1889].

———. *Da'i al-Rashad fi Sabil al-Ittihad wa-l-Inqiyad.* [Istanbul]: al-Matba'a al-Sultaniyya, [no date].

Sayyid-Marsot, Afaf Lutfi. *Egypt's Liberal Experiment, 1922–1936.* Berkeley: University of California Press, 1977.

Schad, Geoffrey D. "Competing Forms of Globalization in the Middle East: from the Ottoman Empire to the Nation State, 1918–67." In *Global History: Interactions between the Universal and the Local*, A. G. Hopkins, ed., 191–228. Basingstoke: Palgrave Macmillan, 2006.

Schayegh, Cyrus. *The Middle East and the Making of the Modern World.* Cambridge: Harvard University Press, 2017.

Schayegh, Cyrus, and Andrew Arsan, eds. *The Routledge Handbook of the History of the Middle East Mandates.* London: Routledge, 2015.

Schindler, Dietrich and Jiri Toman, eds. *The Laws of Armed Conflicts: A Collection of Conventions, Resolutions, and Other Documents.* Dordrecht: Martinus Nijhoff, 1988.

Schlaepfer, Aline. "Between Ruler and Rogue." In *Age of Rogues: Rebels, Revolutionaries, and Racketeers at the Frontiers of Empires*, Hakkı Öztan Ramazan and Alp Yenen, eds., 235–57. Edinburgh: Edinburgh University Press, 2021.

Schlaepfer, Aline, Philippe Bourmaud, and Iyas Hassan. "Fantômes d'Empire: persistances et revendications d'ottomanité(s) dans les espaces post-ottomans." *Revue des mondes musulmans et de la Méditerranée* 148 (2020), last viewed 23 April 2022. (http://journals.openedition.org/remmm/15098)

Schroeder, Paul W. *The Transformation of European Politics, 1763–1848.* Oxford: Clarendon Press, 1994.

Schulz, Matthias. *Normen und Praxis: Das Europäische Konzert der Grossmächte als Sicherheitsrat, 1815–1860.* München: R. Oldenbourg, 2009.

Scott, Rachel M. *Recasting Islamic Law Religion and the Nation State in Egyptian Constitution Making.* Ithaca: Cornell University Press, 2021.

Seale, Patrick. *The Struggle for Syria: A Study of Post-War Arab Politics, 1945–1958.* London: I.B. Tauris, 1986.

Sedgwick, Mark J.R. "Saudi Sufis: Compromise in the Hijaz, 1925–1940." *Die Welt des Islams* 37, no. 3 (1997): 349–68.

Seikaly, Sherene. *Men of Capital: Scarcity and Economy in Mandate Palestine*. Stanford: Stanford University Press, 2016.

Sewell, William H. Jr. "Historical Events as Transformations of Structures: Inventing Revolution at the Bastille." *Theory and Society* 25, no. 6 (1996): 841–81.

———. *Logics of History: Social Theory and Social Transformation*. Chicago: University of Chicago Press, 2005.

Shahin, ʿAzza bint ʿAbd al-Rahim b. Muhammad. *Khayr al-Din al-Zirikli wa-Taʾrikhuhu li-ʿAhd al-Malik ʿAbd al-ʿAziz*. Cairo: Maktabat Madbuli, 2019.

Shalah, Husayn Hadi. *Talib Basha al-Naqib al-Basri wa-Dawruhu Fi Tarikh al-ʿIraq al-Siyasi al-Hadith*. Beirut: Al-Dar al-ʿArabiyya li-l-Mawsuʿat, 2002.

Shambrook, Peter. *French Imperialism in Syria: 1927–1936*. Reading: Ithaca Press, 1998.

Shamir, Shimon. "Midhat Pasha and the Anti-Turkish Agitation in Syria." *Middle Eastern Studies* 10, no. 2 (1974): 115–41.

Shapiro, Ian, and Russell Hardin, eds. *Political Order*. New York: New York University Press, 1996.

Sharkey, Heather J. *Living with Colonialism: Nationalism and Culture in the Anglo-Egyptian Sudan*. Berkeley: University of California Press, 2003.

———. *American Evangelicals in Egypt: Missionary Encounters in an Age of Empire*. Princeton: Princeton University Press, 2008.

Sharma, Surya Prakash. *Territorial Acquisition, Disputes, and International Law*. The Hague: M. Nijhoff, 1997.

Sharp, Walter R. "Review: The Study of International Administration: Retrospect and Prospect." *World Politics* 11, no. 1 (1958): 103–11.

Shaw, Stanford J., and Ezel Kural Shaw. *History of the Ottoman Empire and Modern Turkey*, vol 2. Cambridge: Cambridge University Press, 1977.

Shawcross, Edward. *France, Mexico, and Informal Empire in Latin America, 1820–1867: Equilibrium in the New World*. Cham: Palgrave Macmillan, 2018.

Sheehan, James. "The Problem of Sovereignty in European History." *The American Historical Review* 111, no. 1 (2006): 1–15.

Sheehi, Stephen. "Al-Kawakibi: From Political Journalism to a Political Science of the 'Liberal' Arab Muslim." *Alif: Journal of Comparative Poetics* 37 (2017): 85–109.

Shissler, Ada Holland. *Between Two Empires: Ahmet Ağaoğlu and the New Turkey*. London: New York: I.B. Tauris, 2003.

Shlaim, Avi. *Collusion Across the Jordan: King Abdullah, the Zionist Movement, and the Partition of Palestine*. New York: Columbia University Press, 1988.

Shryock, Andrew. *Nationalism and the Genealogical Imagination: Oral History and Textual Authority in Tribal Jordan*. Berkeley: University of California Press, 1997.

Al-Shubaki, Faruq. *Muhammad Tawfiq al-Bakri: Hayatuhu wa-Adabuhu*. Cairo: Maktabat al-Adab, 2013.

Shubayr, Muhammad ʿUthman. *Ahmad Ibrahim Bik: Faqih al-ʿAsr wa-Mujaddid Thawb al-Fiqh fi Misr*. Damascus: Dar al-Qalam, 2010.

Shumsky, Dmitry. *Beyond the Nation-State: The Zionist Political Imagination from Pinsker to Ben-Gurion*. New Haven: Yale University Press, 2018.

Al-Sibaʿi, Ahmad. *Tarikh Makka*. Riyadh: al-Amana al-ʿAmma li-l-Ihtifal bi-Murur Miʾat ʿAmm ʿala Taʾsis al-Mamlaka, 1999.

Sinanoglou, Penny. *Partitioning Palestine: British Policymaking at the End of Empire.* Chicago: University of Chicago Press, 2019.

Skovgaard-Petersen, Jakob. *Defining Islam for the Egyptian State: Muftis and Fatwas of the Dar Al-Ifta.* Leiden: Brill, 1997.

———. "Levantine State Muftis: An Ottoman Legacy?" In *Late Ottoman Society: The Intellectual Legacy*, Elisabeth Özdalga, ed., 296–310. New York: Routledge, 2005.

Sluga, Glenda. *The Invention of International Order: Remaking Europe after Napoleon.* Princeton: Princeton University Press, 2021.

Smith, Leonard V. *Sovereignty at the Paris Peace Conference of 1919.* Oxford: Oxford University Press, 2018.

Sohrabi, Nader. *Revolution and Constitutionalism in the Ottoman Empire and Iran.* New York: Cambridge University Press, 2011.

Stark, David Charles, and Laszlo Bruszt. *Postsocialist Pathways: Transforming Politics and Property in East Central Europe.* Cambridge: Cambridge University Press, 1998.

Steinmetz, George. "The Colonial State as a Social Field: Ethnographic Capital and Native Policy in the German Overseas Empire before 1914." *American Sociological Review* 73, no. 4 (2008): 589–612.

Stern, Philip J. *The Company-State: Corporate Sovereignty and the Early Modern Foundation of the British Empire in India.* Oxford: Oxford University Press, 2011.

Stirk, Peter M. *The Politics of Military Occupation.* Edinburgh: Edinburgh University Press, 2009.

Stitt, George Marquis Stewart. *A Prince of Arabia, the Emir Shereef Ali Haider.* London: G. Allen & Unwin, 1948.

Stoler, Ann Laura. "Imperial Debris: Reflections on Ruins and Ruination." *Cultural Anthropology* 23, no. 2 (2008): 191–219.

———. "Considerations on Imperial Comparisons." In *Empire Speaks Out: Languages of Rationalization and Self-Description in the Russian Empire*, Ilya Gerasimov, Jan Kusber, and Alexander Semyonov, eds., 33–55. Leiden: Brill, 2009.

Stolz, Daniel A. *The Lighthouse and the Observatory: Islam, Science, and Empire in Late Ottoman Egypt.* Cambridge: Cambridge University Press, 2018.

Tabataba'i, Hossein Modarressi. *Kharaj in Islamic Law.* Tiptree, Essex: Anchor Press, 1983.

Taglia, Stefano. *Intellectuals and Reform in the Ottoman Empire: The Young Turks on the Challenges of Modernity.* London: Routledge, 2015.

De Talleyrand, Charles-Maurice. *Mémoires du Prince de Talleyrand*, 5 vols. Paris: Calmann Lévy, 1891.

Tanenbaum, Jan Karl. "France and the Arab Middle East, 1914–1920." *Transactions of the American Philosophical Society* 68, no. 7 (1978): 1–50.

Tarrazi, Philippe de. *Tarikh al-Sihafa al-'Arabiyya*, 2: 4. Beirut: al-Matba'a al-Amirkaniyya, 1933.

Tate, Joshua C., José Reinaldo de Lima Lopes, and Andrés Botero Bernal, eds. *Global Legal History: A Comparative Law Perspective.* Abingdon: Routledge, 2019.

Tauber, Eliezer. "Sayyid Talib and the Young Turks in Basra." *Middle Eastern Studies* 25, no. 1 (1989): 3–22.

———. "Sayyid Talib and the Throne of Iraq." *Islamic Culture* 63, no. 4 (1989): 31–49.

———. *The Emergence of Arab Movements in World War I*. London: Frank Cass, 1993.

———. "Three Approaches, One Idea: Religion and State in the Thought of ʿAbd al-Rahman al-Kawakibi, Najib ʿAzuri, and Rashid Rida." *British Journal of Middle Eastern Studies*, 21, no. 2 (1994): 190–98.

Taymur, Ahmad. *Aʿlam al-Fikr al-Islami fi al-ʿAsr al-Hadith*. Cairo: Dar al-Afaq al-ʿArabiyya, 2002.

Teitelbaum, Joshua. "Sharif Husayn ibn Ali and the Hashemite Vision of the Post-Ottoman Order: From Chieftaincy to Suzerainty." *Middle Eastern Studies* 34, no. 1 (1998): 103–22.

———. *The Rise and Fall of the Hashimite Kingdom of Arabia*. London: Hurst & Company, 2001.

Thomas, Martin. *The French Empire between the Wars*. Manchester: Manchester University Press, 2005.

Thompson, Elizabeth F. *Colonial Citizens: Republican Rights, Paternal Privilege, and Gender in French Syria and Lebanon*. New York: Columbia University Press, 2000.

———. "Rashid Rida and the 1920 Syrian-Arab Constitution: How the French Mandate Undermined Islamic Liberalism." In *Routledge Handbook of the History of the Middle East Mandates*, Cyrus Schayegh and Andrew Arsan, eds. 244–57. London: Routledge, 2015.

———. *How the West Stole Democracy from the Arabs: The Syrian Congress of 1920 and the Destruction of Its Historical Liberal-Islamic Alliance*. New York: Atlantic Monthly Press, 2020.

Thornhill, Michael T. "Informal Empire, Independent Egypt, and the Accession of King Farouk." *The Journal of Imperial and Commonwealth History* 38, no. 2 (2010): 279–302.

Todd, David. *A Velvet Empire: French Informal Imperialism in the Nineteenth Century*. Princeton: Princeton University Press, 2021.

Toledano, Ehud. *State and Society in Mid-Nineteenth-Century Egypt*. Cambridge: Cambridge University Press, 1989.

———. "The Emergence of Ottoman-Local Elites (1700–1900): A Framework for Research." In *Middle Eastern Politics and Ideas: A History from Within*, Ilan Pappé and Moshe Maʾoz, eds., 145–62. London: Tauris, 1997.

———. "The Arabic-Speaking World in the Ottoman Period: A Socio-Political Analysis." In *The Ottoman World*, Christine Woodhead, ed., 466–79, Routledge, 2012.

Tooze, Adam. *The Deluge: The Great War and the Remaking of Global Order, 1916–1931*. London: Allen Lane, 2014.

Traboulsi, Fawwaz. "The Saudi Expansion: the Lebanese Connection, 1924–1952." In *Kingdom Without Borders—Saudi Political, Religious, and Media Frontiers*, Madawi Al-Rasheed, ed., 65–78. London: Hurst and Company, 2008.

Troeller, Gary. *The Birth of Saudi Arabia: Britain and the Rise of the House of Saʿud*. London: F. Cass, 1976.

Tucker, Judith E. *In the House of the Law: Gender and Islamic Law in Ottoman Syria and Palestine*. Berkeley: University of California Press, 1998.

Türesay, Özgür. "Le temps des almanachs ottomans: usage des calendriers et temps de l'histoire (1873–1914)." In *Les Ottomans et le temps*, François Georgeon and Frédéric Hitzel, eds., 129–57. Leiden: Brill, 2012.

Twitchell, K. S. *Saudi Arabia, with an Account of the Development of Its Natural Resources*. Princeton: Princeton University Press, 1953.

Tusun, 'Umar. *Mudhakkira bi-ma Sadara 'Anna Mundhu Fajr al-Haraka al-Wataniyya al-Misriyya*. Alexandria: Matba'at al-'Adl, 1942.

Al-Tuwayrani, Hasan Husni ibn Husayn. *'Awamil al-Mustaqbal fi Urubba*. Cairo: Matba'at al-Nil, 1310.

Twitchell, K. S. *Saudi Arabia, with an Account of the Development of Its Natural Resources*. Princeton: Princeton University Press, 1953.

Ubicini, A. *Constitution Ottomane*. Paris: A. Cotillon et Cie, 1877.

Al-Ustuwani, 'Abd al-Ghani. *Al-'Arab Min Wara' al-Lahab*. Damascus: Matba'at Khalid b. al-Walid, 1986.

Uzunçarşili, İsmail Hakki. *Ashraf Makka al-Mukarrama wa-Umara'uha fi al-'Ahd al-'Uthmani*. Bayrut: Al-Dar al-'Arabiyya li-l-Mawsu'at, 2003 (Arabic translation of *Mekke-i Mükerreme Emirleri*. Ankara: Türk Tarih Kurumu Basımevi, 1972).

Vasil'ev, A. M. *The History of Saudi Arabia*. London: Saqi Books, 1998.

Visser, Reidar. *Basra, the Failed Gulf State: Separatism and Nationalism in Southern Iraq*. Münster: Lit, 2005.

Vitalis, Robert. *America's Kingdom: Mythmaking on the Saudi Oil Frontier*. Stanford: Stanford University Press, 2007.

Volait, Mercedes. *Antique Dealing and Creative Reuse in Cairo and Damascus 1850–1890: Intercultural Engagements with Architecture and Craft in the Age of Travel and Reform*. Leiden: Brill, 2021.

Walpole, Norman C. *Area Handbook for Saudi Arabia*. Washington, DC: U.S. Govt. Print Off., 1966.

Watenpaugh, Keith David. *Being Modern in the Middle East: Revolution, Nationalism, Colonialism, and the Arab Middle Class*. Princeton: Princeton University Press, 2006.

Weber, Max. *The Theory of Social and Economic Organization*. New York: Oxford University Press, 1947.

Weismann, Itzchak. *Taste of Modernity: Sufism and Salafiyya in Late Ottoman Damascus*. Boston: Brill, 2000.

——. "Abū L-hudā L-Sayyādī and the Rise of Islamic Fundamentalism." *Arabica* 54, 4 (2007): 586–92.

——. *Abd al-Rahman al-Kawakibi: Islamic Reform and Arab Revival*. London: Oneworld, 2015.

Weiss, Max. *In the Shadow of Sectarianism: Law, Shi'ism, and the Making of Modern Lebanon*. Cambridge: Harvard University Press, 2010.

Weitz, Eric D. "From the Vienna to the Paris System: International Politics and the Entangled Histories of Human Rights, Forced Deportations, and Civilizing Missions." *The American Historical Review* 113, no. 5 (2008): 1313–43.

Wempe, Sean Andrew. "A League to Preserve Empires: Understanding the Mandates System and Avenues for Further Scholarly Inquiry." *American Historical Review* 124, no. 5 (2019): 1723–31.

Whidden, James. *Monarchy and Modernity in Egypt: Politics, Islam, and Neo-Colonialism between the Wars*. London: IB Tauris & Co, 2013.

White, Benjamin Thomas. "Addressing the State: The Syrian 'Ulama' Protest Personal Status Law Reform, 1939." *International Journal of Middle East Studies* 42, no. 1 (2010): 10–12.

———. *The Emergence of Minorities in the Middle East: The Politics of Community in French Mandate Syria.* Edinburgh: Edinburgh University Press, 2011.

Wien, Peter. *Arab Nationalism: The Politics of History and Culture in the Modern Middle East.* Abingdon: Routledge, 2017.

Wigen, Einar. "Post-Ottoman Studies: An Area Studies That Never Was." In *Building Bridges to Turkish: Essays in Honour of Bernt Brendemoen,* Éva A. Csató, Joakim Parslow, Emel Türker, and Einar Wigen, eds., 295–312. Wiesbaden: Harrassowitz Verlag, 2018.

Wilder, Gary. *Freedom Time: Negritude, Decolonization, and the Future of the World.* Durham: Duke University Press, 2015.

Wilks, Ann. "The 1922 Anglo-Iraq Treaty: A Moment of Crisis and the Role of Britain's Man on the Ground." *British Journal of Middle Eastern Studies* 43, no. 3 (2016): 342–59.

Williams, Elizabeth R. "Mapping the Cadastre, Producing the Fellah." In *The Routledge Handbook of the History of the Middle East Mandates,* Andrew Arsan, Cyrus Schayegh, eds., 170–182. Abingdon: Routledge, 2015.

Willis, John M. "Governing the Living and the Dead: Mecca and the Emergence of the Saudi Biopolitical State."*American Historical Review* 122, no. 2 (2017): 346–70.

———. "Burying Muhammad 'Ali Jauhar: The Life and Death of the Meccan Republic." Unpublished manuscript.

Wilson, Mary C. *King Abdullah, Britain, and the Making of Jordan.* Cambridge: Cambridge University Press, 1987.

Winter, Michael. "The "Ashraf" and "Niqabat al-Ashraf" in Egypt in Ottoman and Modern Times." *Asian and African Studies* 19, no. 1 (1985): 17–41.

———. *Egyptian Society under Ottoman Rule, 1517–1798.* London: Routledge, 1992.

Wishnitzer, Avner. *Reading Clocks, Alla Turca: Time and Society in the Late Ottoman Empire.* Chicago: University of Chicago Press, 2015.

Wizarat al-Maliyya. *Mizaniyyat al-Hukuma al-Misriyya li-Sanat, 1922–1923.* Cairo: al-Matba'a al-Amiriyya, 1922.

Wright, Quincy. "Sovereignty of the Mandates." *The American Journal of International Law* 17, 4 (1923): 691–703.

———. *Mandates under the League of Nations.* Chicago: University of Chicago Press, 1930.

Wyrtzen, Jonathan. *Worldmaking in the Long Great War: How Local and Colonial Struggles Shaped the Modern Middle East.* New York: Columbia University Press, 2022.

Al-Yafi, Lutfi. *Al-Faqid al-'Azim Fawzi al-Ghazzi.* Damascus: s.n., [1929].

Yaycioğlu, Ali. *Partners of the Empire: The Crisis of the Ottoman Order in the Age of Revolutions.* Stanford: Stanford University Press, 2016.

Yazbak, Mahmoud. "Muslim Orphans and the Shari'a in Ottoman Palestine according to Sijill Records." *Journal of the Economic and Social History of the Orient* 44, no. 2 (2001): 123–40.

Yenen, Alp. "Envisioning Turco-Arab Co-Existence between Empire and Nationalism." *Die Welt des Islams* 61, no. 1 (2021): 75–112.

Yılmaz, Hüseyin. *Caliphate Redefined: The Mystical Turn in Ottoman Political Thought*. Princeton: Princeton University Press, 2018.

Yusufzada, 'Ali. *Kitab Asna Matalib al-Arib fi Mada'ih al-Sayyid Talib Basha al-Naqib*. Cairo: Matba'at al-Mu'ayyid, 1322.

Zaghlul, Ahmad Fathi. *Al-Muhama*. Cairo: Matba'at al-Ma'arif, 1900.

Zahra, Tara. "Against the World: The Collapse of Empire and the Deglobalization of Interwar Austria." *Austrian History Yearbook* 52 (2021): 1–10.

Zamir, Meir. "Faisal and the Lebanese Question, 1918–20." *Middle Eastern Studies* 27, no. 3 (1991): 404–26.

Zamoyski, Adam. *Rites of Peace—The Fall of Napoleon and the Congress of Vienna*. London: HarperPress, 2007.

Al-Zawahiri, Fakhr al-Din al-Ahmadi. *Al-Siyasa wa-l-Azhar: Min Mudhakkirat Shaykh al-Islam al-Zawahiri*. [Cairo]: Matba'at al-I'timad, 1945.

Zeine, Zeine N. *The Emergence of Arab Nationalism; with a Background Study of Arab-Turkish Relations in the Near East*. [3d ed.]. Delmar: Caravan Books, 1973.

Ziadeh, Farhat Jacob. *Lawyers, the Rule of Law and Liberalism in Modern Egypt*. Stanford: Stanford University Press, 1968.

Al-Zirikli, Khayr al-Din. *'Aman fi 'Amman*. 1925; Amman: Al-Ahliyya li-l-Nashar wa-l-Tawzi', 2009.

———. *Shibh al-Jazira fi 'Ahd al-Malik 'Abd al-'Aziz*, 4 parts in 3 vols. Beirut: 1390/1970.

———. *al-A'lam*. Vols. 5 and 8. Dar al-'Ilm li-l-Malayin, 2002 (Shamila electronic edition).

Zürcher, Erik Jan. *Turkey: A Modern History*. 3rd ed. London: I.B. Tauris, 2004.

Abbas Hilmi II, 66, 100–101, 153–154, 183, 205, 206–207, 211–212
Abbas Hilmi Pasha, 155–156
ʿAbd al-ʿAziz, 173, 175–176, 194, 224; avoiding the declaration of conquest in Arabia, 185–189; international law and Hijaz kingdom and, 194–198; Istiqlalis and, 189–193, 215–219; new treaty with the British Empire, 1925, 198–199; Ottoman twilight in Arabia and, 183–185
ʿAbd al-Majid, 211
ʿAbd al-Muttalib, Jabir, 82–83
ʿAbd al-Razzaq al-Sanhuri, 149
Abdülhamid II, Sultan, 4, 14, 34, 71, 100
Abu al-Huda, Hasan Khalid, 212
Abu al-Huda al-Sayyadi, 71–73
Abu-Manneh, Butrus, 72
ʿAfifi ʿUmar, 165
al-ʿAhd al-Jadid, 210
Ali, Mehmed, 79
Alif Baʾ, 213
ʿAbd Allah Bey, 92–93
Allenby, Lord, 44, 133–134, 138–139
Allied Powers, First World War, 5, 8–9, 14, 39, 228; contractual framework of administration, 1919–1940s and, 47–48; peace treaty with Germany, 1919, 49, 50; Principal Allied and Associated Powers treaty, 1920, 48, 49; treaties on occupied territories, 46–47. See also Occupied Enemy Territories Administration (OETA)
Anderson, Benedict, 21, 27
Antonius, George, 199
Appadurai, Arjun, 115
Arab Awakening, The, 199
Arab caliphate: as counter-Ottoman empire, 98–99; dualism and decentralization in, 104–105; ethnicity and, 99–100
Arab Saudi kingdom, 173–176; avoiding conquest in, 185–189; composite polity, 1932, 198–201; Istiqlali network in, 176–183, 189–193; Ottoman twilight in

emerging, 183–185; from the sharifian project to the Saudi Hijazi Kingdom, 1924–1928, 183–198
Arendt, Hannah, 23
Article 22, Covenant of the League of Nations, 51–53
Asʿad, Ahmad, 72
ashrafs, 65–68, 69; Arab kingdom, post-First World War, 113–115; Hijazi Railway as sharifian infrastructure and, 123–129; re-invention of the sharifian emirate and, 76–81; Sharifian commonwealth as Arab kingdom and, 111–113; as source of political authority, 70–76
al-Atassi, Hashim, 214
Austro-Hungarian Empire, 48, 105–106, 116
authority: ashraf as source of, 70–76; under composite system of rule, 11–14, 29; defining, 23–24; Hanafi doctrine of Muslim executive, 158–160; imperial descent and, 66–67; monarchs as constituent fictions and, 27–28; under Occupied Enemy Territories Administration (OETA) (see Occupied Enemy Territories Administration (OETA)); in shariʿa apparatus, post-Ottoman Egypt (see shariʿa apparatus, post-Ottoman Egypt); sources in imperial political orders, 24–26; of subordinated rulers, 30–32
ʿAwn, ʿAbd al-Muʿin b., 79, 212–215
ʿAziz al-Misri, 111–113

Babylonian calendar, 33
Bakhit al-Mutiʿi, Muhammad, 3, 149–150, 165–166
al-Bakri, Muhammad, 73–74, 106–107
Balfour, Lord, 52
Bayly, Christopher, 230
belligerent occupation, 45–46
Bentwich, Norman, 135
Blunt, Wilfrid, 99–100

Bodin, Jean, 59–60

Brilliant, Richard, 6

Britain: Arab caliphate and, 99–100; Article 22 and, 53; British India and, 30; control of territories in the Ottoman Empire, 2–3, 4, 7, 93–94; Sykes-Picot agreement and, 51. *See also* Egypt, British; Occupied Enemy Territories Administration (OETA)

Call of Reason for Union and Obedience, The, 72

Cecil, Lord, 44

Central Powers, First World War, 5

Charmes, Gabriel, 99–100

China, 49

Churchill, Winston, 8

Cohn, Bernard S., 28

Cold War era, 231

Committee of Union and Progress (CUP), 14, 67

composite rule, 11–14, 29; Arab Saudi kingdom, 1932, 198–201; Muslim princely regions in, 91, 92–98

constituent fictions, 25; monarchs as, 27–28

constitutional conventions, 25

contractual framework of administration, 1919–1940s, 47–48

Crabitès, Pierre, 43

Crane, Charles, 221

Dahlan, Ahmad Zayni, 76–77

Darat al-Malik 'Abd al-'Aziz, 77

Dawn, Ernest, 92

decentralization, 107–109

de Jouvenel, Henry, 208–209

Demolin, Edmond, 107–108

al-Din, Khayr, 176

al-Din, Taj, 212

Drummond, Eric, 53

Duraffourd, Camille, 58–59

dynasts, 28

Dynasty of al-Siddiq, The, 75

East India Company, 30

Economy and Society, 23

Egypt, British, 40–47, 94, 147–150; dynastication in, 1919–1923, 150–153; dynasty and constitution in 1920s,

163–164; Khedivial caliph in, 100–101; monarchy and popular sovereignty in, 1914–1928, 160–161; shari'a apparatus and rise of the Grand Mufti in, 154–158

Eich, Thomas, 72

empire: Allied control of Arab regions and, 2–3, 8–9, 14, 39; composite system of rule in, 11–14, 29; example of late Ottoman Syria, 32–37; genealogy and, 66–68; imperial production of local dynastic realm and, 28–32; nation-states emergence after, 1; political cultural legacy of, 4; political order and, 4–5; political order as sociological category of, 22–24; post-World War I relevance of, 1–2; race-talk in, 7; sources of authority in, 24–26; sovereignty and, 3; suspending the right of conquest in British Egypt and, 40–47; theory of transformation of, 4–7

ethnicity and the Arab caliphate, 99–100

expansionism, 5

Fahmi, 'Abd al-'Aziz, 44

Faysal, King, 138–139, 144, 212–214, 222–223

Feldman, Noah, 148

First World War, 1, 5, 8–9, 14; Allied peace treaty with Germany, 1919, 49, 50; national projects emerging from, 21–22; Ottoman declaration of war against the British Empire during, 41–42; treaties on occupied territories, 46–47

Fitzmaurice, Andrew, 39

France: Article 22 and, 53; control of territories in the Ottoman Empire, 2–3, 4, 7; diplomatic uses of the Syrian throne, 1930s, 221–224; land administration in Syria and, 57–59; organic law in, 56–57; strong presidential institution in, 27; Sykes-Picot agreement and, 51; Syria as Franco-Ottoman princely state and, 206–212; Syrian 1928 constitution and, 202–204

Frederick Otho, Prince, 30

French Revolution, 24

Fromkin, David, 8

Fuad, King, 43, 44, 150–153, 164, 169; internationalism and, 153–154; suspension of constitution by, 166
Future of Islam, The, 99–100, 102

genealogy: 'Ali Haydar and Al-Husayn B. 'Ali and institutionalization of sharifian local politics and, 81–85; artistic depictions of, 87–88; *ashraf* as source of political authority and, 70–76; consequences of 1908 coup on the Hamidian ashraf and, 85–87; descendants of the Prophet Muhammad and, 65–66; empire and, 66–68; prophetic kinship and, 68–70; re-invention of sharifian emirate and, 76–81
Genealogy of the Verifiers, The, 71
Gennardi, Philippe, 58
Gentz, Friedrich, 30
Germany, 49, 50
Ghalib, Sharif, 78
al-Ghazi, 'Abd Allah, 77
al-Ghazzi, Fawzi, 216, 219–220
al-Ghazzi, Sa'id, 213
global legal history, 7–11
Gregorian calendar, 34, 36

Hague Conventions, 46
Haiti, 2
al-Hajj Ahmad b. 'Umar b. Muhammad al-Halabi, 119–120
Hallaq, Wael, 147, 156–157
Hamidian regime, 4, 10; 1908 coup on, 85–87; in Syria, 204–206
Hamza, Fu'ad, 191, 193, 200, 202; Istiqlali plan for Saudi emirate of Syria and, 215–219
Hanafi doctrine of Muslime executive authority, 158–160
al-Haqq, Jad, 159–160
Hasan, Sayyid Siddiq, 184
Haydar, 'Ali, 81–85, 206, 210–211, 214–215; 1908 coup and, 86–87; French diplomatic uses of the Syrian throne and, 222–223
Helal, Emad, 156
Herrschaft, 22–23
Hijazi Kingdom, 9–10; from composite polity to Arab Saudi Kingdom and, 1932, 198–201; Hijaz railway, 123–129,

177; international law and, 194–198; Istiqlali network and, 176–183; Saudi state formation and, 173–176
hijri calendar, 33–37
Hikmet, Arif, 205
History of Mecca, 77
Hobsbawm, Eric, 6
Huntington, Samuel, 27
Husayn, Sharif, 80
al-Husayn, 'Ali, 185–186, 212–213
al-Husayn, Faysal, 7, 8; Arab kingdom, post-First World War, and, 114–115; Istiqlali network and, 176–177
al-Husayn, Sharif, 7, 89; Muslim princely regions and, 96–97
Hussein, Saddam, 65

imperial political order, 28–32, 229
India, British, 30
industrialism, 28–29
internationalism, 153–154
al-'Isa, Yusuf, 213
Islam: Arab caliphate and, 98–103; descendants of the Prophet Muhammad and, 65–66; doctrine of Muslim executive authority in Hanafi, 158–160; forms of political regimes under, 3, 228–229; genealogy in (*see* genealogy); prophetic kinship in, 68–70; religious authority in, 23
Istiqlali network, 176–183, 189–193, 202, 203; plan for Saudi emirate of Syria, 215–219; suspended republic in Syria and, 219–221

al-Jabiri, Sa'd Allah, 216
Jacob, Wilson Chacko, 70
Japan, 49
al-Jaza'irli, Sa'id, 206
jihadism, 116

Kamil, Husayn, 42, 147
Kayalı, Hasan, 110
Kelsen, Hans, 26
al-Khuri, Faris, 213
Kings of the Arabs, The, 115, 191–192
Krämer, Gudrun, 148

Laffan, Michael, 70
L'avenir de la Turquie-Le panislamisme, 100
law as autonomy, 26

law as integrity, 26

Law of Province, 1913, 109–111

League of Nations/Covenant of the League of Nations, 2, 3, 7, 9–10, 39, 48, 194, 227–228; Article 22, 51–53; mandate system of, 60; organic law and, 53–57; right of administration and, 50; as site of imperial internationalism, 39; sovereignty and, 39–40; transfer of sovereignty by, 49–50

Lebanon, 55–57

legal structures: bifurcated Ottoman, 1910s, 129–133; legal order and, 26; *qadi* court and Allied occupation, 119–120; shari'a courts, 155–158

legitimacy, 23; relationship between monarchy and, 29–30

Lindley, Mark Frank, 52

local agency, 9

local dynastic realm: example of late Ottoman Syria and, 32–37; imperial production of, 28–32

Lugard, Frederick, 31–32

Lyautey, Hubert, 31–32

al-Madani, Muhammad Zafir, 72

Maghraoui, Abdeslam, 148

Makdisi, Ussama, 66–67

al-Malabi, Sayyid Fadl, 72

Manual of Military Law, 133

March, Andrew, 148

Marx, Karl, 31

Mazzini, Giuseppe, 31

McMahon, Henry, 42

Milner, Lord, 44

monarchomachia, 31

monarchy: debate over usefulness of, 229–230; dynastication in Egypt, 1919–1923, 150–153; imperial production of local dynastic realm and, 28–32; and monarchs as constituent fictions, 27–28; and popular sovereignty in Egypt, 1914–1928, 160–161; Principal Allied and Associated Powers treaty, 1920 and, 48; relationship between legitimacy and, 29–30; utopian federalism and, 91–92

Morimoto, Kazuo, 68

Morocco, 31–32

Muhammad, Prophet, 65–66

Muslim princely regions, 91, 92–98

Nami, Ahmad, 206–210, 215

Napoleon III, 31

naqib, 70

naqib al-ashraf position, 71–76

Nasser, Gamal Abdel, 230–231

nationalism, 13–14, 113; emergence of, 21–22

nation-states, 1, 21–22

Neue Freie Presse, 109

non-belligerent occupation, 45–46

Occupied Enemy Territories Administration (OETA), 45, 120–123, 145–146; administrative authority in, 138–141; authority in government courts in, 137–145; authority in *qadi* court, 1918–1920, 141–145; bifurcated legal infrastructure of Ottoman authority in 1910s, 129–133; dividing occupation authority in, 137–138; Hijazi railway as sharifian infrastructure and, 123–129; law and legitimacy in, 133–137; map of, *121*; *qadi* courts in, 119–120

organic law, 53–57, 203–204

Orientalism, 9

othering of monarchy, 27

Ottoman Empire, the, 2; 1908 coup, 85–87; Arab nationalism and, 113; bifurcated legal infrastructure of authority in, 1910s, 129–133; British and French control of territories in, 2–3, 4, 7, 93–94, 120–121, 228; composite rule in, 11–14; constituted in global legal history, 7–11; constitutional dimension in, 12–13; decentralization in, 1908–1914, 107–109; declaration of war against the British Empire, 1914, 41–42; genealogical authority in (*see* genealogy); Hijazi railway and, 123–129; *hijri* calendar in, 33–37; imperial descent and authority in, 66–67; Islam and monarchy reattached after fall of, 4; as key point of origin for 20th century Arab polities, 10, 226; Law of Provinces, 1913, 109–111; local agency and, 9; Muslim princely regions in composite, 91, 92–98; nationalism ideology in, 13–14; political order and, 4–5, 8; political order in, 5; recycling in, 2, 8, 10; subordinate monarchs in, 30; Syria in late, 32–37; utopian federalism in (*see* utopian

federalism). *See also* Occupied Enemy Territories Administration (OETA)
Ottoman Orientalism, 66–67

Palestine, 10, 15
Paris Peace Conference, 14
Philby, Harry St. John, 199–200
political order, 4–5, 8, 14–15; as assemblage of authority, 23–24; imperial production of local dynastic realm and, 28–32, 229; as sociological category of empire, 22–24; sources of authority in imperial, 24–26
Ponsot, Henri, 204, 210–211, 217
post-Ottoman age, 14–15; dynastication in Egypt, 1919–1923, 150–153; internationalism in, 153–154; multi-time of 20th century world history and, 230–231; political order in, 8, 14–15; shari'a apparatus in Egypt's (*see* shari'a apparatus, post-Ottoman Egypt)
power: constituent fictions and, 25; domination and, 129; legitimacy and, 22, 23; in republican imperial projects, 27
Principal Allied and Associated Powers treaty, 1920, 48, 49
Provence, Michael, 15
Provisional Law of Provinces, 1913, 109–111
Puaux, Gabriel, 224
Puech, Charles, 58–59, 134

qadi courts, 119–120; authority in, 1918–1920, 141–145
Al-Qassab, Muhammad Kamil, 178–183, 190–191, 202; Istiqlali plan for Saudi emirate of Syria and, 215–219
Al-Qibla, 89, 177
Al-Quwwatli, Shukri, 216

al-Rafiq, 'Awn, 77, 80–81
recycling, 2, 8, 10, 14; in Syria, 204–206
Rida, Muhammad Rashid, 101–104, 111–112, 164–165; Istiqlali plan for Saudi emirate of Syria and, 217–219
al-Rifa'i, Ahmad, 72–73
right of conquest: public international law denying, 45–47; suspended in British Egypt, 40–47
al-Rihani, Amin, 115
Rıfaat, Ahmed, 71

al-Sa'id, Nuri, 214
Saint-Jean-de-Maurienne treaty, 1917, 46–47
Salafism, 101–102, 116
Salmoné, Habib Antony, 100
al-Sanhuri, 'Abd al-Razzaq, 166–168
Satia, Priya, 175
sayyid, 69, 70–71, 79
sayyido-sharifology, 68
Sayyid Talib, 72–73, 75, 86, 93
Schayegh, Cyrus, 15
Schmitt, Carl, 25–26
Scott, Rachel, 148
Second World War, 230, 231
şerafet-i tertib, 84
Şevket, Mahmud, 109–110
Sèvres treaty, 1920, 52–53
Sewell, William, 24
Shahbandar, 'Abd al-Rahman, 224
shari'a apparatus, post-Ottoman Egypt, 147–150, 169–170; dynastication, 1919–1923, 150–153; dynasty and constitution in, 163–164; ending the Ottoman caliphate, 161–163; Ottoman Hanafi doctrine of Muslim executive authority in, 158–160; rise of the Grand Mufti and, 154–158; unelected imperial imam doctrine and, 164–169; Wali al-Amr as transformer in, 160–161
sharif, 65–67; elite status of, 68–70; princely state of Syria, 212–215; in Syria, 204–206. *See also* ashrafs
al-Siba'i, 77
sovereignty, 3, 226–228; binding contracts and, 59–60; contractual framework of administration, 1919–1940s, 47–48; denying the right of conquest and, 45–47; flattening of, from composite polity to Arab Saudi Kingdom, 198–201; League of Nations and, 39–40, 227–228; in Muslim princely regions, 95; organic law and, 53–57; practices of granting, in 19th century Europe, 29–31; recognized through treaty, 48; as result of collective decision, Article 22, 51–53; suspended in British Egypt, 40–47; Syrian land administration and, 57–59; transfer between individual legal entities, 49; transfer from individual to collective legal entities, 49–50

Soviet Union, 6

spolia, 5–6, 148

spoliation, 5–6, 8; *in re*, 6, 10, 187; *in se*, 6, 123, 148

Stoler, Laura, 105

subordinated rulers, 30–32

Suez Canal, 44–45

Sufism, 71–72

Sykes-Picot agreement, 1916, 46, 51

Syria, 4, 15, 191–193; 1928 constitution under French administration, 202–204; Article 22 and, 53; as Franco-Ottoman princely state, 206–212; French diplomatic uses of the Syrian throne, 1930s, 221–224; Istiqlali plan for Saudi emirate of, 215–219; land administration in, 57–59; late Ottoman, 32–37; organic law for, 55–56, 203–204; recycling empire in, 204–206; Saudi state formation and (*see* Arab Saudi kingdom); as sharifian princely state, 212–215; suspended republic in, 219–221

Tales of the Alhambra, 115

al-Taqaddum, 34

Al Thunayan, ʿAbd Allah, 66, 76, 184

transfer of sovereignty: between individual legal entities, 49; from individual to collective legal entities, 49–50

Treaty of Lausanne, 1923, 10, 52

Treaty of London, 1915, 46

True Essence of Islam, The, 165–166

Turkish republic, 4, 14

Umm al-Qura, 103, 199

al-ʿUmran, 73

United States, the: organic law in, 54–55; strong presidential institution in, 27

utopian federalism, 89–92; Arab caliphate as counter-Ottoman empire and, 98–99; Arab kingdom, post-First World War, 113–115; dualism and decentralization in, 104–105; emergence of dualist, 105–107; ethnicity and Arab caliphate, 99–100; Khedivial caliph in Egypt and, 100–101; Law of Provinces, 1913, and, 109–111; in Muslim princely regions, 91, 92–98; Ottoman dualism as ethnicity-based idea, 1908–1914, 107–109; post-war context of, 115–116; principles of, 90–91; Rida and al-Kawakibi and caliphate as Muslim federation and, 101–104; Sharifian commonwealth as Arab kingdom and, 111–113

Van Hammel, Joost, 185

Vienna Congress, 29–30

von der Goltz, Colmar Freiherr, 109

Watenpaugh, Keith, 15

Weber, Max, 22–23, 129

world history, multi-time of 20th century, 230–231

Wyrtzen, Jonathan, 230

Yasin, Yusuf, 176; Istiqlali activists and, 193, 194–195; Istiqlali plan for Saudi emirate of Syria and, 216; new treaty with the British Empire, 1925, 198–199; *Umm al-Qura* journal and, 190, 199

Yugoslavia, 14

Zayd, Sharif, 176, 212–215

Zeza Pasha, Ahmed Hamdi, 205

Zürcher, Erik-Jan, 14

A NOTE ON THE TYPE

THIS BOOK has been composed in Miller, a Scotch Roman typeface designed by Matthew Carter and first released by Font Bureau in 1997. It resembles Monticello, the typeface developed for The Papers of Thomas Jefferson in the 1940s by C. H. Griffith and P. J. Conkwright and reinterpreted in digital form by Carter in 2003.

Pleasant Jefferson ("P. J.") Conkwright (1905–1986) was Typographer at Princeton University Press from 1939 to 1970. He was an acclaimed book designer and AIGA Medalist.